COMPARING
PLURALIST
DEMOCRACIES

NEW DIRECTIONS IN
COMPARATIVE AND INTERNATIONAL POLITICS

Series Editors
Peter Merkl and Haruhiro Fukui

Comparing Pluralist Democracies: Strains on Legitimacy, edited by Mattei Dogan

No Farewell to Arms? Military Disengagement from Politics in Africa and Latin America, Claude E. Welch, Jr.

Comparing New Democracies: Transition and Consolidation in Mediterranean Europe and the Southern Cone, edited by Enrique Baloyra

The Rise and Fall of Italian Terrorism, Leonard Weinberg and William Lee Eubank

COMPARING PLURALIST DEMOCRACIES

Strains on Legitimacy

EDITED BY
MATTEI DOGAN

Westview Press
BOULDER AND LONDON

New Directions in Comparative and International Politics

Published in 1988 in the United States of America by Westview Press, Inc.; Frederick A. Praeger, Publisher; 5500 Central Avenue, Boulder, Colorado 80301

Library of Congress Cataloging-in-Publication Data
Comparing pluralist democracies.
  Bibliography: p.
  Includes index.
  1. Democracy.   2. Legitimacy of governments.
3. Pluralism (Social sciences)   4. Comparative
government.   I. Dogan, Mattei.
JC423.C666 1988   321.8   87-8279
ISBN 0-8133-0451-2

Printed and bound in the United States of America

The paper used in this publication meets the requirements of the American National Standard for Permanence of Paper for Printed Library Materials Z39.48-1984.

10   9   8   7   6   5   4   3   2   1

CONTENTS

TABLES AND FIGURES

Figures

ACKNOWLEDGMENTS

The first step of this book was an international conference in July 1985 at the Science Center, Berlin, organized under the joint auspices and support of the Science Center and UNESCO. Twenty-three scholars from eleven countries participated in the meetings. The present volume includes five of the papers presented at this conference, revised for publication, and four chapters prepared specifically for this book. I wish to thank professor Karl W. Deutsch, then director of the International Institute for Comparative Social Research (Wissenschaftszentrum, Berlin), for his generous help in promoting this book. I owe particular thanks to Megan L. Schoeck of Westview Press for her skillful editing.

Jean Stoetzel, author of Chapter 5 and author of the first important publication based on the European Values Study, died in February 1987. This book is dedicated to his memory.

Mattei Dogan

INTRODUCTION:
STRAINS ON LEGITIMACY

Mattei Dogan

In this book, all chapters have a comparative approach; no one chapter deals with a single country. All chapters raise theoretical issues, but they do so by presenting a wealth of empirical data. All deal with the contemporary situation and use the most recent survey data available.

Within this comparative approach, the first question is the extent to which the advanced pluralist countries are similar or different. Like a mountaineer who perceives other mountain ranges only after achieving the summit, pluralist democracies appear similar or contrasting according to the position of the observer. If one compares the 30 advanced pluralist democracies to the 120 nondemocratic regimes, one sees the similarities among the pluralist democracies, what they have in common and what differentiates them as a group from the other countries. But if we consider only the pluralist democracies, we are in a better strategic position to perceive the differences among them. There is a wide range of diversity among pluralist democracies coexisting with basic similarities.

Obviously, many problems could be raised concerning the functioning of pluralist democracies, for instance, the decline of parliament everywhere except in the United States. However, only those issues related to the legitimacy of the political regime are discussed in this book.

CRISES OF LEGITIMACY

Legitimacy is a basic concept, used not only by social scientists but by politicians and by the man in the street. One of the clearest, albeit simple, definitions of legitimacy was given by Seymour Martin Lipset: "the capacity of the system to engender and maintain the belief that the existing political institutions are the most appropriate ones for the society" (Lipset 1981, 64). Juan Linz proposes, as a "minimalist" definition, "the belief that in spite

1

of shortcomings and failures, the political institutions are better than any others that might be established and therefore can demand obedience" (Linz, Chapter 2).

Neither of these definitions includes any mention of how widespread these beliefs must be if the system as a whole is to be considered legitimate. One must remember that "no political system is legitimate for 100 percent of the population, nor in all its commands or forever, and probably few . . . are totally illegitimate—based only on coercion" (Linz, Chapter 2). If our criteria for legitimacy are too demanding, we could arrive at the paradoxical result that none of the pluralist democracies are considered legitimate by an overwhelming majority of the population. As nondemocratic regimes are largely illegitimate by definition, this would mean that no regime on earth is legitimate. In this case, the concept would be useless.

Max Weber's seminal typology of legitimacy—traditional, charismatic, and rational-legal—today has only historical utility. Traditional legitimacy still exists only in a handful of countries, among them Saudi Arabia, Morocco, and some countries with fewer than 2 million inhabitants. Charismatic leadership appears today only in Iran, Libya, and perhaps Cuba. Rational-legal legitimacy is at the base of pluralist democracies, but a distinction must be made between legitimacy and legality. Valéry Giscard d'Estaing, elected by a majority of less than 1 percent, was perceived as a legal but not legitimate president by many Frenchmen when he concentrated too much power in his hands. When the socialist president François Mitterrand remained in power after the conservative victory in the legislative elections of March 1986, many of the French believed that he had the legal right to continue as president, but not a legitimate one. For many Austrians, Kurt Waldheim is a legal president more than a legitimate one. Legality could be the opposite of legitimacy.

Analyzing legitimacy over time presents further problems. Discussing the change of norms and values in post–World War II Germany, Ronald Rogowski invites us to recall the dilemma: "What was once agreed, on good evidence, to be a profoundly authoritarian political culture has now shown itself capable of sustaining high support for democracy for over a generation. If the concept of political culture is to have any explanatory value at all, it must follow that the political culture has changed . . . but if whole societies can be changed so drastically . . . much of the power has gone out of the theory of political culture" (Rogowski 1974, 10–11). There are enormous differences between the beliefs of most Germans during the Weimar Republic, the Nazi regime, and the Bonn Republic. Surveys show fundamentally similar trends in all Western democracies. If the "civic culture" of a country can change so rapidly, it is not a reliable reference. In fact, in many European countries, this concept has never been widely accepted; it has not been accepted in France at all, where it has been considered merely a modern and more sophisticated version of the "psychologie des peuples" of Gustave Le Bon and Gabriel Tarde.

The empirical evidence presented in this book further challenges the concept of civic culture. There is not a British civic culture, nor a German,

French, or Italian one. The differences among countries are differences in degree not of kind, differences of a few percentage points. The differences *within* nations appear greater than the differences *among* nations. There are more similarities in the beliefs of a French and a German social democrat than between a French socialist and a French conservative or between a German social democrat and a German christian democrat.

The rapid cultural changes of the last three decades in the advanced pluralist democracies, as reflected in public opinion, are amazing. Although we lack longitudinal data to demonstrate this point decisively, one does not risk much by arguing that greater cultural changes have occurred in most Western countries in the last thirty years than in the last three centuries. This is true for values concerning religion, nationalism, family, and the work ethic. Peter Merkl, in the first chapter of this book, reviews the data and the literature on this subject. All are characterized by rapid change of a "revolutionary" character.

In the course of their development, democracies have gone through a series of crises of legitimacy. All democracies have had to face five types of crises, four of which have been successfully resolved. The fifth, the current crisis of the welfare state, serves as a major theme for this book. The most important implication of the resolution of each crisis is the manner in which the solution leads, in a dialectical fashion, to the beginning of a new priority, a new crisis. There is no accumulation of crises in the contemporary advanced pluralist democracies, in marked contrast to the situation in the developing countries and in contrast also to the past experiences of several European countries.

FROM NATIONAL INDEPENDENCE TO A RELUCTANCE TO FIGHT FOR ONE'S COUNTRY

The first crisis was the crisis of national independence and the determination of territorial boundaries, largely resolved in Europe by the end of World War I. Some disputes do remain, such as those in the Basque region or Northern Ireland; the issue of Germany's eastern boundaries is now dormant. These exceptions notwithstanding, the central elements of the nation-state solution to this crisis are no longer at issue.

Nation building is not an old phenomenon in Europe. The German and Italian unifications were achieved only a little more than a century ago, and other countries obtained their national independence or unification only in World War I—Hungary, Czechoslovakia, Poland, Yugoslavia, Romania, Estonia, Latvia, Lithuania, Finland—less than two generations ago. In those countries, a child could, as late as the 1960s, hear his or her grandparents tell of the country's fight for independence. A few countries achieved unification a long time ago, as did France, Spain, Britain, the United States, Sweden, and Portugal. Many of these countries, especially the smaller ones, do not have the technical or financial means today with which to defend themselves alone, and they must rely on the protection of the "American umbrella." War is currently inconceivable among the pluralist democracies,

either within Europe, or between North America and Japan. The attitude
of the French people toward the Germans, and vice versa, is one of many
examples that could be given. For three generations, the "hereditary" enemy
of France was Germany, leading to three wars, in which millions of French
and Germans died or suffered. Less than fifteen years after the end of
World War II, in the presence of a potential common danger, a rapprochement
between the two countries began under the leadership of Charles de Gaulle
and Konrad Adenauer. Rapidly, and without much discourse, the economy
of each country became penetrated by the economy of the other. For France,
Germany is now the largest trading partner, and for Germany, France is
now similarly the largest. They are politically and militarily tied together,
for better or for worse. Geopolitics appears to be much stronger than
collective memory.

Since the nations of Europe no longer need to worry about their territorial
integrity (except, of course, for threats from the Eastern giant), many
Europeans seem to have lost their willingness to defend their country. Jean
Stoetzel, in discussing the reluctance to fight for one's country (Chapter
5), confronts the reader with fresh and striking data and challenges some
of the conventional political wisdom. Less than one-half of the European
people declare themselves willing to fight for their own country—a proportion
that differs radically from what it would have been fifty years ago. It was
not asked against whom the respondents thought they would or would not
be fighting, but in the political situation of 1981 the answer must have
been obvious; it was presumably not a question of a possible war among
the countries of Western Europe (except perhaps for Ireland). The important
point is that for the people of the Western European countries, the notion
of a war within Europe has become politically unreal. The unwillingness
to fight therefore refers primarily to fighting against a challenge from the
East.

It is within this framework that the results must be interpreted: about
40 percent of the Europeans refuse to fight and about 17 percent refuse
to decide; only 43 percent declare themselves willing to fight. Nationalism
as a warlike mass movement within Western Europe seems dead, replaced
by a pacifism that looks like defeatism, which could serve as an invitation
to invasion unmet by resistance. "Better red than dead."

Who are those people who say they are willing to fight? Who are those
who do not? In Europe as a whole, the willingness is relatively highest at
the age of forty, well above the age of normal military service. Farmers and
manual workers are slightly more willing to fight than students. Those
willing to fight are persons with higher incomes; homeowners; those who
are happy, in better health, politically more active, more religious, and
better integrated in organizations and families; and those located by their
attitude on the right half of the political spectrum. Those willing to fight
also prefer freedom to equality, have more confidence in the police and in
existing institutions, favor free enterprise, and give "priority to maintaining
order."

Those who refuse to fight are more often under forty or over sixty years
old, have lower incomes, and are better educated. They are more lonely,

feel less happy, and are less satisfied with life. Many are on the left half of the political spectrum, consider "marriage outdated," see justifications for divorce and abortion, and do not prefer "traditional" values.

The second half of Stoetzel's chapter compares the European countries with one another. Here he finds substantial differences among nations. In Germany, Italy, and Belgium, less than 40 percent of the respondents are willing to fight, and in France only 42 percent. In Britain, Denmark, and Spain, more than half are willing to do so. This willingness varies from 25 percent in Belgium to 62 percent in Britain. The number of undecided respondents is largest in Belgium and more than one-fourth in West Germany; it is smallest in Britain and France, suggesting a higher polarization of opinion.

Stoetzel's chapter offers no reasons for the observed differences since reasons cannot be derived from his data. Speculation, however, is not the only alternative. There are readily verifiable facts from political geography and recent history that have a bearing on mass attitudes. For West Germans, fighting for their country means first of all to fight East Germany. Both Germans and Italians carry vivid memories of their defeat in World War II. In addition, most studies of Italian politics since World War II report high levels of alienation and distrust of the government and the political system. Belgium is profoundly split between contending language groups, which the party system has failed to bridge. At the other end of the attitude spectrum, Denmark and Britain are culturally more homogenous. Finally, some Irish respondents may have interpreted fighting for their country as defending it against Britain. These background facts do not furnish anything like a complete explanation, but they deserve to be taken into account.

Stoetzel's chapter is highly professional, with few concessions to popular presentation. He refuses to say anything that cannot be demonstrated directly from his data. His use of percentages on the one hand and of scores on the other may obscure the impact of his findings, but these findings are nonetheless very important. Perhaps his essay will stand as a classic for its time.

As Peter Merkl and Frederick Turner point out in their chapters, there is a significant relationship between reluctance to fight and national pride, and Richard Rose gives detailed information about this relationship. Among those who are proud of their nation, the proportion of those who are willing to fight is naturally much higher than among the people who are not proud. The discrepancy is very high for the United States (73 percent of the proud are willing to fight as opposed to 38 percent of those who are not proud), France (49 percent and 18 percent), and Britain (66 percent and 39 percent) and low for Italy, Belgium, and Japan (Rose 1985, 94).

FROM THE SEPARATION OF CHURCH AND STATE TO THE DECLINE OF RELIGION

The church became dominant and triumphant at a certain moment in all European countries—in the fifteenth century in Spain, the seventeenth century in Italy, and so on. The splendor of Catholic churches and monasteries all over Europe, with their fine marble, sculptures, and gold, testifies to this triumph. At that time of dominance, the church became more an institution of the ruling classes, and in particular of the landed aristocracy, than one of the poor. The alliance between throne and altar rapidly came to include the state, and in some countries the administration of the state was in practice the administration of the church. Kings and emperors were legitimized by religious ceremonies.

All countries had to come to terms with this important transnational institution. In the north, Protestantism facilitated an earlier solution to the question of the relationship between church and state than was possible in the Catholic countries. Nonetheless, even in the latter the issue has been largely resolved, even though a number of social questions—such as birth control, divorce, abortion, and private schools—are still fought largely on religious grounds.

The first breakdown of the alliance of church and state was the Reformation, but it merely replaced that alliance with a new one based on the principle of *cuius regio eius religio* ("he who rules chooses the religion"). American independence was the first real break as it marked a separation not only from England but also from the Church of England. The first European separation of church and state was achieved during the French Revolution, but this did not last long: Napoleon was coronated with the benediction of the pope, brought to Paris for the ceremony.

In many European countries, the fight against domination by the church was long lasting. France dramatically decided on the separation only in 1905, in the wake of the Dreyfus affair. In several countries, the collapse of thrones after World War I brought about a separation of church and state, as was the case in Germany, Austria, Russia, and Turkey. Italy was still deeply divided on this issue as late as the 1970s, when the referendum on abortion symbolically ended church dominance there. Today, in all pluralist democracies, church and state are separated, except in Britain where there is a symbolic unity in the monarch. Ireland is in the final stages of the process.

To the extent that religious symbols or religious obligations have been important as determinations of affect and of legitimacy, this separation may have serious implications. The role of the Church of England, for instance, in the legitimacy of that regime has undergone substantial changes. The traditional legitimacy of the monarch and the aristocracy was also once an issue, but it was ultimately resolved by the collapse of the four major dynasties of Europe during World War I. The crowns in Britain, Scandinavia, the Low Countries, and Spain remain, but they are without real power, even if Juan Carlos's symbolic power has been of importance in the consolidation of Spanish democracy. Curiously, as Lipset points out, many of the most stable democracies retain their monarchs (Lipset 1981, 65–66). This modern form of legitimacy has, dialectally, also led to difficulties. In many countries, the legitimacy of the Republic has been at issue—historically in France, Germany, Austria, and Spain.

The separation appears as a historical achievement of democratic regimes, peacefully accomplished in all countries, even if with strains in some. One example, which appears with particular clarity in Austria and the Netherlands after World War II, is the progressive replacement of the consociational regimes by neocorporatist systems. Consociational democracy in such countries has achieved its historical mission, pacifying religious conflicts and opening the road to neocorporatism. The vertical religious cleavages have been replaced by horizontal social cleavages. In many countries in the late 1960s, survey data and aggregate data showed that religion was of greater value in explaining political behavior than were social or economic cleavages. Since then, the correlation coefficients between religion and politics have been declining as indicators of socioeconomic cleavages grow in importance.

The rapid and heavy decline of traditional values cannot but open the door to new issues. One should not be surprised to find in the surveys that a majority of people approve of birth control, divorce, abortion, and illegitimate children. The church, particularly the hierarchy, fought these reforms fiercely but lost the battle in all countries except Ireland. The church went against the flow then; if it does not in the future adapt itself to new realities, it risks becoming just a sect. Some U.S. bishops, among others, are arguing precisely this point today. In Europe, the doctrinal rigidity of many bishops fuels anticlericalism. It is a tribute to democracy that the political leadership has been sensitive enough to translate into law the feelings of the population in spite of so much pressure against such reforms, particularly in the Catholic countries (notably Italy, Austria, and Ireland).

Today, church attendance is low in most European countries: In 1981, 57 percent in France never attended church, 46 percent in Britain, 43 percent in Denmark, 41 percent in the Netherlands, as opposed to 4 percent in Ireland and 21 percent in Italy—and the figure for Italy should be considered more significant than a figure twice as high in a Protestant country (Harding, Phillips, and Fogarty 1986, 37). Church attendance is not the only indicator we have. Only three-quarters of Europeans believe in the existence of God; only 58 percent believe in the immortality of souls; only 43 percent believe in life after death; only 40 percent, in the existence of paradise; 25 percent, in the existence of the devil; 23 percent, in hell; and only 21 percent, in reincarnation (Stoetzel 1983, 115).

Because of the alliance between church and bourgeoisie, which followed the alliance between aristocracy and church, particularly in the Catholic countries, and because of the process of "de-Christianization" of part of the working class, particularly in central Italy, southern France, and some Spanish and Portuguese regions, it would be very interesting to compare the religious beliefs of the working class and of the bourgeoisie. Such a crosstabulation is not yet available, but one could easily be made since national samples are sufficiently large. For instance, in France in 1968, 50 percent of industrial workers reported that they never attended religious service, as opposed to 41 percent of the entire population. This fact implies that the proportion of the "good bourgeoisie" was not higher than one-third (unpublished survey results obtained by the author).

FROM POLITICAL INTEGRATION
OF THE LOWER STRATA TO NEW FORMS
OF ALIENATION AND PROTEST

Universal suffrage is a recent phenomenon in most pluralist democracies. Only the United States has had universal white male suffrage uninterruptedly for more than two centuries; France has also had a series of periods of such suffrage over the same time span, but uninterruptedly only since 1870. Norway introduced universal suffrage upon independence in 1905, and in most democratic regimes, the change occurred during or immediately after World War I.

Universal suffrage became a source of legitimacy, replacing divine right. Traditional legitimacy has been replaced by democratic legitimacy, occasionally supplemented by charismatic leadership. The importance of this point is particularly clear when we observe that the working-class parties have given up revolutionary goals only in countries with universal suffrage. The socialist movement became the social democratic movement, and was in several cases central to the defense of the republic. By opening the political system to the working class, the legitimacy of the system was strengthened, as Linz points out in Chapter 2.

Universal suffrage was a beautiful conquest, but dialectically this promotion of the lower class has engendered new problems. Contrary to some old illusionary hopes, problems are not miraculously solved by placing a ballot in a box. Voting is to a large degree not rational but a result of the citizen's emotional attachments. As historical battles for the vote recede from memory, suffrage is taken for granted. The source of legitimacy is the electoral process.

The history of pluralist democracies in the last seventy years is no doubt a history of spectacular achievements, but it is also a history of dramatic unrest, alienation, and protest. In each of the last seven decades, despite voting, people have gone to the streets to express their dissatisfaction. Political unrest, protest, alienation, and violence have appeared in all democracies, except Switzerland and Ireland. In fact, as Max Kaase argues, "the propensities for institutionalized and uninstitutionalized political participation are positively correlated" (Kaase, Chapter 3). This statement implies that the development of democratic institutions led, dialectically, to the protest movements that are ubiquitous in the advanced countries. Of course, the degree of protest has varied widely: much more in Weimar Germany, much less in the Netherlands; more in the United States than in Canada. Only in a few countries has civil war resulted. Important comparative data—on levels of protests, demonstrations, political strikes, riots, and deaths from violence in the pluralist democracies—are presented and discussed in Chapter 3.

One of the important questions, besides the comparison of protest across space, is the comparison of levels of protest across time. Unfortunately, as Max Kaase points out, "longitudinal data for even one country—not even to mention comparative data—are still very rare" (Kaase, Chapter 3). Analysis of the existing data suggests that in many countries, dissatisfaction has increased over the last twenty years. A distinction must be made between passive dissatisfaction with the working of the democratic regime and active protest, more or less violent, by political minorities. The analytical and theoretical difficulties are many, and Kaase reviews them. A substantial minority in all pluralist democracies is dissatisfied, but the reasons are not always easy to discover. The existence of a strong Communist party in France and Italy appears related to dissatisfaction and alienation; which is cause and which is effect is less clear.

Both the development of universal suffrage and the crisis of traditional legitimacy have led to new vertical cleavages within society. As the unifying symbols of monarch or church disappeared, cultural and linguistic cleavages emerged. Narrowly based parties, taking advantage of universal suffrage, came into existence, some of which were also based on religious cleavages. To varying degrees, minorities in each country hesitated to give the regime full legitimacy. Meanwhile, economic cleavages became more salient in most countries. This is not to say that class conflict is becoming more severe, but it is true that an increasing number of elections are being fought on economic issues at the expense of other types of issues.

Political protest and alienation cannot be understood without reference to legitimacy, as Kaase argues. Given the existence of many legal forms of political participation, especially in comparison with authoritarian or total-itarian regimes, it is important to analyze the reasons why dissatisfied individuals sometimes choose illegal forms of protest. One important factor in this choice is efficacy. Over the last three decades, Europeans, Americans, and Japanese have increasingly come to admit that forms of participation other than voting can be effective.

Political unrest, demonstrations, alienation, and protest can sometimes be healthy reactions. Some types of scandals can explode only in true democracies. The Watergate scandal and the Dreyfus affair pay homage to the U.S. and French democracies. The resignation of President Leone, involved in a financial scandal, did not weaken the Italian democracy; on the contrary, it was perceived as a healthy symptom. Civil rights movements can indicate vigor and not weakness in a democratic regime. As Peter Merkl writes, "political turmoil and violence serve only a symbolic function, perhaps to teach the government and the majority supporting it a painful lesson" (Merkl, Chapter 1). Kaase, referring to several authors, asks if it is not good for democracy "to have skeptical, distrustful citizens, citizens who are aware . . . of the human frailties of political leaders and by virtue of their distrust keep the arrogance of political power from taking over" (Kaase, Chapter 3). Popular protest against the malfeasance or simple errors of leaders not only does not endanger the legitimacy of the regime but can even reinforce it.

FROM THE REDISTRIBUTION OF NATIONAL INCOME
TO THE GORDIAN KNOT OF FREEDOM/EQUALITY

The salience of economic issues, combined with universal suffrage, has led to another crisis, which logically follows from a system of one-man, one-vote. A majority of voters may favor the transfer of some wealth from the rich to the less well-off when the income of the average citizen is inferior to the income of the median voter. The problems of redistribution vary widely, and they are controversial in all pluralist democracies, but the fundamental solution—that there should be *some* redistribution—remains.

The history of the last seventy years is also, and perhaps first of all, the history of progressive income redistribution, with ups and downs. The phenomenon has been widely analyzed. Inequality has obviously retreated to various degrees everywhere, sometimes by wise compromises, sometimes as a result of violence. This redistribution has taken two basic forms: higher incomes for lower-status individuals and what economists call "public goods." Comparing indices of inequality today with those of fifty years ago is the simplest way to measure the changes, particularly the blossoming of the middle classes along with the improvement in the social conditions of the working classes. Because of the spectacular increase of the middle classes, it is becoming more meaningful to distinguish between the upper and lower halves of the society by drawing a line through the center of the middle class.

The demand for more equality comes from the lower half of society, which stands to gain from it. This demand is resisted by the upper half, arguing in favor of greater freedom. So, the redistribution of national income becomes a competition between more equality and more freedom. A common denominator of all surveys on legitimacy and values is the trade-off between liberty and equality.

In the European Values Study, a choice between precisely these two values was presented to samples in ten European democracies. Overall, 49 percent preferred personal freedom to social equality while 35 percent expressed the reverse preference. Freedom was most preferred in Great Britain, 69 percent to 23 percent, while in Italy, Spain, and West Germany narrow majorities opted for equality over freedom.

Social equality and personal freedom are in a sense associated. If they were totally separated, society would experience deep splits. In a very inegalitarian society, there is no freedom. It is possible to conceive of an egalitarian society without freedom, but such a society cannot be democratic. In the democratic regimes, there is nevertheless a point at which equality is detrimental to freedom and vice versa. This point represents the social equilibrium between the two halves of society. More equality for the lower half implies less freedom for the upper half. Very often elections are decided by a margin of less than 2 percent, as in the United States, Britain, France, Germany, and Austria. For the floating voters just above the median, further reductions of socioeconomic inequality could mean less freedom for themselves, or vice versa; more socioeconomic inequality could mean that their incomes would go above the average income.

Competitive democracies are marked by a competition between egalitarians, who want more social equality, and the individualists, who want more personal freedom in all fields, including the economic sphere, and consequently are not in favor of more social redistribution. As Frederick Turner points out, "there is some structural conflict" between freedom and equality (Turner, Chapter 6). The median voters try to undo the Gordian knot according to their own interests. The only result is a rotation of governments following electoral oscillations.

Furthermore, as income was redistributed, economic efficiency came to be impaired. There may be a crisis of efficiency rather than a crisis of legitimacy, in the sense discussed by Lipset in *Political Man* (1981, 68–70). That is, an inefficient regime may remain stable so long as it is viewed as legitimate by the most important sectors of society, as was the case in Scandinavia, Switzerland, and the English-speaking democracies during the Great Depression.

POLITICAL LEGITIMACY AND
MISTRUST OF THE ECONOMIC SYSTEM

One basic fact is striking to any observer: The list of the thirty richest countries in the world overlaps almost exactly with the list of the thirty pluralist democracies. There are only two exceptions. Why India is democratic remains a very interesting problem not only for specialists on India but for all comparativists. Many factors could be cited, starting with the ubiquity of agricultural smallholders, religious influence, the British legacy, the caste system, and other vertical cleavages of this enormous subcontinent. The other exception is Costa Rica, but this country is, nevertheless, the richest in Latin America and also is characterized by a preponderance of small agricultural proprietors. (A number of ministates could be discussed, but these need not detain us.) In addition to being rich countries, these pluralist democracies—even Sweden—are all based on market economies and private ownership of the means of production. They are basically capitalist.

Schumpeter's prediction of nearly a half century ago, that capitalism would not survive, has not yet come to fruition. It is true that Schumpeter did not indicate a firm date for the transition. He was partly right in the sense that none of the economic systems of the pluralist democracies are still exclusively capitalist—they are all mixed economies with a high proportion of the GNP controlled by the government.

Is it accidental that the pluralist democracies are also the richest countries in the world, with only East Germany and Czechoslovakia approaching the same level of wealth? Even if we admit that all these rich countries have mixed economies today, it remains true that they were already rich before their economies became mixed; their wealth resulted from the capitalist economic system, as it did even in East Germany and Czechoslovakia. Historically, democracy has grown on capitalist soil.

Nevertheless, survey research today shows that there is substantially more support for democracy than for capitalism. This gap is one of the main questions Juan Linz raises in Chapter 2, where he compares the legitimacy of democracy with the legitimacy of the socioeconomic system: "To what extent does the legitimacy of the democratic system contribute to the legitimation or delegitimation of the socioeconomic system, or inversely, does the legitimacy of the socioeconomic order reinforce the legitimacy of the political system or in the case of illegitimacy contribute to its delegitimation?" (Linz, Chapter 2). The essence of Linz's answer to this question is that "the commitment to political democracy is compatible with an alienation from or a dissatisfaction with the economic system since there is the hope that it can be changed by democratic means in the shorter or longer run. . . . This was the basis of the success of social-democratic socialism" (Linz, Chapter 2).

As long as political leaders refrain from large-scale intervention in the economic system, "political institutions and leaders do not necessarily have to be blamed for the failures of the economic system" (Linz, Chapter 2). However, we know that in these mixed economies, intervention is inescapable, by regulation alone or by taxation/redistribution. For this reason, the performance of the economic system, more or less controlled by the government, can have in some circumstances an important impact on the legitimacy of the political regime itself. But as Peter Merkl argues, economic failures do not necessarily damage political legitimacy, for "if the long list of policy failures could not keep Thatcher from being returned in triumph, why should we imagine that the economic and social failures might diminish the legitimacy of British government?" (Merkl, Chapter 1). The same is true for Reagan: "There is no evidence that U.S. legitimacy has suffered in the least from the negative responses to his economic policies" (Merkl, Chapter 1).

Even if the government ceases to intervene now, it will be held responsible for its nonintervention since it intervened in the past. There are two aspects of this responsibility, efficiency and equity. The first refers, obviously, to productivity and to strictly economic performance. Equity refers to questions of social justice, fairness, and the role of employees in the management of companies, among other things. A wealth of data on these issues has been presented by Linz in Chapter 2, by Lipset and Schneider in *The Confidence Gap* (1987), by McClosky and Zaller in *The American Ethos* (1984), and by the European Values Study.

These two questions of efficiency and equity are fundamental when one analyzes the desirability of what, in the final chapter of this book, are presented as the alternatives: civic society or statist society.

DECLINING SUPPORT FOR THE REGIME
IN A CRISIS OF UNEMPLOYMENT:
HYPOTHETICAL PROJECTIONS

In Chapter 4, Ulrich Widmaier asks what would happen between 1983 and 2000 to the legitimacy of governments and of basic constitutional democratic regimes if unemployment were to rise to an average of 20 percent of the work force by the year 2000. He uses a simulated world model, limited to the domestic politics of five countries—the United States, the United Kingdom, Germany, France, and Italy—based on aggregate and survey data. The model uses real data for the period from 1970 to 1983 and is simulated from 1983 to 2000. The model distinguishes among three levels of political stability: support for the incumbent government, support for the political regime, and support for the polity. The focus of the analysis is directed toward the long-term development of regime legitimacy (support) to the year 2000. Exogenous macroeconomic indicators drive the model until 1983; afterward it is assumed that unemployment will rise from its 1983 level continuously to 20 percent in the year 2000. All other exogenous variables remain at their 1983 level.

Despite some considerable variation in terms of levels and changes in the six countries under study, the results show tendencies toward an accelerating erosion of regime legitimacy. Since the underlying scenario is not any more likely to become reality than other scenarios, the results cannot be interpreted as predictions or forecasts; they are warnings.

For his "real world" period 1970–1983, Widmaier finds large national differences, which persist in substantial part throughout the projected period. His model thus shows contrasting national levels but a similar common trend, albeit of different strength for each country. The higher the legitimacy of a basic political regime at the start of the period, the greater is its projected loss of legitimacy to 2000 if high unemployment should persist. In Britain, where regime legitimacy was about 65 percent in 1970 and 1980, it is projected to drop to 50 percent by 2000.

That a majority of adults should lose confidence in their political regime does not necessarily mean, of course, that they could agree on an alternative to it, as data presented by Kaase demonstrate. However, such a regime might survive only precariously, through the disunity of its opponents, with little inner strength against external challenges.

Even more thought provoking are Widmaier's projections of the popularity of governments as distinct from that of basic political regimes. His model projects political cycles: As a new government comes into office, it is relatively popular thanks to the campaign promises it made. As unemployment persists, government popularity drops, and only when a new administration or government comes in does popularity recover. It remains at a very low level in Italy and France. If these projections are realistic, the likelihood of minority governments, insecure coalitions, and weak governments is likely to increase in all six countries. Furthermore, such a projected unemployment rate for the entire working population would also imply a much higher rate for the younger generation. If, tomorrow, one out of every three young persons is unemployed, more than an erosion of legitimacy will occur—we will confront the ghost of Weimar!

To be sure, Widmaier's model projections represent warnings that under-line what may happen if policies are not changed and if high levels of unemployment should come to be accpeted as normal. Neither is preordained. Policies may change for many reasons, and some people may consider the estimate of 20 percent unemployment probable. Nonetheless, Widmaier's data to 1983 and his projections to 2000 deserve careful attention.

CROSSNATIONAL SIMILARITIES
OF ADVANCED WELFARE STATES

Richard Rose emphasizes the commonalities among the situations of the various pluralist democracies by studying public programs in such areas as education and income maintenance: The "similarities are greater within a given program across national boundaries than among different programs within a country" (Rose, Chapter 8). One implication of this finding is that all pluralist democracies face similar crises of the welfare state.

Differences among the various programs within each country are far greater than are those of the same program across the pluralist democracies. This fact permits a useful typology of programs for all advanced countries: money-intensive programs, employee-intensive programs, and law-intensive programs. Within each category, there are several basic kinds of programs: Income-maintenance programs, for instance tend to be of the first type in all countries. In addition to this similarity of program orientation, and despite differences in total government spending as a proportion of GNP across countries, the shares of each type of program within the total budget are strikingly similar: "Spending on income maintenance tends to be double that on education and health, and about three times that on defense, and public employment in education and health tends to be eight to ten times that for income-maintenance programs" (Rose, Chapter 8). Statistical analyses of differences in spending and employment for different programs within and across nations confirm that the variations among pluralist democracies are less important than the variations within each one. The same is true for levels of different kinds of taxation. These similarities in public spending and employment are as remarkable as those in values and culture.

Rose argues that since the crossnational differences are relatively small, policy analysts need to learn from the experiences of other countries confronting similar issues. This need is particularly important as the pluralist democracies increasingly confront the crisis of the welfare state. Given the great similarities among countries, the experiences of any one country cannot be ruled out for others a priori. Chapter 9 provides a prospective analysis of the crisis of the welfare state, taking precisely this fact as its point of departure.

Public programs are not simply a matter of redistribution. About half of the public expenditure is not distributed to identifiable individuals, families, or corporations; that is, about half of government spending goes to public goods from which all citizens benefit. Much of this second half goes not only to low-income individuals and families but to all, such as child allowances or national health insurance, or at least everyone can expect to benefit from a given program at some time in their lives, as is the case with social security or unemployment insurance. If everyone benefits from governmental largess—even if some individuals pay substantially more for the privilege—then eliminating programs is very difficult politically. Each program develops a clientele, which may be as large as the entire population, and taking benefits away risks losing political support. Dealing with the crisis of the welfare state by eliminating programs inevitably involves, therefore, strains on the legitimacy of the regime. All pluralist democracies face this problem.

A NEW TEST OF LEGITIMACY:
THE CRISIS OF THE WELFARE STATE

The crisis of the welfare state is the last in a series of crises experienced by democracies. It appears as a dialectical development from the previous crisis of redistribution. The main challenge to the legitimacy of the regime tomorrow will probably be provoked by the shrinking of the welfare state.

Social legislation has in general recognized in law the aspiration of a majority of the population. Such a process is an achievement for Western democracies, and dissatisfaction with a regime on the part of a minority of the population should be interpreted in part at least as a demand for further reforms.

In analyzing the crisis of social security in Chapter 7, I describe two developments among the highly developed Western pluralist democracies: the rising ratio of pensioners to the working population and increasing health care costs. The uniform tendencies of all these countries, apart from minor instances of imitation, suggests parallel but autonomous structural developments. The analysis stresses increasing cleavages in each country between the growing number of retirees and the dwindling number of working contributors, between the employed and the longtime unemployed, and between the interests of actual patients and hospital administrators and those of contributors to health costs. Within the framework of that chapter I do not stress the crosscutting ties that mitigate these cleavages, especially family ties: between retirees and their children, who would have to support them; between the employed and unemployed; between the badly sick and the more healthy. Furthermore, shifting a larger share of welfare costs to taxes on consumption would increase the overlap between taxpayers and beneficiaries. Productivity in Western countries has grown during the last forty years by an annual average of about 3 percent, and actual per capita income in most of these countries has grown by not much less. If the demographic trends I point out in Chapter 7 continue, productivity would need to increase more than threefold in the next thirty-five years, as would per capita income, in order to make the anticipated welfare burdens bearable.

The Western democracies have reached such a level of penetration of the society by the state that we cannot avoid asking how much further the welfare state can continue to grow. Indefinitely? In contrast to the previous crises—when the ultimate resolution was foreseeable from the outset—the new crisis of the welfare state does not offer a clear alternative, even if criticizing big government is fashionable.

Any discussion of this problem must begin with two basic facts. First is the impossibility of an exponential growth of the welfare state, particularly of the social security system. If present trends continue, the financial bankruptcy of these programs is inevitable. We hear the same leitmotiv in country after country, even in those where these programs are comparatively small, as in the United States. Among the many factors contributing to this irresistible growth, it suffices to mention only one here: Contemporary medicine is capable of cheating death, postponing by six months or one year the last day of a moribund patient. If every citizen has the right to cheat death, then the most important industry may become health care for the elderly. The only conceivable solutions to such a perspective are either euthanasia (but its implementation would create enormous problems) or a ceiling on terminal health care costs under which each individual has the right to allocate his or her medical expenses, as is the case under some medical plans in the United States. But neither of these two solutions is likely to be widely adopted in the near future.

The second basic fact is the existence of a majority in all countries in favor of the maintenance of the public social security system. How can we explain this phenomenon? One explanation is that, with few exceptions, survey questions about social benefits are in a sense superficial, even naive. Asking someone if he or she is in favor of social security is like asking a child if it would like to play football with the moon. If the questions in surveys on social security were phrased to include alternatives or constraints, then the results would certainly be different.

Politicians ignore neither of these two basic facts, and they adapt themselves to the situation by continuing to let the budget increase because reelection is an immediate problem and bankruptcy of the system a more remote one. They refrain even from discussing the latter problem. They pass the buck to experts and higher civil servants who, not having to face electoral pressure, are able to tell the truth. But their warnings go unheeded, mere howling in the wind.

One way to deal with this complex problem is to hypothesize two opposite trends, as is done in the final chapter of this book, by considering both a continuation of the growth of government and a dramatic reversal of that trend. Both perspectives are beset with pessimism.

Up to a certain level, the welfare state facilitated political consensus, and it continues to do so today. The legitimacy of pluralist democracies is nourished in large part by the safety net provided by the state against illness, unemployment, and old age and by the support given for education, housing, and so on. The legitimate state is a paternalistic one. Any attempt to reduce this social coverage implies a risk of electoral defeat for those who dare try. The Reagan-Thatcher experiments are supported by a large segment of the population in each country, but not by the majority. Prime Minister Thatcher controls a majority of the House of Commons, but her party represents less than half the electorate. President Reagan has not been able to cut social security, only smaller social programs, and the majority of the Congress belongs to the rival party. The Chirac government in France actually increased taxation for social security. In the past, whenever a government has tried to reduce the budget, it has faced serious difficulties. Contracting government is difficult because it is too easy for the opposition to propose further expansion.

One way to avoid delegitimation is to hand the hot potato over to the electorate itself by referendum. It does not matter if the decision taken by the electorate is a wise one or a myopic one; it would in any case be a legitimate one. There is no recourse to vox populi. If an electorate makes the wrong decision, because the referendum was not preceded by a sufficiently illuminating debate on the parameters, there is still the possibility of holding a new referendum on the same issue.

The second alternative is the indefinite growth of government, the statist society. This is also a pessimistic perspective. It is not necessary to recall here the literature on the difficulty of aggregating interests within an overloaded government (see Dogan and Pelassy 1987 and Rose 1980), and few people would reject the supposition that an overloaded government is a less efficient government. A long period of inefficiency brings erosion of legitimacy not only of the incumbents in power—as Lipset and Schneider (1987) have shown for the United States—but, over the long term, of the political system itself.

Perhaps this pessimism is unwarranted. In the past, most democratic regimes have overcome adversities and crises; the past performance of democratic regimes permits a grain of hope.

REFERENCES

Abrams, Mark; David Gerald; and Noel Timms. 1985. *Values and Social Change in Britain*. London: Macmillan.

Dogan, Mattei, and Dominique Pelassy. 1987. *Le Moloch en Europe: Etatisation et Corporatisation*. Paris: Economica.

Harding, Stephen; David Phillips; and Michael Fogarty. 1986. *Contrasting Values in Western Europe*. London: Macmillan.

Lipset, Seymour Martin. 1981. *Political Man*. Expanded ed. Baltimore: Johns Hopkins University Press.

Lipset, Seymour Martin, and William Schneider. 1987. *The Confidence Gap: Business, Labor, and Government in the Public Mind*. 2d ed. New York: Free Press.

Noelle-Neumann, Elisabeth. 1985. "National Identity and Self-Esteem." Paper presented at the World Congress of the International Political Science Association, Paris, August 15–19.

McClosky, Herbert, and John Zaller. 1984. *The American Ethos: Public Attitudes Toward Capitalism and Democracy*. Cambridge: Harvard University Press.

Orizo, F. A. 1983. *Espana entre la Apatia y el Cambio Social*. Madrid: Editorial Mapfre.

Rezsohazy, R., and Y. Kerkhofs, eds. 1984. *L'Univers des Belges: Valeurs anciennes et valeurs nouvelles dans les annees 80.* Louvain: Ciaco.

Rogowski, Ronald. 1974. *Rational Legitimacy: A Theory of Political Support.* Princeton: Princeton University Press.

Rose, Richard. 1980. *Challenge to Governance: Studies in Overloaded Politics.* London: Sage Publications.

————. 1985. "National Pride in Cross-National Perspective." *International Social Science Journal,* 103, 37:1.

Stoetzel, Jean. 1983. *Les Valeurs du temps present: Une enquete europeenne.* Paris: P.U.F.

1
COMPARING LEGITIMACY AND VALUES AMONG ADVANCED DEMOCRATIC COUNTRIES

Peter H. Merkl

Until the seventeenth century in Europe, and in many countries long after that time, it was easy to define the legitimacy of authority in a given state. Nearly all societies were aristocratic and hierarchic, and the foremost aristocratic family, by lawful inheritance, supplied the legitimate king. All other aristocratic families, in descending order, likewise had to be the lawful successors of previous aristocrats or to have been solemnly elevated to their rank by a legitimate king. Religious sanction usually reinforced the legitimate authority of secular rulers, and there was no need to make the legitimacy of His Most Christian Majesty dependent on any particular standards of righteousness or performance (Friedrich 1963, chapter 6). Once rulers had to adopt justifications and rationalizations of their authority, such as Sir Robert Filmer's theory of the divine right of kings, they were well on their way to losing it. Even the most well-reasoned statements, such as Thomas Hobbes's *Leviathan*, were just as likely to be applied in support of their challengers as to themselves.

DEMOCRATIC LEGITIMACY

With legitimism in retreat before popular sovereignty over subsequent centuries, and with the eventual rise of democratic governments, new and far more complex definitions had to be found both for internal and for international legitimation of authority (Cranston 1986). And the problems only began with formulations such as Thomas Jefferson's, who wrote "It accords with our principles to acknowledge any government to be rightful which is formed by the will of the people substantially declared," and elsewhere "that every [nation] may govern itself according to whatever form it pleases, and change these forms at its own will; and that it may transact its business through whatever organ it thinks proper, whether King, convention, assembly committee, President, or anything else that it may choose. The will of the nation is the only thing essential to be regarded" (Cranston 1986, 39).

Behind Jefferson's word *it* there lurked a whole world of modern political change and development: How indeed would "it" have to be organized— in parties, elections, laws, institutions—to be capable of "substantially" articulating "its" will? How exactly were the citizens of a legitimately constituted modern democratic state to know the extent of their obligation to obey its laws and commands? If democratic legitimacy and political obligation appeared in need of cogent redefinition in Jefferson's day, they have been questioned even more closely in the last twenty years under the onslaught of various new challenges of our age, as we can see in the following chapters. One challenge has been the broadly based participatory and generational upheaval in most advanced democracies, which has been described in the studies of Ronald Inglehart (1977), Samuel Barnes and Max Kaase (1979), and others. Democratic legitimacy seems a fragile vessel amid the praetorian waves of this participational revolution. The emphatic demands for the "democratization" of societies that had long considered themselves democratic illustrates the nature of the challenge. The student revolts of the late 1960s, the ethnic rebellions of the 1970s, the feminist challenge to a male-dominated order, the environmental protests against bureaucratic planning and management, and the pacifist questioning of the domestic and international order of our democratic "warfare states" supply further evidence to the critiques of democratic legitimacy. Since the early 1970s, there has indeed been a great deal of new literature on the "legitimacy crisis" of democratic states (Habermas 1973, Offe 1972, Denitch 1979) as well as on the "confidence gap," or simply "crisis of democracy" (Lipset and Schneider 1983, Crozier, Huntington, and Watanuki 1975)—although the Cassandras of this crisis are not in agreement about its precise causes and likely effects on democracy.

Most of the essays in this book also focus in one way or another on this crisis of democratic legitimacy and values, frequently citing new comparative opinion polls on the subject. In this chapter, I shall attempt to bring together, compare, and summarize the various arguments and the evidence with a skeptical eye, bearing in mind the nature of democracy and the difficulties of measuring legitimacy or the absence of it (cf. Eckstein 1971, Gurr and McClelland 1971). Since democracy, unlike its predecessors, has a natural correction process built into it by which dissatisfied majorities can replace their rulers and even minorities can try to persuade the majority of the merits of their complaints, democratic legitimation appears to be a matter of procedure rather than of substance. A duly elected government has the right, within reason, to carry out its mandate and to expect reasonable obedience from its constituents—until the next election. Short of a well-organized effort, not necessarily by a majority, the government is unlikely to fall even if considerable numbers of the citizens, for one reason or another, refuse to carry out its orders. As long as the advanced democratic countries do not face massive attempts to overthrow them, in other words, the legitimacy of their governments may be safe in spite of such challenges as I have noted.

OPERATIONALIZING LEGITIMACY

Generally speaking, the conventional definitions of democratic legitimacy have emphasized three elements: (1) the presence of a community, or nation, united by a consensus with regard to political values—no small order among multiethnic or multicultural countries but in the form of a successful national government a powerful builder of legitimacy; (2) a solemnly and widely accepted legal and constitutional order of democratic character; and (3) an elective government responsive to the expressed needs of the people. The legitimate authority of the government in this scheme, unlike its monarchic antecedents, is narrowly circumscribed as to its functions[1] and largely stripped of the personal features of ascriptive authority. The political obligation of the citizenry is similarly limited and contingent not on an actual act of consent—for example, by the election of government leaders—but on the character of the government: "If it is a good, just government doing what a government should, then you must obey it; if it is a tyrannical, unjust government trying to do what no government should, then you have no such obligation" (Pitkin 1971, 19–20). Although some authors stress as the basis of democratic obligation the principle of utility (Rawls, the Utilitarians; Walzer 1970, x–xvi; Wilkinson 1977, 13–14; Rogowski 1974, 45ff.)—the state's effectiveness in providing for the general welfare—others prefer to argue that political obligation is derived from the implied consent (by election) of a majority of the citizenry (social contract theory); still others, like Hamma Pitkin, say "it is not whether you have consented but whether you ought to" (Pitkin 1971, 20–21).

What can we do to operationalize these concepts of political philosophy, to bring them down to the level of empirical public opinion research? Certainly, a sense of identification with one's nation or political community can be measured and even compared across national boundaries. The history of modern nationalist movements supplies plenty of evidence to suggest that nationalism, or patriotism, is one of the most powerful legitimizing forces of our age, strong enough to compel even human sacrifice, and yet its extraordinary power requires leaders of the movement to be neither democratic nor self-effacing functionaries. Once victorious, moreover, nationalism can lend a regime an overwhelming aura of legitimacy, again without internal democracy or a democratic leadership style (Friedrich 1963, 245). David Easton has called such a sense of obligation by identification one kind of *diffuse* regime support—to distinguish it from more *specific* kinds of support—and has pointed out its generation by processes of political socialization (see also Easton 1965, chapters 11–13, and Easton 1975, 444–445). Religion has the potential of being an equally legitimizing force, but so far we lack the data to distinguish degrees of religious loyalty from other religious values.

We only need to recall the draft resistance movement in the United States during the Vietnam era, a most dramatic instance of the basic values of U.S. legitimacy under challenge, to see the next dimension of this complex. A corollary of identification with one's political community is the obligation to serve one's country in any capacity, in this case to defend its territory and interests among rival powers (Walzer 1970, chapters 4–5). The civic duty to risk life and limb for one's country has been commonly limited to young, healthy males. Viewed in the broader context of diffuse system support involving one's family, home, and local community, however—both in terms of socialization and of symbolic maintenance and defense (not so much physical defense)—this duty is bound up with many other societal maintenance functions, such as an obligation to maintain families and to contribute to the local community. It also has its parallel obligation for young, healthy women, namely childbirth and family roles. Long neglected by political philosophers and very controversial today, this latter obligation has been under an analogous challenge as that of the young men. Just as young men have asserted a right not to risk their bodies and lives for the political community without their consent, young women have begun to assert a similar right—by insisting on family planning and abortion rights—and there has been a precipitate drop in the marriage and birthrates in many industrialized countries.

These issues, moreover, are related. In West Germany, for example, as the drastically reduced number of conscriptable males is expected to shrink further to 200,000 a year in 1990 and 150,000 in 1995, serious consideration is being given to opening the military to females, perhaps even to drafting them (Enloe 1983). Refusing to pay taxes to the state; open tax rebellion à la Mogens Glistrup in Denmark or Howard K. Jarvis in California; or a growing tolerance of tax evasion, social security fraud, or of corruption in public office also may demonstrate the erosion of legitimacy of a state. A recent survey undertook to measure the tolerance toward these offenses among nine European nations and found that France and Belgium are the most permissive on this score while Denmark and, surprisingly, Italy frown the most on such antisystem behavior (Stoetzel 1983, 41). Whether we conceive of this growing refusal to serve the community as an additional limitation on the already limited concept of political obligation in liberal democracies, or as a species of Herbert Marcuse's "great refusal," it clearly diminishes the diffuse support system of legitimacy in contemporary democracies.

The acceptance of the legal and constitutional order as a source of legitimacy can also be measured through polls about popular satisfaction with democracy. Since most advanced democracies, not to mention the most recent, are not yet so far removed from earlier more authoritarian forms of government, and since there are usually movements of the far Right or far Left advocating a return to authoritarianism for reasons of their own, the acceptance of democracy can usually be contrasted with a preference for authoritarian rule. Criticisms that a contemporary democratic state is not democratic enough, or different concepts of democracy, are more difficult to handle in that the critics may still be supportive of democratic government in principle while finding the current regime wanting. Measurements of public support, diffuse or specific, for particular institutions—parliament, the courts, the executive—also fit into this rubric even though they may make considerable demands on the level of knowledge of many respondents (Ehrmann 1976, 50–53). Replacing more specific questions with general ones about "trust" or "confidence" in the national government or particular institutions is not necessarily a step closer to regime legitimacy, because respondents tend to understand such questions largely as "confidence in particular office-holders" and what they do (Lane 1979, 63–64; Ladd 1976–1977, 544f.).

Finally, we get into the murky area of what a sense of well-being, attributed to government policies, may contribute to building up diffuse system support over a period of time where it is weak or lacking.[2] There are elaborate Marxist and non-Marxist theories of an alleged "legitimation crisis" in European democracies that postulate a permanent legitimation deficit of advanced capitalistic societies that requires continuous socioeconomic improvements (often via economic growth) in the lives of the majority of citizens (see Habermas 1973, Offe 1972, Wolfe 1977). There are neo-utilitarian theories that make regime legitimacy dependent on the effectiveness and efficiency of government in providing more life satisfaction for the worst-off part of society and, eventually, good and equal satisfaction for everyone (Honderich 1976, 78–82). Some theorists blame structural problems, such as the government overload that results from endless differentiation of organized interests, policy specialization, and government growth; the growing gap between the provision of private and of collective goods; or the failing capacity of government to steer society (see Widmaier, Chapter 4). Even rampant consumerism is sometimes seen as a way of filling the void in the life satisfactions of postindustrial societies. Other theorists see the legitimation crisis in the hypertrophic development of certain policies, such as "the elephantiasis of social security"; the new dilemmas posed by technological development, as in the most expensive new medical technology, which has outgrown the ability to provide fairly for all in an egalitarian welfare state (see Dogan, Chapter 7); or nuclear energy. The rise of government spending on health and pensions in all OECD countries against a background of economic stagnation and relative decline (see Rose, Chapter 8) transforms these structural dilemmas of the democratic welfare state into insuperable financial tests of government performance and, hence, of regime legitimacy.

There are, of course, comparable international polls on life satisfaction and individual happiness, and they may often correlate positively with other indicators of a sense of legitimacy. Taken by themselves, however, they bear little relevance to it, for people could be subjectively just as happy, or perhaps even happier, in a state of anarchy or in a primitive stateless society. It might be more meaningful, if rather specific, to investigate public reactions to particular policies and governments, such as Thatcherism and Reaganism. Such an investigation may raise a whole complex of questions about ideology and life satisfaction—with or without the welfare net—that are related to questions of diffuse and specific system supports. In a more general vein, we can also relate values and ideologies to an existing regime on the assumption that substantial concordance between governors and the governed, and perhaps even among rivaling elites, contributes to the legitimacy of a system. The lack of such concordance, for example, between alien rulers and their colonial subjects, has often been blamed for the quick disintegration of legitimate rule in former colonies (Von der Mehden 1973, 78–79). By the same token, a basic disagreement among rival elites over the values underlying regime legitimacy may well doom a regime over the long run (Field and Higley 1979).

REBELLION OR SYSTEM NONSUPPORT?

Questions about what makes a democratic regime legitimate obviously have their obverse side in phenomena that weaken or counteract democratic legitimacy. Every one of our measuring rods is likely to reveal such a negative factor, although we must not forget that governments, once established, have great staying power that may see them through temporary crises and permit them in time to recover, as long as their adversaries cannot muster the organized power to overthrow them. There is a difference between a lack of regime support that is owing to indifference, parochialism, or ethnically/culturally divided countries—as can be observed in many nations, especially of the Third World—and the threat of a well-organized, militant minority animated by a different concept of legitimate order (Friedrich 1974, 111–112).

The rise of youthful rebellion and a counterculture in the 1960s, however ephemeral, was more of a fundamental challenge to the values on which legitimacy was founded in the advanced democracies even though there was never a serious attempt to overthrow, nor the likelihood of such an outcome. The economic and structural problems of the 1970s, by way of contrast, demoralized governments to the point where they felt helpless and doubted their own ability to cope with them. The breakup of the social-democratic consensus in Europe and its liberal equivalent in the United States, the rise of ethnic challenges, and the collapse of conservative rule in Italy, West Germany, and France each ushered in a sense of anomie and malaise—including the confidence gap (Lipset and Schneider 1983), the perennial budget deficit and overload crisis (Crozier, Huntington, and Watanuki 1975), and plenty of political alienation and protest (see Kaase, Chapter 3)—but not exactly the crisis of legitimacy prophesied by some of the writers of the early 1970s. Instead of the ballyhooed legitimacy crisis, one could argue, in fact, that in some countries there ensued a veritable orgy of deliberate government manipulation of the sentiments of diffuse system support. In place of attempts to solve the vexing problems, governments in the United States and Britain, for example, simply created a popular euphoria of flag-waving and patriotic self-congratulation while pursuing their neoconservative policies abroad and at home.

Let us briefly review the significance of the negative side of the indicators of legitimacy. Patriotism and pride of nationality clearly have their limits among ethnic minorities in a nation-state, even though we must not imagine that all Basques and Catalans categorically deny the legitimacy of the Spanish state or even that they may refuse to serve in its army or pay its taxes (see Chapter 6). Nevertheless, such a refusal for whatever reason—the motive could be private, religious, or even economic as often as political—would detract from the power of the state to command obedience and to muster its forces against an adversary. But we must not forget that such refusal is likely to involve only small numbers of citizens and to be anomic in character. Most important, the essence of legitimacy, its "rightful and proper" character, is not so easily impaired by a small number of nonbelievers or dissidents who may hardly stand out among the vast masses of people who are indifferent or parochial. A rather different situation is suggested by organized minorities that reject democracy as a system or want to overthrow it and replace it with another system *without* the consent of a majority. Thus, there is a difference between finding a radical minority bent on revolutionary action and gathering opinions of an undefined group of people who say they completely reject the present system. The latter should perhaps be characterized as alienation only. By the same token, people who say they are unhappy are not necessarily denying the democratic legitimacy of the state, nor do they necessarily have an alternative legitimate order in mind.

Actual measurements of protest, turmoil, and alienation are more relevant to legitimacy even though they may add together separate, unrelated incidents as easily as recording one unified rebellion. There is something essentially undemocratic about the use of political violence or terror in a democratic system (Wilkinson 1977, 78)—even though violence may be used against a dictatorship or foreign domination in order to attain more democracy—in that such action ignores the will of the majority. Even an impassioned commitment to the oppressed does not in principle excuse violence against a democratically elected government and its representatives. It is not implausible, though, to imagine that violence may be justified as self-defense against repressive state violence, especially if the silent majority that gave legitimacy to the elected government is not adequately informed or callous about the repression its government inflicts upon a minority (see also Honderich 1976, 90–113). One could also argue that such a government is an *imperfect democracy* that enjoys only a part of the immunity owed to truly democratic government.

Finally, with policy questions we arrive once more at the murky business of separating personal, structural, and ideological motives, or of separating implied system nonsupport from expressed disapproval of incumbent leaders, particular policies, and administrations in office. Counting the numbers of people who feel that the Thatcher government has failed to handle the economic situation properly or that her government's economic policies are not fair to all concerned falls far short of establishing a legitimacy deficit in Britain. This failure is in fact the reason why there is no inherent contradiction between the outpouring of patriotic support at the time of the Malvinas/Falklands crisis and the high level of disapproval of Thatcher's economic and social policies. On the other hand, a poll asking 100 French people whether, in general, they "trust or distrust" their various representatives and groups gave the following results.

	Trust	Distrust	Don't Know
Mayors	73	16	11
Senators and deputies	45	37	18
Government ministers	35	46	19
Politicians	29	54	17
Political parties	22	58	20

These results do indicate that there are elements of diffuse support or the absence of it in France, again without suggesting that the French will revolt tomorrow against their national executive leaders and parties while retaining their mayors and the national parliament (Hastings and Hastings 1984, 88). Expressions of a lack of trust in particular institutions—parliament, the executive, courts, higher education—are probably understood the same way, as references to the people who run them.

ORDINAL COMPARISON OF SYSTEM SUPPORTS

Nearly all the data I compare in this chapter appear in the chapters of this book. Because of the varying character and inclusiveness of existing data sets measuring aspects of system support among industrialized democracies, however, I have transformed them all into rank orderings and brought them together on Table 1.1.* in order to show patterns. Ordinal comparison has the advantage of simplifying the relative differences between high and low ratings and permits us, at least visually, to perceive these differences while discounting the varying coverage—many of the data sets include only European countries. A second ordinal table, Table 1.2, records the negative side of the same questions or adds scales of nonsupportive behavior. The relative magnitude of the entries (some scales account for less than 10 percent of the responses) has been noted in the notes for the tables.

The various columns differ, of course, in their relevance to general system support as will be detailed later. But, at first glance, there is a noticeable

---

*For the reader's convenience, all numbered tables and figures in this book have been grouped at ends of chapters.

concordance at both ends of most of the scales. For example, Britain and Ireland rank rather high on most of the scales of support, among the top three or at least among the top half of items 1–3 and 12–14 and almost nowhere near the bottom. The United States, to the extent that it is included, generally appears even higher in the ratings. Italy, Belgium, and frequently France, on the other hand, are almost invariably close to the bottom in system support, and so is Japan whenever it is included. The Scandinavian countries, the Netherlands, and Luxembourg are usually in the middle, if included, and West Germany seems to vary up and down in unpredictable ways.

Taking the rankings one by one, being proud of one's nation (index item 1) is obviously one of the most crucial in that it reflects identification with one of the elements, the population, of the conventional theory of the state.[3] The 1982 rankings of the United States, Britain, Italy, and West Germany, interestingly, are still the same as in the Almond and Verba survey of 1959, but now France, Ireland, and Spain are also placed in the appropriate order. No one will be surprised to see the United States, with its carefully maintained and reinforced civic religion, in first place.[4]

In the case of France, the alignment was complicated by long-standing patterns of revolutionary patriotism and, more recently, by the patriotic agonies of losing an empire—a motive shared by the higher-ranking British and, at least subjectively, also by many right-wing Americans who still mourn the passing of the age of U.S. omnipotence. Postwar conservative regimes in West Germany, Japan, Italy, Spain, and France muted their nationalism and, especially in the European nations, transmuted it into a new enthusiasm for European cooperation and unification. In the case of West Germany under Konrad Adenauer, this enthusiasm even took the form of a rejection of the tradition of national unification and unity—for example, with respect to the Saar—and it is only now, forty years after the end of World War II, that there is a serious revival of scholarly discussions about "the German question" (Weidenfeld 1983, chapters 1 and 4). Nazi crimes, the truncation of the territory of prewar Germany, and its division into irreconcilable West and East Germanies, moreover, have left a deeply seated sense of *identité manquée* ("lack of identity") that continues to show up in public opinion polls (Schweigler 1974, 184–188; Merkl 1974, chapter 2). None of these data deny the latent presence of national pride among Germans, Japanese, French, Italians, and Spaniards—even of the left wing—but it certainly explains their reluctance to wax as exuberantly patriotic as Americans on the Fourth of July or Englishmen after the reconquest of the Malvinas/Falklands.

WILLINGNESS TO FIGHT FOR ONE'S COUNTRY

The willingness to fight for one's country (items 2 and 3), the "state's territory," is a second major index of system support at a most basic level, even if the actual decision to go or refuse to go when drafted may relate to many other things, such as a respondent's perception of whether the country or its basic interests are under attack, peer pressure, and the coercive power of the state to penalize those people that refuse to serve.[5] The willingness to fight, in any case, represents a much higher potential cost to the citizen—injury, illness, imprisonment by the enemy, death, and at least prolonged absence from home—than a mere statement of national pride. Once again we find the United States at the very top with 71 percent (versus 20 percent negative) willing to fight, which must be a considerable recovery from the low point of the Tet offensive of 1968 and the rest of the Vietnam years. A considerable distance lower are Britain with 62 percent (versus 27 percent), Denmark with 58 percent (versus 22 percent), and Spain with 53 percent (versus 27 percent)—all countries where it is evidently still considered sweet to die for the homeland.

At the other end of the scale, we find the familiar World War II trio as well as France, Belgium, and the Netherlands. In all of these countries, the unwilling outnumber those willing to fight by a considerable margin. In Italy, the former constitute a majority (57 percent); in Japan, they outnumber the latter 40 percent to 20 percent. In Italy, France, and Belgium, the low rate may well be related to a high degree of individual self-regard, paired with a considerable cynicism toward civic duties, but Italy, Belgium, and West Germany also share the syndrome of a sense of belated and unfinished nationhood. Japan and West Germany, furthermore, learned their antimilitaristic lessons of 1945 all too well, with the result that there are profound pacifistic, and especially antinuclear, sentiments in both nations to this day. The West Germans, in particular, have always been aware of their exposed location in central Europe, which makes a defense of their territory a likely prescription for total self-destruction (Merkl 1987).

Jean Stoetzel made a major effort to correlate the willingness to fight among the European nations with other attitudes of the more than 15,000 respondents in nine countries. Those willing to fight appeared to be much better adjusted, enjoy better health and a sense of being the master of their own lives, and be more self-confident. They were also happier, more optimistic, more satisfied, less lonely, and less obsessed with a sense of meaninglessness and death. They were more active in their leisure time, belonged more to associations, exhibited more trust in others and in governmental institutions, and had more faith in moral values, family life, and a pride of nationality. Stoetzel also discovered considerable national differences in correlation with different factors: In Denmark, for example, willingness to fight varied according to the Left-Right continuum; in West Germany, it depended more on other life satisfactions; in France, religious attitudes correlated highly, unlike in Ireland where people willing to fight also condoned political terrorism and assassination. In Britain, home ownership and income were highly associated with the willingness to fight, although there and in Ireland, Italy, and West Germany working-class respondents were generally more willing to serve than were the white-collar and independent respondents (see Stoetzel, Chapter 5). Altogether, the European Values Study found only 43 percent willing to serve (40 percent were not, and 17 percent were undecided), and their responses varied by age and sex. Men under forty, older respondents, and women were noticeably less willing to defend their country than were male respondents between forty and sixty (Stoetzel 1983, 57), who grew up in the shadow of World War II and the Cold War. There is little reason to assume that these European findings would not apply also to the United States and Japan.

IDENTIFICATION WITH "THE SYSTEM"

Identification with one's nation and with defense of one's country are relatively easy and straightforward compared to identification with "the system," which is a complex and multifaceted relationship. There is identification with the democratic process by itself, which often invites principled disagreement about different ideals of democracy—such as representative versus direct democracy or procedural versus substantive principles—and about institutional details and reforms.

Commitment to democracy also has to be understood in the context of what system preceded it and may be viewed as an alternative. In a posttotalitarian or postdictatorial system, such as existed in West Germany in the late 1940s or in Spain during the first years after the death of General Francisco Franco, commitment to democracy in the midst of the psychological, social, and economic residues of the previous regime—and in the face of the threat of a coup or relapse—means something quite different from a commitment to "radical democratization," which the student movements and other new social movements have championed since the mid-1960s in many advanced industrial countries.

There is a big difference also between asking West German respondents whether they believe "democracy as we have it in the FRG, is the best form of government, or can . . . imagine a better one"—in other words, a question about an ideal type, even if not further defined—and asking for an assessment of a real system: What would you generally say about democracy in the FRG, that is, about our political parties and our entire political system? Are you satisfied, somewhat satisfied, or not satisfied with it? These two questions—the first asked in 1967 with 74 percent (versus 4 percent) affirmative responses; the second, in 1972 and 1976 with 90 percent (versus 7 percent and 6 percent, respectively)—do not form the basis of a longitudinal measurement (cf. Conradt 1980, 234). Some respondents, for instance, may feel that the political system of the FRG does not conform to their ideal of democracy. Others may respond to the policy overtones of the second version and consider certain West German policies unacceptable or undemocratic. In fact, both questions were repeated in 1978 and drew different levels of affirmative responses, 71 percent and 90 percent, respectively.

The question, Are you satisfied with the way democracy works in _____? also has strong policy overtones (Table 1.1, 4 and 5) and, in this form, would probably be understood by the public more in terms of satisfaction with the present government than as long-term support for the regime. Averaging the rankings over eight years, of course, helps to strengthen the long-term aspects and may even help to measure trust in government if the results show only a low level of fluctuation. There is nothing wrong, certainly, with measuring popular reactions to particular policies as long as we are clear about what we are doing and have a theory about policy satisfaction's being an important part of democratic legitimacy. I shall return to the policy angle later. The response scales of Table 1.1 for items 4 and 5 deviate from those of items 1–3 in an important way. Suddenly the West Germans are near the top, for motives that seem somewhat obscure. The West Germans' place on both scales may actually have become lower since 1983, as the fallout from assorted government scandals and the government's handling of the consequences of Chernobyl have penetrated the civic consciousness. But the high rating of West Germany, nevertheless, seems to confirm the evidence to be gained elsewhere (Rausch 1983, 130–142) of the consolidation of system support in that country.

To illustrate, the West German constitution, the Basic Law, got off to a poor start: In 1956, only 29 percent expressed approval of it, 6 percent were opposed, 14 percent were undecided, and 51 percent said they did not know the document (in 1979, 64 percent repeated the last statement). But in the late 1970s, 68 percent expressed confidence in the constitution and rejected the thought of a complete recasting of the occupation-era document, which has never been popularly ratified. Only 14 percent supported a revision.[6] In the mid-1970s, a rising percentage (68 percent in 1974 and 79 percent in 1976) agreed that "we have a good political order in the FRG," and the positive responses to the question about satisfaction with democracy (Table 1.1, 4 and 5) remained at the 76–80 percent level until the 1980s. Then they began to drift down to 66 percent in 1982, probably in reaction to the candidacy of Franz Josef Strauss for chancellor in 1980 and the antimissile deployment campaigns of 1981 (Rausch 1983, 132–135).[7]

The next group of items on Table 1.1, items 6–8, still fits into this picture because, in its disaggregated form, it reveals another salient aspect of the mysterious ups and downs of the FRG on the scales. The high rating of West Germany on the reform-plus-defense scale, it turns out, is due not so much to a devotion to gradual societal improvement and reform but to an unusually large percentage of respondents (38 percent)[8] who feel that the status quo "must be valiantly defended against all subversive forces" (see Linz, Chapter 2). Bearing in mind the rising German hysteria about subversive "system-changers" and terrorism in the 1970s,[9] I consulted the annual Eurobarometer percentages on this question and found the following development (see Figure 1.1): West German defensiveness about "our present society" has been rising ever since the social-liberal coalition took power in late 1969 and reached a peak in 1978 that exceeded the 1981 measurement of Table 1.1, 8. After some repressive measures against radicals and terrorists, in fact, some of the defensive mania may have been transmuted into a spirit of "gradual improvement by reform," which may also account for the high "satisfaction with how democracy functions" reported above for the late 1970s.

The findings are buttressed further by the global Human Values Study of 1981 and 1982, which split the options of the same question a different way, namely, into overall acceptance, gradual improvement, and complete rejection of the system—without mention of radical change or revolutionary action. The changes are amazing: far larger numbers now admitted to profound alienation (without committing themselves to revolutionary action, cf. Table 1.2, 7), and larger numbers also said they accepted their existing law, government, and society—the West Germans led with a very high 43 percent, more than twice as high as the next two, Australia (21 percent) and Canada (18 percent). Fifty-four percent of the Germans, at the bottom end of the scale, opted for gradual improvement—both percentages are very similar to the FRG's 38 percent for defense of the status quo and 53 percent for gradual reform on the Eurobarometer scales. The relative position of France and Italy on both scales, i.e., higher on reform than on defense/ acceptance also conforms to this interpretation.

The parallel character of the two surveys also helps us, one, to put the European data in global comparison with Japan, the United States, Canada, and Australia and, two, to give an intra-European refinement to the broad-stroke global picture. On the gradual reform scale, evidently, Japan, Canada, and the United States can be grouped with Spain and Sweden, and the Benelux countries and Denmark are closer to the British attitude than to the German one. On the acceptance/defense scale, by the same token, Australia and Canada belong with the Netherlands and Denmark (Belgian responses seem to differ because of a high percentage of don't knows), and the United States appears closer to Britain than to the lowest group, which includes Japan along with France, Italy, Belgium, Spain, and Sweden. If we sum up the scores of both the Human Values Study items (Table 1.1, 9 and 10) and compare that total with the combined Eurobarometer scale (Table 1.1, 6), we obtain the following ranking: The highest rankings go to West Germany, Japan, Canada, the United States, and Australia; then come Britain, France, and Italy, in that order. This order is the obverse of the complete system rejection rankings (Table 1.2, 7) and would place Spain and the Netherlands still above this highest group of West Germany, etc., in diffuse system support. Surprisingly, Ireland, Denmark, and Belgium would rank below France and Italy.

CONFIDENCE IN POLITICAL INSTITUTIONS

Although not part of the comparative tables (except Table 1.4), few measurements of declining system support caught the attention of the U.S. public as dramatically as the precipitous drop of confidence in various political institutions in the 1970s. In the United States, at least, the confidence gap in such long-established institutions as the presidency, Congress, and the Supreme Court seemed to signify an alarming lapse in the traditional and rational elements of legitimate authority in the system (see Table 1.3). These trends were explored in considerable detail by Samuel Huntington

(Crozier, Huntington, and Watanuki 1975, 79–83) and by Seymour M. Lipset and William Schneider (Lipset and Schneider 1983) and found to apply, with minor variations, to a host of political and social institutions, including the media. But Lipset and Schneider also concluded significantly that the lack of confidence mostly applied to the leadership and performance of the institutions and organizations and that belief in the basic soundness of the institutional system remained very high (Lipset and Schneider 1983, 27–28). The overall trend for confidence in institutions was a steep decline during the Vietnam and Watergate years, followed by a modest recovery for some and stagnation or further decline for others (labor, business, religion, and the press) (Table 1.3).[10]

Both European and Japanese scholars tell us that similar trends also characterized the political landscape in their countries in the 1970s—without benefit of Vietnam involvement, Watergate crisis, or disillusionment with President Carter (Flanagan 1982; Crozier, Huntington, and Watanuki 1975, 16–18, 26–29, 50–52, 142–145). People everywhere—especially the young—are disenchanted with big organizations, including government, and with their flawed channels and procedures for coping with the demands of the public.

The European Values Study ranked different institutions with respect to the confidence they enjoyed among the 15,000 respondents in nine nations. Europeans rated the police, army, and the courts above the average—before education, organized religion, and their respective parliaments; below average were executives, major companies, the press, and the unions, in that order (Stoetzel 1983, 84). Table 1.4 shows the results of a Gallup International survey of 1981/1982 for a ten-country Western European average (EUR), six of the larger European countries, Japan, and the United States. Japan diverges significantly from the Europeans by placing the courts and police at the top, followed by the press, education, and the army. The bureaucracy, parliament, and the unions come before major companies and the churches. The United States gives the first three places to army, police, and the churches; next come education, the civil service, Congress, the courts, and major companies; and finally, the press and the unions. The uniformly high position of the police in the United States—especially vis-à-vis the courts—is hard to explain, and there are many other surprises in individual countries: Italians evidently place their press far above the Chamber of Deputies and the Senate while the British rate Parliament rather low on the totem pole.

By comparison, the Lou Harris ranking of U.S. institutions on Table 1.3 places medicine, higher education, and the Supreme Court before the military followed by the presidency and organized religion. Congress, major companies, and the press rank the lowest except for the trade unions (but see also Lipset and Schneider 1983, 203). Over the fifteen years from 1966 to 1981, this rank order changed very little except for a relative promotion of the presidency and the Supreme Court on the scale (Lipset and Schneider 1983, 68). But all along, as Lipset and Schneider have shown, the negative perceptions of the leadership of these institutions have been accompanied by the widespread conviction (68–80 percent) that given better leaders, they could be made to work very well. The confidence gap, in other words, clearly distinguishes between the leaders and the institutional offices they hold.

VALUES AND SATISFACTIONS

Items 11–15 on Table 1.1 deal with values and life satisfaction in a way we have already encountered in Stoetzel's correlations with the willingness to fight for one's country. Religious values alone (item 11) may not strike the reader as the most likely correlate with diffuse system support, but it is hard to ignore the extent to which the ranking resembles those of items 1–3 on the same table. As I explained at the beginning, political and religious communities are analogues that can and historically did powerfully reinforce each other just as much as they may be arrayed against each other. In a modern society, being religious often reinforces patriotism and diffuse system support. We can also compare the rankings of Table 1.1, item 11, with the mention of "living in a religious manner" among the life goals of the global human values surveys (Hastings and Hastings 1982, 499ff.). The following percentages of the adult populations mentioned living religiously as a life goal (multiple choices were permitted): United States and Canada 55, France 49, Italy and Britain 44, West Germany 21, and Japan 13. The percentages are only half as large as those of the Gallup survey, or still less, but only France appears to be out of place. The European Values Study includes a ranking of religious practice (church attendance) that helps to illuminate the position of at least the European countries on a scale from 1 to 1,000: Ireland 977, Spain 516, Italy 464, Belgium 361, the Netherlands 349, West Germany 304, Britain 202, France 157, and Denmark 88 (Stoetzel 1983, 263). It is clear that France ranks even below Protestant England and far lower than the other Catholic countries, even those in which religiousness is also closely identified with being right of center (Stoetzel 1983, 264, 272, 287).

Furthermore, as Frederick Turner has pointed out, religiousness is by no means a reliable indicator of moral views (see Turner, Chapter 6). In the European Values Study, countries were also ranked according to their permissiveness (degree of "willingness to excuse") with regard to a long list of transgressions of varying severity.[11] The ranking on a summary index from the most permissive on down is France 317, the Netherlands 311, Denmark 282, Spain 268, West Germany 264, Britain 262, Belgium 261, Italy 238, and Ireland 212. This order is very different from the one for religious values on Table 1.1 (see also Hastings and Hastings 1982, 526ff.).

The two scales for life satisfaction and the one for happiness (Table 1.1, 12–14) again rate attitudes that positively related to the willingness to fight (see Stoetzel, Chapter 5). It is not implausible to expect that people who are very dissatisfied with their family life, personal fortune, or economic future will have less of a stake in the country, though they might just as well take out their unhappiness on a wartime enemy—i.e., be more willing to fight. On the other hand, there are highly subjective and also cultural factors involved in making people pronounce themselves "very happy"— the ancient Greeks would have feared the envy or disdain of the gods. Forty percent of the Brazilians, who might be considered to have a lot less to be happy about than people in other countries, declared themselves to be "very happy," and another 36 percent said "fairly happy." Only 16 percent of the French and 12 percent of West Germans said they were "very happy" (and 51 percent and 49 percent, respectively, said they were "fairly happy" [Hastings and Hastings 1982, 538ff.]). I shall come back to this dimension later in discussing unhappiness.

PERFORMANCE AND SYSTEM SUPPORT

Even though international differences in the economic and social indicators rarely seem to guarantee a higher degree of life satisfaction—otherwise the West Germans and the French ought to be much happier than the Brazilians— it still is true that within one country over a period of time, the perceived success of economic policies and their benefits for the individual help to reinforce diffuse system support. By same token, we would expect economic downturns, cutbacks, and policy failures to weaken diffuse system support, although an enlightened citizenry might be able to differentiate between the effects of bad policies and factors beyond the government's control.[12] If the citizens can do that, they may even support a well-designed policy of austerity, especially if they thought it was fair. Beyond the short-term economic and social causes and effects, an enlightened electorate might also make a rational choice between policies that emphasize either economic freedom (free enterprise) or the equality produced by socialist economic policies (Table 1.1, 15). Although long-range differences on this score are more likely to represent an entrenched history of liberalism (as in the United States, Britain, and France) than a short-range choice, this dimension also places West Germany in the egalitarian camp while Japan surprisingly comes out on the libertarian side (see also Turner, Chapter 6).

But we would do well to bear in mind the importance of the exact wording of questions, for another international poll that asked respondents to choose between "individualism and socialism" in their country's social conditions produced quite different results (Hastings and Hastings 1982, 549). Predictably, majorities in France, the United States, Canada, and Australia—in that order—opted for individualism, but so did the West Germans (59:37), in fact more than in the United States. On the other hand, the Japanese (71:25) and Italians (54:30) chose socialism, and so did the respondents in Britain (64:26), where especially the lower classes heavily supported it. Like most value choices, of course, this option per se is not a factor for or against system legitimacy except as it may contribute or detract from a consensus on values.

There was also an attempt to gauge the extent to which different postindustrial nations accept the pivotal role of such common economic mechanisms as collective bargaining and of the relative importance of the two "social partners," major companies and trade unions (Table 1.1, 16). I could also have examined (but did not) the balance of consensus on economic intervention by the state. All these parameters raise a lot of questions, and most of them cannot be answered because of a lack of comparative data. Raising them, however, will place what can be demonstrated into the proper context, at least as long as we remember its rather indirect and still largely unproven impact on system legitimacy.[13]

In spite of the glaring difference between the relatively robust U.S. and the weak British economic performances,[14] the political success in recent years of the administrations of Prime Minister Margaret Thatcher and President Ronald Reagan, with their distinctive economic policies, sheds some more light on a confused situation. The positive climate of British public opinion toward the welfare state dropped dramatically between 1963 and 1968. In 1963, opinion was still expansive regarding pensions and housing—although some 1962 polls had already noted a growing resistance to family subsidies, unlimited unemployment benefits, and rent subventions—but in 1968, 33 percent agreed that too much was being spent on social welfare. Eighty-nine percent thought that the availability of the (unemployment) dole made people less willing to work, and 78 percent believed that the presence of so many social services meant that people worked less hard than they used to (Golding and Middleton 1982, 228–229). Under the battering of the energy crisis of the seventies, these sentiments turned into a veritable torrent of media propaganda against the welfare cheats and dole scroungers and, eventually, supplied the popular basis for Thatcherism. But did the British like the tough medicine they had prescribed for themselves? Obviously not as Tables 1.5 and 1.6 show: During the period of 1980 to the end of 1982, the proportion of those who thought the government's economic policies were not fair to all concerned grew from about two out of five to almost three out of five (Table 1.5). There was, moreover, a difference of opinion as to whether the government did too much for the well-to-do and too little for the working class and for people with small incomes or pensions (Table 1.6).

On a less moralistic question, Do the government's policies for tackling the economic situation give you the feeling that they are or are not handling the situation properly? Thatcher's government did only a little better: The negative responses consistently hovered around 53–58 percent while the positive ones were in the neighborhood of 30–36 percent (Hastings and Hastings 1982, 125, 130–134; 1984, 6, 138); in early 1981, the negative responses even rose to 71 percent (January) and 66 percent (May). Percentages of 52–68 particularly criticized the government's failure to control the rise in prices, and 40–59 percent expressed general dissatisfaction with the government and, especially, its cuts in public spending (Hastings and Hastings 1982, 131; 1984, 139). Only rarely did the government's supporters outnumber its critics (June and July 1982) and even then never with a majority. There was, however, a strong partisan perspective to the responses; for example, in 1980, 72 percent (versus 20 percent who did not) of respondents identified with the Conservative party expressed approval while 93 percent (versus 4 percent) of Labour supporters disapproved.

A series of 1982 polls on specific policy issues brought out more fully the issue at stake: The respondents felt "less favorably" on tax policy (46 percent versus 17 percent), Common Market policy (43 percent to 28), the level of unemployment (72 percent to 4), and the cost of living, but on the Falklands issue 64 percent were favorable (versus 24 percent who were not), and right after the Falklands operation (which in an early poll even netted 84 percent approval versus 13 percent), "Thatcher as prime minister" received 39 percent favorable responses (versus 32 percent).

One could go on with this list of particular policies[15] and show that none of Thatcher's policies, except the Falklands operation (and, barely, her perceived record on law and order), even drew a plurality of approval over disapproval (Hastings and Hastings 1984, 174-175). Even in February and March of 1983, 50 percent of the respondents expressed dissatisfaction (versus 41-42 percent who were satisfied) with the way the government was running the country, a sharp reduction from the 68 percent who were dissatisfied (versus 23 percent satisfied) before the Falkland crisis (Hastings and Hastings 1984, 175-176). It is difficult to deny in this case that it was the little tail of the Falklands venture that wagged the large dog of public opinion, for despite disapproval of practically every single Thatcherite policy, Thatcher's government promptly won the mid-1983 elections in a landslide. If the long list of policy failures could not keep Thatcher from being returned in triumph, why should we imagine that the economic and social failures might diminish the legitimacy of British government?

The U.S. experience with the "Teflon presidency" of Ronald Reagan supplies a parallel example of policy disapproval by majorities on nearly every issue, even if we grant that Grenada and the postures of relentlessly fighting the "evil empire" fall short of the drama and significance of the Falklands operations. Even the earlier public support of the military buildup has long turned into rejection by the majority, and yet Reagan's extraordinary ability to communicate and manipulate symbolic national values seems to succeed even when his policies have gone astray according to the public. Unlike the British public, which from the start responded to Thatcherism with skepticism, the U.S. public at first seemed rather impressed with Reaganomics: In 1981, 42 percent predicted that the president's economic policy would be a success (versus 41 percent who said the opposite) while nearly half the respondents expected a healthy economic expansion. But even then, large majorities believed that "the rich and big business will be much better off" (69-75 percent) and "the elderly, the poor, and the handicapped will be especially hard hit" (64-71 percent). By May of 1982, a majority of 53 percent (versus 30 percent) was ready to pronounce the president's economic program a failure as the recession of 1982 began to make itself felt (Hastings and Hastings 1984, 48–49). By September of the same year, 58 percent (versus 39 percent) had become convinced that the country was in a depression even though the unemployment rate in the United States, to cite one example, never took on British proportions.

Actually, the presidential budget cuts turned out to be much more selective than the president's initial rhetoric would have led anyone to expect: The victims were mostly Aid for Families with Dependent Children (AFDC), unemployment insurance, CETA training jobs, and the social security benefits for student aid and disability—in other words, mostly minorities, women, indigents, and the handicapped were affected. Programs benefiting the broad constituencies of the elderly (social security, Medicare), veterans, and even low-income youth (school lunches, head start, summer youth jobs) remained intact (Dolbeare 1982, 260–261).

The choice of targets was rather carefully based on public opinion polls taken while President Carter was in office: In April 1980, results were for all federal welfare programs, 69 percent for cuts, 28 percent opposed; for food stamps, 65 percent for cuts, 32 percent opposed; for social security, 23 percent for cuts, 74 percent opposed. When his successor was about to take office in January 1981, the polls showed that 82 percent (versus 15 percent) wanted Medicare benefits hardly changed at all and 77 percent preferred the same for social security while 53 percent (versus 41 percent) advocated 10–50 percent cuts in the food stamp program and 58 percent (versus 38 percent) wanted to see federal unemployment benefits curtailed. School lunches (63 percent were against substantial cuts) and Medicaid (57 percent) were to be left intact, but the CETA program and welfare funds granted to lower levels of government were singled out for cuts (Hastings and Hastings 1982, 145–147).

The big welfare backlash in the United States, as in Britain—in continental Europe the backlash was much smaller even though those nations' tax burdens and expenditures on income maintenance and public health care are generally much larger than those in the United States[16]—by no means cut the safety net right across the board. The United States also had the good fortune of having an energetic labor market, which expanded mightily if at lower wage levels, while European unemployment seemed nearly impervious to government measures. Before the 1982 congressional elections, a large majority (73 percent)—even among Republican voters (62 percent)—insisted that voters ought to tell Republicans it is neither right nor fair to give breaks to the rich while making it tougher for the elderly, the poor, and the handicapped (Hastings and Hastings 1984, 1980). In any case, President Reagan too was reelected by a landslide in 1984. There is no evidence that U.S. legitimacy has suffered in the least from the negative responses to his economic policies, or even from his relatively less friendly reception by blacks, women, and the poor. On the contrary, some of his magic has undoubtedly rubbed off on diffuse system support as the patriotic pride of many has been rekindled by his consummate showmanship.

STRAINS ON THE WELFARE STATE

Because of their pronounced anti-welfare-state images (as distinguished from some of the actual policies) both Reaganomics and Thatcherism raise the question whether the safety net programs, in particular public health care and old age pensions, are losing their power to generate diffuse systems support, a power demonstrated clearly during the days of depression and crisis management in many advanced countries in the 1930s.[17] The over-extension of the democratic welfare state and the excessive tax burden it caused (Hicks and Swank 1984, 81–119) were criticized early by the British press, but soon Americans too were speaking of "the welfare mess" and whacking the bushes for instances of welfare fraud. Although they would hesitate to bad-mouth welfare, the West German Christian Democrats have built entire national election campaigns around dramatizations of the growing budget deficit attributed to the "big spenders" in the Social Democratic party: In images and words clearly connecting current deficits to the legitimacy crisis of the Weimar Republic and the dire straits suffered during the years of great inflation (1923) and depression, they have conjured up a sense of impending disaster for the value of the German mark and for the living standards of West Germans, along with the danger of Communist subversion and the political chaos to follow.

The by now almost universal giant budget and tax overload crisis, inevitably, has forced democratic nations to make painful choices (see Dogan and Rose, Chapters 7 and 8). Where in the panoply of the current welfare state, which eats up most of the money, is the budget ax to fall? And, by implication, what services or aspects may turn out to be immune to even the great fiscal crisis? (Lockhart 1984). What is the difference between reinforcing a sense of national solidarity in adversity against a laissez-faire background of the 1920s and 1930s and the effect of relatively minor cutbacks in overdeveloped social security and health coverage systems today? Perhaps the earlier instance did involve a sense of legitimacy while today's problems do not. And given the current situation, will the public understand that the most advanced social security systems may indeed have developed a bad case of elephantiasis and that health care rights are on the verge of becoming a bottomless pit? (see Dogan, Chapter 7). Will people appreciate the importance of tax cuts now and understand the financial dilemmas that have been revealed by the program approach to budget analysis? (see Rose, Chapter 8, and Schmidt 1983, 1–18).

It would appear necessary to disassemble some aspects of these rather complex questions before we can try to answer any of them. To begin with, the voting public in most advanced countries is very poorly informed about its own entitlements. First, a 1980 Swedish poll (Hastings and Hastings 1982, 70) ascertained that only 6 percent of a national sample (versus 81 percent who overestimated it) could answer the question, How many households receive household subsidies? within a margin of 25 percent of the correct answer, and only 39 percent could indicate the average size of this subsidy—10 percent were correct—within a margin of 0–20 percent. Forty-nine percent were much further off the mark. Second, there are moralistic dimensions—the work ethic versus the dole and social altruism versus neglecting the less fortunate—intersecting with pragmatic, even technical, questions of good administration and distribution. The welfare state in the United States, for example, has been inhibited (compared to continental Europe) by the work ethic and vitiated by a welter of structural complications ranging from federalism to grossly inadequate access and distribution.[18] As long as the system still has to learn to distribute basic health care to some people who are currently not served at all, it seems rather premature to worry about whether the highest quality of health care and medical technology—such as kidney dialysis or heart transplants—is getting too expensive for general distribution (Morris 1984, 383–395).

In the 1970s and early 1980s, the public attitudes in France and West Germany toward their health care systems were quite satisfied (two-thirds) and in Canada, Britain, and the United States even more so (over 80 percent). Yet 15 percent of the U.S. respondents—versus only 5 percent on the Continent—complained that they could not afford to be sick. Low-income respondents in all advanced countries particularly appreciate good public health care whereas the better-off and right-of-center respondents are more likely to prefer fewer health benefits (and other social security costs)—and lower taxes. Still, dissatisfaction with public health care has been mounting, for example, in the United States and Italy (Andrain 1985, 117–119, 197–199). In the United States, in particular, protectiveness against health cuts rose from 58 percent (versus 35 percent cutters) in September 1981 to 73 percent (versus 21 percent cutters) in November 1982. Protective attitudes regarding care for the elderly, poor, and handicapped rose from 79 percent (versus 15 percent) to 81 percent (versus 7 percent) in the same period, and social security support jumped from 71 percent to 81 percent (versus 22 percent and 12 percent, respectively [Hastings and Hastings 1984, 184]).

In Great Britain, Thatcher had barely been in office a year when a May 1980 poll revealed that 59 percent (versus 24 percent) of the adult population was not made "more favorable toward her government" by public spending cuts in themselves, about the same percentage that had disapproved of her government's spending policies and the way it ran the country (58 percent and 57 percent, respectively). The same polls also ascertained that 64 percent (versus 29 percent) disapproved of the government's health service policies and that barely 44 percent (versus 42 percent) supported its old age pensions policy, a balance that turned negative (46 percent versus 42 percent) before the year was out (Hastings and Hastings 1982, 127–132).

The percentages of people who were prepared either to leave health, education, and welfare benefits intact or to "save" them even if it meant increasing taxes also rose from 79 percent in March 1980 to 82 percent in March 1981. In March and July 1980, 68–70 percent also felt the government was spending too little on the National Health Service (versus 4 percent too much) while 22 percent thought the expenditure was about right. Old age pensions in the same polls gained the support of 54–59 percent ("too little" spending) and of 31–38 percent who believed the spending level to be about right (Hastings and Hastings 1982, 142–143). By August and September of 1982, 79 percent and 72 percent, respectively, disapproved of the government's health service policies, and 47–48 percent had the same reaction toward its old age pensions. When asked in March 1983 what the priorities in consumer spending ought to be over the coming years, public health (with 26 percent) headed the list (Hastings and Hastings 1984, 175, 182). Almost the same question had been asked in Sweden three years earlier, and health and dental care (24 percent) and care of the elderly (23 percent) had headed a long list. The same items also drew the lowest mention among twenty-six items on a list of possible spending cuts—only 3 percent for the elderly and 8 percent for health (Hastings and Hastings 1984, 144).

How do all these results fit into our consideration of aspects of legitimacy in advanced democracies? It appears that in recent years spending on health and pensions has grown prodigiously in all OECD countries (see Dogan and Rose, Chapters 7 and 8, and Hicks and Swank 1984), fueling the compulsion of governments to overspend. This compulsion has followed the trends toward the aging of populations and spiraling health costs and been aggravated by a relative economic stagnation or decline (see Dogan, Chapter 7). But when the budget crunch was borne home and aggravated by a new insistence on tax cuts, health and pensions turned out to lead a charmed life among all the programs of the welfare state—perhaps because both involve life-threatening crises beyond an individual's control. It is also possible that a conservative hard-heartedness on these two issues is indeed seen as so unjust that it touches on the sense of legitimacy. And yet, the trend toward the privatization of economic concerns—from private supplements to health and pension coverage to simple neglect, holes in the safety net, or the vagaries of a growing underground economy—also is beginning to nibble away at the solid foundations of the democratic welfare state. It is not inconceivable that the privately insured and the simply uninsured may one day again outnumber those dependent on the public safety net. If that day arrives, will it also make system legitimacy once more vulnerable to major crises, or will it start a new cycle of welfarism?

LEGITIMACY, PROTEST, AND ALIENATION

Low system support is not prima facie a cause of delegitimation unless, of course, it should reach levels that undermine a state's credibility and its capacity to function. A state can be compared to a voluntary organization that "claims the monopoly of the legitimate use of physical force within a given territory" (Weber 1946, 78) and can function only when given that monopoly, of territorial control, and the voluntary obedience of its members. A loss of control over significant parts of a state's territory, as in secessionist rebellions, effectively challenges its monopoly of the use of force—guerrilla movements and private armies (rather than terrorism) can be a threat and, most of all, massive refusals to obey will diminish and can even lead to the disintegration of its organized power. The democratic countries under consideration in Table 1.2 have not been threatened by either effective secessionist rebellions—only autonomist movements—or guerrilla armies. Antisystem behavior has been limited to political turmoil, most of it anomic in character, and to individual refusals to obey that rarely reach a degree of organization such as the anti-Vietnam draft resistance movement in the United States or taxpayer revolts in Denmark and elsewhere. Both the draft resistance movement and the tax challenges, moreover, were met, not with head-on confrontation, but by individualized court action or by giving draft resisters a nonrebellious way out in the form of conscientious objection and alternative service.

Table 1.2 might help us gauge the state of the challenges to democratic legitimacy. The striking agreement between the relative lack of pride of nationality (item 1) in Japan, West Germany, France, and Italy—Spain's can be accounted for by ethnic antagonisms—and the unwillingness of the same respondents to fight for their respective countries (items 2 and 3) is our first glimpse of *incivisme* in those countries—and we might as well add the Benelux countries to the list. Although the significance of lacking national pride may be mired in cultural ambiguities, an unwillingness to fight seems to mirror two discrete elements: the pacifist movements in some countries (West Germany, Japan, the Benelux countries, and probably the Scandinavian ones if they had been included) and the Communist parties in others (Italy, France). Britain's peace movement evidently was not strong enough to overcome the patriotic impulse.

On the next three items (4–6), those respondents opting for radical change by revolutionary action again seem to live in countries with strong Communist and other revolutionary movements (Italy, France, Greece) or cultural-ethnic rebellions (Ireland, Spain, Belgium). The West German response now lies at the other end of the scale, as do the responses from Denmark, Sweden, and Norway. The dominant role of social-democratic parties in those countries (and perhaps also Britain and the Benelux countries) clearly has preempted discontent with moderate reformism.

Item 7, "completely reject present system," interestingly, appears to measure something quite different, namely, alienation in a more passive form. The large number of alienated, 20–26 percent, in France, Italy, and Britain is a surprise, although Max Kaase has pointed out that it is quite possible to be alienated, even violent, and yet neither interested in nor capable of challenging the political order. Democracy itself defuses discontent by facilitating peaceful change in power, and people in democratic countries are by and large rather satisfied with their lives and with their systems. At the same time, people have clearly become more distrustful of their leaders and institutions and more capable of upsetting the applecart (see Kaase, Chapter 3).

We have the data to look at both the extent to which people in these countries may be unhappy or dissatisfied with their lives and systems and the extent to which they have engaged in antisystem behavior. Individual unhappiness, (Table 1.2, 12), whatever it may portend in this connection, once more gathers our democracies into the camps of the unhappy Axis countries plus Spain and France versus the happy Britain, Ireland, and the United States. The late British psychoanalyst Don W. Winnicott, in his book *Home Is Where We Start From*, wrote: "The unhappy will try to destroy happiness [of others]. Those who are caught up in the prison of the rigidity of their own defenses will try to destroy freedom [of everybody]." But can we really equate, as Winnicott suggested, a healthy individual childhood development with a healthy social and political structure or the "envy of freedom" of a slave, with his or her own unhappiness and constricted character, with social repression? In the polls cited on Tables 1.1 and 1.2, satisfaction with one's life (Table 1.1, 12–13) changes the sequence on Table 1.2, although Italians, French, and Germans are still on the dissatisfied side, along with the Greeks. Satisfaction with democracy (Table 1.1, 4–5) carries the change still further by showing Italians, French, Belgians, and the Irish as being the most dissatisfied while the Germans and Greeks are happy with their political systems. The changes show that we cannot simply link personal unhappiness with dissatisfaction with the system, though for Italy, France, and Belgium it seems true enough.

The indicators of political turmoil and deaths from political violence (Table 1.2, 8–11) in the years 1973–1977 and 1948–1977 show that Greece, France, Italy, Britain, and Ireland were among the most turbulent countries while a lot of the countries at the opposite end of the scales had no record of turbulence at all. The scales differ in minor ways, but most of the principal nations at the top are familiar entries (especially Greece, France, and Italy). The words *turmoil* and *deaths* are reminiscent of Douglas H. Hibbs's study of mass political violence which, like the *World Handbook of Political and Social Indicators*, contains strong evidence that a high degree of economic development is related to less turmoil and violence (Hibbs 1973). Hibbs's "collective protests" (riots, demonstrations, and political strikes) are not really meant to bring down the governmental system of democracy while his "internal war" (armed attacks, assassinations, and deaths from political violence) is not capable of it. There is an overwhelming impression that in advanced democratic countries, political turmoil and violence serve only a symbolic function, perhaps to teach the government and the majority supporting it a painful lesson.

On the other hand, we must not underestimate the long-range erosion of legitimacy that may result from prolonged, massive anomie and anarchy, which could also be related to the processes by which contemporary governments succumb to "overload" or lose their capacity to steer society. Perhaps the loss of legitimacy of the social partners (Table 1.2, 14) precedes that of the entire system. Ulrich Widmaier, with the help of the Globus model, has predicted such an inexorable erosion of legitimacy for most systems (see Widmaier, Chapter 4). However, he exempts Italy—which is in a prominent place on the Table 1.2 scales—because "legitimacy can only be lost when it is there," and for historical reasons, the Italian government has never achieved a high measure of it (Grew 1978, 273–279). This theory of declining system performance is quite different from the political alienation theories as well as from the well-known theories of value change of R. Inglehart, which have demonstrated the generational change of system-supporting attitudes since the 1960s.

Jean Stoetzel links the unwillingness to fight for one's country with various other negative attitudes in an almost Manichaean way: The people who won't fight also tend to be less happy or less satisfied with their lives, more pessimistic about their futures, lonely, less active in leisure and in associations, less tolerant of unusual neighbors, and less confident of the police and all institutions. They express less interest in marriage, home life, and parent-child relations; they more often find life meaningless and are obsessed with death (see Stoetzel, Chapter 5). There was also an international poll on how often people feel that life is meaningless, and it ranked nations as follows, from the most morose on down:[19] Spain (42 percent feel that way often or sometimes), France (34 percent), Italy (33 percent), West Germany (27 percent), Britain (26 percent), Japan and Belgium (25 percent), Ireland (24 percent), Denmark (20 percent), and the Netherlands (17 percent) (Hastings and Hastings 1984, 529). Perhaps William Shakespeare should have set his *Hamlet* on the Mediterranean shores rather than in Denmark— and even Hamlet was more concerned with settling a private score than with overthrowing a government.

CONCLUSIONS

I began with the elusive problems of defining legitimacy and wrestled with ways to translate the almost indefinable into testable propositions, such as that pride of nationality might measure identification with the community and willingness to fight might measure identification with territorial control. But these two elements of identification can also be related to a welter of social attitudes such as an attachment to home and family, trust in strangers and in political institutions, and a willingness to contribute to one's society to the best of one's ability. Thus, personal happiness and life satisfactions may also play a role. A third element is identification with the governmental system, democracy, and with specific support of particular institutions that may feed back into diffuse system support. Another feedback may come from policy performance. The other side of the coin, the impact of system nonsupport, is harder to explain simply by considering the negative side of these supportive attitudes or actions. States rarely collapse from modest numbers of bad patriots, draft dodgers, or tax evaders alone, even though massive resistance would obviously be a serious problem. Active rebellion or revolution is a different matter, even if pursued only by small minorities. A confidence gap with regard to leaders, governments, and policies also may not signify a crisis of legitimacy—we do not really know.

These concepts were then used to generate, from various international polls, two ordinal tables that rank advanced democratic nations on a list of variables. Some patterns soon evolve from the comparison, such as the high levels of system support in the United States, Britain, and Ireland and the low levels in Italy, Greece, Belgium, and France on most accounts. But there are also other patterns, such as the lack of national pride and low willingness to fight in countries either conquered or ultimately defeated in World War II. On satisfaction with democracy, furthermore, the Greeks and the Germans—with the enthusiasm of new disciples—are near the top of the list, and on another measure of system acceptance/gradual reform, West Germany again ranks high along with Canada, Australia, the United States, Japan, Spain (also new disciples), and the Netherlands while France, Italy, and Britain rank the lowest. Clearly, there is more diffuse support in West Germany, and less in Britain, than at first meets the eye. And Italy is ever the low legitimacy wonder.

Examining more specific supports for particular institutions, such as parliaments and courts, we have looked at the U.S. confidence gap of the 1970s and noted that the lack of confidence applied more to the leadership and performance of those institutions than to the United States institutional system as such. Comparing confidence in institutions among the European democracies and Japan, we found an astonishing agreement among them all about having high respect for the police and army and respecting least the press (except in Japan) and the trade unions. Between the top and the bottom of these scales, however, there are some differences among nations— particularly among the United States (which ranked churches and education above the courts), Japan (where judges and journalists enjoy higher prestige), and the European nations. Japan gives the least respect to churches and other indicators of religious values, such as "living religiously" as a life goal or church attendance, but it ranks high on a sense of individual morality. The United States, Ireland, and the other Catholic nations of Europe rate religion highly, but this rating does not correlate at all with their relative "permissiveness" toward various moral transgressions, nor with their "happiness" and even less with their preferences for freedom over equality or "socialism" over individualism.

Do economic success and welfare state performance bolster the legitimacy of a regime? Arguing from the evidence *a contrario*, examination of the popular reactions to Thatcherism and Reaganomics showed that one patriotic exercise, like the Falklands/Malvinas operation or President Reagan's skillful invocation of patriotic symbols, clearly outweighed the effect of negative majority opinions of the two leaders' entire social and economic policies and helped get them both reelected. Although their personal political successes may not mean greater legitimacy for the regimes, there can be little doubt that the patriotic hoopla did enhance diffuse system support and that feedback from the social and economic policies made little difference. Regarding Reagan's and Thatcher's intended welfare cuts, the public's preoccupation with tax cuts and with trimming back the exuberant jungle of the democratic welfare state has definite limits in the public mind: Public opinion balks at reducing the heavy expenditures on public health care and old age pensions—and the politicians act accordingly—the two public welfare functions most closely connected with individual physical survival and hence, perhaps, most likely to involve an individual sense of the legitimacy of the system. To paraphrase Thomas Hobbes, the political obligation of citizens of the great Leviathan ends when the state (aside from military duty) is unable or unwilling to protect the lives of its citizens from the brutish state of nature.

What then is the state of legitimacy in the advanced democratic countries today? Is it endangered by failures of performance, as many social scientists have suggested? In the short run, considering policy failures and public reactions, this possibility does not seem to be the case even though conflicting public moral quandaries and confusions tend to obscure this fact. As long as democratic governments shrink from recklessly risking the health and lives of their constituents—through ill-motivated wars or major lapses of public health and social security—their legitimacy is not in danger. Nuclear accidents and other life-threatening mistakes, of course, may also endanger legitimacy.

Is it alienation and protest that put democratic legitimacy in jeopardy, as other scholars insist? Probably not, until the democratic states' monopoly of legitimate force and territorial control are really threatened, which does not appear to be the case in any of the countries considered—with the possible exception of Northern Ireland. By its very nature, democracy can peacefully handle popular pressure for change without violence or revolution. Lack of national pride on unwillingness to fight, and other forms of refusal or alienation have not yet impaired legitimacy anywhere; most of the time they do not even draw it into question. Pacifism and Communist oppositions so far have not presented significant challenges to democratic legitimacy, and turmoil and political violence, including terrorism, have not taken on worrisome magnitudes.

Is it the generational change in values and life-style, then, that has so visibly increased public resistance to many of the civic duties—fulfilling military service, paying taxes, contributing to societal maintenance—that earlier generations took more or less for granted? The answer really hinges on an evaluation of the concepts of political and social obligation among the new social movements of today's advanced democracies. Alienation aside, we must not ignore the very considerable moral motivation behind today's pacifists, ecologists, feminists, and even tax rebels, especially since liberal democratic thought, long before Henry David Thoreau, has always stressed a very limited and individualistic notion of what citizens owe to their state. The movements named only deny a person's specific obligation to be drafted, slowly poisoned, forced into marriage and childbearing, or to pay certain taxes without one's specific consent. They have rarely put anarchy above democratic legitimacy on their banners. If it is true, moreover, that legitimacy does not suffer from modest amounts of alienation and protest as long as its basic moral premise is still acknowledged, these value changes are no menace to it either. Even Jean Stoetzel's Manichaean forces, system-supporting people versus those who tend to view life as meaningless and are obsessed with death, suggest no deliberate challenge but, rather, a vast anomic army of the wayward and walking wounded who have been left behind in the processes of social integration.

NOTES

1. This statement, of course, is not to deny that today's "big government" is far more intrusive into our lives and has a vastly greater "reach" than its predecessors.

2. See especially the literature on how growing support for parliaments and executives may have turned into diffuse system support (cited in Easton 1975, 444–445).

3. The others are the state's territory and the governmental system.

4. The emphasis on patriotic image-building of the last years, and especially its exploitation during the Olympic Games of 1984 and the Statue of Liberty celebrations of 1986, must be unrivaled in any postindustrial society.

5. The last-mentioned dimension also involves the question of whether and how easily conscripts can opt for noncombatant alternative service. Many advanced industrial societies permit such an alternative.

6. In late 1968, after a year of student revolt, only 43 percent expressed approval, and 23 percent wanted revision. In 1972, 23 percent expressed the opinion the constitution was an obstacle to the realization of genuine democracy in West Germany (cited in Rausch 1983, 130–131).

7. For comparison, see also the polls on the revision of the Canadian constitution (Hastings and Hastings 1982, 89–98).

8. This percentage is exceeded only by the Norwegians (45 percent) for reasons unknown to me. Most others are around 20 percent, with Denmark and Holland at 24 percent.

9. The "system-changers" were mostly young socialists (Jusos) and feminists in the early 1970s. The Baader-Meinhof group and later terrorist formations functioned throughout the 1970s, with a peak of activity in the second half.

10. Gallup surveys for the seventies show generally higher figures but comparable trends except for the Congress, which they show in further decline.

11. The list begins with car theft, political assassination, and drug abuse—these are the least excusable transgressions among Europeans and rank above corruption, resisting the police, and tax evasion. The list ends with self-defense, divorce, abortion, and euthanasia, in reverse order (Stoetzel 1983, 30–38).

12. There are occasional polls, for example in Britain, that ask the respondents whether they believe certain economic problems to be beyond the control of government.

13. An excellent review of systematic attempts to establish either a social learning relationship between system support and perceptions of the performance of political incumbents, or a structuring hypothesis (i.e., that the level of system support influences one's evaluation of the performance) can be found in Muller and Williams (1980, 34–37). They suggest a reciprocal relationship rather than a one-way causation between the two variables. There are, of course, also some neo-Marxist models of the "legitimacy crisis of advanced capitalist states" (Habermas, Offe) which consider

that economic inputs are the only sources of democratic legitimacy and therefore expect prolonged recession or "stagflation" to bring on a terminal legitimacy crisis.

14. Britain was the last among eight typical industrial nations with an annual real growth of 3.3 percent in the period 1959–1973 (U.S., 4.2 percent) and slipped further during the oil shock era of 1974–1979 to 1.2 percent (U.S., 2.3 percent). In 1980, Britain lost 2.3 percent (U.S., 1.3 percent) while most of the other nations continued at 2.3–4.3 percent (Dolbeare 1982, 89).

15. The polls also asked, Do you approve of the way the government is handling—defense? cost of living and prices? economic and financial affairs generally? strikes and labor relations? full employment? education? the health service? housing? old age pensions? immigration? roads? taxation?

16. The overall tax rate of 17 percent of individual earnings in 1976 and the marginal tax rate of 32 percent in the United States were far lower than in Scandinavia and the Netherlands (27–35 percent and 47–63 percent, respectively). The percentages of the U.S. GNP that went for income maintenance (7.4 percent) and public health care (3.0 percent) again were smaller in the mid-seventies than those of the Benelux countries (14–19 percent and 4.2–5.1 percent, respectively) or France and Germany (12.4 and 5.3 percent, respectively) (OECD 1978, Dolbeare 1982).

17. Such a power was demonstrated both in the fall of the crisis-stricken Weimar Republic and in the successful crisis management of the New Deal in the United States and, say, Sweden during the Great Depression.

18. For example, for one reason or another, about one in six U.S. adults, or an estimated 37 million people, have no medical insurance at all, including temporary or part-time workers, many self-employed people or people employed in very small businesses that provide no health insurance benefits, retired people too young to qualify for Medicare, and people not poor enough to qualify for Medicaid.

19. Oddly enough, a companion question, How often do you think about the meaning and purpose of life? produced a somewhat different lineup: France, Italy, West Germany, Japan, Denmark, Britain, Ireland, Belgium, Spain, and the Netherlands.

REFERENCES

Almond, Gabriel A., and Sidney Verba. 1963. *The Civic Culture*. Princeton: Princeton University Press.

Almond, Gabriel A., and Sidney Verba, eds. 1980. *The Civic Culture Revisited*. Boston: Little, Brown and Company.

Andrain, C. F. 1985. *Social Policies in Western Industrial Societies*. Berkeley: University of California, Institute of International Studies.

Baker, Kendall L., Russel J. Dalton, and Kai Hildebrandt. 1981. *Germany Transformed: Political Culture and the New Politics*. Cambridge: Harvard University Press.

Barnes, Samuel, Max Kaase, et al. 1979. *Political Action: Mass Participation in Five Western Democracies*. Beverly Hills, Calif.: Sage.

Conradt, David P. 1980. "Changing German Political Culture." In Gabriel A. Almond and Sidney Verba, eds., *The Civic Culture Revisited*, pp. 212–272. Boston: Little, Brown and Company.

Cranston, M. 1986. "From Legitimism to Legitimacy." In A. Moulakis, ed., *Legitimacy/ Legitimate*, pp. 36–43. New York: De Gruyter.

Crozier, Michel, Samuel P. Huntington, and Joji Watanuki. 1975. *The Crisis of Democracy*. New York: New York University Press.

Dahl, Robert A. 1982. *Dilemmas of Pluralist Democracy: Autonomy Vs. Control.* New Haven: Yale University Press.

Denitch, Bogdan, ed. 1979. *Legitimation of Regimes: International Frameworks for Analysis.* Beverly Hills, Calif.: Sage.

Dolbeare, Kenneth M. 1982. *American Public Policy: A Citizen's Guide.* New York: McGraw-Hill.

Easton, David. 1965. *A Systems Analysis of Political Life.* New York: John Wiley.

_____ . 1975. "A Re-Assessment of the Concept of Political Support." *British Journal of Political Science* 5:435–457.

Eckstein, H. 1971. *The Evaluation of Political Performance: Problems and Dimensions.* Beverly Hills, Calif.: Sage.

_____ . 1979. *Support for Regimes: Theories and Tests.* No. 44. Princeton, N.J.: Woodrow Wilson Center for Monographs.

Ehrmann, H. W. 1976. *Comparative Legal Cultures.* Englewood Cliffs, N.J.: Prentice-Hall.

Enloe, C. 1983. *Does Khaki Become You? The Militarization of Women's Lives.* London: Pluto Press.

Euro-Barometer. 1983. No. 20 (December), A 32–36.

Field, G. L., and J. Higley. 1979. "Elites, Insiders, and Outsiders: Will Western Political Regimes Prove Nonviable." In Bogdan Denitch, *Legitimation of Regimes: International Frameworks for Analysis,* pp. 141–160. Beverly Hills, Calif.: Sage.

Flanagan, Scott C. 1982. "Changing Values in Industrial Societies." *Comparative Political Studies* 14:403–444.

Friedrich, C. J. 1963. *Man and His Government.* New York: McGraw-Hill.

_____ . 1974. *Limited Government: A Comparison.* Englewood Cliffs, N.J.: Prentice-Hall.

Gallup, George, Jr. 1984. *Forecast 2000: George Gallup Jr. Predicts the Future of America.* New York: Morrow.

Gamson, William A. 1968. *Power and Discontent.* Homewood, Ill.: Dorsey Press.

Geiger, T. 1978. *Welfare and Efficiency: Their Interactions in Western Europe and Implications for International Economic Relations.* Washington, D.C.: National Planning Association.

Gerth, H., and C. W. Mills, eds. 1946. *From Max Weber.* New York: Knopf.

Girod, R., P. de Laubier, and A. Gladstone, eds. 1985. *Social Policy in Western Europe and the United States, 1950–1980.* New York: St. Martin's Press.

Golding, P., and S. Middleton, 1982. *Images of Welfare: Press and Public Attitudes to Poverty.* Oxford: Robertson.

Grew, R., ed. 1978. *Crises of Political Development in Europe and the United States.* Princeton: Princeton University Press.

Gurr, T., and M. McClelland. 1971. *The Performance of Political Systems: A Twelve-Nation Study.* Beverly Hills, Calif.: Sage.

Habermas, Jürgen. 1973. *Legitimationsprobleme im Spätkapitalismus.* Frankfurt am Main: Suhrkamp.

Hastings, Elizabeth Hann, and Philip K. Hastings, eds. 1982. *Index to International Public Opinion, 1980–81.* Westport, Conn.: Greenwood Press.

_____ . 1984. *Index to International Public Opinion, 1982–83.* Westport, Conn.: Greenwood Press.

Hibbs, D. A. 1973. *Mass Political Violence: A Cross-National Causal Analysis*. New York: Wiley.

Hicks, A., and D. Swank. 1984. "On the Political Economy of Welfare Expansion: A Comparative Analysis of 18 Advanced Capitalist Democracies, 1960-1971." *Comparative Political Studies* 17 (April), pp. 81-119.

Honderich, T. 1976. *Political Violence*. Ithaca, N.Y.: Cornell University Press.

Ingelhart, Ronald. 1977. *The Silent Revolution: Changing Values and Political Styles Among Western Publics*. Princeton: Princeton University Press.

Jahrbuch der offentlichen Meinung (JOM). 1968-1973. Allensbach, West Germany: Institute für Demoskopie.

Ladd, E. 1976-1977. "The Polls: The Question of Confidence." *Public Opinion Quarterly* 40 (Winter), pp. 544-552.

Lane, R. 1979. "The Legitimacy Bias: Conservative Man in Market and State." In Bogdan Denitch, *Legitimation of Regimes: International Frameworks for Analysis*, pp. 55-80. Beverly Hills, Calif.: Sage.

Lijphart, Arend. 1984. *Democracies: Patterns of Majoritarian and Consensus Government in Twenty-one Countries*. New Haven: Yale University Press.

Lipset, Seymour Martin, and William Schneider. 1983. *The Confidence Gap: Business, Labor, and Government in the Public Mind*. New York: Free Press.

Lockhart, C. 1984. "Explaining Social Policy Differences Among Advanced Industrial Societies." *Comparative Politics* 16 (April), pp. 335-350.

Merkl, Peter. 1974. *German Foreign Policies, West and East*. Santa Barbara, Calif.: Clio Press.

——. 1987. "The Evolution of West German Public Opinion on Detente Since 1970." In W. Hanrieder, *Arms Control, the Federal Republic of Germany, and the Future of East-West Relations*. Boulder, Colo.: Westview Press.

Merkl, Peter, ed. 1983. *West German Foreign Policies Dilemmas and Directions*. Chicago: Council of Foreign Relations.

Morris, R. 1984. "The Future Challenge to the Past: The Case of the American Welfare State." *Journal of Social Policy* 13 (Oct.), pp. 383-416.

Moulakis, A., ed. 1986. *Legitimacy/Legitimate*. New York: De Gruyter.

Muller, E. N., and C. J. Williams. 1980. "Dynamics of Political Support-Alienation." *Comparative Political Studies* 13 (April), pp. 33-59.

Muller, Edward N., and Thomas O. Jukam. 1977. "On the Meaning of Political Support." *American Political Science Review* 71 (Dec.), pp. 1561-1595.

Offe, Claus. 1972. *Strukturprobleme des kapitalistischen Staates*. Frankfurt am Main: Suhrkamp.

Organization for Economic Cooperation and Development (OECD). 1978. *Public Expenditure Trends*. Studies in Resource Allocation no. 5. Paris.

Pitkin, Hamma. 1971. "Obligation and Consent." in D. W. Hanson and R. B. Fowler, *Obligation and Dissent: An Introduction to Politics*, pp. 19-32. Boston: Little, Brown and Company.

Plant, R. 1982. "Jurgen Habermas and the Idea of Legitimation Crisis." *European Journal of Political Research* 10 (Dec.), pp. 341-352.

Powell, Bingham G., Jr. 1982. *Contemporary Democracies: Participation, Stability, and Violence*. Cambridge: Harvard University Press.

Rausch, H. 1983. "Politisches Bewusstsein und politische Einstellungen im Wandel." in W. Weidenfeld, ed., *Die Identitat der Deutschen*, pp. 119-153. Munich: Hanser.

Rogowski, R. 1974. *Rational Legitimacy: A Theory of Political Support.* Princeton: Princeton University Press.

Sartori, G. 1962. *Democratic Theory.* Detroit: Wayne State University Press.

Schmidt, M. G. 1983. "The Welfare State and the Economy in Periods of Economic Crisis: A Comparative Study of Twenty-Three OECD Nations." *European Journal of Political Research* 11 (March), pp. 1-26.

Schmitt, Hermann. 1983. "Party Government in Public Opinion: A European Cross-National Comparison." *European Journal of Political Research* 11 (Dec.), pp. 353-375.

Schweigler, G. 1974. *Nationalbewusstsein in der BRD und der DDR.* Dusseldorf: Bertelsmann.

Simmons, A. J. 1979. *Moral Principles and Political Obligations.* Princeton: Princeton University Press.

Steinberg, J. 1978. *Locke, Rousseau, and the Idea of Consent: An Inquiry into the Liberal Democratic Theory of Political Obligation.* Hartford, Conn.: Greenwood Press.

Stoetzel, Jean. 1983. *Les Valeurs du Temps Present: Une Enquete Europeenne.* Paris: Presses Universitaires de France.

Taylor, Charles Lewis, and David A. Jodice, eds. 1983. *World Handbook of Political and Social Indicators.* 2 vols. 3d ed. New Haven: Yale University Press.

Von der Mehden, F. 1973. *Comparative Political Violence.* Englewood Cliffs, N.J.: Prentice-Hall.

Walzer, Michael. 1970. *Obligations: Essays on Disobedience, War, and Citizenship.* Cambridge: Harvard University Press.

Weber, M. 1974. *The Theory of Social and Political Organization.* Ed. with an introd. by Talcott Parsons. New York: Oxford University Press.

Weidenfeld, W., ed. 1983. *Die Identitat der Deutschen.* Munich: Hanser.

Wilkinson, P. 1977. *Terrorism and the Liberal State.* London: Macmillan.

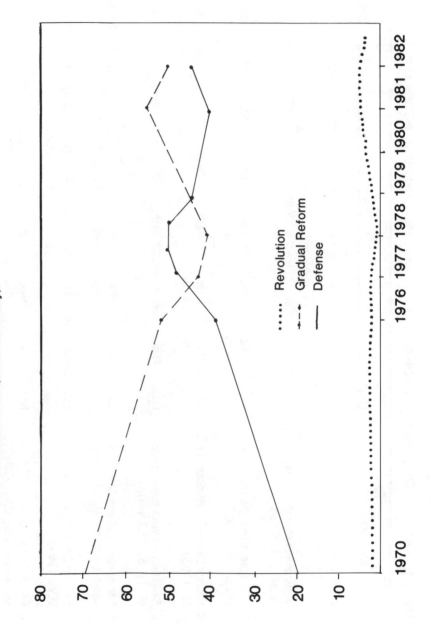

Figure 1.1 Revolution, Reform, and Defense Against Subversives, 1970–1982.
Source: Eurobarometer (West Germany).

TABLE 1.1 -- Ordinal Comparison of Indices of System Support Among Industrialized Democracies

Index Item	High									Low
1. Pride in nationality (GI 1982)	U S	Ire.	GB	Sp.	It.	Fr.	Jap.			FRG
2. Willingness to fight for one's country (EVS 1981)	Dk.	GB	Sp.	Ire.	Neth.	Fr.	FRG	Belg.		It.
3. Willingness to fight for one's country (GI 1982)	U S	GB	Sp.	Ire.	Fr.	FRG	It.			Jap.
4. Satisfaction with democracy (E 1983)	Dk.	FRG Gr.	GB Lux.	Neth.	Belg.	Fr.	Ire.			It.
5. Satisfaction with democracy (E 1976–1983 avg)	Lux.	FRG	Dk.	Gr.	Neth.	GB	Ire.	Belg.	Fr.	It.
6. For gradual reform & defense against subversion (EVS 1981)	Sp.	Neth.	FRG Nor.	It. GB	Fr. Swed.	Ire.	Dk.			Belg.
7. For gradual reform only (EVS 1981)	Sp.	Swed.	It.	Ire.	Fr.	GB	Dk.	Neth.	Belg. FRG	Nor.
8. For defense against subversion only (EVS 1981) (continued)	Nor.	FRG	Neth. Dk.	Sp.	GB	Ire. Fr., It.	Belg.			Swed.

Note: E = Eurobarometer   EVS = European Values Study   GI = Gallup International

Index Item	High											Low
9. Accept law, government and society (HVS 1980–81)	FRG	Aus'l	Can.	GB	US	Jap.	It.					Fr.
10. For gradual improvement within governmental system (HVS 1980–81)	Jap.	Can.	US	Fr.	Aus'l	It.	GB					FRG
11. Religious values (GI 1982)	US	Ire.	Sp.	It.	GB	FRG	Fr.					Jap.
12. Life satisfaction (E 1983)	Dk.	Lux. Neth.	GB	Belg. Ire.	FRG	Fr.	Gr.					It.
13. Life satisfaction (E 1976–1983 avg)	Dk.	Neth.	Lux.	Belg.	Ire.	GB	FRG	Fr.				It. Gr.
14. Happiness, very and quite happy (GI 1982)	GB	Ire.	US	Fr.	FRG	Sp.	Jap.					It.
15. Value freedom more than equality (H&H 1982–83)	US	GB	Fr.	Ire.	FRG	Jap.						Sp.
16. Legitimacy of trade unions and companies (EVS 1981)	Fin.	Nor.	Ire.	Swed.	Dk.	Fr.	GB	Neth.	FRG	Sp.	Belg.	It.

Note: E = Eurobarometer EVS = European Values Study GI = Gallup International
H&H = Hastings and Hastings HVS = Human Values Study

NOTES TO TABLE 1.1

1. The question was, How proud are you to be _____? and the table does not show the extreme differences between the proud groups (U.S., Ireland, GB, Spain, and even Italy) in which 80–96 percent said they were "very" or "quite proud" and the least proud (Japan and the FRG) in which around 30 percent said they were "not very" or "not at all proud" of their nationality.

2. These rankings were established by Jean Stoetzel by giving a score of 100 to respndents who said they would not fight, 200 to those giving no answer, and 300 to those who expressed a willingness to fight for their country. The highest group (Denmark, GB, Spain) received a ranking between 226 and 237; the lowest (Belgium and Italy), in the 170s (see Stoetzel, Chapter 5).

3. The question was, Of course we all hope that there will not be another war, but if it were to come to that, would you be willing to fight for your country? In France, West Germany, Italy, and Japan, the negative responses were higher than the positive ones. The question made no attempt to account for the likely differences in perception of whether a given war might be "justified," or purely a matter of defending one's country, or not.

4.–5. The question was, On the whole, are satisfied with the way democracy works in _____? The responses fluctuated somewhat from year to year, presumably in reaction to the flow of events and issues, but not enough to make for major differences between the two scales. In the case of Greece, where the surveys only began in 1981, I used the last three years as an average to compare to the eight-year averages of the other countries (see *Eurobarometer* no. 20 [Dec. 1983], A 32–36.

6.–8. The question gave respondents a choice among (a) radical change by revolutionary action, which accounted for only 1–8 percent of the responses; (b) gradual societal improvements by reforms, the choice of large majorities (49–75 percent); and (c) "Our present society must be valiantly defended against all subversive forces," the choice generally of between 14 and 24 percent, except for the evidently very defensive Norwegians (45 percent) and West Germans (38 percent). The "loaded" wording of the third choice made it advisable to present three rankings, including (b) and (c) separately and combined.

9.–10. The question gave three choices: (a) acceptance of "the overall existing law, our present system of government and our society," (b) gradual improvement within the existing system of government, and (c) complete rejection of the present system and desire for complete social change (see Table 1.2). The responses for (a) ranged from 43 percent (FRG) and 21 percent (Australia) to a low of 8 percent (Italy) and 6 percent (France). The responses for (b) began with 84 percent (Japan) and ended with 54 percent (FRG).

11. There were two questions, one about belief in God, life after death, and heaven and hell and the other asking for a self-assessment, Are you a religious person?—regardless of church attendance. In spite of the diversity of religious views and their linkage to political cleavages in different countries, the rankings were almost identical, contrasting the ultrareligious United States, Ireland, Spain, and Italy with secular Japan (see Turner, Chapter 6, for a discussion of the varying significance of religious values in different countries).

12.–13. The question was, On the whole are you satisfied with the life you lead? and, as expected, the responses were considerably more sanguine than those regarding satisfaction with how democracy works. Fluctuations over the years were minor and Greece was handled as indicated in the note for items 4. and 5. (see *Eurobarometer* no. 20 [Dec. 1983], A 15–24).

14. The question was, Taking all things together, would you say you are very happy, quite happy, not very happy, not at all happy? As Frederick Turner points out, some countries (Japan, Italy) impose considerable psychocultural impediments in the way of persons' calling themselves "very happy." Nevertheless, we should not ignore the 13–23 percent (in the FRG, Spain, Japan, and Italy) who call themselves "not very" or "not at all happy."

15. This item is the result of half of a question asking respondents to choose between freedom and equality in a zero-sum way, and the responses ranged from about 70 percent in favor of freedom over equality (US, GB) to a slight preference for equality in Spain, Japan, and West Germany (Hastings and Hastings 1984, 604).

16. This item is the average of two rankings, one rating the importance of trade unions and the other that of major companies in each country. I added the national percentages saying that either "social partner" mattered "a great deal" or "quite a lot" and averaged them. Although some strikingly polar views were produced (Britain was near the top in appreciation for major companies and at the bottom regarding trade unions and Denmark was nearly the opposite), on the whole the method appeared to bring out a measure of support for the "social partners" (see Linz, Chapter 2).

TABLE 1.2 -- Ordinal Comparison of Indices of System Non-Support Among Industrialized Democracies

Index Item	High							Low
1. Not proud of nationality (GI 1981)	Jap.	FRG	Fr.	It. Sp.	GB	Ire.		US
2. Unwilling to fight for one's country (EVS 1981)	It.	Belg.	Fr.	FRG	Neth.	Ire.	Sp.	GB	Dk.
3. Unwilling to fight for one's country (GI 1981)	It.	Fr.	FRG	Jap.	Ire.	Sp. GB		US
4. Radical change by revolutionary action (EVS 1981)	Fr.	Sp.	It.	Belg.	GB, Ire. Swed.	Neth. Dk.		FRG Nor.
5. Radical change by revolutionary action (E 1983)	Gr.	Fr. Ire.	It.	Neth. Belg.	GB	FRG Lux.		Dk.
6. Radical change by revolutionary action (E 1976–1983 avg)	Fr.	It. Gr.	Ire.	Belg.	Neth.	Lux.	FRG	Dk.
7. Completely reject present system (H&H 1980–81) (continued)	Fr.	GB	It.	Aus'l.	US	Can.	Jap.	FRG

Note: E = Eurobarometer   EVS = European Values Study   GI = Gallup International
H&H = Hastings and Hastings

TABLE 1.2 (Continued)

Index Item	High → Low
8. 1973–1977 turmoil per capita (WH III, vol.2 1983)	Gr. GB Ire. Fr. It. US Dk. Neth. Nor. Swed. FRG Belg. Can. Jap.
9. 1948–1977 turmoil per capita (WH III, vol.2 1983)	Fr. Gr. It. US Ire./GB Dk. FRG Can. Nor. Swed. Jap. Neth.
10. 1973–1977 deaths per capita from political violence (WH III, vol.2 1983)	GB Ire. Gr. It. Neth. Fr. Swed. FRG Nor. Belg. Jap. US Can. Dk.
11. 1948–1977 deaths per capita from political violence (WH III, vol.2 1983)	It. Gr. GB Ire. Belg. US FRG Jap. Swed. Can. Neth. Dk. Nor.
12. Not very or not at all happy (GI 1981)	It. Sp. Jap. FRG Fr. US Ire. GB
13. Potential separatism scale (WH III, vol.2 1983)	Belg. Can. Sp. GB Turk. Fr. US (etc.)
14. Low rating of unions and companies (EVS 1981)	It. FRG Sp. GB/Neth. Swed. Ire./Fin. Dk. Belg./Fr., Nor.

Note: E = Eurobarometer   EVS = European Values Study   GI = Gallup International
H&H = Hastings and Hastings   WH = World Handbook

NOTES TO TABLE 1.2

1. This item is the negative side of the earlier question on national pride, based on the "not very" and "not at all proud" responses to the same question (Table 1.1, 1). These responses ranged from 31 percent in Japan and 29 percent in the FRG to 3 percent in the U.S.

2. These are the negative responses to the question of the European Values Study (Table 1.1, 2), and they range from around 50 percent for Italy (57 percent), Belgium, France and the FRG to between 22 and 25 percent for the three lowest.

3. This is the negative side of the International Gallup survey on the same question (Table 1.1, 3). In addition to the high Italian score (57 percent), it includes negative pluralities of 40–46 percent for France, the FRG, and Japan; in the U.S. only 20 percent and in the other three only 27–31 percent declared they were not willing to fight for their country.

4. These responses form only a small minority and range between 2 and 8 percent of each national sample. There were three choices—gradual reform, defense of the status quo against subversives (see Table 1.1, 6–8), and this one, which read: "The entire way our society is organized must be radically changed by revolutionary action."

5.–6. Again, the percentages for 1983 only run from 2–8 percent but in 1976, France and Italy each had 13 percent giving this response. The 1976–1983 averages presumably give more of a long-range profile.

7. This is one of the three options of the Human Values Survey reprinted in the *Index to International Public Opinion 1980–81*. The other two were (1) acceptance of existing law, system of government, and our society and (2) gradual improvement within the existing system of government. The negative side was "I completely reject the present system and want complete social change" and it produced much larger percentages than items 4–6. They ranged from 26 percent (France), 24 percent (GB), and 20 percent (Italy) to 3 percent (FRG).

8.–11. These are events data per capita from the *World Handbook of Political and Social Indicators* (1983). "Turmoil" means the incidence of protest demonstrations, political strikes, and riots. The second category denotes actual deaths from such events. The averages of nearly three decades are intended to overcome temporary fluctuations in each country.

12. This is the negative side of the responses to the happiness question on Table 1.1, 14. The responses ranged from 4 percent (GB) to 20–23 percent (Spain and Italy).

13. This scale measures the percentages of a nation's population, given the presence of separatist movements, that would be likely to secede in countries that have appeared in our other scales.

14. These are the combined responses to the question on Table 1.1, 16, that rated a country's trade unions and major companies as having "not very much" importance or "none at all." There were a few countries (Finland, GB) in which the ranking of unions was diametrically opposed to that of the major companies, but in most cases combining the rankings produced a reasonable index of nonappreciation of the social partners. The "not very much" response generally ranged between 30 and 50 percent; the "none at all," between 10 and 20 percent.

TABLE 1.3 -- Proportion of Public Expressing "Great Deal of Confidence" in Leadership of Institutions

	1966	1971	1972	1973	Change 1966-1973	Sept. 1974	Apr. 1975	Feb. 1979	Sept. 1981
				(in percent)					
Government									
Federal Executive	41	23	27	19	- 22	18	13	17	24
Congress	42	19	21	29	- 13	16	14	18	16
Supreme Court	50	23	28	33	- 18	35	29	28	29
Military	62	27	35	40	- 22	31	24	29	28
Social Institutions									
Major companies	55	27	27	29	- 26	16	20	18	16
Organized labor	22	14	15	20	- 2	18	14	10	12
Higher education	61	27	33	44	- 17	39	36	33	34
Medicine	72	61	48	57	- 15	48	43	30	37
Organized religion	41	27	30	36	- 5	32	32	20	22
Press	29	18	18	30	+ 1	26	26	28	16

Question: "As far as people running these institutions are concerned, would you say you have a great deal of confidence or hardly any confidence in them?"

Source: Selected from Louis Harris and Associates, Confidence and Concern: Citizens View American Government, Committee Print, U.S. Senate, Committee on Government Operations, Subcommittee on Intergovernmental Relations, 93rd Congress, 1st Session, December 3, 1973, and selections from later Harris surveys.

TABLE 1.4 -- Confidence in Institutions (in percent)

					Positive responses only				
	US	Jap.	GB	Ire.	FRG	Fr.	It.	Sp.	EUR*
Police	76	67	86	86	71	64	68	63	71
Armed forces	81	37	81	75	54	53	58	61	60
Legal system	51	68	66	57	67	55	43	48	57
Educational system	65	51	60	67	43	55	56	50	55
Church	75	16	48	78	48	54	60	50	52
Parliament/Congress	53	30	40	51	53	48	31	48	43
Civil service	55	31	48	54	35	50	28	38	40
Major companies	50	25	48	49	34	42	33	37	39
Press	49	52	29	44	33	31	46	31	32
Labor unions	33	29	26	36	36	36	28	31	32

* EUR = European average

Question: "How much confidence do you have in each of the institutions [above]: a great deal, quite a lot, not very much or none at all?"

Source: Rearranged from Hastings and Hastings 1984, p.605.

TABLE 1.5 -- Great Britain: Fairness of Economic Policies (in percent)

	Mar. 1980	May 1980	Aug. 1980	Sept. 1980	Dec. 1980	Jan. 1981	May 1981	Mar. 1982	Sept. 1982	Oct. 1982	Apr. 1983
Fair	25	24	23	19	15	18	16	19	21	21	22
Not fair	65	64	70	74	76	74	77	78	71	72	71
Don't know	10	12	7	7	9	8	7	3	8	7	7

Question: "Do you think that the government's economic policies are or are not fair to all concerned?"
Source: SSLT polls, Hastings and Hastings 1982, pp.126-136; 1984, p.66.

TABLE 1.6 -- Great Britain: Fairness to Social Class (in percent)

	Well-to-do	Middle-class	Working class	People on Pensions or Small Incomes
Enough	26	33	19	16
Too much	62	15	3	2
Too little	3	40	73	78
Don't know	9	12	5	4

Question : "Do you think this government does enough, too much or too little for [the groups above]?"
Source: Hastings and Hastings 1982, p.135.

2
LEGITIMACY OF DEMOCRACY AND THE SOCIOECONOMIC SYSTEM

Juan J. Linz

INTRODUCTION

Legitimacy is an idea of central importance in political thought and science, although the concept has proven difficult to use in comparative research.[1] As with so many other concepts, we know—or believe we know—what we mean when we consider the rule of Somoza illegitimate and that of the government of a prime minister in an European democracy legitimate, but the question would be more complex in the case of the first secretary of the Communist Party of the Soviet Union today. The belief in the legitimacy of rule is a value judgment, and depending on our values we, as aggregates of citizens and organized groups like the military, are willing to believe in the right of a ruler to give commands, to find obedience, to impose sanctions against those who want to overthrow him, etc. As Max Weber has underlined, there are different bases for that belief. Rulers themselves may feel more or less convinced of their legitimacy (on a variety of grounds), their staffs might be ready to obey commands only within certain limits and according to certain rules, and citizens might obey only out of fear or self-interest— comply but not out of a conviction that it is their duty to do so.

To avoid the many complexities of the notion of legitimacy, I shall use a minimalist definition: the belief that in spite of shortcomings and failures, the political institutions are better than any others that might be established and therefore can demand obedience—in order to make the definition more minimal, to lower the threshold even further, one might add, "in a particular country" after "that might be established." Legitimacy, therefore, would implicitly involve comparison among alternatives (real or imaginary), and their absence assures a minimum of support even when an outside observer would assume a widespread lack of legitimacy. I do not need to stress that no political system is legitimate for 100 percent of the population, nor in all its commands or forever, and probably very few that are totally illegimate— based only on coercion—stay in power for any length of time.

In this chapter, I shall start from the assumption that today, at least in the advanced stable democracies of the Western world and even in some that have been recently established, the institutions of political democracy enjoy widespread legitimacy and only minorities question seriously the desirability of a democratic system of government—although more might question specific institutions, to say nothing about their trusting particular parties in power or particular incumbents. Trust might be an indicator of legitimacy, be derived from it, and contribute to its reinforcement, but trust should not be confused with belief in legitimacy, nor should it be confused with favorable judgments about the efficacy and performance of a system. In fact, belief in legitimacy is put to a test—like loyalty in Hirschman's *Exit, Voice, and Loyalty*[2]—in the case of failures in performance, i.e., when there are conflicts between self-interest and the demands of the system and its legitimate incumbents.

The other side of the equation is legitimacy of the social and economic system, which again should (and can) be kept separate from trust in the agents of the system or its concrete performance. Some readers may object to applying the term *legitimacy* to a social and economic system, arguing that this is an unwarranted extension of the use of the term—at least the Weberian conception of binding commands and commitments. I do not ignore the validity of the objection, but I would like to argue that beliefs similar to those of political legitimacy apply to the socioeconomic system, whose function in many respects is similar. I shall, therefore, without further analysis and with all kinds of reservations, use for convenience the expression, legitimacy of the social and economic system.

The social system involves many dimensions that are not directly linked with the economic institutions, like the position of linguistic, ethnic, national, regional, and religious groups in society. In this chapter, however, I shall focus on the socioeconomic system and ignore those other dimensions. In fact, one could distinguish analytically between the economic system and the social structure it helps generate; I say helps since the fiscal and welfare policies of states today contribute much toward shaping the social system. In reality, it is highly probable that judgments about the economic system are to a large extent colored by judgments about the social, particularly the stratification, system. I shall return to this point later since the democratic political system can (and does) modify both, although its policies might have a greater impact on one or the other, and it is obvious that successful welfare states have contributed to the legitimacy of their economic systems— although their legitimacy can also be weakened when their structural demands conflict with welfare state structures and policies.

Once more I use a minimalist definition of legitimacy: the belief that a particular society's economic system, in spite of shortcomings and failures, is better than any other alternative system that might be established in that society. Without going into a discussion of all possible alternative economic systems, one can distinguish between a system based on private ownership of means of production, independent entrepreneurship, a dominance of market mechanisms, a relatively free disposal of profits, free labor, etc., and one with very low limits for private ownership of means of production, practically no independent entrepreneurial initiative, a dominance of public planning mechanisms, no legitimate profits going to owners and/ or managers, limits on labor mobility, etc. These two systems can be described loosely as "capitalist" and "socialist," but there are a number of mixed systems as well.

The boundaries between different types of economic systems are certainly unclear. Many of these systems that a committed socialist ideologist would describe as "capitalist" would be considered by a neoliberal of the Chicago School as "socialist," and any delimitation of a type or types between extremes would be even more debatable. The terms themselves, irrespective of the substantive content they denote, have, like the term *democracy*, different connotations for different people and arouse positive or negative feelings. As in the case of the democratic political system, responses of the population, particular groups, and institutions (like the churches) are largely independent of the system's actual performance (in the short and medium run), the evaluation of specific institutions of the system, and the capacity or incapacity of the people who had positions in the system. Even so, all those and many other factors (for example, national or foreign control, a noneconomic characteristic) contribute to their generalized and diffuse beliefs.

Economic systems based on the same or similar institutions and processes differ in the degree to which they are considered legitimate in different societies. On the basis of some empirical evidence, one could go so far as to argue that within European capitalist systems, the differences in opinion about "the system" are likely to be much greater than in the belief in the "democratic system." It is also likely that the differences among countries in evaluating the performance of the economic systems will diverge even more.

To explain the differences in beliefs about the legitimacy of the economic system in different countries would be an important and exciting task for historians, sociologists, and economists interested in comparative research; to account for the stability or variability of those beliefs would be another. To avoid misunderstanding, belief in the legitimacy of the economic system does not coincide, although it correlates, with voting for or against "socialist" parties, nor with class position. Of the many complex factors involved, it should not be forgotten that there has always been a nonleftist anticapitalism of traditional conservatives, religiously oriented groups (even the Catholic church in its pre-Vatican II pronouncements), and particularly fascism.[3] I shall take the differences in beliefs as a given in characterizing different European societies and exploring some problems derived from the relationship between the belief in the legitimacy of political democracy and the belief in the legitimacy of the economic system. I assume a relative autonomy of both systems and the possibility of actions and processes initiated in or in response to one or the other system on the basis of their legitimacy or illegitimacy.

The legitimacy question is a complex one because it is not always easy to isolate it from the judgment about the performance of the institutions, the individuals who occupy the decision-making positions in them, and the actual situation when research is undertaken. Undoubtedly, the specific moment in the business cycle—boom or depression, inflation or unemployment, or stagflation—might have a lot to do with the opinions and attitudes one might use as indicators. But just as the legitimacy of political authority is put to its real test when its commands do not coincide with citizens' interests—as a dramatic example, when one is asked to die for one's nation—the belief in an economic order is probably best tested when its performance is temporarily not at its best. In this sense, today is a good moment for such inquiries.

Given the nature of economic institutions—and their goals of creation and allocation of goods—it is undoubtedly more difficult for people to separate those institutions, as objects of loyalty, from their actual performance than it is to do so for other institutions. In fact although legitimacy—and the expression of it in feelings of loyalty—and the term *loyalty* itself do not seem incongruous when applied to a nation, the state, or a party, they do not sound proper when applied to an economic system, although we talk about loyalty to a brand name or a neighborhood store and Hirschman has shown its significance for economic analysis. Loyalty to an enterprise on the part of its workers and customers reduces economically disturbing processes like high labor turnover, absenteeism, financial difficulties, flight of deposits, and refusal of credit, all factors that would prevent the reequilibration of economic units after a failure or a bad moment and thereby put limits on the "creative destruction" process described by Joseph A. Schumpeter.[4]

It is interesting to note that economic behavior can sometimes be based on sentiment rather than rational calculation or self-interest. Such behavior is microeconomic and contributes to stability, like loyalty to political institutions and parties reduces electoral volatility, sudden and excessive swings in the political pendulum, and the rise of antisystem parties or movements (like the rise of nazism in the thirties). Such beliefs and behavior ultimately have macroeconomic and macrosocial consequences, like flight of capital, a drop in savings rates, investment behavior, productivity, etc. Unfortunately, the research on economic behavior has been less comparative than that on political behavior, and we therefore have a less comparative perspective on how the legitimacy and the perceptions of delegitimation of the economic system affect the actors in an economic system: entrepreneurs, savers and investors, workers. We link economic behavior mostly to changes within a national economic system rather than to differences between economic systems. Since such behavior affects the total societal performance, which is also attributed to the political system, it is politically relevant.

The questions may be asked, Can we speak of the legitimacy of a political system or are we really dealing with the legitimacy of a social and/or economic system? To what extent can one speak of the legitimacy of the political system as distinct from a social-economic system? The answers are far from unambiguous. The logical possibilities are one aspect; another is their likelihood in social reality and their stability. Naturally, in both cases one deals, not with 100 percent legitimacy, but with greater or lesser legitimacy.

The four logical possibilities are

Political System

		Legitimate	Illegitimate
Economic	Legitimate		
System	Illegitimate		

The cases of congruence, both legitimate or both illegitimate, are not as problematic as those of incongruence. The situation of dual illegitimacy is to be found in quite a few authoritarian regimes, particularly those I have called "sultanistic,"[5] in which the ruler appropriates not only political but also economic power—as a major owner of wealth and through his, his family's, and his clients' power, he controls economic opportunities. Both kinds of power are likely to have little legitimacy, and the social order is likely to be tainted by a generalized illegitimacy because of its corruption by the ruler. The regimes of Somoza, Trujillo, Papa Doc, and even to some extent the shah of Iran come to mind as examples. Other societies in which an authoritarian regime is a social and an economic oligarchy but whose privileged status is not based on tradition or performance are close to the same situation, but other authoritarian regimes are to be found in the mixed cases: Either the political rule enjoys very limited legitimacy without an equal level of questioning of the social-economic order (probably Uruguay before redemocratization), or less often, there is a combination of a certain degree of political legitimacy with a questioning of the socioeconomic system.

No relatively stable regime fits the extreme situation of illegitimacy of both the political regime and the social order, although regimes in which an ethnic, racial, or religious group occupies a hegemonic position and allows democratic processes within the ruling majority segment of the population while being rejected by another part of the population would be such a case. The rejection might be combined with a rejection of the social-economic order, like in South Africa; the existence of the state, like Israel for the Palestinians or Ulster for the Catholics; or the distribution of power within unsuccessful consociational arrangements, like Lebanon and Cyprus, without necessarily questioning the economic system as much.

The "normal" democracies fall mainly into one of two types: both the democratic political institutions and the social and economic order enjoy considerable legitimacy or the democratic institutions enjoy such a legitimacy but the legitimacy of the social-economic system is questioned. In general, it would seem that political democracy would always enjoy greater legitimacy than the economic order, although not necessarily all political institutions more than all economic institutions, and even less the incumbents of political power at a given moment versus the economic elites. The combination of a democratic political system's having less legitimacy than the social-economic system—to put it bluntly, democracy less than capitalism—is an unknown situation. There is, however, the possibility that in Eastern Europe a socialist economy might be more legitimate than the political system, but Eastern European countries are not democracies.

The political system, democratic or not, in principle should enjoy higher legitimacy than the private economic system, since in principle the former is serving "public," collective goals while private business is serving "private" goals and making profits (in addition to other things that might be conceived of as serving public goals). The terminological differences among "retribution" of officials, "profits" of business, and "honoraria" of professionals reflect this different evaluation. It is obviously conceivable that public officials might pursue mainly private ends and might appropriate more resources than businessmen, that corruption might be more profitable than business, but this is seen as the exception and certainly not the normal pattern in democratic politics. However, there is always the dilemma: Who is more corrupt, the one who bribes or the one who demands bribes? It can be argued that it is the economic system that corrupts the political, although anyone doing business in certain societies will know it can be the other way around. The compatibility between the higher legitimacy of the democratic political system and its institutions and the questioning of the economic system and its institutions is the result of a number of factors.

INTERDEPENDENCE OF DEMOCRATIC LEGITIMACY AND "LEGITIMACY" OF THE ECONOMIC SYSTEM

Since in principle the sovereign state, and in it the democratically elected authorities, can change the social and economic structure, the commitment to political democracy is compatible with an alienation from or a dissatisfaction with the economic system since there is the hope that it can be changed by democratic means in the shorter or longer run. Only the narrowing of the time perspective leads to a voluntaristic response of minorities who do not think that it is right and/or necessary to wait for change until a majority consensus is reached. The Marxist model of social and economic development under capitalism indirectly—in relatively advanced industrial societies—gave support to the democratic hope of the anticapitalists since they could expect to become the majority through an increase in numbers and the gaining of consciousness because of the action of parties and trade unions. This was the basis of the success of social-democratic socialism.[6] Underdevelopment and the disillusionment with the class consciousness attainable through trade union and electoral politics might logically lead to a Leninist voluntarism and the rejection of Western models of political democracy. Incidentally, this belief in the possibility of social and ideological change leading sooner or later to a majority consensus contrasts with the permanent minority status of ethnic, linguistic, national, and religious minorities in modern states and explains their potential for radicalism and their frequent denial of legitimacy to majoritarian democracy (unless they reduce or compromise their demands).

Democracy—in making power divisible; creating the hope for alternation; giving a share of power to the opposition in local or regional government, parliament committees, and coalition governments; and in giving autonomy and representation to institutions like trade unions—allows for partial change, reform rather than revolution, and agreements that do not represent either the status quo or total change. The critics of the social system can achieve some of their goals, and the people who are hostile to change can expect to defend part of their interests by limited concessions, conditions that can lead to change and reform although they normally frustrate total change.

Democratic participation and sharing in power indirectly legitimize the social order since they postpone the demand for radical change and assure respect for—"legalize"—those aspects that are not the immediate object of change. However, they also weaken principled resistance to any change. The slowness of changes in basic values and opinions under conditions of freedom and absence of violence can reduce the fears of the people who have something to lose, but it also dampens the enthusiasm and hopes of those who in the absence of "democratic visibility"—the counting of votes— could believe that they represent "the people," the majority.

The moment of transition to democracy from an authoritarian system is one in which neither the people advocating change nor those against it know their actual strength, and therefore, both hopes and fears can be exaggerated. Such a situation makes compromise on democratic institutions difficult and the desire to manipulate them (through electoral laws, limits on democratic decision making, etc.) strong. The real significance of electoral results is also likely to be the object of distorted interpretations. Therefore, the relationship between democracy and the legitimation of the socioeconomic order can be better understood in long-lasting and relatively stable democracies.

Although political democracy can be legitimate for those who advocate radical social change, even though they may not expect to achieve it immediately, it also can be acceptable to those opposing it as long as they can hope to attain a consensus for their position or for limited change. If the conflicts were between only a privileged minority and an underprivileged majority, or if the situation were perceived as such, it would seem doubtful that those so privileged would agree to fully democratic political institutions (particularly if they are in control, as in many authoritarian regimes).

However, in addition to inaccurate perceptions of social inequality, those who are privileged have reasons to believe that such a majority is unlikely to effect radical change under democratic conditions. One reason is they believe the less privileged are far from united in their interests. The conviction of the privileged about the capacity of the system to satisfy demands and their capacity to convince others of their superior ability to manage the society and economy is another. A third is their belief in the need for the entrepreneurial function (as justification of their privileged position). In practice, the awareness that conflicts other than those over the socioeconomic order divide society—religious, cultural, linguistic, rural-urban, foreign policy, etc.—and find expression in democratic politics makes it possible for the privileged to accept the institutionalized "uncertainty" and "risk" of political democracy.

Even more, they could and can count on the legitimation of their position by other legitimate social traditions, values, and institutions in the religious and cultural realm. The legitimation of private property by religion and law, which predate modern economic systems and political democracy, has limited the impact of radical criticism of the socioeconomic order of capitalism. The status structure, as distinctive from class structure, that survived from the prebourgeois society (*Stand* vs. *Klasse, Bildung* vs. *Besitz*, to use the classical German terms) served as a protective structure during the industrial revolution, a point rightly emphasized by Schumpeter,[7] perceived and used by conservatives like Disraeli, and central to studies about the British "tory worker" by McKenzie and Silver among others.[8] The role of religion was perceived by the bourgeoisie, who turned away from their laicism and anticlericalism as the proletariat started challenging the bourgeoisie, and by members of the nineteenth-century labor movement, particularly Marxists and anarchists, who therefore considered the fight against religion as a step in making class consciousness possible. These developments heightened the importance of religious cleavages in European democratic politics, often contributed to a weakening of the left, and when cumulated rather than cross-cutting led to a polarization that threatened or destroyed the viability of democracy (for example, in Spain and Austria).

The growing distance between the educated elite, the religious institutions and believers, and the professional and bureaucratic elites from the economic system, particularly under the influence of the intellectuals, has been seen as a change that would make the survival of the capitalist system unlikely, despite its undeniable achievements and the undeniable failures of existing fully socialist systems. This is the central point in the Schumpeterian analysis of the breakdown of capitalism, in which intellectuals rather than the labor movement play the decisive role.[9] Today, Schumpeter would probably add the religious "intelligentsia" and the leaders under their influence. In fact, while defending the traditional social order of individual private property, the churches had never fully reconciled themselves to capitalism and the "amoral" character of the market (in fact, the amoral character of the democracy, so formally homologous to each other). The secularization process undoubtedly contributed to the weakening of this legitimizing role, independent of changes in value orientations. These processes did not have the consequences Schumpeter expected in advanced industrial and democratic societies because the democratic process allowed the leaders of the working class, trade unionists, and politicians to gain a better understanding of the economic system, the market, the functions of accumulation and entrepreneurship, etc., and of the costs of alternative systems, so that they adopted "rational" and limited reforms as their program.

The question that must be raised is to what extent the consequences will be different in countries now undergoing both the process of capitalist economic development and the process of political democratization. To what extent will the privileged—including entrepreneurs, managers, professionals, and bureaucrats, not only landlords who are a numerical minority—be willing to risk democracy when they perceive that those who traditionally have supported the existing social order as god given, to be accepted with forbearance and corrected by brotherly love and charity rather than radical change, abandon them? When those traditional supporters question the existing social order radically from a religious perspective, often using the same language of their political opponents and sometimes giving them their blessing, using the theology of liberation? Can political democracy be accepted, in principle, as legitimate by sectors of society under conditions in which numerical and ideological hegemony converge and the uncertainty of outcomes of democratic processes is replaced by certainty? Under such conditions, how effective can other mechanisms, like legal-procedural guarantees and civil liberties, be in reversing what might be a temporary political and social alignment? Hirschman, in his discussion of the role of ideological forces behind the entrepreneurial function (including O'Connor's accumulation) and the redistributive function, notes:

> In Latin America the ideological mutation just discussed—the withdrawal of intellectual support from one function and its shift to the other—was particularly evident in Chile, Argentina, and Brazil. Strongly entrenched social groups were left in these countries without any ideological fig leaf; an uncomfortable and perhaps precarious position. In this manner it may be possible to account for the readiness of these groups to use force, which served to make up, as it were, for the lost ideological support. For as Rousseau pointed out long ago in his *Essay on the Origin of Languages*, force is a substitute for "eloquence" and "persuasion."[10]

The belief in the possibility of "ideological" legitimation of the existing social order—or a modified version of it—is the basis for the acceptance of democracy in such situations. Many people would argue that the result would not be real democracy, and that the numerical and ideological hegemony would achieve real democracy, but we might ask ourselves, Will it be democracy with freedom or will those who have everything to lose (and know it) and who control so many resources—wealth, skills, the instruments of violence—give up without a fight? The answer might be, Why not then revolution and their defeat and destruction, since they are not ready to surrender voluntarily? To answer yes, one would have to be sure that the revolution would win, that those groups are really dispensable, and that their functional equivalent would not reemerge but this time in a society based on hegemonic power and a tradition of violence. I for one would not be sure of all those conditions. That is why political democracy based on partial legitimation of even an unjust social order might still be a better alternative.

One can, therefore, conclude that the high legitimacy of a democratic system, although often compatible with widespread or intense disagreement about the legitimacy of the socioeconomic system, is not easily compatible with a overwhelming delegitimation of a preexisting economic system. Here one encounters the age-old question of the possibility of a democratic transition to advanced socialism (not the welfare state, a mixed economy, etc., in relatively wealthy and advanced societies).

In principle, a democratically elected leadership can use its position to question an economic system and to achieve a democratic majority in order to transform the system democratically, which might well endanger the institutional processes. In addition, as the neoliberals have continuously stressed, the functional requirements for the free formation of alternative opinions (not only about socioeconomic issues) may well depend on certain types of socioeconomic institutions.

The different degrees of legitimacy of the political and the socioeconomic systems therefore pose a number of interesting problems, which I can only hope to outline here. The central question would be, To what extent does the legitimacy of the democratic system contribute to the legitimation or delegitimation of the socioeconomic system, or inversely, does the legitimacy of the socioeconomic order reinforce the legitimacy of the political system or in the case of illegitimacy contribute to its delegitimation? There is an inherent tension between democracy and *any* socioeconomic order: No social group can be assured—or believe it is assured—of a total safeguarding of its interests. In principle, this uncertainty is compensated for by the fact that no one can win once and for all; victors immediately face the prospect of having to defend their position in the future. The submission pro tempore to the rule of democracy is based on both the belief in the legitimacy of the democratic rules and procedures and the self-limiting character of those rules. That legitimacy belief is never absolute but conditional on the protection of the minority rights; but to what extent and in what way, in a modern state with its growing power, those rights can be effective is a more complex question than the legal recognition of civil liberties.

The other condition is a social one, and no democratic principles can assure it, the absence of permanent political hegemony. It is not and cannot be assured normatively. It is the result of the social structure, of the ideological climate, of the organizational capacity of conflicting interests, of deliberate decisions of political actors, and, unfortunately more so every day, of the action of the state. Without the hope of reversing or changing in the long run the political balance of power by democratic means, the willingness to participate in the democratic process becomes doubtful. Social hegemony as the basis of political hegemony undermines the second condition for a stable democracy.

LEGITIMACY OF THE SOCIAL AND ECONOMIC SYSTEM
IN EUROPEAN DEMOCRACIES

The data from the European Values Study of 1981[11] allow us to explore some of the legitimacy problems comparatively. The social order of Western European democracies is not questioned radically (see Table 2.1): In 1981 only 5 percent of the population of the democracies included in the study felt that "the entire way our society is organized must be radically changed by revolutionary action." Those ready to take such a position were a small minority (even in France 8 percent, Spain 7 percent, and Italy 6 percent), less than those voting for Communist and extreme left parties. However, the feeling that societies must be gradually improved by reforms is widespread: 64 percent as the average; 70 percent in Latin Europe. The maximum was in Spain, 75 percent; followed by Sweden 72 percent, Italy 70 percent, and France 68 percent. The most conservative position; "Our present society must be valiantly defended against all subversive forces," was curiously weak in Spain, 9 percent, and highest in West Germany, 38 percent (where the revolutionary option was especially weak, 2 percent), and Norway, 45 percent. The European average was 22 percent.

Private ownership of the means of production—business and industry— is still the dominant form of economic organization in Western democracies although public ownership is quite important in a number of them (see Table 2.2). To what extent do people believe that owners should run the business or appoint managers? There is a wide range between Northern Ireland and Great Britain, where 57 and 50 percent, respectively, thought so, and France, where only 19 percent did. The European average was 34 percent. Below average, in addition to France, were Spain, Sweden, Italy, and the Netherlands, but in the three last countries, 59, 47, and 47 percent, respectively, believed that owners and employees should select managers. Even in France and Spain the sum of those favoring pure private ownership and codetermination made up a majority of 67 and 54 percent.

The two socialized choices, "The state should be the owner and appoint the managers" and "Employees should own and select the managers"—that is, state socialism and self-management—were the preference of only 14 percent of the Europeans as an average, but 29 percent of the Spaniards, 20 percent of the French, 14 percent of the Italians, and 11 percent of the Dutch favored one of those two choices.[12] Those who most favored state ownership were the Italians, 8 percent, and the Spaniards, 7 percent, while self-management was preferred by 22 percent of the Spaniards, 17 percent of the French, and 10 percent of the Dutch.

The data suggest that the challenge to the economic system varies considerably from country to country. However, contrary to what some readers might have expected, it is not greater in countries that traditionally have had a large vote for social democratic parties and in which those parties have governed many years. The failures of the public sector in Italy and Spain do not seem to have decreased the preference for it, and its recent expansion in France has not resulted in a high preference for state ownership. The relatively low appeal of self-management in Italy (6 percent) is surprising in view of that country's syndicalist tradition and the importance of factory committees, but it might reflect the position of the Italian Communist party. In Spain, the self-management idea had enormous appeal after Franco's death, reaching 29 percent in 1977, but it had dropped to 22 percent by 1981, and according to another survey early in 1983, it had dropped even further to 14 percent. In 1976-1977, even center parties like the Christian Democrats included the idea in their programs, but since then one has heard little about it. Interestingly enough, countries whose social structure we consider relatively similar, like the Scandinavian countries or Belgium and the Netherlands, differ considerably. For example, among the last two, respectively, 6 and 10 percent favor self-management and 34 and 30 percent, pure private property. It is important to realize that those national differences are not just a reflection of a greater inclination of the electorates toward the left or the right since respondents who placed themselves on the same points on a ten-point, left-right scale also differed considerably in their preferences by country (see Table 2.3).

The pattern repeats itself with some changes in attitudes toward authority at work (see Table 2.4). The response, "People should follow the instructions of their superiors even when they do not fully agree with them," was highest in Norway (60 percent), followed by Denmark (57 percent), Great Britain and Northern Ireland (each 49 percent), the Republic of Ireland (45 percent), Sweden (40 percent), and the Netherlands (39 percent). It was equal to the European average of 33 percent in Belgium, and Spain, West Germany, France, and Italy fell below that average.

The most interesting discrepancy between the attitudes toward property and authority is found in West Germany, where only 28 percent accepted the authority principle. Perhaps because of the Nazi experience and the reeducation and the new ideological currents among youth, the idea that "no one should be expected to follow their superior's instructions on a job without being convinced that the instructions are right, rather than as a matter of principle" is particularly strong. Agreement with this opinion was expressed by 51 percent of the Germans, 57 percent of the French, 41 percent of the Spaniards, 40 percent of the Finns, and 39 percent of the Italians.

These data indicate that the challenge to the socioeconomic order of capitalism is quite different in Western democracies and that the voting patterns reflect that difference only imperfectly.

The "Legitimacy" of the Social Partners

The socioeconomic system of Western European democracies is based on the legitimacy of the social partners—unions and employers' organizations—who in neocorporate systems make many of the major decisions affecting the economy with the approval of the government, which gives their actions binding character.[13] It is therefore important that both should enjoy a certain level of approval. Unfortunately, we have at hand only a rating of the trade unions, not one of the employers' organizations, so in this analysis I will use the rating of "major companies"—which often carry much weight in those organizations—as a makeshift substitute. Taking the "European average," one can place each country as above or below that average in an interesting typology (see Tables 2.5 and 2.6).

There are two countries in which the rating of both trade unions and major companies is below or barely above average, and no one will be surprised, in view of the discussion of the legitimacy of the social order, to find that those two countries are Italy and Spain. Indeed, both unions and business received the lowest rating in Europe in Italy. Only in three countries—Great Britain, Northern Ireland, and Belgium—does one find the rating of business above average and that of the unions below. The constant conflict with the unions and the absence of effective neocorporative solutions in Britain would be congruent with those data.[14]

In four countries, Denmark, Sweden, West Germany, and the Netherlands, major companies are below average and trade unions above, and also in four, both unions and major business are above the European average— the Republic of Ireland, Norway, Finland, and France (in the last, unions were rated close to the average and business slightly higher, perhaps because of pride in a number of large enterprises, many of them nationalized). It is not clear why some of the countries in these two groups should rate major companies higher or lower, but certainly the rating of trade unions reflects the level of institutionalization of socioeconomic conflicts, particularly in Scandinavia, the Netherlands, and apparently in the Republic of Ireland. The position of West Germany is closer to the average than those of the other countries, both for business and the unions, and therefore closer to the conflict point.

The countries in which the ten institutions included in the survey were rated above the European average, with the exception of Denmark, were also those in which business was rated above average and, with the exception of Great Britain, trade unions were similarly rated.

Images of Economic Systems

An interesting problem is the discrepancy between the evaluation of actual socioeconomic systems as models and the judgments about them in the abstract. The data from research on attitudes toward the economic system in Spain (1983) allow us to explore this problem further (see Table 2.7).[15]

In Spain, few people consider any of the communist societies a model, and a significant number consider Western, even purely capitalist, systems like those in the United States and Japan as models. However, when it comes to characterizing purely socialist and capitalist economies by assigning certain characteristics to them, socialist systems are ahead in the positive characteristics, except for wealth and technological advance—see responses for justice, freedom, and humaneness. In addition, the socialist systems are seen as only slightly more repressive (16 percent versus 13 percent).

The socialist ideal is not shattered by the negative realities of "real socialism," although they are dimly perceived, and the positive reality of capitalist societies, although not ignored, does not modify the negative evaluation of capitalism.

"Legitimacy" of Educational Institutions, the Press, and Business

Since Schumpeter discussed the question, Can capitalism survive? in the chapter, "Growing Hostility," in which he put so much emphasis on the role of the intellectuals and perhaps more particularly on the journalists, the tension between the producers of culture and some forms of mass culture and capitalism has been a central theme. The "adversary culture," as Daniel Bell has emphasized, plays a central role in undermining some of the value assumptions on which capitalism is based.[16] Unfortunately, in the research there have been no questions about the "legitimacy" and "performance" of intellectuals, or the cultural institutions and the media in different countries or even in one country, so I cannot relate such responses to the attitudes toward the economic system. One does not know to what extent a positive response to intellectuals is associated with a negative one toward entrepreneurs and capitalists.

At the risk of going beyond what the data might show, I utilize instead the responses in the European Values Study concerning how much confidence people have in different institutions—the press, the education system, and major companies (see Table 2.8). In the thirteen countries of Europe, counting Northern Ireland separately, we find that the average for the educational institutions is 2.61, somewhat above the 2.49 for all institutions and greatly above the 2.29 for major companies and 2.22 for the press. These data suggest that the more established part of the intellectual community, the academic community, is perceived by the population differently from the press (although I would be happier if the term *the press* would have been *the journalists* since the press also involves other aspects of the institution, like economic and political control). It is noteworthy that in all the countries of Europe educational institutions are also rated higher than major companies, although the differences vary from 0.59 to 0.20, being largest in some of the smaller European countries—the Netherlands, Norway, Finland, and Denmark as well as Italy—and smallest in Great Britain, France, West Germany, Spain, and Belgium.

The position of the press is quite different from that of the educational institutions, and in some respects this fact makes one question to what extent the media have a legitimacy that would allow them to play the delegitimizing role that Schumpeter attributed to them. In all of the countries included in the study, with the exceptions of Italy, Spain, and West Germany, major companies enjoy a more favorable rating than the press (see Table 2.9). This is particularly true for Great Britain, with a difference of 0.31; France, 0.22; and Finland, 0.10 (the European average difference is 0.7).[17] I should however note that the two countries in which capitalism receives the lowest support are also two of the three countries in which the press is rated practically the same or higher than major companies—Italy, 0.03, and Spain, 0.17.

"LEGITIMACY" AND "EFFICIENCY"
OF POLITICAL DEMOCRACY AND CAPITALISM:
SOME ILLUSTRATIVE DATA

One can examine—illustrate—the problems with some data from research in 1983 on attitudes of Spaniards toward the economic system and some data kindly made available to me by Elisabeth Noelle-Neumann from a study by Demoskopie in Germany.[18] I wish I could deal with these problems comparatively and over time, but the data are not available.

Both the German and the Spanish studies attempted to probe into what one might call the legitimacy of democracy and capitalism and the perception of the efficiency of both systems. There were, particularly in one of the alternatives on capitalism, differences in wording that limit the comparability. Even so a number of common patterns and some interesting differences appear clearly.

The Spanish statement was, The capitalist economy of private initiative is the best economic system for a country like ours, and The capitalist economy of private initiative allows that the economic problems we Spaniards have to face are being solved. The German statement was, Capitalism as the economic system that lives from the wealth of ideas of everyone is the best for our country, and With capitalism as economic system we can solve the economic problems that we have in the Bundesrepublik. In both countries the respondents were asked to agree or disagree with two other statements: (1) Democracy is the best political system for a country like ours (for our country, in Germany) and (2) With democracy we can solve the problems we (Spaniards) have (we have in the Bundesrepublik).

Both in Spain and the Bundesrepublik, the legitimacy of political democracy enjoys high support among those who expressed an opinion, 89.7 percent and 85.8 percent, respectively; both were higher than the same evaluations of capitalism, 48.4 percent and 48.6 percent, respectively (see Table 2.10). When one turns to the efficiency of democracy, and its capacity to solve the problems of the country, and that of capitalism, there is a parallel pattern but, not so surprisingly, differences between Spain and the Bundesrepublik. Respectively, 67.4 percent and 74.2 percent believed in the efficiency of democracy and 34.1 percent and 43.1 percent in the efficiency of capitalism. The difference in the legitimacy of democracy and capitalism is, respectively, 41.3 percent and 37.2 percent, while that regarding efficiency is 33.3 percent and 31.1 percent. There is, however, a difference between the efficiency of both democracy and capitalism in the two countries: 6.8 percent in favor of German democracy and 9.0 percent in favor of German capitalism, a difference I would surmise reflects reality rather than differences in perception.

Given these distributions, it is logical that the most positive combination—those believing in the legitimacy (vaguely defined) of both democracy and capitalism and in the efficiency of both—should be more widely accepted in the Bundesrepublik (33.5 percent) than in Spain (21.4 percent). The proportions denying legitimacy and efficiency to *both* systems are small, 9.0 percent in the Bundesrepublik and 3.8 percent in Spain, a more surprising finding. In Spain, under a socialist government, the proportion of those believing in the legitimacy *and* the efficiency of democracy but denying both to capitalism is 30.8 percent, a slightly larger proportion than in the Bundesrepublik, 28.2 percent. The proportion of those believing in the legitimacy of democracy but not in its efficiency *and* not in either in the legitimacy or the efficiency of capitalism is also larger in Spain, 12.2 percent compared to 8.3 percent.

Let me emphasize that although correlated with the vote for socialist and conservative parties, the general attitudes toward the economic and political systems are largely independent from party preference. According to the German data, 24.0 percent of the Social Democratic party (SPD) respondents opted for the most favorable combination of the legitimacy and efficacy of both democracy and capitalism, to which one could add the 6.3 percent who only questioned the efficacy of capitalism. Obviously, the proportions of Christian Democratic Union (CDU) respondents were larger, respectively, 48.3 percent and 5.7 percent. The proportion of SPD respondents positive on legitimacy and performance of democracy but negative or undecided on both counts for capitalism was 39.8 percent. If SPD respondents were less than "socialist" in their attitudes toward the economic system, a minority of CDU respondents, committed democrats, responded negatively to capitalism, 22.9 percent; to which one might add those favorable to the legitimacy of democracy but unhappy with its performance and negative with regard to capitalism, 4.6 percent.

The Spanish data show a somewhat similar pattern, although more polarized and consistent. Among Partido Socialista Obrero Español (PSOE) respondents, 18.5 percent were positive toward both democracy and capitalism on legitimacy and efficacy, compared to 31.3 percent among Alianza Popular (AP) respondents, to whom we might add those positive except on the performance of capitalism, respectively, 8.3 percent and 10.6 percent. The proportion of democratic socialists negative on both the legitimacy and efficacy of capitalism was slightly larger than in Germany, 43.7 percent, but the proportion of conservative AP respondents was smaller than in Germany, 7.0 percent, a difference that is easily understood given the minority position of the AP in the electorate. The fact that 16.3 percent were positive with regard to capitalism on both counts but also negative on both with regard to democracy has no equivalent in the CDU electorate.

Interaction Between the Legitimacy
and Efficiency of Political Democracy
and the Economic System

Many analyses of the crisis of democracy and the rise to power of fascism, particularly nazism, have linked that crisis directly with the challenge to the legitimacy of capitalism and its loss of efficiency because of the world depression. Those theoretical approaches have focused on only one of the possible relationships: the direct impact of the crisis of capitalism on the stability of democracy (crisis of capitalism leads to breakdown of democracy), without exploring alternative relationships. One, the crisis of capitalism added to or combined with a crisis or weakness of legitimacy of democracy leads to a breakdown that would not have happened without that initial weak legitimacy of democracy preceding or coinciding with the economic crisis (low legitimacy of democracy plus crisis of capitalism leads to breakdown of democracy). Two, in the case of high legitimacy of democracy, the crisis of capitalism would not lead to the breakdown of democracy, although it could lead to some level of crisis (high legitimacy of democracy plus crisis of capitalism leads to crisis within democracy but no breakdown). The data now being analyzed by Eckart Zimmermann,[19] particularly the contrast between the Netherlands and Germany, could seem to support the second alternative, or at least suggest that the relationships between the economic crisis and its different indicators and the rise of fascism and the crises of democracy are not that simple. Without entering here into that historical-sociological debate, I want to suggest some structural reasons why the crisis in the performance of the economic system should not always affect the evaluation of the performance of democracy and even less of its legitimacy.

A factor that has to be introduced here is the process of attribution (Zurechnung) of social consequences, which in different societies, democracies, and economic systems might vary considerably. In principle, in a liberal political democracy with a capitalist market economy, the "attribution" is made to the economic actors rather than to the political actors: to enterprises, banks, the world economic system, and when there is institutionalized bargaining, to employers' organizations and trade unions. The political actors can, up to a point, attribute the crisis of performance to those actors— depending on their left-right position more to employers or more to trade unions—and only when the ties of those organizations to political parties are too close will they be unable to distance themselves from the results of their actions. In addition, the "internal democracy" of those organizations allows for a distinction between incumbent officeholders and the organizations, as survey data for the United States analyzed by S. M. Lipset and W. Schneider show.[20]

In turn, the democratic system allows for a distinction between the system as a method of legitimation of authority and the people who exercise power for the time being (until the next election). Only when all the parties that sustain the legitimacy of the democractic system against an antisystem opposition (or oppositions) are also responsible for its efficiency is an acute loss of efficiency likely to be detrimental to the legitimacy of the "system."

Democracy can, therefore, allow for attribution of low efficiency to quite different sectors, to different actors, and/or to different institutional levels before reaching the point of attributing it directly to the "political system" instead. This process is much less likely in the case of totalitarian and authoritarian systems, which control (often only in theory) wide areas of social life without recognizing (in principle) their autonomy and in which a distinction between the "political system" and the government is not possible since there is no institutionalized opposition that could take over the government by peaceful means without changing the system. A dis-aggregate, dispersed, and multilevel attribution of failures poses inherent limits to the delegitimation of the democratic system as the result of failures of performance of the economy.[21] Today's growing awareness of the worldwide interconnectedness of modern capitalist economies, together with the aware-ness and acceptance of the limits to national economic sovereignty, also contributes to that dispersion of attribution (and accountability) and perhaps paradoxically protects Western political democracies from the loss of efficiency of the economic system. This situation might, among other factors, account for the different impact of the crises of the thirties and the present.

The attribution process is in part a function of ideological frameworks, and certainly in an orthodox-vulgar-Marxist view, in which any "bourgeois" government is only the managing committee of the bourgeoisie, the dis-tribution of attribution and accountability would be more difficult. In this context it would be interesting to know the processes of attribution in different democratic societies, the degree to which there is belief in the capacity of the state to solve problems (not of a specific regime alone).[22] In principle, the belief in a free market economy, in capitalism as an economic system, should lead to less faith in the capacity of the government (irrespective of its being leftist or rightist) and ultimately the state to solve problems.

In the Spanish survey, the responses to the question, One trusts that the state can solve the problems of our society because it has the means to do so: Would you say that the state can solve all the problems, the majority of problems, many problems, only some, none? showed that few people believed that "none" was the answer. Close to one-third opted for the modest expectation, "only some"; over one-third, "many"; and a minority, "the majority" or even "all." More unexpected was the result that those considering capitalism the best system and those disagreeing did not differ too much, although they did differ in the direction of our hypothesis as 22.5 percent of the former and 28.6 percent of the latter answered "all" or "the majority" compared to 39.8 percent and 32.3 percent, respectively, answering "only some" or "none."

The failures of performance of a society, its difficulty in solving or its failure to solve problems, should therefore affect political institutions dif-ferently. One could perhaps argue that in the Weimar Republic, the right, with its Prussian Staatsgläubigkeit ("faith in the state"), was particularly likely to attribute the low efficiency to the "system" (which to start with the rightists believed had low legitimacy), a situation that might not occur as much in societies in which the expectations about the capacity of the state and its bureaucracy are lower. In turn, perhaps, one could find here one of the sources of the lower legitimacy of the capitalist economic system in countries with a Napoleonic tradition than in Anglo-Saxon societies that have a weaker state. Those differences should also account for differences in attribution of the failures of the socioeconomic system.

In a capitalist economy, the blame for crises can be imputed to a variety of factors: the impersonal forces of the market, the monopolies that destroyed the free market mechanism, the trade unions that introduced distortions into the labor market, the collusion between employers' organizations and trade unions that favored inflationary tendencies, the intervention of the state that distorted the normal functioning of the capitalist system, more recently the organizations of consumers and environmentalists, and last but not least, the world capitalist economic system. This multiplicity of imputation possibilities frees the political system from being made responsible for a crisis as long as it does not claim to be able to solve more problems than it can handle. Governing parties are not likely to do so, and a democratic opposition that hopes to govern within the constitutional and institutional limits of the regime is also unlikely to go too far in making such a claim. In such a context, only a disloyal opposition will attribute the crisis not only to the party in power but to "the system," the economic as well as the political. In fact, a rightist antisystem party, like the Nazi and the German antidemocratic conservatives, can attribute the crisis to the regime.

However, such an interpretation of an economic crisis presupposes a delegitimation of the political system as an instrument of an "illegitimate" economic system, as Communist parties have done; as alien to the national tradition and supported by forces hostile to it, like the Nazis did; or as imposed from the outside, like the "vulgar" dependency theory would. The crisis then would only confirm that negative—alienated—view of the political system. In a basically legitimate democratic system, with an opposition expecting or hoping to govern, the multiple centers of imputation, the multiple factors accounting for failures in the efficacy of the economic system, would lead people to see the government as a guarantee against irresponsible or selfish economic interests.

The difficulties in the functioning of the capitalist system would make the political system and the democratically elected political leaders more deserving of legitimacy and trust. Taking this perspective, a crisis in the economic system does not necessarily carry with it a crisis of the political system. Political institutions and leaders do not necessarily have to be blamed for the failures of the economic system, which might explain the fact that during the Great Depression, a number of democratic governments acquired a greater stability as was indicated by the greater continuity of governments than before 1929.[23] The economic crisis contributed to the breakdown of democracy where it was not fully legitimated—as in Germany and Austria— but the already consolidated democracies of Scandinavia, the United Kingdom, and the Benelux countries gained new strength and in Scandinavia were able to successfully integrate the working class into the polity with new and innovative policies. Overstating somewhat the point, one could say that the crisis in the economy, rather than threatening democracy, helped in its full institutionalization.

It could be argued that in many democracies, the legitimacy of the political system compensates for the lesser legitimacy of the social economic system. Democratic politicians, even those opposed to or critical of the capitalist system (as long as they do not actually disrupt it or destroy it), have taken the place of the protective strata of Schumpeter. We should also not forget that those preindustrial strata that maintained the legitimacy of the political and social systems while the capitalist industrial revolution was taking place were often far from sympathetic to entrepreneurial and capitalist values.

In fact, one could go further and note that the left often comes to power democratically during periods of economic crisis, when the resources for reform are scarce and even austerity measures have to be taken, which conservatives might sometimes be unable to do. The left indirectly and paradoxically might contribute to the stability of capitalism since its victory contributes to a strengthening, at least temporarily, of the political system that presumably should serve to challenge the economic order but is forced under the circumstances to leave it unchallenged. The experience of a leftist government that is unable to make major changes, even the prospect of having to assume power under such circumstances, itself will lower the expectations of changes in the economic system that the left would generate out of power during periods of prosperity. Paradoxically, the legitimacy of political democracy reinforced by the supporters of the left in a democratic context makes it more difficult to attack the economic institutions directly when such an attack would come into conflict with the desire for stability of the political leadership and the legal order that the state sustains.

As Robert Fishman has shown in his research, the desire of the working-class leaders at the plant level to help in the consolidation of Spanish democracy after Franco contributed to a moderation of their economic demands.[24] The responses of plant leaders of both the communist Comisiones Obreras (CCOO) and especially the socialist Unión General de Trabajadores (UGT) trade unions in Barcelona and Madrid show their willingness to limit labor demands for the sake of consolidation and stability of democracy (see Table 2.11). Of the CCOO leaders surveyed in those two industrial centers, 63 percent agreed with a statement to that effect, 77 percent of the UGT leaders surveyed did so, and 65 percent of all those interviewed agreed. Certainly, economic considerations—like the need to maintain the competitiveness of the Spanish economy or the need to fight inflation— were not ignored by those leaders, but economic considerations were considered less compelling than the concern for democracy in moderating labor demands. The legitimacy of the democratic state and its legal system becomes an obstacle to the pursuit on the part of the working class of economic goals that might be in conflict with that system.

There is, in addition, a certain asymmetry between the legitimation of democracy and any socioeconomic system. In the case of democracy, it is a procedure and its preconditions—civil liberties—that are legitimated, but the substantive content can be changed and does change depending on the will of the electorate. Intellectually, it is possible to separate the concrete reality of a society at a given time from the democratic institutional framework. On the other hand, it is much more difficult, if not impossible, for the average citizen to separate the principles of an economic system—like those of a capitalist market economy—from the social and economic realities of a concrete society.

This situation means that it should be easy to believe in democracy while being highly critical of its temporary manifestations, the substantive content given by an electorate to the political system. With an equally critical attitude toward an economic system like capitalism it is more difficult, except at an analytical level, to believe in the excellence of the system. Therefore, it is easier to question the economic system and to conceive of an alternative.

Furthermore, both democracy and the market economy are vulnerable to the criticisms that they are not justified by the substantive social order they produce, and that no specific individuals can be made responsible for them—responsibility lies instead with a myriad of individual acts of voters, producers, and consumers that are difficult to subject to moral considerations. This problem accounts for the difficulties that some religious, moral, and intellectual leaders have in identifying with democracy and/or capitalism and the surprising attraction for them of different authoritarian and socialist systems.

PERCEPTIONS OF JUSTICE AND INJUSTICE AND "LEGITIMACY"

It is tempting to think that the attitude toward the economic system would be a reflection of the perception of the justice or injustice of the socioeconomic order, or the other way around since it would be difficult to determine which of the two comes first, that is, which is the "independent variable." The Spanish data, on which I base my thinking, suggest a considerable and somewhat surprising independence of both attitudes (see Table 2.12).

Obviously, the people who do not recognize the "legitimacy" (in our vague sense) of capitalism nor its efficiency are more likely to consider the system unjust (15.6 percent "very unjust"; 45.3 percent "fairly unjust"), but the people who are positive to capitalism on both questions are not that far apart in their responses (respectively, 6.2 percent and 32.4 percent). Fewer of those negative on both counts consider it very just or fairly just (1.4 percent and 8.5 percent), but among the most positive the proportions are only 1.4 percent and 14.6 percent). Therefore, the deviations from the average distribution of attitudes in the population are less extreme than one would expect, with the more procapitalist most likely to say "neither just nor unjust" (43.3 percent versus 35.9 percent as the average for the population and 28.2 percent of the most negative).

People who consider the economic system "very unjust" are more likely to deny that the capitalist economic system is either the best possible or able to solve the problems (58.2 percent); among those saying "very just," the proportion is smaller (38.1 percent) but not that much (see Table 2.13). Among the latter, the most positive response to capitalism is larger (26.8 percent) but not that much more than among those saying "very unjust" (15.2 percent). Even if one adds those who in principle are favorable to capitalism—irrespective of efficiency—one finds only 48.8 percent in the first group and 27.9 percent in the second. There is, therefore, a considerable independence between both attitudes.

The feeling that the economic system is "very unjust" is not associated, even in Spain, with a belief that a communist country is a model to follow in organizing social and economic life (see Table 2.14). In the Spanish survey, only 2.8 percent thought Cuba was such a model; 3.8 percent, the USSR; 2.9 percent, China; and 2.4 percent, Yugoslavia. In contrast, 29.8 percent mentioned Sweden as a model; 26.8 percent, Germany; 12.8 percent, Japan and 16.5 percent, the United States; 10.7 percent, the United Kingdom; and 8.6 percent, France. While 42.3 percent of those surveyed rejected the USSR and 19.0 percent the United States as models, the proportions among those most dissatisfied with the socioeconomic order were 31 percent and 26 percent, respectively.

The most negative attitudes toward capitalism were not associated with communist countries to any significant extent. Those respondents were most likely to consider Sweden a model (35.4 percent), and there was an almost equal rejection of the United States (30.5 percent) and the USSR (31.9 percent). A positive attitude toward capitalism was not linked with one likely to consider the United States as a model (25.7 percent), although that response was compatible with considering Sweden as such (23.5 percent).

The realities of different societies, their success combined with ideological perceptions, seem to be stronger than any ideological identifications (which might have been stronger fifty or sixty years ago). But one could equally well argue that the vague ideological responses are to a large extent not much affected by the realities of the societies that presumably are the realization of those ideal models.

Again according to the Spanish data, the experience of having been treated unjustly—or the perception of having been so treated—in the workplace, in a bank, by the electricity company, or while buying something leads to a slightly larger proportion of people being negative toward both the legitimacy and the efficiency of capitalism (respectively, 51.8, 46.4, 45.8, and 45.3 percent, compared to the population, 40.2 percent). Similarly, the proportions of those most positive on both counts were fewer (21.0, 26.8, 25.4, and 23.8 percent, respectively, compared to 26.2 percent among the population). The greatest number favorable on both counts, 27.6 percent, perceived unfair treatment in a municipal office, and the smallest, 21.0 percent, perceived it in the workplace (see Table 2.15).

The data would seem to indicate that the general perception of injustice of the economic order is correlated more with the attitudes toward the economic system—although not too strongly—than with the actual experiences of injustice in private business and public services.[25] Only the respondents who had no feeling of having been treated unjustly in any of the seven contexts listed (26 percent of the population) were less likely to be negative on both legitimacy and efficiency (32.1 percent), but they were hardly more favorable on both (28 percent).

The perception of injustice of the economic system is associated with a slightly larger proportion reporting they had been treated unjustly than among those saying that the system is very just (a small minority): 2 percent more in the workplace and 4 percent more by the bank or the electricity company (see Table 2.16). There was no difference connected with buying a product, but a somewhat larger number in dealing with an office of the state (8 percent). There was little difference (−1 percent) in relation to social security, −7 percent with regard to the municipality, and 9 percent fewer said they had never been treated unjustly.

These data would indicate little difference in one's actual experience of injustice and the basic attitude toward the economic system, and the same might be said regarding that attitude and grievances against the administration of the state.

THE ECONOMIC SYSTEM
AND INTERMEDIARY STRUCTURES:
TRADE UNIONS AND EMPLOYERS' ORGANIZATIONS

Opinion about the behavior of trade unions and employers' organizations in economic conflicts is likely to respond both to generalized, diffuse attitudes and specific responses to particular situations and to the most recent large-scale conflict; therefore, comparison among countries and social sectors within countries would present methodological problems. However, by considering the problem in the context of "the last years," we might be able to obtain a basic attitude.

In the Spanish survey, there was a related question with four logical possibilities: (1) trade unions and employers' organizations both act with a sense of responsibility; (2) the trade unions act responsibly in moderating workers' demands without cooperation of the employers' organizations; (3) the employers act responsibly without trade union cooperation; and (4) neither of the two act with consideration for the interests of the country. The responses showed a wide range of opinions (including 19 percent without one). Twenty-two percent were positive to both, 35 percent were negative to both, 19 percent were more favorable to the trade unions, and 5 percent were more favorable to the employers' organizations. For our purposes, the interesting question is, How much do these responses correlate with the "basic" attitudes toward the capitalist system? and the data show a wide dispersion of attitudes. Among the most procapitalist, 26 percent believed both act responsibly (compared to 22 percent among the most negative), 10 percent the employers (versus 2 percent), 13 percent the trade unions (versus 27 percent), and an equal number (37 percent) neither trade unions nor employers (14 percent of the procapitalists and 12 percent of the anticapitalists expressed no opinion).

The differences are congruent with the basic attitudes but far from large or polarized. In addition, a significant number (37 percent), irrespective of the perception of the economic system, were critical of both parties in the institutionalized conflict in modern democratic class society, in the name of some larger general interest—perhaps a resonance of the *bonum comune* ideology of catholicism or the "national interest" of fascism? The proportions of pro- and anticapitalists without opinion were practically the same (14 and 12 percent, respectively), except for those with no opinion about the desirable economic system. Once more, when we turn to the concrete functioning of an economic system, different perceptions of reality (that might or might not correspond to that of an unbiased outside scholarly observer) turn out to be almost as important as the "basic" more ideological preferences. Those preferences are related to a conflictual relation between workers and employers, but among those most negative toward capitalism, 12 percent expected improvement for the working class through conflict compared to 85 percent through cooperation; among those most favorable toward capitalism, the figures were 2 percent and 95 percent, respectively.

The Spanish data provide evidence for the legitimation—or at least acceptance—within a democratic context of trade unions and employers' organizations. Only 23 percent of the respondents felt that trade unions should not give support to political parties, and only 31 percent felt the same way about employers' organizations. Among those who were most procapitalist the figures were 20 percent and 23 percent, respectively; among those who were most negative toward capitalism, 25 percent and 38 percent.

RELATIVE DEVELOPMENT AND THE PERCEPTION OF ENTREPRENEURS AND WORKERS

The commitment to advanced socialization of an economy is linked to a negative perception and evaluation of entrepreneurship no matter what the country, but also with a more negative one of the entrepreneurs in a less developed country. Although people obviously have no adequate knowledge of "European" entrepreneurs versus Spanish entrepreneurs, the responses to a question in the Spanish survey for the attribution of certain characteristics to one and the other showed a more negative image of the Spanish, both among partisans of private enterprise and among partisans of a socialized economy, particularly the latter. It is the relative backwardness of economic development that contributes to the lesser acceptance of the "free enterprise" system, but the negative view is also a general attitude. For example, among those favorable to socialization, 33 percent thought European entrepreneurs were exploiters, and 58 percent thought the Spanish were while among partisans of free enterprise, the gap was only 3 percent. Similarly, the responses of the former to the belief that making money was the only motivation for European and Spanish businesses were 36 percent and 60 percent, respectively, but the gap among partisans of free enterprise was only 6 percent.

In the Spanish case, where rapid economic development in which entrepreneurs certainly played a role had taken place in the sixties, a negative image is surprising. Perhaps past low performance and other factors associated with economic development, particularly under an authoritarian regime as well as in an ideological climate, could not be overcome by success. If this situation were true for developing countries, entrepreneurial achievements might not always or easily be translated into a legitimation of the entrepreneurial function. Success without the support of other legitimizing factors or institutions would therefore not be sufficient. If this were the case, entrepreneurship in a second round of development could be discouraged, particularly since after rapid growth one would expect some "creative destruction" crisis of the less competitive enterprises that would reinforce that persistent hostility. To this hostility, one must also add the dissatisfactions generated by rapid and sudden economic development. Disadjustments that result from rapid urbanization, dissatisfactions generated by the mass consumption of certain goods like automobiles, and the disappointments of the consumer after the acquisition of certain goods (which have been noted by Hirschmann in his discussion of disappointment) would then reinforce hostility in spite of success.

The relative economic position of countries, as much or more than actual performance in the immediate past or rates of growth, seems therefore to be an important factor in delegitimizing capitalism. The survey data in this case confirm the analysis of Andrew C. Janos, a political scientist–historian of the origins of radicalism, particularly among the intelligentsia, in Hungary.[26]

Parallel to this negative evaluation of the national entrepreneurial class there is a reversal in the evaluation of workers. The responses on this point were more negative among the partisans of free enterprise and more positive among those of advanced socialization than the evaluation of workers in more advanced societies.

IDEOLOGICAL POSITIONS AND ATTITUDES
TOWARD ACTUAL ECONOMIC PROCESSES

A good example of how the concrete attitudes toward economic actions have become largely independent from the ideological image of the economic system is the relatively small differences in how the larger profits of an enterprise should be distributed (once the normal profits have been paid). Among the people who considered themselves "most capitalist" and "least capitalist," such profits should be distributed among shareholders (13 percent and 2 percent, respectively), shareholders and personnel (36 percent and 25 percent), and the personnel (6 percent and 7 percent). There was an agreement on investment to modernize (44 percent and 42 percent), to expand in order to create more jobs (59 percent and 74 percent), to invest in research (10 percent and 11 percent), and to not pay the profits as taxes (1 percent and 3 percent). Contrary to the people who perceived an inevitable conflict between accumulation and redistribution, there was considerable consensus on the need for accumulation, although linked in the present economic situation to job creation.

Another example of the inconsistency between ideological position and the response to concrete situations is that when asked to opt for only public television, both public and private, or only private, the proportions opting for a mixture were 78.2 percent of the procapitalists and 74.3 percent among those negative toward capitalism; among the same groups, 12.9 percent and 20.0 percent, respectively, chose public monopoly. It is significant that among the procapitalists, those not considering democracy legitimate were more favorable to either public monopoly or exclusively private television.

NEW SOURCES OF DELEGITIMATION
OF THE SOCIOECONOMIC SYSTEM

The opposition to the socioeconomic order in the nineteenth century and until late in the twentieth century was largely based on property relations, including in many countries those between landowners and tenants, poor farmers and farm laborers, and more specifically employers and manual workers. Sooner or later most of the countries resolved these conflicts with agrarian reforms, rural-urban migration and increased wealth of the remaining farmers, and the institutionalization of industrial labor conflict.

However, new sources of grievances, hostility, and moral indignation against the socioeconomic order of industrial societies have appeared with the spread of postmaterialist values, to use the expression of Ronald Inglehart.[27] These values are more diffuse in nature, often difficult to define, and directed against both economic and social institutions, including public ones, and governments that do not control their activities. From those positions have emerged and still can emerge new generalized delegitimations of the "system," conceptualized as "capitalist" but really industrial-urban society.

The risks of technology, aesthetic considerations, and dysfunctions and displeasures associated with widespread affluence and consumption by the masses turn into new sources of hostility toward capitalism.[28] Those responses, with their implicit elitist view of the past, are most likely to be articulated by the privileged, the intellectuals, but diffused by the media to the masses, whose disappointment with their newly improved position is likely to be even greater in view of the expectations of pleasure they had placed on acquiring it and the sacrifices doing so had required.[29] Instead of the frustration of rising expectations, they are disappointed with the satisfied expectations. This disappointment can be blamed on the economic system that presumably generated those needs rather than on oneself, needs defined a posteriori as "false." Such a disillusion is likely to be greater for the people who, because of their more limited economic means, must content themselves with goods of lower quality, cheaper housing, and crowded vacation places and who must sacrifice other pleasures they would have otherwise pursued, like everyday leisure, fancier foods, etc. An improvement in one's standard of living that seemed unattainable turns into a new source of discontent. This pattern is particularly possible in rapidly developing, still semideveloped societies.

However, the question might be asked, If the climate of opinion is critical of the economic system, how much greater would the hostility be if there had not been a massive improvement? Certainly in Spain to have improved one's position with respect to one's parents "very much" was associated with a more favorable attitude toward capitalism (59.1 percent versus 48.6 percent for those in the same position and 53.7 percent for those whose position had improved considerably). For those in a much worse or considerably worse position, that proportion was reduced even more, to 35.8 percent and 34.3 percent, respectively). However, the fact that as a percentage of the population, the first group composed 5.2 percent and the latter 0.9 percent, and those "considerably better" 18.5 percent compared to 1.8 percent "considerably lower," should not be forgotten. Certainly if downward social mobility had exceeded intergenerational upward mobility (subjectively perceived, let us not forget), the climate of opinion would have been appreciably less favorable.

One problem concerning the legitimacy of the socioeconomic system that largely cuts across the left-right dimension is the international character of the capitalist system, particularly since multinational corporations are today a basic component of the system. Institutions that escape the "national sovereignty"—multinationals, finance capitalism, the church (and in the past Masonry), and the internationals of political parties—were and are perceived as a threat by many people. As long as democratic politics is nation-state politics, there is an inherent tension in the capitalist economic system to the extent that it is international. In this context, nationalism both of the right and increasingly of the left, brings into question an important aspect of the capitalist system, whose rationality is not always compatible with the national interest—at least in the short run—as defined by political leadership.

CONCLUSION

I realize that the line of analysis suggested in this chapter might contribute to an explanation of the exceptions to the basic relationship established between economic development—industrialization, GNP per capita, standard of living, etc.—and political democracy. Perhaps independent of economic development, the widespread illegitimacy of capitalism—particularly among elites but independent of the vote for socialist parties, due to a variety of factors—contributed to the social instability that in turn contributed to the political crisis. In that case, one could account for the different political impact of comparable economic crises, for the political instability that was independent of the efficacy of the capitalist economic system in different countries. In such a case, the destabilizing impact of the crisis of capitalism would really be a function of the prior weak legitimation of the political system. The Weimar Republic would be one such case as would some of the crises of democracy in Latin America.

On the other hand, the early and evolutionary institutionalization of political democracy would then have contributed to the early and successful institutionalization of the capitalist economic system, or more generally a modern economy. It would have contributed to the legitimacy of capitalism and, as a consequence, to continuous development and the capacity to resist economic crisis, thereby indirectly contributing to the reinforcement of political stability. As I have already pointed out, this situation would apply to the Benelux countries; to the United Kingdom, in spite of the intensity of labor conflicts; and to the impact of the depression in the United States during and after the New Deal.

This analysis, therefore, would prevent one from claiming some inevitable outcomes of an economic crisis for the stability of democracy since it provides for a more complex analysis of the interaction between the political and the economic systems.[30]

Paradoxically, the problem for latecomers to economic development and/ or democracy would not be so much the relative performance of both democracy and the modern economy as the difficulty of transforming efficacy into legitimacy, given the initial and continuous delegitimation resulting from the comparison of those societies with early, successful societies. It would be the diffusion of all the delegitimizing ideologies and images formulated in the advanced societies before the institutions of capitalism and democracy took hold, which have only a limited impact in them, that would make their consolidation in societies that developed later more difficult, irrespective of performance.

Only an internal comparison of alternatives—an awareness of the costs of an unsuccessful revolution, of the destructive attacks on the economic system, of the authoritarian counterrevolutionary regimes, of the repression of and at the same time inability to solve structural economic problems— might lead to a different and perhaps more realistic frame of reference than crossnational comparisons. It is perhaps such an internal comparison, derived from bitter historical experience, that might contribute decisively to the legitimation of both democracy and a more or less modified capitalist system in some of the countries that have lived under authoritarian regimes in recent decades, both in southern Europe and in the Southern Cone of Latin America.

In those countries, political democracy might have become a value in and by itself, irrespective of some of the difficulties for efficacy and even if democracy does not lead immediately to the destruction of capitalism. In those societies, a radical questioning of the economic system probably would require a break with the institutions of political democracy or endanger the consensus on which they are based—a respect for minorities with strong feelings and interests, the self-limitation of democratic processes emphasized by Schumpeter. Perhaps such a positive evaluation of democratic institutions, irrespective of their capacity to change the social and economic system, might allow the capitalist economic engine to continue functioning and under worldwide favorable circumstances achieve a reasonable level of performance. Such success would ultimately legitimize many of the system's institutions, particularly with regard to relationships between employers' organizations and trade unions and the entrepreneurial function, but it would not necessarily provide the capitalist system with a legitimizing ideological climate of opinion like the one it engendered in early democracies and the industrial countries of the West. Obviously, such an analysis makes it difficult to predict the future of those countries, but it would allow political and economic actors to make use of the stability or at least partial stability of those societies, which would provide the conditions for economic development and democratic politics.

NOTES

I want to acknowledge the support of the Instituto de Estudios Económicos of Madrid and its director, Víctor Mendoza Oliván, for the study of economic mentalities and the assistance of Data in carrying out the survey. Elizabeth Noelle-Neumann of Demoskopie was kind enough to make available the German data. I also am grateful to Rocío de Terán and Patricia Craig for research assistance and to Megan L. Schoeck for her excellent editing.

1. For a review of the historical evolution of the idea of legitimacy, see Thomas Würtenberger, "Legitimitat, Legalität," in Otto Brunner, Werner Conze, and Reinhart Kosellick, eds., Geschichtliche Grundbegriffe: Historisches Lexikon zur politisch-sozialen Sprache in Deutschland, 3:677–740 (Stuttgart: Klett-Cotta, 1982).

2. Albert O. Hirschman, Exit, Voice, and Loyalty: Responses to Decline in Firms, Organizations, and States (Cambridge: Harvard University Press, 1970), chapter 7.

3. There is no systematic comparative analysis of the anticapitalism of the right or of Catholic and above all fascist anticapitalism, which leads to the distorted view that only the left takes a hostile or critical stance. It would be important to know more specifically which aspects of capitalism are the foci of Catholic and fascist criticism. In the case of traditional Catholicism, both the "ethos" in the Weberian sense and the moral irresponsibility of the market are probably the more salient aspects. Fascism focuses more on the lack of communal-national solidarity and the "bourgeois" style of life—on its consumption side, often combined with a glorification of the entrepreneur as producer but also with an emphasis on planning versus the "anarchy" of the market.

4. Joseph A. Schumpeter, Capitalism, Socialism, and Democracy (New York: Harper and Brothers, 1950), Chapter 7, pp. 81–86.

5. For a discussion of "sultanistic" regimes, a concept derived from Max Weber's use of the term, as a distinctive type, see J. Linz, "Totalitarian and Authoritarian Regimes," in Fred Greenstein and Nelson Polsby, eds., Handbook of Political Science, vol. 3 (Reading, Mass.: Addison Wesley, 1975), pp. 175–411, especially 259–263.

6. Günther Roth, in The Social Democrats in Imperial Germany (Totowa, N.J.: Bedminster, 1963), has analyzed how Marxist theory was used in a context in which the success of revolution was improbable and limited freedom led to a process of "negative integration." This process ultimately, after many difficulties and crises, led to contemporary social-democracy. Italians have found it fruitful to apply some of this analysis to the evolution of the Italian Communist party after World War II.

7. Schumpeter, Capitalism, Socialism, and Democracy, pp. 134–139, on the role of protective strata. See also the essays in the volume edited by Arnold Heertje,

Schumpeter's Vision: Capitalism, Socialism, and Democracy after 40 Years (New York: Praeger, 1981); Daniel Bell, "The New Class: A Muddled Concept," in Daniel Bell, *The Winding Passage: Essays and Sociological Journeys, 1960–1980* (New York: Basic Books, 1980), pp. 144–164; and the texts of F. A. Hayek quoted there.

8. Robert McKenzie and Allan Silver, *Angels in Marble: Working-Class Conservatives in Urban England* (London: Heinemann, 1968); Erich A. Nordlinger, *The Working-Class Tories* (Berkeley: University of California Press, 1967); Ralph Samuel, "The Deference Voter," *New Left Review* (January–February 1960), pp. 9–13; W. G. Runciman, *Relative Deprivation and Social Justice* (Berkeley: University of California Press, 1966); and David Butler and Donald Stokes, *Political Change in Britain* (New York: St. Martin's Press, 1969), pp. 104–115.

9. Schumpeter, *Capitalism, Socialism, and Democracy.*

10. Albert O. Hirschman, "The Turn to Authoritarianism in Latin America and the Search for Its Economic Determinants," in David Collier, ed., *The New Authoritarianism in Latin America* (Princeton: Princeton University Press, 1979), pp. 91–92.

11. Data are from the European Values Study sponsored by the European Values Study Foundation. For information on the study see Jean Stoetzel, *Les valeurs du temp present: Une enquête* (Paris: Presses Universitaires de France, 1983), and national analyses in the process of publication. The tabulations for the thirteen countries have been prepared by Social Surveys (Gallup Poll) Ltd., London. The author participated with Gordon Heald of Gallup UK, Elisabeth Noelle-Neumann and Renate Köcher of Demoskopie, Helene Riffault and Jean Stoetzel of Faits of Opinion, and Francisco A. Orizo of Data in designing the survey, which was conducted in 1980 and 1981.

12. Whatever indicators are used, three of the countries in the values study stand out: France, Italy, and Spain. It is therefore no accident that they should be below the European average of 5.2 on the left-right scale (from 1 to 10) with a mean, respectively, of 4.93, 4.63, and 4.89. The Spanish data of the European Values Study have been analyzed by Francisco Andrés Orizo, *España entre la apatía y el cambio social: Una encuesta sobre el sistema europeo de valores; el caso español* (Madrid: Mapfre, 1984).

13. The literature on "corporatism" in Western democratic industrial societies is too extensive to quote here. For a contribution with bibliographic references, see the different essays in Suzanne Berger, ed., *Organizing Interests in Western Europe: Pluralism, Corporatism, and the Transformation of Politics* (Cambridge: Cambridge University Press, 1981), and in particular the chapter by Philippe C. Schmitter, "Interest Intermediation and Regime Governability in Contemporary Western Europe and North America," pp. 285–327. It is interesting to note that the ranking of countries by their societal corporatism by Schmitter (p. 294), to the extent that they were included in the values study, coincides with the rating of trade unions. Finland is an exception since that response in the attitude study placed unions higher than the ranking on corporatism would lead one to expect. Belgians on the other hand rated unions lower than the ranking on corporatism would warrant if the rank order were the same. The countries lowest in the corporatism ranking of Schmitter, the United Kingdom and Italy, were also among those that placed the unions below average.

14. In the United States there has been, for the period I have data (1966–1981), always a larger population having "a great deal of confidence" in leaders of major companies than of organized labor. See Seymour Martin Lipset and William Schneider, *The Confidence Gap: Business, Labor, and Government in the Public Mind* (New York: Free Press, 1983).

15. The Spanish data used in this chapter are from a study of economic mentalities of Spaniards directed by me with the sponsorship of the Instituto de Estudios Económicos. The survey was planned and executed in 1983 with the collaboration of Manuel Gómez Reino of Data.

16. Schumpeter, *Capitalism, Socialism, and Democracy*, pt. 2, specifically Chapter 13, pp. 143–155, and Daniel Bell, *The Cultural Contradictions of Capitalism* (London: Heinemann, 1976), passim. Elisabeth Noelle-Neumann, in E. Noelle-Neumann and Burkhard Strümpel, *Macht Arbeit Krank? Macht Arbeit Glücklich? Eine aktuelle Kontroverse* (Munich: Piper, 1984), pp. 35–39, has proposed an interesting approach to the study of the impact of intellectual ideas transmitted by the media on attitudes toward society by comparing responses to questions formulated in "media language" and in "everyday language."

17. In the United States in the mid sixties and early seventies there was a large proportion expressing "a great deal of confidence" in the leaders of the major companies than in the press (51 and 28 percent, respectively, in the mid sixties and 28 and 20 percent in the early seventies). However, there was a shift to 20 and 24 percent, respectively, as an average for eight surveys between August 1974 and January 1977 (see Lipset and Schneider, *The Confidence Gap*, pp. 48–49).

18. The German data are from a survey by the Institut für Demoskopie, Allensbach, in April-May 1984. I want to thank Professor Elisabeth Noelle-Neumann for undertaking this study and making the data available to me.

19. Eckart Zimmermann, "The World Economic Crisis of the Thirties in Six European Countries: Causes of Political Instability and Reactions to Crisis: A First Report" (Paper presented at the European Consortium for Political Research [ECPR], Salzburg, 1984); "Pitfalls and Promises in the study of Crisis Outcomes in Liberal Democracies: Towards a New Approach," *International Political Science Review* 3 (1983), pp. 319–343; and "Zur vergleichenden Analyse politischer Systemkrisen in demokratischen Industriegesellschaften: Skizze eines Forschungsplans," *PVS: Politische Vierteljahresschrift* 24 (1983), pp. 259–284.

20. Lipset and Schneider, *The Confidence Gap*.

21. This point is made by Daniel Bell when he notes: "The virtue of the market is that it disperses responsibility for decisions and effects. The public household concentrates decisions and makes the consequences visible" (Bell, *The Cultural Contradictions of Capitalism*, p. 235).

22. Habermas has suggested that with the extension of politico-administrative functions into a general regulative function, to which concrete service functions must be added, a *Generalzuständigkeit* ("general responsibility and imputability") of the state for failures appears in Jürgen Habermas, *Strukturwandel der Öffentlichkeit* [Berlin: Neuwied, 1976], p. 289). For a discussion of the development of the theoretical debate in contemporary social thought about legitimacy in capitalist societies (particularly Claus Offe's pursuance of the theme), see Manfred Kopp and Hans-Peter Müller, *Herrschaft und Legitimität in modernen Industriegesellschaften: Eine Untersuchung der Ansätze von Max Weber, Niklas Luhmann, Claus Offe, Jürgen Habermas* (Munich: tuduv, 1980), pp. 125, 140–148, 150–155. The hypothesis requires empirical verification, although the answers obtained in the Spanish survey about the capacity attributed to the state and answers to questions about whom Europeans make responsible for the economic crisis would suggest caution about such a *Generalzuständigkeit*. For example, there was little difference in the proportion of Spanish socialist (PSOE) and conservative (AP) respondents attributing the high unemployment in their country to the world recession (52.1 and 54.9 percent) and not much in assigning responsibility to the government (35.3 and 28.6 percent). They did, however,

diverge in their assigning responsibility to big business and/or the banks, 28.0 and 13.4 percent, respectively; the trade unions, 4.2 and 12.3 percent; and the "climate of discord," 19.7 and 39.4 percent, among a list offered.

23. Juan J. Linz, "Crisis, Breakdown, Reequilibration," in J. Linz and Alfred Stepan, eds., *The Breakdown of Democratic Regimes* (Baltimore: Johns Hopkins, 1978), pp. 110–112. On the relationship between the world economic crisis and the rise of fascism, see the works by Zimmermann cited in note 19 and J. Linz, "Political Space and Fascism as a Late-Comer: Conditions Conducive to the Success or Failure of Fascism as a Mass Movement in Interwar Europe," in Stein U. Larsen, Bernt Hagvet, Jan P. Myklebust, eds., *Who Were the Fascists?* (Bergen: Universitetsforlaget, 1980), pp. 153–189, especially pp. 170–173. My analysis obviously questions the Marxist interpretations of fascism as "instrumental" or "functional" for the survival of capitalism and its rise as a response to the great economic crisis. I agree with Daniel Bell, *Cultural Contradictions of Capitalism*, p. 250, in not thinking that formal democracy in countries such as Sweden, England and the United States can "easily" be replaced. The strength of democracy derives from an autonomous tradition of liberty, not the "needs" of the capitalist system. Even adding countries like Spain and some in Latin America to the list would not change that conclusion.

24. Robert Fishman, "Working-Class Organization and Political Change: The Labor Movement and the Transition to Democracy in Spain" (Ph.D. dissertation, Yale University, 1985).

25. The difference between the attitudes of people generalizing about "society" and those reflecting personal experiences of the respondents, the former more negative and the second more positive, has also been noted for Germany by Elisabeth Noelle-Neumann in Noelle-Neumann and Strümpel, *Macht Arbeit Krank?* pp. 37–40.

26. Andrew C. Janos, *The Politics of Backwardness in Hungary 1825–1945* (Princeton: Princeton University Press, 1982), chapter 4, particularly pp. 167–173, and conclusions, pp. 313–323.

27. Ronald Inglehart, *The Silent Revolution: Changing Values and Political Styles Among Western Publics* (Princeton: Princeton University Press, 1977).

28. In this context, it might be noted that more Germans who are most negative toward both democracy and capitalism on the two dimensions of legitimacy and efficacy are found in the electorate of the Greens, 13.6 percent, compared to 2.8 percent in that of the CDU and 3.4 percent in that of the SPD. Those questioning the performance of democracy and negative toward capitalism, not recognizing either its legitimacy or its effectiveness, were also numerous among the Green voters— 14.9 percent compared to 4.5 percent among those of the CDU and 9.3 percent among those of the SPD.

29. Albert O. Hirschman, *Shifting Involvements, Private Interest, and Public Action* (Princeton: Princeton University Press, 1982), chapter 1, "On Disappointment," pp. 9–24.

30. After writing this chapter, I read again Albert O. Hirschman, "Rival Interpretations of Market Society: Civilizing, Destructive, or Feeble?" *Journal of Economic Literature* 20 (December 1982), pp. 1463–1484, and realized how it would be possible to formulate some of its themes about the interrelation between democracy and capitalism and mutually legitimizing and delegitimizing effects in a way that would be quite homologous to his chart on p. 1481. There is also a similarity with his conclusion that "however incompatible the various theories may be, each might still have its 'hour of truth' and/or its 'country or group of countries during some

stretch of time' " (in this case, the theories about capitalism and democracy that I have—largely implicitly—been debating). My conclusion is in the same spirit as when he writes, "after so many failed prophecies, is it not in the interest of social science to embrace complexity, be it at some sacrifice of its claim to predictive power?"

Table 2.1 Attitudes of Europeans Toward Revolution and Reform

	Want Revolutionary Change (%)	Want Gradual Reform (%)	Resist Subversive Forces (%)	Don't Know (%)	(Number of Cases)
Total	5	64	22	10	(15,589)
Great Britain	4	66	22	8	(1,231)
Northern Ireland	1	67	23	8	(312)
Republic of Ireland	4	67	18	11	(1,217)
West Germany	2	53	38	9	(1,305)
Netherlands	3	59	24	13	(1,221)
Belgium	5	56	17	21	(1,145)
France	8	68	18	6	(1,199)
Italy	6	70	18	6	(1,348)
Spain	7	75	9	10	(2,303)
Denmark	3	60	24	13	(1,182)
Sweden	4	72	14	10	(886)
Norway	2	46	45	8	(1,246)
Latin Europe	7	70	16	7	(4,850)
Northern Europe	3	59	29	10	(6,431)

Note: In this and subsequent tables in the chapter, the figures in parentheses are the number of cases in the surveys on which the percentages are based. The percentages do not always add up to 100% because of rounding or, in some cases, the inclusion of "don't know" or "no answer" responses.

Source: European Values Study, 1981. Country tabulations prepared by Social Surveys, Ltd., London.

Table 2.2   Attitudes of Europeans Toward Control of
            Business

	Owners Run or Appoint Managers (%)	Owners & Employees Select Managers (%)	State Owns and Appoints Managers (%)	Employees Own and Appoint Managers (%)	Don't Know (%)	(Number of Cases)
Total	34	41	4	10	11	(15,589)
Great Britain	50	37	2	7	4	(1,231)
Northern Ireland	57	24	1	7	11	(312)
Republic of Ireland	47	34	3	7	9	(1,217)
West Germany	47	37	2	7	7	(1,305)
Netherlands	30	47	1	10	12	(1,221)
Belgium	34	34	3	6	24	(1,145)
France	19	48	3	17	13	(1,199)
Italy	29	47	8	6	11	(1,348)
Spain	21	33	7	22	17	(2,303)
Denmark	41	41	1	8	9	(1,182)
Sweden	29	59	1	7	4	(886)
Norway	36	51	2	5	6	**(1,246)**
Latin Europe	24	44	6	14	13	(4,850)
Northern Europe	46	38	2	7	8	(6,431)

Source: European Values Study, 1981. Country tabulations prepared by Social Surveys, Ltd., London.

Table 2.3 Opinion on How Enterprises Should Be
Run by Self-Placement on the Left to
Right Scale (1=10) in Three Countries

Left-Right		Pure Private Property	Codetermination	State Run	Self-Management	No Answer	(Number of Cases)
Total	Spain	21	33	7	22	17	(2303)
	France	19	48	3	17	13	(1200)
	West Germany	47	37	2	7	7	(1305)
1/2	SP	4	26	10	55	5	(165)
	FR	12	30	5	47	6	(103)
	WG	33	30	4	32	2	(52)
3/4	SP	11	43	8	31	8	(490)
	FR	8	58	2	26	6	(253)
	WG	26	56	2	12	4	(257)
5/6	SP	29	38	6	17	10	(625)
	FR	19	54	3	12	13	(426)
	WG	49	41	1	5	5	(491)
7/8	SP	35	30	12	12	10	(264)
	FR	29	51	1	6	13	(155)
	WG	64	27		4	6	(283)
9/10	SP	43	15	11	19	12	(57)
	FR	45	34	3	9	9	(35)
	WG	59	27	12	1	2	(67)
No answer,	SP	19	26	4	17	3	(702)
don't know	FR	26	34	4	12	24	(178)
	WG	46	26	3	5	21	(178)

Source: European Values Study. The data for
France kindly made available by Jean Stoetzel.

Table 2.4 Attitudes of Europeans Toward Authority at Work

	Should Follow Instructions (%)	Must be Convinced First (%)	Depends (%)	Don't Know (%)	(Number of Cases)
Total	33	42	20	4	(15,589)
Great Britain	49	34	14	3	(1,231)
Northern Ireland	49	25	23	3	(312)
Republic of Ireland	45	26	25	4	(1,217)
West Germany	28	51	18	3	(1,305)
Netherlands	39	33	21	8	(1,221)
Belgium	33	31	23	12	(1,145)
France	25	57	15	2	(1,199)
Italy	24	39	34	4	(1,348)
Spain	29	41	21	9	(2,303)
Denmark	57	21	13	10	(1,182)
Sweden	40	32	26	2	(886)
Finland	43	40	16	2	(994)
Norway	60	32	4	4	(1,246)
Scandinavia	48	31	17	4	(4,308)
Northern Europe	38	41	17	4	(6,431)

Source: European Values Study, 1981. Country tabulations
prepared by Social Surveys, Ltd., London.

Table 2.5 Degree of Trust of Trade Unions and Major Companies in Western Europe, 1981

	Great Deal (%)	Quite a Lot (%)	Not Much (%)	None (%)	Don't Know (%)	Great Deal (%)	Quite a Lot (%)	Not Much (%)	None (%)	Don't Know	(Number of Cases)
Total	5	28	43	21	3	6	33	39	17	5	(15,589)
Great Britain	5	21	50	22	2	11	37	40	8	5	(1231)
Northern Ireland	4	19	57	20	0	10	45	39	7	1	(312)
Republic of Ireland	8	28	47	14	1	13	36	39	10	2	(1,217)
West Germany	5	31	47	16	1	4	30	46	19	1	(1,305)
Netherlands	5	34	46	12	4	4	30	47	15	4	(1,221)
Belgium	4	26	27	23	11	4	33	34	14	15	(1,145)
France	4	32	36	20	8	3	39	29	14	15	(1,199)
Italy	5	23	40	32	0	5	28	37	29	0	(1,348)
Spain	7	24	45	20	4	9	28	41	19	3	(2,303)
Denmark	10	39	36	11	4	4	29	48	14	6	(1,182)
Sweden	8	39	38	16	0	3	33	43	20	0	(886)
Finland	10	47	34	6	3	4	37	45	12	3	(994)
Norway	8	48	36	7	1	4	41	48	6	2	(1,246)
Scandinavia	9	42	36	11	2	4	34	45	14	2	(4,308)
Latin Europe	5	27	40	25	4	5	32	35	21	6	(4,850)
Northern Europe	5	27	47	18	2	7	33	42	14	4	(6,431)

Source: European Values Study, 1981. Country tabulations prepared by Social Surveys, Ltd., London.

Table 2.6   Rating of Trade Unions and Major
            Companies in European Societies

	Major Companies		Trade Unions	
	Above Average	Below Average	Above Average	Below Average
Finland	2.34		2.64	
Norway	2.43		2.58	
Denmark		2.25	2.51	
Sweden		2.19	2.39	
Netherlands		2.24	2.32	
Republic of Ireland	2.52		2.31	
West Germany		2.19	2.26	
France	2.37		2.22	
Belgium	2.31			2.12
Spain		2.28	2.19	
Great Britain	2.53			2.09
Northern Ireland	2.57			2.06
Italy		2.10		2.00

Note: European averages are trade unions, 2.18;
major companies, 2.29; all institutions, 2.49.

Source: European Values Study, 1981.

Table 2.7   Survey Responses in Spain, 1983, to Words
Characteristic of Capitalist and Socialist
Economies (in percent)

	Capitalism	Socialism	Difference in Favor or Against Socialism	Proportion of Those Attributing the Characteristic to Both Capitalism and Socialism
Unemployment	31	10	21	14
Freedom	19	23	4	11
Inequality	37	8	29	8
Technological Advance	22	13	9	19
Wealth	25	6	19	9
Egoism	29	7	22	10
Power	25	14	11	21
Profit (Lucro)	23	4	19	6
Justice	8	28	20	21
Scarcity	7	13	6	21
Humaneness	5	13	8	18
Progress	17	17	0	16
Planning	7	33	26	30
Efficacy	7	11	4	14
Repression	13	16	3	15
Corruption	23	9	14	17
No Answer	12	16		98

The survey question was: which of the words on this list are
those that describe best what you think of the capitalist
economy of private initiative? And of the socialist economy
(where there are no private enterprises)?

Source: Economic Mentalities Study in Spain (1983).

Table 2.8 Rating by Europeans of the Education System,
           the Press, and Major Companies

	Education System	Major Companies	Differ- ence	Press	Difference MC/P	ES/P
European Average	2.61	2.29	-32	2.22	+ 7	+39
Great Britain	2.73	2.53	-20	2.22	+31	+51
Northern Ireland	2.98	2.57	-41	2.25	+32	+73
Republic of Ireland	2.85	2.52	-33	2.45	+ 7	+40
West Germany	2.42	2.19	-23	2.23	- 4	+19
Netherlands	2.83	2.24	-59	2.17	+ 7	+66
Belgium	2.46	2.31	-15	2.23	+ 8	+23
France	2.57	2.37	-20	2.15	+22	+42
Italy	2.60	2.10	-50	2.13	- 3	+47
Spain	2.53	2.28	-25	2.45	-17	+ 8
Denmark	2.75	2.25	-50	2.20	+ 5	+55
Sweden	2.59	2.19	-40	2.15	+ 4	+44
Finland	2.86	2.34	-52	2.24	+10	+62
Norway	2.97	2.43	-54	2.40	+ 3	+57

Source: European Values Study, 1981. Country tabulations prepared by Social Surveys, Ltd., London.

Table 2.9   Ratings of Major Companies and the
            Press by Europeans

	Major Companies		Press	
	Above Average	Below Average	Above Average	Below Average
Northern Ireland	2.57		2.25	
Great Britain	2.53		2.22	
Republic of Ireland	2.52		2.45	
Norway	2.43		2.40	
France	2.37			2.15
Finland	2.34		2.24	
Belgium	2.31		2.23	
Spain		2.28	2.45	
Denmark		2.25		2.20
Netherlands		2.24		2.17
Sweden		2.19		2.15
West Germany		2.19	2.23	
Italy		2.10		2.13

Source: European Values Study, 1981. Country
tabulations prepared by Social Surveys, Ltd.,
London.

Table 2.10 Legitimacy and Efficiency of Political Democracy and
Capitalism in the FRG and Spain (proportion of the
total sample with opinions).

Democracy		Capitalism Leg.-Eff. + +	Capitalism Leg.-Eff. + -	Capitalism Leg.-Eff. - +	Capitalism Leg.-Eff. - -	Totals for Democracy
Leg.-Eff.	FRG	33.5	7.1	3.8	28.2	72.6
+ +	Spain	21.4	11.1	2.8	30.8	66.1
	diff.	+12.1	- 4.0	+ 1.0	- 2.5	+ 6.5
Leg.-Eff.	FRG	2.1	2.4	.4	8.3	13.2
+ -	Spain	5.1	5.6	.7	12.2	23.6
	diff.	- 3.0	- 3.2	- .3	- 3.9	-10.4
Leg.-Eff.	FRG	.4	.4	.2	.6	1.6
- +	Spain	.2	.2	.2	.7	1.3
	diff.	+ .2	+ .2		- .1	+ .3
Leg.-Eff.	FRG	1.7	1.0	1.0	9.0	12.7
- -	Spain	3.5	1.3	.2	3.8	8.8
	diff.	- 1.8	- .3	+ .8	+ 5.2	+ 3.9
Totals	FRG	37.7	10.9	5.4	46.1	100% = 1,035
for	Spain	30.2	18.2	3.9	47.5	100% = 3,952
Capitalism	diff.	+ 7.5	- 7.5	+ 1.5	- 1.4	

Source: Economic Mentalities Study in Spain (1983); Institut für
Demoskopie Survey in Germany (1984).

Note: The following proportions have been excluded from the table
for Spain: with no opinion on legitimacy of democracy, 3.9;
capitalism, 9.1; neither democracy nor capitalism, 4.0. Total not
included in typology, 17.3 of 3,952.

108

Table 2.11 Motives that Workplace Leaders in Barcelona (B) and Madrid (M) Consider
Justified Reasons to Limit Labor Demands in the Current Context (in percent)

	CCOO[a]			UGT[a]			Other Unions			Independents			Total		
	B	M	Total	B	M	Total	B	M	Total	B	M	Total	B	M	Total
Importance of creating a situation favorable to consolidation and stability of democracy	48	76	63	71	81	77	57	53	55	44	74	57	53	75	65
Need to maintain competitiveness of Spanish economy in international market	21	43	33	37	53	46	43	35	39	49	55	51	34	47	41
Need to fight inflation	26	43	35	37	53	46	50	41	45	46	55	50	36	48	42
Need to develop and strengthen workers' organizations before attempting sharper struggles	48	65	57	69	72	71	36	41	39	44	42	43	51	61	56
Danger of plant closings	58	72	65	74	77	76	86	59	71	72	71	71	68	72	70
Lack of support of other unions	39	51	45	49	43	45	21	24	23	44	29	37	41	42	41
Lack of a willingness of workers to support strikes with the determination necessary	77	83	80	80	70	74	36	71	55	56	65	60	69	75	72
N=	66	75	141	35	47	82	14	17	31	39	31	70	154	170	324

[a] CCOO = Comisiones Obreras, a union close to the Communist party; UGT = Unión General de Trabajadores, the socialist union linked to the Partido Socialista Obrero Español (PSOE).

Source: Robert Fishman, "Working-Class Organization and Political Change: The Labor Movement and the Transition to Democracy in Spain" (Ph.D. dissertation, Yale University, 1985). The data are from a sample survey made in 1981.

Table 2.12 Attitude Toward the Legitimacy and Efficacy of Capitalism and the Perception of the Justice of "Our Economic System"

Attitude Toward Capitalism			The Economic System Is						
Legitimacy	Efficacy		Very Just	Fairly Just	Neither Just nor Unjust	Fairly Unjust	Very Unjust	Don't Know	(Number of Cases)
yes	yes		1.4	14.6	43.3	32.4	6.2	2.1	(1,032)
yes	no		2.1	9.9	42.5	35.5	8.9	1.1	(600)
yes	n.a.			14.6	36.4	32.0	5.9	11.1	(44)
no	yes		1.5	10.9	44.0	37.6	6.0		(138)
no	no		1.4	8.5	28.2	45.3	15.6	1.0	(1,567)
no	n.a.			20.7	31.3	37.0	5.8	5.2	(25)
no and other answers			1.0	7.4	34.8	34.3	8.8	13.8	(519)
Total			1.4	10.4	35.9	38.5	10.7	3.1	(3,925)

Source: Economic Mentalities Study in Spain (1983).

Table 2.13 Injustice of the Economic System and Attitude Toward the
Legitimacy and Efficacy of Capitalism in Spain, 1983
(in percent)

		The Economic System Is						
Capitalism		Very Just	Fairly Just	Neither Just Nor Unjust	Fairly Unjust	Very Unjust	No Answer	Total
Legitimacy-	Efficacy+							
+	+	26.5	36.9	31.7	22.1	15.2	18.5	26.3
+	-	22.3	14.5	18.1	14.1	12.7	5.1	15.3
-	+	3.7	3.7	4.3	3.4	2.0		3.5
-	-	38.1	32.8	31.4	47.0	58.2	11.4	39.9
No Answer		9.4	12.3	14.4	13.3	11.8	65.0	14.9
N =		56	409	1,408	1,510	420	117	3,925

Source: Economic Mentalities Survey in Spain (1983).

Table 2.14 Country Seen as Model "To Organize the Social
and Economic Life of Our Country" (in percent)

	Total		Capitalism Leg. + Eff.		Capitalism Not Leg. + Not Eff.	
	Model	Rejects	Model	Rejects	Model	Rejects
U.S.S.R.	3.8	42.3	1.8	54.0	6.0	31.9
Cuba	2.8	18.3	0.8	23.1	4.9	15.2
China	2.9	16.1	1.9	16.1	3.6	15.0
Yugosl.	2.4	4.9	1.6	4.5	3.7	4.3
Sweden	29.8	1.5	23.5	1.2	35.4	1.4
Germany	26.9	2.0	27.7	1.9	24.7	2.3
U.K.	10.7	5.8	14.5	3.7	7.1	9.2
France	8.6	5.3	9.6	5.1	8.3	4.2
Japan	12.8	5.2	15.1	3.7	10.7	6.8
U.S.	16.5	19.0	25.7	7.8	9.2	30.5
N =	3,434	3,336	965	940	1,456	1,418

Source: Economic Mentalities Survey in Spain (1983).

Table 2.15   Personal Experience of Having Been Treated Unjustly in Different Contexts and Attitudes Toward the Legitimacy and Efficacy of Capitalism

	Considers the Capitalist System					
	Leg. and Eff.	Leg. and Not Eff.	Not Leg. and Eff.	Not Leg. and Not Eff.	Other Answers N.A.	
Has Not Been Treated Unjustly	27.9	13.1	3.6	32.1	20.2	(1023)
Has Been Treated Unjustly						
in the work place	21.0	14.3	3.8	51.8	7.0	(541)
by the bank	26.8	13.7	3.6	46.4	7.2	(446)
by the electric company	25.4	15.0	3.0	45.8	8.5	(735)
while in buying something	23.8	15.9	3.8	45.3	8.6	(735)
by a government office	27.0	17.0	3.8	43.3	7.0	(1132)
while solving something in the municipal office	27.6	15.2	3.5	41.6	9.2	(994)
by the social security administration	23.3	16.1	3.5	45.2	8.6	(1615)
Total	26.2	15.3	3.4	40.2	11.7	(3760)

Source: Economic Mentalities Study in Spain (1983).

Table 2.16   Injustice of the Economic System and Actual
              Experiences of Unjust Treatment in Spain (in percent)

Treated Unjustly	Considers the Economic System					Total of Respondents
	Very Just	Fairly Just	Neither Just nor Unjust	Fairly Unjust	Very Unjust	
In the workplace	15	14	11	16	17	14
By the banks	12	15	10	11	16	11
By the electric company	23	23	16	19	27	19
While buying something	25	20	17	19	25	19
By the municipality	37	30	22	26	30	25
By an office of the state	28	28	26	30	36	29
By the social security administration	50	43	37	43	49	41
Not treated unjustly	30	23	29	24	21	26
No answer	1	3	4	4	4	4
N =	58	412	1,415	1,524	422	3,952

Source: Economic Mentalities Study in Spain (1983).

3
POLITICAL ALIENATION
AND PROTEST

Max Kaase

This chapter reviews the empirical data from various sources with respect to political alienation and political protest. But first, four major problems must be defined: (1) What are the conceptual meanings and foundations of alienation and protest? (2) What is the relationship of these concepts to other, similar concepts, and what is their place in ongoing discussions in the social sciences? (3) Which types of countries should be included in the analysis? (4) Which types of data are necessary to perform the analysis and to what extent are such data available? In the two final sections, the available empirical evidence is presented and put into broader perspective.

One further specification is necessary regarding the thrust of the chapter. This is *not* a theoretical piece. There will be no thorough and systematic discussion of the concepts of political alienation and protest, their theoretical foundations, and the multiplicity of meanings associated with them. Rather, the approach will be strictly empirical, descriptive, and pragmatic: What longitudinal data bases are there to characterize the development of political alienation and political protest in competitive democracies after World War II? Needless to say, such a task cannot be meaningfully achieved without some theoretical foundation.

ON THE MEANING OF POLITICAL ALIENATION
AND POLITICAL PROTEST

The concepts of alienation and protest both reach well beyond the political sphere, and it is assumed here that their major theoretical elements remain unchanged regardless of which subsystem they are analytically related to. *Political* alienation and protest refer to that subsystem of the total social system that is responsible for the creation and implementation of decisions binding the whole system.

Political Alienation

The concept of alienation is one of the classic concerns—and therefore one of the classic concepts—of the social sciences. In a review and evaluation of its use, Peter C. Ludz (1975) points to its etymological roots as indicating "the individual's separation or estrangement from other men, from his country, or from the gods" (Ludz 1975, 11). Ludz then shows the multiplicity of meanings of alienation, the normative bases and implications of the concept, and the empirical work that originated from those foundations (for a similar account see also Hart 1978, 1–31). It is important to note that alienation can be plausibly conceptualized as a mental state of a given individual—notwithstanding the macrostructural conditions that may and usually will create this state. As an individual property, alienation is therefore accessible through the individual himself and requires the individual's subjective assessment of his or her own situation. The subjectivity of alienation is one of the many examples from empirical research in which subjective states cannot be logically deduced from the objective situation of the individual. (Conspicuous examples are provided by many of the quality of life studies [see Strümpel 1974].) Thus, survey research is the most adequate data-generation procedure for collecting reliable information on individual alienation.

Given the Marxist theoretical heritage, it is not surprising that alienation has been studied with respect to the workplace. The second major area of studies in alienation, Ludz (1975, 35) observes, has been politics. Ada Finifter (1972, 190–191) proposes a four-dimensional conceptualization of political alienation: (1) political powerlessness—the individual feels he or she has no influence whatsoever on the actions of the government; (2) political meaninglessness—the individual believes that political outcomes do not follow a discernible pattern, are unpredictable; (3) perceived political normlessness—the individual believes that the normal procedures of political decisionmaking and government have broken down; and (4) political isolation—the individual rejects political norms and goals widely held by other members of the society. In summarizing much of the research on political alienation, James D. Wright (1976, 4) argues that dimensions one and three of Finifter's typology are the ones most commonly dealt with in the theoretical literature and are also most prevalent in empirical research. As William A. Gamson writes: "Political alienation includes both an efficacy (or input) dimension and a trust (or output) dimension. . . . The efficacy dimension of political alienation refers to people's perception of their ability to influence; the trust dimension refers to their perception of the necessity for influence" (Gamson 1968, 42).

It needs to be noted that the theoretical ambiguity of the alienation concept forbids any a priori decision with respect to the proper number of dimensions representing the concept. As will become evident later in the chapter this point is an important but nevertheless a futile one: There are so few longitudinal data on political alienation available that one simply has to take what is there if any conclusions are to be reached at all.

Political Protest

The concept of political protest at first seems to be unambiguous in that it refers to those activities by citizens or groups that are directed at preventing undesired political outcomes by uninstitutionalized political means. On closer inspection, this conceptualization is unsatisfactory. In competitive democracies, particularly, every utterance of protest ("against them") automatically—in a dialectical sense—contains an element of support ("for us"). Thus, *voice* would seem a much more appropriate term for any form of political participation. On the other hand, the colloquial meaning of *protest* carries with it a connotation that is more specific in the sense that it refers to a particular type or form of participation that indicates a challenge of and to the institutionalized channels of political participation and the political authorities.

That rationale was used to distinguish between institutionalized (conventional) and noninstitutionalized (unconventional) forms of participation—the latter were regarded as political protest. For theoretical as well as for empirical reasons, voting was excluded from institutionalized participation, and all violent acts were excluded from noninstitutionalized participation (Barnes, Kaase, et al. 1979, 71–72, 86). In other research, those activities have been included as separate dimensions. In addition, a theoretically meaningful distinction between violent, aggressive political participation (political violence) and civil disobedience (nonlegal, nonviolent political participation like rent or tax strikes) has been suggested (Muller 1979, 3–68; Schmidtchen and Uehlinger 1983, 202–217). Finally, Kaase, Barnes, et al. (1979, 45) have pointed out that noninstitutionalized unconventional political participation involves, in addition to the legality aspect, a legitimacy dimension and the two are *not* identical (see also Zimmermann 1983, 34–46). The conventionality of any given particular activity, the degree to which it is widely accepted as legitimate by the public, is not stable over time but can change depending on the extent of its use and the experience the public accumulates vis à vis the activity. (Of course, changes may also occur regarding the legality dimension.)

These considerations lead to the types of political participation and protest itemized in Table 3.1, and some remarks regarding the table are in order. First, columns three and four are by definition empty since illegal institutionalized participation is a contradiction (except in case of a system change). Second, the logic of the legitimacy dimension implies that the extent to which certain participatory acts are evaluated by the people as legitimate at any given time is always an empirical question. This point explains why certain acts appear with question marks in two columns of the table (lawful demonstration in columns five and six and political strikes in seven and nine). Beyond the empirical nature of the assessment, a decision also has to be made concerning which percentage to use for the cutting point between legitimacy and illegitimacy. This figure can obviously not be decided on a priori grounds; one needs a theoretical rationale for justification. Needless to say, the movement of activities over time among the columns of the table and the clarity of their location provide very useful information regarding the state and evolution of any given political system.

Although political protest cannot be exclusively defined by behavioral acts, it is—unlike the intrapersonal concept of political alienation—most clearly reflected by such acts. This point is important to keep in mind since it provides for a much broader data base: In addition to survey data, one can use official records and press reports (see Taylor and Jodice 1983, Powell 1982, Zimmermann 1983).

RELATED CONCEPTS

If political alienation means estrangement from the political system, then its opposite—identification with or a sense of belonging to the political system—certainly needs to be considered as well (Gamson 1968, 39), especially since speculations about a grave legitimacy crisis in Western democracies played an important role in politics and political science in the 1970s (for a detailed account see Kaase 1980, 1982). The complexities and ambiguities of the legitimacy concept are too numerous to be dealt with in this chapter. For this discussion, it is only necessary to state that on the macro level, legitimacy refers to the authority structures in a given society and their varying bases; on the micro level, it refers to the beliefs of the individuals in the rightfulness of the social and political order.

The systematic relationship between legitimacy and alienation is explicitly addressed by Gamson (1968, 41). However, in referring to the seminal work by David Easton (1965), Gamson does not use the term *legitimacy*, but rather its conceptual equivalent in Easton's writings, political support. Most consequential in Easton's ideas about political support is the distinction between specific support—directed at the incumbent authorities—and diffuse support—directed at the regime institutions and the political community (Easton 1975, Gamson 1968, 50–51). Easton explicitly considers four hier-archically organized objects of political trust (the output dimension): the incumbent authorities, the political institutions of a regime, the public philosophy of a regime, and the political community. The complexities of combining the dimensions of input and output with the hierarchy of objects of political trust (for a thorough analysis see Westle 1987) have not yet been appropriately mastered by Easton himself nor by others. It is no wonder, then, that the resulting empirical research on legitimacy beliefs— as will be shown later in the chapter—has been ambiguous, confusing, and noncumulative. Nevertheless, whatever is there is highly pertinent to the study of political alienation.

Moving from alienation and legitimacy to protest, it is widely accepted that protest is a specific category on the overall dimension of political participation (Fuchs 1983, 277). Provided a satisfactory theoretical rationale is given, all types of political participation or nonparticipation can be regarded as indicators of political protest. Given the central role of political parties in Western democracies, this consideration makes all elements of party-related activities and orientation prime candidates for empirical scrutiny.

CHOICE OF COUNTRIES

To the extent that political systems and subsystems of nation-states came into being through evolution and sociostructural differentiation, it can safely be assumed that alienation and protest are two modes of political orientation and behavior that are always present in any given society. If one takes into account the diversity of human nature and interests, one can conceive of no situation in which a mixture of consensus and dissent is not inevitable; it is the ratio of both plus a variety of other factors that determine the situation's consequences. From this observation, one can also conclude that anyone interested in alienation and protest could study any society at any given time to much advantage. Nevertheless, the number of possible units of analysis, their variety, the differences in knowledge about them, and the differences in the length of their existence make such a procedure rather impractical.

If concentrating on only one subset of systems for a limited period of time seems plausible and necessary, one must still decide which criteria to use in choosing the subset and time period to study. A first choice might be to study contemporary phenomena. As citizens of today we are most naturally concerned with political life today and what it probably will be in the future. Still, however, the past must always be considered if one is to properly understand what is happening currently. A decision to limit the analysis to competitive democracies (Powell 1982, 1–11) clearly reflects a value judgment but, also, the democratic ideology of these countries gives their citizens a much broader political role and potential than citizens of authoritarian or totalitarian regimes have. Not only do citizens in competitive democracies have a well-defined legal framework for political participation, their free consent is central to the legitimacy of the system, and they can go beyond set legal limits in challenging the given political structures. If they succeed in legitimizing their challenges, appropriate structural and legal consequences will ensue in the long run (thereby probably enhancing the legitimacy of the system). If they do not succeed, turmoil and unrest might result. Thus, the challenging role of alienation and protest in democratic societies—which lack a coercive potential to be put (or threatened) to quick and uncontrolled use by the political authorities—makes that role a relevant topic for research from the perspective of the maintenance of liberal democracy. An additional consideration, of a more practical nature, helps to further justify the choice to look just at competitive democracies. Alienation and protest also involve the measurement of attitudes, and such data are only freely available and open to close scrutiny in such democracies.

Finally, for better theory building, comparative research within a defined framework of social and political similarity/dissimilarity among nations can help in the assessment of the impact of causal factors that are at variance across the set of selected units of analysis (for the detailed argument see Przeworski and Teune 1970). Research across time makes such an approach even more valuable since it can show any within-system variance of central explanatory variables.

Therefore, the empirical analysis of political alienation and protest should be based on longitudinal data from those twenty-five to thirty-five nations that qualify as competitive democracies. As will become obvious from the data requirements discussed in the next section, such an analysis is not feasible because of the lack of appropriate empirical information.

DATA REQUIREMENTS AND AVAILABILITY

The selection of what empirical data are deemed necessary for any given analysis should depend exclusively on theoretical grounds. Still, beyond this "golden rule" a variety of factors is involved in crossnational comparative research, and those factors require at least some mention since they are also relevant for the production and evaluation of data bases.

First, since societies are vertically (hierarchically) organized, there is the problem of level of analysis. Erwin Scheuch (1968) has pointed out that macro properties cannot be measured by simply aggregating individual-level data. Thus, there has to be a correspondence between the level of analysis and the level of measurement. In concrete terms, the analysis of the political beliefs of a citizenry requires the measurement of individual beliefs, fortunately a basically easy and reliably executable task through sampling and survey research. Of course, this approach can be generalized toward the measurement of individual beliefs of any *part* of the citizenry, e.g., members of strategic groups such as elites or participants in social movements.

Second, the methodology of comparative research as well as the functional school of comparative politics has alerted scholars to the problem that truly comparative research requires the definition of functional equivalents among systems, which demands an intimate knowledge of the internal operation of each system. Third, and very important, the validity of any measurement of not directly observable constructs such as beliefs, attitudes, and values depends on the link between theory and analysis. To the extent that the theory in question is not sufficiently specified and/or that its specification is not generally accepted, a wide variety of practical applications is possible. As Ludz (1975) has pointed out, the ambiguity of the theory of political alienation is a perfect case in point. The various approaches to the empirical study of legitimacy beliefs or political support are also examples of this problem (Westle 1987).

Fourth, crossnational comparisons can be hindered by different sampling procedures (quota versus random, personal versus household); varying completion rates among and within countries over time; differences in interviewer staff composition (selective noncompletion, interactions between study topic and interviewers); different sample sizes; different contextual settings (temporal proximity of past general election); etc.

Fifth, data from official (statistical) records may not be equally reliable, may use different categorizations, may come from varying points in time, may have different measurement intervals, and may not be similarly available for all countries.

Sixth, data collection (especially for surveys based on national samples) is so expensive that longitudinal data for even one country—not to mention comparative data—are very rare. This problem exists despite individual and collective efforts to improve the existing data bases. Examples of the former include efforts by Almond and Verba (1963), Verba, Nie, and Kim (1978), and Barnes, Kaase, et al. (1979); examples of the latter include the biannual Eurobarometer surveys sponsored by the European Commission in Brussels; the various national social surveys in the United States, Britain, and Germany; the surveys by the U.S. National Election Study; and the German electoral data project.

Last, and most important, the internal structure of the social sciences (with respect to the professional reward system and to negligence in working toward a better research infrastructure) has not yet been able to move the profession sufficiently away from static, structural approaches to dynamic approaches. This deficiency is surely reflected by the lack of impetus to create longitudinal data bases. Even more, however, it surfaces in the constant mismatch between theoretical conceptualizations and the research design of empirical studies (lack of dynamic multilevel analyses). Needless to say, these deficiencies feed back to the level of theoretical sophistication so far achieved.

THE EMPIRICAL EVIDENCE

In this section, I will emphasize *trends* in political alienation/legitimacy and protest whenever possible. Data referring to only one point in time will be reported only if they are available for more than one country.

Satisfaction with Democracy

The most interesting longitudinal crossnational survey data base presently consists of the biannual studies sponsored by the European Commission (EC) in Brussels, the results of which are published in the so-called eurobarometers (Commission 1983). From this data base the results of three questions were selected for presentation in tables in this section: satisfaction with life as a whole, satisfaction with the way democracy works in any given country, and assessment of the need for revolutionary social change.

Three remarks are in order before discussing the results in greater detail. First, even though it is unusual to have longitudinal survey data for a span of eight years, the data still fail to adequately cover the particularly interesting periods of the "quiet" fifties and early sixties or the "unrestful" late sixties and early seventies. Second, there is little point in deploring conceptual and operational ambiguities in the wording of the questions. Whatever the data measure, it is interesting to look at the results in longitudinal perspective, thus assuming that whatever fallacies there are in the data will not *systematically* vary over time so that an adequate assessment of aggregate change is at least possible. Third, there cannot and will not be any major effort to explain the different *levels* of satisfaction/dissatisfaction among countries.

Such an effort would require a much more detailed and thorough analysis of the situation in each country than can be achieved in this chapter.

Let us look first at Tables 3.2 and 3.3. It is well known from the literature on quality of life studies that the average level of satisfaction with private matters is always substantially higher than the level of satisfaction with public affairs (for the most recent documentation of this effect see Glatzer 1984). A similar result from electoral research, that citizens are always by far more satisfied and optimistic in personal economic matters than in their evaluation of the overall economic situation, is equally well documented (Kinder 1981, Kinder and Kiewiet 1981). The distance of citizens from the body politic and their need to rely on outside information and evaluation, especially by the mass media, most probably account for this result. Thus, it is not surprising that the same assessment emerges from the Eurobarometer data. With just one exception (Luxembourg in 1976) citizens in the EC countries are always—and usually substantially—more satisfied with their personal lives than with the way democracy works. As an indicator of the dimension of diffuse support, the results do not convey an impression of enthusiastic approval. Still, considering the systematic difference in evaluation of private and public matters, they, in general, do not seem to signal widespread alienation from the democratic order. What is even more striking is the absence of any clear-cut trend in either direction. This lack is remarkable because of the substantial economic difficulties that the EC countries have been facing since 1974.

This analysis is corroborated by the data displayed in Table 3.4. The question that produced these data was somewhat awkward in its response categories, and the meaning of the category represented in the table, "the entire way our society is organized must be radically changed by revolutionary action," is not at all clear. But setting these reservations aside for the moment, even these data do not reveal a widespread and deeply rooted opposition to the sociopolitical system. They do document, however, that in each of the countries—with varying magnitude—a sizable part of the population has substantial grievances against the society it lives in. Whether these citizens are particularly resourceful and active is an important question, but it could be answered only by making a thorough secondary analysis of the Eurobarometer data.

Certain changes in these data within countries may well be attributed to particular political events such as changes in government or governmental crises. However, Italy and France deserve special mention in the sense that in life satisfaction as well as in political satisfaction they—at times or generally—fall way below the averages of the other countries (the distrust of Italians vis à vis political matters has been documented in the literature since the Five Nations Study [Almond and Verba 1963]). It is possible that the existence of strong Communist parties might be partly related to the generally higher level of political alienation in these two countries. One sophisticated macropolitical analysis (Powell 1982, 123–132) shows that extremist parties are often associated with the level of citizen turmoil:

"There is good reason to believe that this relationship reflects the precipitating effects of such parties' activities on citizen's frustrations, as well as the presence of severe discontent" (p. 132).

Input Alienation (Absence of Internal Efficacy) and Output Alienation (Absence of External Efficacy)

One major deficiency of the data presented so far is that they do not include the United States (although other, not directly comparable, data clearly indicate an identical pattern for the United States [see Lipset and Schneider 1983, 126-159]). In this section, such data are presented, but unfortunately they are available only as time series data. Alienation has come to be conceptualized as the lack of two separate subdimensions: *internal efficacy*, the belief of the individual that he or she is politically efficacious, and *external efficacy*, the belief of the citizen that the authorities or the regime are responsive to citizen demands (for a good summary discussion of these concepts and the respective measurement instruments see Abramson 1983, 135-145). The distinction between internal and external efficacy is recent and obviously reflects the U.S. public's response to political events (Converse 1972). However, the validity of the distinction has been demonstrated for the United States (Abramson 1983, 141-145) as well as for other countries (Barnes, Kaase, et al. 1979, 573-574).

Basically, both measures are based on items that were developed at the Survey Research Center (SRC; later, Center for Political Studies, CPS) at the Institute for Social Research, University of Michigan. There are six individual items, to which respondents can agree or disagree (in parentheses is the first year measurements are available; I = internal efficacy, E = external efficacy):

1. People like me have no say in what the government does (1952). (I)
2. Voting is the only way that people like me can have any say about how the government runs things (1952). (I)
3. Sometimes politics and government seem so complicated that a person like me cannot really understand what is going on (1952). (I)
4. I don't think that public officials care much about what people like me think (1952). (E)
5. Generally speaking, those we elect lose touch with the people pretty quickly (1968). (E)
6. Parties are only interested in people's votes, not in their opinions (1968). (E)

This is not the place to discuss the methodological issues that have arisen from the utilization of these items and the ensuing scales or indices (for details see Wright 1976, 89-110; Abramson 1983, 141-145), but one difference must be noted. Whereas Lipset and Schneider (1983, 19-24) and Barnes, Kaase, et al. (1979, 573-574) believe the first three items constitute the internal efficacy dimension and the last three items constitute the external efficacy dimension, Abramson (1983, 143–144) uses only the first four items and attributes items 2 and 3 to internal efficacy and items 1 and 4 to external efficacy. This difference has to be kept in mind, particularly with respect to the longitudinal analyses Abramson presents.

However, whether one looks at the percentage distributions among the individual items over time—as Lipset and Schneider do—or at indices combining several of those items—as Abramson does—in both cases very clear and consistent results emerge. First of all, internal efficacy in the United States increased from 1952 to 1968 and then remained fairly stable at a level of a little less than 50 percent for those respondents who scored medium or high. The rise in internal efficacy was mostly due to the fact that people no longer believed that voting is the only way one can influence politics. (This result will be taken up again in the discussion of political protest.) Converse (1972) first thoroughly analyzed this phenomenon; he could do so because the most spectacular increase in efficacy occurred between 1964 and 1968. In building on Converse's analysis, Abramson suggests that three different processes determined the changes in internal efficacy: "the rising levels of personal political effectiveness among the college educated, the declining levels among the two lower educational groups [some high school/eight grades or less], and changing educational levels among the electorate" (Abramson 1983, 179). Considering the demographic change, the change in average level of education obtained, and the positive correlation between education and internal political efficacy (an average of 0.35), one would clearly have expected a rise in internal efficacy over time. That this rise did not materialize points to the operation of other, offsetting factors, a point to which I will return later.

As I mentioned before, truly longitudinal data for internal efficacy outside the United States are generally not available. For a much shorter period of time covering the years from 1959 to 1972, Baker, Dalton, and Hildebrandt (1981, 27–30), do document an increase in internal efficacy in West Germany. Although the determinants and the meaning of the development reported by Noelle-Neumann and Piel (1983, 339), are not clear, their data show a seminal increase in the level of political interest displayed by the West German population from 27 percent in 1952 to 57 percent in 1983. Wright in his analysis (Wright 1976, 119–125) finds that in Canada, West Germany, the Netherlands, and Switzerland in the 1968–1972 period, there were levels of political alienation that matched those in the United States. The data (mean scores) from the 1973–1976 Eight Nation Study for the three-item internal efficacy index are as follows (Zentralarchiv 1979, 455; the range of the index is from 1 = low efficacy to 4 = high efficacy):

United States (1974)	2.3
Netherlands (1974)	2.2
Switzerland (1976)	2.2
Great Britain (1973/1974)	2.1
Germany (1974)	2.0

Italy (1975)	2.0
Finland (1975)	2.0
Austria (1974)	1.7

These data indicate that the United States has the highest average of internal efficacy, but, with the exception of Austria, all other countries rate somewhat but not exceptionally lower on that measure.

The impression conveyed by those data that levels of internal political efficacy have been moderate and stable is not at all matched when one moves on to the dimension of external political efficacy, which reflects citizens' feelings about the responsiveness of the political authorities to citizen demands. Notwithstanding a particularly interesting developmental pattern among black U.S. citizens, the data register a strong and linear decline in external efficacy in every SRC/CPS study from 1960 to 1980, a decline that occurred at similar rates among all citizens—roughly 55 percent in 1960 to about 35 percent in 1980. The cross-sectional data for the three-item efficacy index from the Eight Nation Study read as follows (Zentralarchiv 1979, 455; 1 = low efficacy, 4 = high efficacy):

Netherlands	2.3
United States	2.2
Switzerland	2.1
Great Britain	2.1
Germany	2.1
Finland	2.0
Austria	1.9
Italy	1.9

As before, these data cannot be amended to introduce a longitudinal perspective. Nevertheless, they indicate that the eight countries are less divided in this respect than on the internal efficacy score, and that in 1974 the United States ranked only slightly above average in feelings of external efficacy.

This is not yet the point to speculate about the social and political factors that cause the developments in political efficacy. Obviously, the decline of external efficacy is related to the public's general evaluation of government and other large social and political organizations and institutions.

Legitimacy Beliefs, Political Trust, and Political Support

Arthur Miller (1974) was the first scholar to observe a substantial decline in what he then called political trust. However, his conclusions were immediately contested by Jack Citrin (1974), and the inconclusive course of this debate is unfortunately typical of many of the later arguments in this respect. As Muller and Jukam (1977), as well as Muller, Jukam and Seligson (1982), have rightfully observed, a large part of the conceptual confusion in the political trust debate has originated from the inadequate conceptual underpinning of and ensuing operationalizations in the SRC/ CPS trust items. The major deficiencies lie in the inability to separate out the two Eastonian dimensions of specific (authority related) and diffuse (regime as well as political community related) support.

Political trust and political support are here used as synonyms. Both refer to the idea that political authorities cannot operate unless their decisions meet with some acceptance on the part of the citizens without prior consultation: "The effectiveness of political leadership, then, depends on the ability of authorities to claim the loyal cooperation of members of the system without having to specify in advance what such cooperation will entail. Within certain limits, effectiveness depends on a blank check" (Gamson 1968, 43). Political trust refers to a set of distinct political objects, of which the authorities and the regime are the most important. I believe that both dimensions of trust are elements in an encompassing notion of legitimacy beliefs that can also embrace the internal and external efficacy measures previously discussed.

Before turning to the empirical evidence, one additional conceptual consideration is in order. Wright (1976) has challenged the notion that a widely shared political consensus among the citizenry is a necessary condition for a stable democracy. He has argued that it is the particular mix of consenters, assenters, and dissenters—plus other conditions—that determines the stability of democratic polities. Both Hart (1978) and Sniderman (1981) push this argument further. They both ask—in a normative frame of reference—whether unconditional political trust is such a positive citizen attitude at all. Is it not much more important for a good democracy to have skeptical, distrustful citizens, citizens who are aware—as were the founding fathers of the U.S. Constitution—of the human frailties of political leaders and by virtue of their distrust keep the arrogance of political power from taking over? These questions cannot be answered by empirical evidence alone, but they do help to put the following data into perspective.

The data presented by Abramson is representative of the wealth of other information confirming the trend described below. I shall start with the concrete SRC/CPS trust items that made up the political trust scale used by Abramson (1983, 319–320):

1. How much of the time do you think you can trust the government in Washington to do what is right—just about always, most of the time, or only some of the time? (1958)
2. Do you think the people in the government waste a lot of the money we pay in taxes, waste some of it, or don't waste very much of it? (1958)
3. Do you feel that almost all of the people running the government are smart people who usually know what they are doing, or do you think that quite a few of them don't seem to know what they are doing? (1958)

4. Do you think that quite a few of the people running the government are a little crooked, not very many are, or do you think that hardly any of them are crooked at all? (1958)
5. Would you say the government is pretty much run by a few big interests looking out for themselves or that it is run for the benefit of all the people? (1964)

Items 1–4 were used by Abramson to build the scale; item 5 was excluded because it was first asked in 1964 and not in 1958 as the other four items were. The Eight Nation Study employed a political trust index consisting only of item 5 plus a slightly changed version of item 1 (Barnes, Kaase, et al. 1979, 575):

6. How much do you trust the government to do what is right? Do you trust it just about always, most of the time, only some of the time, or almost never?

Abramson (1983, 193–238) as well as Lipset and Schneider (1983) have thoroughly analyzed the trends in the distribution of political trust among U.S. citizens. The evidence they came up with is overwhelming: There was a massive and steady decline in political trust from the mid-1960s until 1980. There is no question that the downward change from a high of about 75 percent in 1964 to about 30 percent in 1980 truly deserves to be called spectacular. It is more than unfortunate that similar longitudinal analyses for other Western democracies are not possible because of the lack of comparable data. Again, the Eight Nation Study permits at least a limited comparison between the United States and seven European democracies. It must be noted that the two items constituting the political trust index are the two that witnessed the largest decline among the individual items (Abramson 1983, 230). The data read as follows (Zentralarchiv 1979, 456; 1 = low political trust, 4 = high political trust):

Austria	2.9
Switzerland	2.9
Germany	2.8
Netherlands	2.6
Great Britain	2.4
Finland	2.3
United States	2.1
Italy	1.7

Tentative as these data can be at least, they nevertheless suggest that the substantial decline in political trust in the United States has not been paralleled in all Western democracies. Surely, from one data point in time no conclusions can be deduced. Still, it seems that the shattering events of the Vietnam War and the Watergate affair have left a special mark on the political beliefs of people in the United States. Unfortunately, France was not included in the Eight Nation Study. Looking back at the location of Italy and France in Tables 3.2–3.4, it does not come as a surprise that of all the eight nations studied, Italy displays the by far lowest level of political trust.

Scheuch speculated as early as 1976 that the suspected decline in political legitimacy reflected an increasing skepticism of citizens against all big organizations. This point was corroborated not only by data presented in Crozier, Huntington and Watanuki (1975) but also by unpublished data collected by the Infas Institute in Bad Godesberg for West Germany and soundly substantiated by the Lipset and Schneider analysis. They write:

> It would appear that the individuous sentiments expressed about large organizations reflect a general anti-elitist, anti-power ideology much more than a sense of personal maltreatment. Americans apparently believe that incontrolled, self-oriented power will always be used against the public interest, and that those in charge, if not watched closely, will act to benefit themselves— at the expense of the public if they are politicians, against the interests of consumers and their own employees if they are corporation executives, and against the interests of the community and even their own members if they are union leaders. [Lipset and Schneider 1983, 382]

The only other country for which—to the best of my knowledge— longitudinal data on legitimacy beliefs/political trust/political support are available is West Germany. There are two likely reasons for the availability of these data: The reconstitution of the German democracy after World War II was a process of immense interest to foreign as well as German scholars, and in the Institut für Demoskopie there existed a survey research organization that built a longitudinal data base reaching back almost to the foundation of the Federal Republic in 1949. Germany is particularly interesting because, as Boynton and Loewenberg (1973) have so aptly demonstrated, the establishment of a firm basis for diffuse support depended on the creation of specific support for Konrad Adenauer and the ruling political parties through the success of their policies—particularly the "economic miracle." This particular sequence from specific to diffuse support raises the question whether it is typical for the establishment of all democracies or whether other conditions and sequences prevail.

Boynton and Loewenberg's conclusions are supported and enlarged by a series of secondary analyses based on data from the Institut für Demoskopie as well as other data sources (Conradt 1980; Weil 1981; Baker, Dalton, and Hildebrandt 1981, 21–37; Pappi 1982; Küchler 1982). The development of diffuse support for the political institutions of the Federal Republic plus the emergence of democratic attitudes is very well summarized by Pappi (1982, AB 82). More recently, the still high support for the political institutions of West Germany is being increasingly qualified because of a more skeptical evaluation of actors and institutions, undoubtedly partly the result of the increase in internal political efficacy referred to before.

The question remains: To what extent does the historic specificity of Germany's development make it a deviant case in the sense of producing a time lag between the creation of specific and diffuse political support and the ensuing erosion because of structural properties of the democratic process? The analyses of the United States and the less systematic observations of many other democracies seem to indicate that particular political events *plus* a change in public values, ideology, and perceptions in postindustrial polities act together to create a climate of suspicion against the established political process and large political, economic, and social actors. There is no doubt that this suspicion has been magnified through the looking glass of the mass media and their negativist style of reporting. One important question that as of now cannot be clearly answered is whether distrust has already extended to cover objects of not only specific but also diffuse support, in particular the general system of democracy. In his analysis of the U.S. Congress, Dennis (1981, 347–348) concludes that diffuse support has been declining, too. By contrast, Lipset and Schneider (1983, 384–385) maintain that it is exactly the still high level of diffuse support that has prevented a manifestation of negative consequences from the low level of support for the political authorities and leaders.

In order to answer such questions in a reliable way a good deal of additional conceptual and empirical effort will have to be carried out. Work by Muller and his associates (e.g., Muller, Jukam, and Seligson 1982) indicates one direction to be taken. Still, one cannot help but wonder why political scientists in the past have devoted so little good thinking and empirical work to the central question of legitimacy beliefs.

Turnout, Voting, and Political Parties

As more and more democracies travel the road toward party government, the presently central role of political parties in and for the democratic process is increasingly highlighted—notwithstanding the vastly different role parties play in the United States. In this section three variables are briefly discussed that can be regarded as indicators of the legitimacy of political parties and the electoral process. I must mention that none of the three indicators is unambiguous in its meaning; this problem, however, shall not concern us here.

The first variable is *turnout* at general elections. If political systems are not in crisis and polarization, a high turnout can be interpreted as a measure of citizen identification with the electoral process and its main actors. Fortunately, several analyses have been recently published that study turnout comparatively and longitudinally (Dittrich and Johansen 1983, Mair 1984). These studies are in agreement that no clear-cut pattern of changes in turnout is visible, in particular not the kind of general decline that might indicate increasing dissatisfaction with party government and party democracy. Rather, country-specific factors are obviously in operation, which in some countries enhance and in others lower turnout. It does, though, not come as a surprise that electoral participation in the United States has substantially suffered along with the other measures of political identification. As Verba, Nie, and Kim observed in 1978, the institutionalized links between political parties and social groups as well as the parties organizationally simply are too weak to survive such a heavy attack on the political motivation of the citizens. In this sense, the turnout data for European party systems may indeed conceal the extent to which citizens might have already turned their backs on the political parties.

That all is not well on the Western party front indeed is signaled by the other two variables, voting volatility and party identification. Voting volatility refers to the changes in aggregate party strength across two or more elections. This chapter is not the right spot to take up the thorny issue of individual change versus aggregate change, but it can be said that analyses by Pedersen (1983) and Maguire (1983) demonstrate that the last two decades have indeed witnessed an increasing trend in aggregate voting volatility. As a note of caution, however, one should keep in mind that this volatility is substantially reduced if *party* volatility measures are replaced by measures of *block* volatility. Thus, even though there is some empirical evidence for the waning away of the established links between social and political cleavages (see Lipset 1981), there can be no question that many of those links are still alive and well (as is demonstrated by Bartolini and Mair 1984 for the socialist voting bloc).

It is by now well-established by empirical evidence that in the United States there has been a strong decline in the number of citizens identifying with a political party and in the intensity of their emotional attachment (Abramson 1983, 69-131, especially 127). Comparable longitudinal party identification data are not generally available for European democracies. Kaase (1980) has shown that there was virtually no decline in the extent and strength of party identification between 1970 and 1980 in Germany; an analysis for the United Kingdom (Särlvik and Crewe 1983, 333-336), by contrast, indicates a considerable decline in extent and even more of a decline in strength of party identification between 1964 and 1979. Peter Mair (1984), in his secondary analysis of the Eurobarometer data between 1975 and 1981 for Belgium, France, Germany, and the Netherlands (these were the times and countries in which the party identification question was identically asked), demonstrates a decline in partisanship and found the same decline to be true for the brief period between 1978 and 1981 in the other EC countries as well.

Political Protest

The comparative survey studies of Almond and Verba (1963) as well as of Verba, Nie, and Kim (1978) only covered institutionalized conventional political participation. The empirical study of direct action politics through surveys began to flourish in the seventies, although to this point the Eight Nation Study (Barnes, Kaase, et al. 1979) has been the only crossnationally comparative study to be published. One major criticism that could be leveled against this study is that it did not—in contrast with Muller (1979)—

concentrate on *actual* participation but rather extended its reach to include also potential participation (for details of conceptualization and operationalization see Barnes, Kaase, et al. 1979, 57-96). A replication of the study with a large sample of sixteen–fifty-year-old Germans in 1976 strongly sustained the 1974 results (Infratest 1980). In addition, in three of the eight countries of the political action study (Germany, Netherlands, United States) a panel replication was conducted in 1980/1981. Unfortunately, these comparative longitudinal results will not be made available to the public until the publication of a comparative book on the panel. Thus, no detailed longitudinal analyses of any of the protest measures are possible at this time (for some such comparisons see Kaase 1983). It can, however, be said that there is no *general* trend toward increased uninstitutionalized participation—the Netherlands and Germany witnessed a decline, the United States an increase.

One of the most important results from the 1974 study (Barnes, Kaase, et al. 1979, 151) is that the propensities for institutionalized and uninstitutionalized political participation are positively correlated. There is an inclination by active citizens to jointly use both modes of political participation, a finding that has turned out to be very robust across a variety of other studies. This result is relevant because it speaks against a concept of political protest that automatically equals such protest with turmoil and undemocratic postures.

The lack of comparative longitudinal survey data on the development of attitudes toward uninstitutionalized political participation permits no firm conclusions with respect to future developments in these attitudes and behaviors. However, there exists—collected through the World Handbook of Political and Social Indicators Project (Taylor and Jodice 1983)—a longitudinal base of behavioral event data on protest and related activities embracing the time between 1948 and 1977. One volume of the *Handbook* deals with political protest and government change and contains a set of relevant indicators (Taylor and Jodice 1983):

- A *protest demonstration* "is a nonviolent gathering of people organized for the announced purpose against a regime or government or one or more of its leaders; or against its ideology, policy, intended policy, or lack of policy; or against its previous action or intended action" (p. 19).
- A *political strike* "is a work stoppage by a body of industrial or service workers or a stoppage of normal academic life by students to protest a regime and its leaders' policies or actions" (p. 21)—it should be noted that economically oriented strikes were not coded in this category.
- A *riot* "is a demonstration or disturbance that becomes violent. If destruction of property . . . is an essential component of the observed behavior the event is not a demonstration. . . . The second distinguishing characteristic of a riot is the event's apparent spontaneity. Violent action against persons or property that was the work of a discrete and identifiable group was coded as an armed attack" (p. 29).

- *Deaths from political violence* "is a useful indicator of the magnitude of internal war. Political deaths were coded as an attribute of other events rather than as events in and of themselves" (p. 43).

Taylor and Jodice (1983, 5–7) rightfully point out that scholars of political violence go far beyond descriptive analyses of the occurrence of political violence and the conditions associated with that occurrence. However, for the purposes of this chapter it suffices to document the frequency of acts of political protest over time. Consequently, the Taylor and Jodice data are arranged in five-year intervals for the total period from 1948 to 1977; unfortunately, more recent crossnational event data are not available. Tables 3.5 and 3.6 cover the dimension of political turmoil (combining the indicators of protest demonstrations, political strikes, and riots) and the number of deaths from political violence, respectively. Both tables are standardized according to population size.

There are many ways one can look at the data in Table 3.5, but I shall draw only three major conclusions. First, there is no evidence whatsoever of an increasing amount of political turmoil over time that would signal and corroborate in *behavioral* terms the much-suspected legitimacy crisis. Second, the data clearly indicate the preponderance of country-specific conditions determining the extent of political turmoil (obvious examples are the United Kingdom, Ireland, Portugal, and Greece—the latter two being countries that are experiencing true system change). Third, "an amazing number of countries switched from peaceful to violent, or from violent to peaceful, or occasionally both ways" (Taylor and Jodice 1983, 6–7). This conclusion points to the complexity of interaction among factors that finally produce actual political protest and violence and therefore forbids any simple generalization.

These analyses are amended by the data on deaths from political violence (Table 3.6). Such events are apparently rather rare occurrences and reflect even more the specific political circumstances of the polities in question (the United Kingdom and Ireland are once again the cases in point).

CONCLUSIONS

The analyses presented have amply demonstrated that in empirical political science conceptually well-founded information on a broad variety of relevant problems is still largely missing, particularly for Europe. What is needed is consistent cumulative research, not a permanent "reinvention of the wheel." In addition, it should have become clear that dynamic multilevel theorizing and multilevel research designs are equally amiss.

Beyond these general criticisms, the data presented in this chapter indicate that certain elements of political alienation in Western democracies are widespread and have been increasing in size. Wright (1976) has taken one possible approach to these results in pointing to the fact that most likely there has never been a time in democratic nations when an all-embracing identification of the citizens with their polities existed. He questions the idea of a general consensus about the political community and explains the relative stability of democratic regimes according to the precarious balance of a small number of active dissenters, a large number of neutral assenters, and a sizable group of active consenters. In addition, his and other analyses of the social and political composition of the politically alienated suggest that these citizens are among the least resourceful, least skillful, and least motivated and therefore are neither interested in nor capable of truly challenging the political order.

Wright's scenario may appear too cynical to be true. Another explanation is offered by Sniderman (1981) who otherwise shares many views with Wright. Based on data from the San Francisco Bay Area Study, Sniderman finds that even among the most politically alienated and embittered Americans in the region there is hardly anyone who can think of a preferable alternative to the existing polity. As Sniderman says: "The disaffected are politically suspicious, resentful, disillusioned; given the right chance, they will translate their feelings into actions, and sometimes violent ones at that. And the point I have meant to make is this: one can be alienated, genuinely so, and yet identify with the political order—as the disaffected do. . . . Time has witnessed the eclipse of alternative conceptions of a political order in America" (Sniderman 1981, 141). One is tempted to add that this point is true for other parts of the world too, certainly for the Western European nations.

Two more considerations that help to explain why Western democracies have not yet faltered are offered by Lipset and Schneider (1983, 385–392). One factor, which is consistently buffered by empirical evidence, is that people in Western democracies are by and large satisfied with and optimistic about their personal lives. In late 1983, 16 percent of the citizens living in the EC countries said they were very happy, and 61 percent said they were fairly happy (Commission 1983, A31). The second factor is that the democratic system of government, faulty as it may seem, still permits "throwing the rascals out"—i.e., a peaceful transition of political authority between competing groups. Surely, as public opinion data show in abundance, this positive effect seems to wear off rather swiftly. Still, the chance for transition is institutionally guaranteed, which is no small asset when one looks at other systems of government.

I am not arguing that all is well in democracy land; quite the contrary is true. Politicians will have to face the fact that their constituents have become more distrustful of them and at the same time feel politically more efficacious than before (at least in parts of the citizenry). If, for instance, Schmitt's 1983 analysis, which shows a strong correlation between government stability and support for party government, is sound, then that fact would indicate that playing government-change games—as in Germany (1982) and so frequently in Italy—is not appreciated and is not conducive to a positive evaluation of democratic government. In addition, Powell (1982) has pointed to the problems of but also to the structural alternatives available for democratic governance. Whereas having an unstable government seems to be the price frequently paid by representational systems, these systems also facilitate integration into the legitimate (and legal) political process by new groups, definitely decrease political turmoil, and enhance voter participation. It is in these systems that the positive functional aspects of uninstitutionalized political participation, which is frequently enforced in majoritarian systems, becomes particularly visible (Powell 1982, 222).

It is an open question whether the demand for increased political participation by the citizens has a firm developmental basis or just reflects a cycle of engagement and disengagement (Hirschman 1982). Nevertheless, broader and more numerous institutionalized channels of participation would help citizens gain more influence and at the same time learn more about the constraints that are immanent in the political process. The implementation of such channels of participation could neutralize much of the emotional negativism that is directed at the political process through the mass media and at the same time help the faltering legitimacy to recover.

REFERENCES

Abramson, Paul R. 1983. *Political Attitudes in America.* San Francisco: Freeman.

Almond, Gabriel A., and Sidney Verba. 1963. *The Civic Culture.* Princeton: Princeton University Press.

Baker, Kendall L., Russel J. Dalton, and Kai Hildebrandt. 1981. *Germany Transformed: Political Culture and the New Politics.* Cambridge: Harvard University Press.

Barnes, Samuel H., Max Kaase, et al. 1979. *Political Action: Mass Participation in Five Western Democracies.* Beverly Hills, Calif.: Sage.

Bartolini, Stefano, and Peter Mair. 1984. "The Class Cleavage in Historical Perspective: An Analytical Reconstruction and Empirical Test." Florence: European University Institute. Manuscript.

Boynton, G. R., and Gerhard Loewenberg. 1973. "Der Bundestag im Bewusstsein der Öffentlichkeit 1951-1959." *Politische Vierteljahresschrift* 14:3-25.

Citrin, Jack. 1974. "Comment: The Political Relevance of Trust in Government." *American Political Science Review* 68:973-988.

Commission of the European Community, ed. 1983. *Eurobarometer* no. 20. Brussels.

Conradt, David P. 1980. "Changing German Political Culture." In Gabriel A. Almond and Sidney Verba, eds., *The Civic Culture Revisited,* pp. 212-272. Boston: Little, Brown and Company.

Converse, Philip E. 1972. "Change in the American Electorate." In Angus Campbell and Philip E. Converse, eds., *The Human Meaning of Social Change,* pp. 263-337. New York: Russell Sage.

Crozier, Michel, Samuel P. Huntington, and Joji Watanuki. 1975. *The Crisis of Democracy.* New York: New York University Press.

Daalder, Hans, and Peter Mair, eds. 1983. *Western European Party Systems.* Beverly Hills, Calif.: Sage.

Dennis, Jack. 1981. "Public Support for Congress." *Political Behavior* 3:319-350.

Dittrich, Karl, and Lars Lørby Johansen. 1983. "Voting Turnout in Europe, 1945–1978: Myths and Realities." In Hans Daalder and Peter Mair, eds., *Western European Party Systems*, pp. 95–114. Beverly Hills, Calif.: Sage.

Easton, David. 1965. *A Systems Analysis of Political Life*. New York: John Wiley.

———. 1975. "A Re-Assessment of the Concept of Political Support." *British Journal of Political Science* 5:435–457.

Finifter, Ada W. 1972. "Dimensions of Political Alienation." In Ada W. Finifter, ed., *Alienation in the Social System*, pp. 189–212. New York: John Wiley.

Fuchs, Dieter. 1983. "Protest." In Ekkehart Lippert and Roland Wakenhut, eds., *Handwörterbuch der Politischen Psychologie*, pp. 276–283. Opladen, West Ger.: Westdeutscher Verlag.

Gamson, William A. 1968. *Power and Discontent*. Homewood, Ill.: Dorsey Press.

Glatzer, Wolfgang. 1984. "Zufriedenheitsunterschiede zwischen Lebensbereichen." In Wolfgang Glatzer and Wolfgang Zapf, eds., *Lebensqualität in der Bundesrepublik*, pp. 192–205. Frankfurt and New York: Campus.

Hart, Vivien. 1978. *Distrust and Democracy: Political Distrust in Britain and America*. Cambridge: Cambridge University Press.

Hirschman, Albert O. 1982. *Shifting Involvements: Private Interest and Public Action*. Princeton: Princeton University Press.

Infratest. 1980. *Politischer Protest in der Bundesrepublik Deutschland*. Stuttgart: Kohlhammer.

Kaase, Max. 1980. "The Crisis of Authority: Myth and Reality." In Richard Rose, ed., *Challenge to Governance*, pp. 175–193. Beverly Hills, Calif. and London: Sage.

———. 1982. "Legitimacy Beliefs and the Democratic Order: Theory, Facts, and Fiction." Paper presented at conference on Representation and the State: Problems of Governability and Legitimacy in Western European Democracies. Palo Alto: Stanford University.

———. 1983. "Political Action in the 80s: Structures and Idiosyncrasies." Paper prepared for the Sixth Annual Scientific Meeting of the International Society of Political Psychology. St. Catherine's College, Oxford University, July 19–22.

———. 1984. "Politische Beteiligung in den 80er Jahren: Strukturen und Idiosynkrasien." In Jürgen W. Falter, Christian Fenner, and Michael Th. Greven, eds., *Politische Willensbildung und Interessenvermittlung*, pp. 338–350. Opladen, West Ger.: Westdeutscher Verlag.

Kinder, Donald R. 1981. "Presidents, Prosperity, and Public Opinion." *Public Opinion Quarterly* 45:1–21.

Kinder, Donald R., and D. Roderick Kiewiet. 1981. "Sociotropic Politics: The American Case." *British Journal of Political Science* 11:129–161.

Küchler, Manfred. 1982. "Staats-, Parteien-, oder Politikverdrossenheit?" In Joachim Raschke, ed., *Bürger und Parteien: Ansichten und Analysen zu einer schwierigen Beziehung*, pp. 39–54. Opladen, West Ger.: Westdeutscher Verlag.

Lipset, Seymour Martin. 1981. "Whatever Happened to the Proletariat?" *Encounter* 56:18–34.

Lipset, Seymour Martin, and William Schneider. 1983. *The Confidence Gap: Business, Labor, and Government in the Public Mind*. New York: Free Press.

Ludz, Peter C. 1975. *Alienation as a Concept in the Social Sciences. Current Sociology* 21:1.

Maguire, Maria. 1983. "Is There Still Persistence? Electoral Change in Western Europe, 1948–1979." In Hans Daalder and Peter Mair, eds., *Western European Party Systems*, pp. 67–94. Beverly Hills, Calif.: Sage.

Mair, Peter. 1984. "Party Politics in Contemporary Europe." *West European Politics* 7:128–134.

Miller, Arthur H. 1974. "Political Issues and Trust in Government: 1964–1974." *American Political Science Review* 68:951–972.

Muller, Edward N. 1979. *Aggressive Political Participation*. Princeton: Princeton University Press.

Muller, Edward N., and Thomas O. Jukan. 1977. "On the Meaning of Political Support." *American Political Science Review* 71:1561–1595.

Muller, Edward N., Thomas O. Jukam, and Mitchell A. Seligson. 1982. "Diffuse Political Support and Antisystem Political Behavior: A Comparative Analysis." *American Journal of Political Science* 26:240–264.

Noelle-Neumann, Elisabeth, and Edgar Piel, eds. 1983. *Allensbacher Jahrbuch der Demoskopie 1978–1983*. Vol. 8. Munich: K. G. Saur.

Pappi, Franz U. 1982. "Die politischen Institutionen der Bundesrepublik Deutschland: Zum Legitimitätseinverständnis der Bevölkerung." *Ausserschulische Bildung*, pp. B 72/AB 82–AB 82/B 79.

Pedersen, Mogens N. 1983. "Changing Patterns of Electoral Volatility in European Party Systems, 1948–1977: Explorations in Explanations." In Hans Daalder and Peter Mair, eds., *Western European Party Systems*, pp. 29–66. Beverly Hills, Calif.: Sage.

Powell, Bingham G., Jr. 1982. *Contemporary Democracies: Participation, Stability, and Violence*. Cambridge: Harvard University Press.

Przeworski, Adam, and Henry Teune. 1970. *The Logic of Comparative Social Inquiry.* New York: John Wiley.

Särlvik, Bo, and Ivor Crewe. 1983. *Decade of Dealignment*. Cambridge: Cambridge University Press.

Scheuch, Erwin K. 1968. "The Cross-cultural Use of Sample Surveys: Problems of Comparability." In Stein Rokkan, ed., *Comparative Research Across Cultures and Nations*, pp. 176–209. Paris and The Hague: Mouton.

————. 1976. *Wird die Bundesrepublik unregierbar?* Cologne: Arbeitgeberverband der Metallindustrie.

Schmidtchen, Gerhard, and Hans-Martin Uehlinger. 1983. "Jugend und Staat." In Ulrich Matz and Gerhard Schmidtchen, eds., *Gewalt und Legitimität*, pp. 105–264. Opladen, West Ger.: Westdeutscher Verlag.

Schmitt, Hermann. 1983. "Party Government in Public Opinion: A European Cross-National Comparison." *European Journal of Political Research* 11:353–375.

Sniderman, Paul M. 1981. *A Question of Loyalty.* Berkeley: University of California Press.

Strümpel, Burkhard, ed. 1974. *Subjective Elements of Well-Being.* Paris: Organization for Economic Cooperation and Development.

Taylor, Charles Lewis, and David A. Jodice, eds. 1983. *World Handbook of Political and Social Indicators*. 3d ed. Vol. 2, *Political Protest and Government Change*. New Haven: Yale University Press.

Verba, Sidney, Norman H. Nie, and Jae-on Kim. 1978. *Participation and Political Equality*. Cambridge: Cambridge University Press.

Weber, Max. 1956. *Wirtschaft und Gesellschaft*. 2 vols. Cologne: Kiepenheuer und Witsch.

Weil, Frederick David. 1981. "Post-Fascist Liberalism: The Development of Political Tolerance in West Germany Since World War II." Ph.D. dissertation, Harvard University.

Westle, Bettina. 1987. "Zur Theorie und Empirie politischer Legitimität." Ph.d. dissertation, University of Mannheim.

Wright, James D. 1976. *The Dissent of the Governed*. New York: Academic Press.

Zentralarchiv für Empirische Sozialforschung. 1979. *Political Action: An Eight Nation Study 1973-1976*. Cologne.

Zimmerman, Ekkart. 1983. *Massenmobilisierung: Protest als politische Gewalt*. Zurich: Edition Interfrom.

Table 3.1 Types of Political Participation and Protest

Institutionalized Participation				Noninstitutionalized Participation: Protest					
Legal		Illegal		Legal		Illegal			
						Legitimate		Illegitimate	
Legit-imate	Illegit-imate	Legit-imate	Illegit-imate	Legit-imate	Illegit-imate	Non-violent	Violent	Non-violent	Violent
Voting and other activities related to the institutionalized political process, e.g., campaigning, communal activities particularized contacting	Voting for extremist parties(?)			Boycotts(?), lawful demonstrations(?), citizen initiative groups	Boycotts(?), lawful demonstrations(?)	Civil disobedience (?), political strikes (?), rent strikes (?), tax strikes (?)	?	Civil disobedience ? political strikes (?), rent strikes (?), tax strikes (?)	Personal violence, violence against things

Table 3.2   General Satisfaction with Life

	Year and Month of Survey[a]							
	1976	1977	1978	1979	1980	1981	1982	1983
	Oct.-Nov.	Oct.-Nov.	Oct.-Nov.	April	April	April	Oct.	Oct.
Belgium	1.7[b]	1.7	1.7	1.7	1.8	1.8	2.0	2.0
Denmark	1.6	1.5	1.5	1.5	1.5	1.5	1.5	1.5
Germany	2.0	1.9	1.9	1.9	2.0	2.0	2.0	2.1
France	2.2	2.2	2.2	2.3	2.3	2.2	2.2	2.2
Ireland	1.8	1.7	1.8	1.8	1.8	1.8	1.9	2.0
Italy	2.5	2.4	2.4	2.4	2.4	2.3	2.4	2.4
Luxembourg	1.8	1.7	1.8	1.7	1.7	1.7	1.7	1.7
Netherlands	1.7	1.7	1.7	1.6	1.6	1.7	1.6	1.7
United Kingdom	1.9	1.8	1.8	1.9	1.9	1.9	1.8	1.9
Greece						2.5	2.4	2.3

a) Data derived from samples usually between 900 and 1,100 respondents; average sample size in Luxembourg was 300. Respondents were selected either through quota or multistage random sampling. Different sampling procedures sometimes applied across countries.

b) Data entries are means based on the following category labels: Very satisfied (= 1); Fairly satisfied (= 2); Not very satisfied (= 3); Not at all satisfied (= 4). Missing data are excluded from calculation. The percentage of missing data rarely exceeds 1-2 percent.

Source: Eurobarometer nr. 20 (December 1983), pp. A15-A24.

Table 3.3   Satisfaction with the Way Democracy Works

	Year and Month of Survey[a]							
	1976 Oct.-Nov.	1977 Oct.-Nov.	1978 Oct.-Nov.	1979 Oct.	1980 Oct.	1981 Oct.	1982 Oct.	1983 Oct.
Belgium	2.4[b]	2.4	2.6	2.5	2.8	2.7	2.6	2.5
Denmark	2.5	2.3	2.3	2.1	2.3	2.2	2.4	2.0
Germany	2.1	2.1	2.1	2.0	2.2	2.2	2.2	2.2
France	2.6	2.5	2.7	2.7	2.8	2.4	2.6	2.6
Ireland	2.4	2.2	2.3	2.4	2.6	2.3	2.6	2.7
Italy	3.3	3.1	3.1	3.1	3.1	3.1	3.1	3.1
Luxembourg	1.7	2.0	2.2	2.0	2.1	2.1	2.3	2.3
Netherlands	2.3	2.3	2.4	2.4	2.5	2.4	2.6	2.5
United Kingdom	2.5	2.3	2.5	2.5	2.5	2.5	2.4	2.3
Greece						2.4	2.2	2.2

a) Data derived from samples usually between 900 and 1,100 respondents; average sample size in Luxembourg was 300. Respondents were selected either through quota or multistage random sampling. Different sampling procedures sometimes applied across countries.

b) Data entries are means based on the following category labels: Very satisfied (= 1); Fairly satisfied (= 2); Not very satisfied (= 3); Not at all satisfied (= 4). Missing data are excluded from calculation. Missing data vary between 5 and 10 percent; in Belgium, between 10 and 20 percent.

Source: Eurobarometer, nr. 20 (December 1983), pp. A32-A36.

Table 3.4   Percentage of Respondents Claiming the
            Way Society is Organized Must Be
            Radically Changed by Revolutionary Action

	Year and Month of Survey[a]							
	1976 Oct.-Nov.	1977 Oct.-Nov.	1978 Oct.-Nov.	1979 Oct.	1980 Oct.	1981 Oct.	1982 Oct.	1983 Oct.
Belgium	5[b]	4	6	7	6	8	9	6
Denmark	4	3	4	2	1	2	2	2
Germany	2	2	2	3	4	4	3	3
France	13	8	12	10	9	5	5	8
Ireland	7	7	7	7	7	4	7	8
Italy	13	10	9	9	6	6	7	6
Luxembourg	2	4	5	2	5	4	3	3
Netherlands	5	4	6	6	4	6	5	7
United Kingdom	7	6	5	7	6	9	5	5
Greece					9	8	7	9

a) Data derived from samples usually between 900
and 1,100 respondents; average sample size in
Luxembourg was 300. Respondents were selected
either through quota or multistage random sampling.
Different sampling procedures sometimes applied
across countries.

b) Entries are percentages based on all
respondents including missing data. Missing data
average between 5 and 10 percent; in Belgium
between 10 and 20 percent.

Source: Eurobarometer, nr. 20 (December 1983),
pp. A38-A47.

Table 3.5 Turmoil in Democracies 1948-1977[a]; Events per Capita[b]

Country	1948-1952 Per Capita	Rank	1953-1957 Per Capita	Rank	1958-1962 Per Capita	Rank	1963-1967 Per Capita	Rank	1968-1972 Per Capita	Rank	1973-1977 Per Capita	Rank	Total Number of Events
United States	2.43	(16)	3.32	(10)	27.34	(6)	67.89	(2)	47.68	(3)	14.82	(8)	3199
Canada	4.37	(14)	1.91	(12)	7.26	(12)	17.81	(5)	22.89	(9)	4.83	(17)	117
Ireland	26.95	(7)			3.53	(17)	48.68	(3)	223.43	(1)	86.23	(4)	116
United Kingdom	7.11	(13)	0.79	(13)	23.59	(7)	10.82	(8)	81.48	(2)	93.93	(3)	1205
France	28.51	(5)	31.31	(1)	32.84	(3)	7.80	(11)	23.88	(8)	33.07	(5)	739
Belgium	89.14	(2)	15.78	(5)	73.19	(1)	16.90	(6)	7.27	(16)	6.09	(16)	187
Netherlands	3.96	(15)	2.79	(11)			4.88	(14)	1.53	(20)	10.30	(11)	29
Luxembourg									29.50	(7)			1
West Germany	26.40	(8)	10.69	(6)	4.33	(15)	16.43	(7)	18.45	(11)	7.13	(15)	465
Switzerland	2.13	(17)			5.59	(13)	1.71	(18)	17.56	(12)	15.30	(7)	26
Austria	64.89	(3)	5.76	(8)	28.38	(5)	2.76	(16)	4.03	(17)	10.61	(10)	82
Italy	62.65	(4)	18.06	(4)	19.70	(8)	10.01	(9)	32.48	(6)	25.81	(6)	847
Portugal	1.19	(18)			58.92	(2)	7.58	(12)	35.92	(5)	430.27	(1)	468
Greece	10.58	(11)	27.63	(2)	3.60	(16)	73.68	(1)	46.63	(4)	189.25	(2)	306
Turkey			7.97	(7)	18.54	(9)	7.06	(13)	10.23	(13)	9.03	(12)	164
Denmark	28.18	(6)	22.52	(3)	32.74	(4)	2.10	(17)	8.12	(14)	13.93	(9)	49
Sweden	7.13	(12)					9.04	(10)	18.64	(10)	7.24	(14)	33
Norway	18.38	(9)			5.59	(13)	32.23	(4)	2.58	(18)	7.49	(13)	24
Finland	129.71	(1)			11.29	(10)			2.17	(19)	4.30	(18)	60
Japan	14.94	(10)	5.57	(9)	16.26	(10)	2.93	(15)	7.86	(15)	1.62	(19)	457

a) According to a suggestion by Charles L. Taylor, protest demonstrations, political strikes and riots were treated as constituting one single dimension of turmoil, i.e., of small threats to the system with (mostly) the intent to change some kind of government policy. Therefore, the event counts for the three activities were summed up to create a single indicator of turmoil.

b) The absolute number of events is misleading information if not standardized according to the population size of a given country. Although this standardization may well give rise to other objections, for the descriptive purposes of this chapter it seems perfectly adequate. Standardization was achieved by dividing the absolute number of events by population size and multiplying by a factor of 10,000 to arrive at a number reasonable for comparisons among countries. The population size used for standardization was always taken from the middle year of the given time period, i.e., 1950, 1955, and so on. All data were taken from the file documented in Taylor and Jodice 1983, #22-36.
    The data were supplied by the Zentralarchiv fur Empirische Sozialforschung of the University of Cologne.
    My thanks go to Dieter Fuchs and his colleagues from the Central Archive who provided me with the computations.

Table 3.6 Deaths from Political Violence in Democracies, 1948-1977; Events per Capita

Country	1948-1952 Per Capita	Rank	1953-1957 Per Capita	Rank	1958-1962 Per Capita	Rank	1963-1967 Per Capita	Rank	1968-1972 Per Capita	Rank	1973-1977 Per Capita	Rank	Total Number of Events
Greece	12,295.80	(1)					5.85	(3)	3.41	(8)	33.59	(4)	9,341
United Kingdom	1.19	(9)			0.57	(9)			99.86	(1)	159.50	(1)	1,463
United States	1.44	(7)	0.54	(7)	2.38	(7)	12.66	(2)	4.69	(7)	0.84	(15)	434
Turkey			1.26	(6)	16.72	(3)	15.73	(1)	14.48	(3)	29.59	(5)	267
Italy	13.90	(3)	3.53	(1)	4.58	(6)	0.77	(7)	6.91	(4)	20.54	(6)	259
France	0.72	(10)	1.84	(3)	21.67	(2)	0.41	(9)	1.97	(13)	7.94	(8)	164
Belgium	4.63	(5)			6.56	(5)			71.59	(2)	2.03	(13)	81
Portugal					27.19	(1)	2.17	(5)	2.32	(11)	43.37	(3)	66
West Germany	1.20	(8)	1.78	(4)			0.68	(8)	5.44	(6)	2.92	(10)	61
Japan	1.20	(8)							2.01	(12)	0.99	(14)	60
Ireland			3.42	(2)	0.21	(10)			6.77	(5)	150.11	(2)	50
Denmark	32.78	(2)											14
Netherlands											9.56	(7)	13
Canada							3.05	(4)	1.40	(14)	0.44	(16)	12
Austria	5.77	(4)	1.44	(5)	1.12	(8)	1.38	(6)	2.69	(9)	2.65	(11)	10
Sweden									2.49	(10)	4.82	(9)	6
Finland	2.49	(6)			6.77	(4)							4
Norway											2.50	(12)	1
Luxembourg													
Switzerland													

Source: Taylor and Jodice 1983; 48-51.

4
TENDENCIES TOWARD AN EROSION OF LEGITIMACY

Ulrich Widmaier

Critical writers from the Marxist or neo-Marxist tradition have postulated an accelerating erosion of capitalism caused by its increasing internal contradictions and, as a consequence, the collapse of its political super-structure, i.e., the bourgeois state (see Habermas 1973, Offe 1972). Do empirical findings on the decline of regime legitimacy in Western liberal-democratic systems finally support these long-standing "predictions"? The answer to this question seems to be yes insofar as a significant number of recent studies based on time series data come to the conclusion that the legitimacy of Western liberal democracies has declined over the last ten to twelve years (see Kaase, Chapter 3); Barnes, Kaase, et al. 1979, Dennis 1981, Lipset and Schneider 1983, Abramson 1983). The answer to the question is clearly no insofar as the theoretical explanations offered and the implications drawn by these studies differ from the neo-Marxist perspective despite some terminological and prima facie similarities.

For many neo-Marxist analysts, one of the state's functions is to legitimize the dominant mode of production and distribution. Because of increasing contradictions in the welfare state, the government must absorb more and more functions, which will lead to a declining overall performance in terms of legitimate allocations. This "overload" argument can also be found among liberal writers, but the problem is seen by them as a political one caused by the "logic" of politics in the advanced industrial societies. The question is asked, How can political regimes maintain legitimacy under the conditions of a modern society characterized by increased differentiation of organized and/or articulated interests?[1]

This question also characterizes the departure for this analysis. But before moving on and attempting to investigate this question, I have to define what I mean by regime legitimacy. Regime legitimacy, as understood in this chapter, refers to the beliefs of a significant number of citizens in a political system that the institutionalized rules of the political structure are acceptable and meaningful in comparison with conceivable others. In this sense regime legitimacy goes beyond the performance of a particular incumbent government and its resulting popularity. Regime legitimacy in these terms is also compatible with what Easton (1975) calls diffuse regime support. This definition also implies that I am not differentiating between an input (efficacy) and an output (trust or performance) dimension (Gamson 1968). On the empirical level, then, the problem is to find an "operationalization" of the concept that is as independent as possible from the notion of government popularity (authority or specific support, in Easton's terms).

This definition is certainly a minimalist one, but my intention is not to deepen the definitional or analytical aspects. Rather, the objective is to take some admittedly imperfect measurements of regime legitimacy in five Western democratic nations[2] and use them to derive parameters for a formal political model that has been constructed to analyze alternative long-term future developments in the area of political stability. This model was designed to meet the needs of the GLOBUS Project, an attempt to construct a global simulation model for twenty-five major countries of the world. The model is concerned with the long-run future (i.e., thirty years from now) in domestic and foreign economic and political arenas.[3]

On the domestic political side this emphasis implies that the reelection chances of particular incumbent governments are less relevant for the model than the future development of regime legitimacy. But repeated bad performance of various incumbent governments may have a cumulative impact. The models could be seen as politico-economic models that have been adapted to simulate the long-term implications of short-run developments.

It has been argued that regime legitimacy goes beyond the concept of government popularity. Nevertheless, legitimacy is gained or lost through the performance of political elites, especially incumbent ones. Depending on political institutions, party systems, and political culture, ongoing persistent dissatisfaction or frequent disappointment with incumbent governments more or less independent of their ideological composition will erode regime legitimacy. The belief of citizens in democratic institutions and procedures is treated as a stock that can be augmented or depleted by government performance. The lag in the process can be very long and may vary from country to country. In general, the personal popularity of a president or chancellor over a relatively short period (e.g., two years) will contribute fewer positive flows to the stock of regime legitimacy than an economic crisis over a long period (e.g., eight to ten years) under different governments will generate negative flows. The net effect is a decline in regime legitimacy. Government popularity is included in the politico-economic modeling literature either as election results (Kramer 1971) or as the results of a survey question asking whether the voter approves/is satisfied or not with the performance of a government or its chief representative.

Some additional remarks on the structural properties of the model are necessary. A political system is represented in several layers: a governmental level, which deals with government policies, their impact on society and the economy, and the reaction of citizens to government performance; a regime layer, which tries to capture changes in regime legitimacy on the basis of long-term and accumulated government performance;[4] and a so-called polity level, which tries to represent the support for the nation-state of the national political community.

This chapter is not a technical report on the modeling exercise (that is presented in Widmaier 1982, 1984), and therefore I will not go into details of the structure of equations and estimation procedures. It must suffice to say that the changes in the level of government popularity (specific or authority support in Easton's terms) have been econometrically estimated on the basis of quarterly data of socioeconomic indicators for the years 1960–1980 and an election cycle variable. It is important to note that it is not the reported current values of the socioeconomic indicators that are used. Instead, the model employs a continuously adapting expectation mechanism. The difference between what there is (say 5 percent unemployment) and what people expect there to be (e.g., 3 percent) is utilized in the simulation as well as in the estimation routines.

It is assumed that the existing popularity deficit of an incumbent government on election day constitutes the initial lead of the newly elected government. If afterward "objective" conditions do not change, this initial lead will continuously decline with a speed given by a decay parameter (for details of this concept see Hibbs 1982, Widmaier 1984). The parameters generated via the estimation procedure are used for the simulation of the model. The relationship between government popularity and diffuse regime support is less rigorously empirically based. Technically speaking, changes in the stock of regime legitimacy are caused by a continuously lagged and weighted influence of changes in government popularity. The weighting system is dynamic and based on the government popularity surplus or deficit (relative to the country-specific majority margin). The parameters are chosen to reproduce historical patterns as indicated by the survey data. The polity level changes very slowly as a result of developments on the regime level. More important, the existence of large separatist movements or big ethnic minorities in opposition to the nation-state affects the regime and government levels negatively (i.e., increases their depreciation factor).

THE MEASUREMENT OF REGIME LEGITIMACY (1970–1983)

Conceptually and methodologically more difficult (because based on limited quantitative information) is the modeling and empirical grounding of the determinants of changes in regime legitimacy. From a time series perspective, the choice among measurements is limited. For the European countries I decided to use the Eurobarometers[5] question, On the whole, are you very satisfied, fairly satisfied, not very satisfied, or not at all satisfied with the way democracy works? The data combining the two positive reply categories are shown in Table 4.1.

Even a short inspection of the data shows considerable differences among the four countries both in the level of satisfaction and in change over time. It is assumed that the question roughly captures the same political dimension in the four countries, i.e., there is no serious systematic measurement error.[6]

For the United States the most common indicator for regime legitimacy or diffuse regime support (Easton 1975) is the political trust scale developed by Robinson, Rusk, and Head (1968). There has been, however, considerable debate about the validity of the scale (Miller 1974, Citrin 1974), and recently Muller, Jukam, and Seligson (1982) have also questioned its validity and reliability. The thrust of the criticism is basically directed toward using expressions like "the people in Washington" or "the government" as a generalized institution. It is argued, and I tend to agree, that the scale is not independent of incumbent government performance, i.e., government popularity.[7] As a consequence, issues like Watergate, Vietnam, and Carter's foreign policy caused a drop in the positive reply categories from approximately 80 percent in the 1960s to 56 percent in 1970 and 38 percent in 1980. Based on the objections mentioned, I argue that the conclusion that regime support (or legitimacy) in the United States is rapidly eroding is premature or even wrong. This argument is clearly supported by more recent data that indicate a substantial resurgence of trust in government (for details see Citrin and Green [1985]). Unfortunately there is no comparable time series available for a better and more valid indicator, but we do have results for the support-alienation scale developed by Muller, Jukam, and Seligson (1982), which can serve as an anchor to rescale the trust scale values as reported by Abramson (1983). In 1978 the ratio between the political trust items and the support-alienation scale in terms of positive (i.e., support/trust) replies was 2.25 (90 percent versus 40 percent)—using a nonlinear transformation to weight low percentages of the political trust scale higher (100 percent = 1.0; 40 percent = 2.25; 1 percent = 10.0). Table 4.1 shows the resulting data for the United States, data I will be using for the modeling effort.

Theoretically and empirically there are two different aspects of the issue of regime legitimacy in a comparative and dynamic perspective: (1) the level of regime legitimacy at a given time and (2) the degree and direction of change over time. Therefore, we may empirically find political systems in which the level of regime legitimacy is low or high while the change over time is strong or weak. If we translate these two alternatives into a four-box figure, we can empirically locate the five countries into four cells (see Figure 4.1). Change in regime legitimacy can again take several forms. First, there may be basically a linear decline (or increase). Second, one may observe a strong or weak variation with the changes of government popularity. Third, downswings may be stronger/weaker than upswings but with both more or less dependent on government popularity. Almost all of these patterns exist for the five countries studied.

For the United States our rescaled political trust values show no variation of regime legitimacy with government popularity. On the other hand, we observe a moderate secular decline over the last ten years, which reflects the negative trend in the political trust measure. The data for the United Kingdom indicate strong movements on the regime level with particularly high values in 1977 and 1982. The latter can be at least partially explained by the Falklands/Malvinas War. In 1977 government popularity (Labour) was relatively high, probably because the Callaghan government had some success in its battle against inflation (inflation dropped below 10 percent). In other words, we observe variation of the regime legitimacy measure with government popularity.

In France regime legitimacy also displays considerable changes over time, but contrary to the British case the peaks can be "explained" by presidential elections, which tend to mobilize citizens politically and thereby generate a feeling of political influence and control. No negative trend can be observed. In the FRG, however, we find a negative development over time with some recoveries at times when federal elections take place (like in France). This phenomenon has also been recently observed by Berger, Gibowski, and Roth (1984), but their analysis, based on monthly data for the FRG, also shows that satisfaction with the political regime is viewed from a party preference perspective, i.e., in case the Christian Democratic Union (CDU) party wins, a CDU voter will see democracy and the political regime more positively. In that sense an upward push in regime legitimacy around election times reflects the positive feelings toward democratic rule by the "new majority."

In terms of regime legitimacy Italy is an outlier towards the low end of the spectrum. Over the whole observation period only around 18–20 percent of the Italian electorate was very or fairly satisfied with the way democracy works in their country. This low figure means that more Italian citizens are satisfied with the performance of a particular incumbent government than with the democratic procedures and rules under which the government operates. Furthermore, the low percentage figure is very stable over time with no indication of further decline, which indicates a stable and almost cynical attitude of the majority of Italians toward their political regime.

Assuming for the moment that the data on regime legitimacy measure roughly the same dimension across the five countries, how can the differences both in level and in changes over time be explained? In this chapter, it is not possible to extensively treat the country-specific structures and issues that could account for the observed variations. Nevertheless, some comparative and country-specific explanations should be offered.

The fact that regime legitimacy in the United States is relatively high and only moderately declining has its roots in the traditional positive and almost religious feelings of U.S. citizens toward their political tradition, which is characterized by an anticolonial war leading to a democratic and constitutional political system. The institutionalization of human and civil rights has especially shaped the attitudes of Americans in this respect. The belief in the nation and its basic constitutional principles seems to be dissociated from any performance of incumbent presidents. Nevertheless the cumulation of political failures and scandals during the last generation caused a decline of regime legitimacy, which can—under certain conditions—continue and even accelerate in the future. As pointed out earlier, I do not believe in the pessimistic outlook that the political trust scale results seem to suggest (those by Dennis 1981, e.g.). Based on my interpretation I assume a weak relationship between development of government popularity and regime legitimacy. In order to deplete the stock of legitimacy severely, persistent and strong negative trends in government popularity have to occur. (This argument will also serve as a basis when I derive parameters for the U.S. model.)

In West Germany, after the reconstruction of democracy, the constitutional order and the principles of democracy were subject to a "positive taboo" at least until the end of the 1960s. During the period of the student rebellion in 1968 the taboo was questioned for the first time. Democracy was no longer accepted just as a formal and legal mechanism to regulate the process of acquisition and loss of power in a society but was challenged on the basis of its substantive and actual allocation decisions.

Moreover, we know from Almond and Verba (1963) that Germans have a weak affective relation with their political system and are more output oriented. Despite some criticism and later findings (Conradt 1980, e.g.), this result seems to still be valid.[8] The economic crisis from 1973 onward, with its lower outputs, has probably contributed to a moderate erosion of regime legitimacy as measured by the Eurobarometer survey question. Dissatisfaction with the way democracy works can be voiced of course from opposite political perspectives: Some people may reject the regime because of its weakness in solving political problems (output dimension), others may criticize it because of its restricted political participation possibilities (input dimension). I do not differentiate between these two political ideologies here and assume that both have an equally damaging effect on the legitimacy of existing democratic institutions.

From a historical comparative perspective the Federal Republic may be much more prone than the United States to lose the legitimacy of its political system. This proposition is based on historical events and the assumption that the time span since 1948 has not been long enough to consolidate the legitimacy of a *legale Herrschaft* ("legal authority") (Weber 1956). Improvements in regime legitimacy must be accomplished via increasing support for the parties that form the incumbent governments, but the rising share of votes for the Green party is not pointing in that direction. The existing moderate election cycle of regime legitimacy is dominated by a moderate negative trend.[9]

The data for both France and the United Kingdom show similar characteristics. Regime legitimacy varies with political events and consequently with government popularity. But the time series correlations are weak ($<.2$), which indicates that the relationship is not systematic—i.e., that not all causes of rising and declining government popularity also have an impact on regime legitimacy. In France, more than in Germany, elections seem to have a positive effect on regime legitimacy. The fact that more French citizens have positive feelings toward democracy around presidential election times does generate a cyclical pattern of regime legitimacy instead of a negative trend.

At least for the United Kingdom this observable pattern is somewhat surprising. Given the long-standing British tradition of democratic institutions and their "dignified" character (Bagehot 1867), one would expect regime legitimacy to float way above the daily political debate and the current popularity of Her Majesty's government. This is obviously not the case. Only in times when the glory of the British Empire comes back temporarily does satisfaction with the way democracy works reach the 60 percent level among the British electorate. At other times it varies around 50 percent. Compared with France, the data do not indicate the presence of an electoral cycle as strongly. The variation in the percentages seems to be generated by political events rather than by changing political majorities, but in fact, the persisting economic crisis has heated up the distributional issues in Britain. Therefore, one could infer that the middle classes and the working-class voters have different perceptions about the functioning of democracy depending on whether a Labour or a Conservative government is in power. Since I am not in a position to foresee "positive" exogenous shocks to British democracy (like the Falklands/Malvinas War), I have to rely in the modeling exercise on the existence of an electoral cycle with a moderately strong connection to government popularity.

Before finally discussing the simulation results, some remarks on the Italian situation should be made. As stated above, Italy has a stable but low measure of regime legitimacy. Neither political events nor elections have an observable impact on the measure. The latter, of course, is quite understandable. Italian citizens do vote, but they are never replacing or forming a government via this act. The center and the center-left coalition, with some minor modifications in party composition, has stayed and most probably will remain in power. The only issue is whether the Communists participate in and/or tolerate the fragile but nevertheless persistent coalition government. In classical democratic theory such a situation is qualified as a damaging factor for democratic rule. In addition, Italy and its government have not been successful in improving the country's economic conditions and certain structural problems (north-south gap) in recent years. Contrary to this interpretation, which is based on official economic statistics, some analysts (among them Dogan in Chapter 7) have observed an "economic miracle" in Italy based partly on a booming underground or shadow economy. The political regime can hardly get full credit for that particular achievement, and economic success that is obviously much better realized outside the official and legal sphere does not help the legitimacy of the political system very much. In that sense, both phenomena can exist at the same time: an "underground economic miracle" and a low and stable level of regime legitimacy.

Another critical factor for Italy is the substantial income gap between blue-collar workers and professional, managerial, and high administrative employees. According to Frank Parkin, the average salaries of the latter are about seven times as high as those of the unskilled workers. This proportion compares to about five times in France, two and a half times in the United States, three and a half times in England, and only about two times in West Germany (Parkin 1971, 118).

The combination of these broad factors is, among other things (e.g., the existence of a strong Communist party), responsible for the very low percentages of satisfaction with the operation of Italian democracy. But the data also seem to support another hypothesis, which is reflected in the modeling effort: The further a level has been depleted, the less further depletion is likely to occur. In that sense one can reach stability on a low level. But whether such a low level of satisfaction and support will be sufficient for the regime to survive a major challenge or crisis is another question.

THE SIMULATION RESULTS
TO THE YEAR 2000

The results displayed in five of the figures in this section were generated via a simple experiment. I took the estimated/calibrated models and simulated them until the year 2000. The exogenous inputs to the models are given by time series data for several socioeconomic indicators (see Widmaier 1982). The model begins with 1970 values, and until 1983 the exogenous time series data were used. From 1983 to 2000 I assumed that unemployment would rise in all five countries from the 1983 level to 20 percent, maybe too pessimistic a hypothesis. All other indicators (prices, income, etc.) remained constant on their 1983 value (see Figure 4.2 for an example).[10]

Each of the five country figures shows three lines: one for government popularity, a second for regime legitimacy, and a third (of less interest here) for polity support. In all five cases, government popularity follows a more or less regular pattern after 1983. Given the sharp rise in unemployment and the fact that the other indicators remain constant, all incumbent governments lose their reelection. My goal, however, is not to predict the change of governments until the year 2000 (which would be a rather ambitious undertaking) but to explore the impact on regime legitimacy if such a negative development would occur.

I am trying to avoid a general discussion about the comparative validity of the operationalizations. Doing so does not mean that I am not aware of the problems involved in comparing nations on the basis of such relatively simple indicators. I prefer, however, to look more at the implied dynamics of the model and take the data as given.

Looking at the simulation results for Italy (Figure 4.3), it is interesting to realize what stability means in a dynamic modeling context. In a comparative perspective the very low level of regime legitimacy (i.e., satisfaction with democratic procedures) must be alarming, and consequently Italy should be a country in which democracy is or will be shortly in trouble (see Kaase, Chapter 3). In a dynamic perspective (i.e., changes over time) Italy appears to be the most stable of all the five countries. In a sense this fact indicates that socioeconomic and political conditions no longer matter. Legitimacy can only be lost when it is there. But once it is lost, its lack does not cause a collapse of the system. It is even difficult to argue that the system will be more prone to collapse than other systems with higher levels of legitimacy. Unless the widespread dissatisfaction is organized and channeled (which might be quite difficult because of the existing political apathy and cynicism) little will happen. Rapid changes within short time periods are probably more damaging than a continuous low level of legitimacy. Still, I do not predict for Italy a stable political future independent of what the Italian economy does. I am just trying to make the point that in Italy certain factors do not matter that much. This situation is reflected in the model parameters and consequently leads to the result shown in Figure 4.3.

On the model for the United States almost the opposite problem can be observed (see Figure 4.4). Given the estimated and/or calibrated model parameters, the U.S. support levels start very high (97 percent) and then take a deep dive. At the end of the 30-year simulation period the percentage of the population supporting the regime has dropped to less than 60 percent. This decrease is caused by the fact that the small but continuous decline of the legitimacy variable between 1970 and 1980, despite some positive developments on the government popularity level, leads to a parameter constellation that weighs negative trends in presidential popularity higher than positive ones. This somewhat surprising result is of course dependent on the time series constructed for the United States. But the usage of the political trust scale results (Abramson 1983) would have made the situation even more dramatic.

For the Federal Republic of Germany, the simulation results, again surprisingly, do not look too bad (see Figure 4.5). Regime legitimacy does drop with a pause in the early eighties, from about 80 percent in 1970 to about 60 percent in the year 2000. Not surprisingly, the SPD-FDP coalition does continue because there is no endogenous process in the model that could predict the political reorientation of a coalition partner.

The results for France and the United Kingdom (see Figure 4.6 and 4.7) reflect clearly the more cyclical character of satisfaction with democracy in those countries. Nevertheless, the persistent negative developments in government popularity after 1983 (except for the positive shifts that result from the election mechanism) do cause a decline in regime legitimacy. The nonlinear pattern of government popularity reduction between election dates is generated by a nonlinear election cycle variable that operates with different weights in all five individual country models.

What has been accomplished by this analysis, what can be learned from the exercise? The purpose of the simulation work was to illustrate the long-term implications of current empirical trends and relationships with the help of a formalized computer model. I have been able to demonstrate that under certain conditions (rise of unemployment to 20 percent from

1983 to the year 2000 with other indicators remaining constant on their 1983 values), regime legitimacy will decline in all of the five countries under study. In some it will decline more rapidly than in others. A 20 percent unemployment rate may look rather high from a 1984 perspective, but 10 percent unemployment rates were considered to be impossible not too long ago.

Admittedly the socioeconomic scenario is not too sophisticated, but a complex one would have been much more difficult to present and the results due to counteracting influences would have been less easy to interpret. Increases in unemployment plus a stagnation in household incomes (i.e., wages and salaries plus welfare benefits) will generate more severe distributional conflicts in the nations under study. In that sense these variables are indicators of a widespread dissatisfaction among different groups in society.

We know, of course, that presumably such a socioeconomic future will not occur, but the results nevertheless demonstrate a potentially dangerous development in democratic political systems if future government performance is poor—be it in fighting unemployment or be it in solving other pressing issues. Government policies do affect the legitimacy of the political regime. In some countries the erosion of regime legitimacy has already taken place (Italy), in some it may accelerate in the future (U.S., FRG). This erosion may also imply a loss of governmental stability. Minority or weak coalition governments may emerge as the dominant type, a situation that would change the character of party government and democracy in these countries. Democracy as a form of government cannot survive just as a purely formal mechanism.[11] The acutal allocation decisions must also yield positive outcomes for a significant number of people in a political community.

A POSSIBLE EXPLANATORY THEORY

Thus far, I have presented empirical information and simulation work showing that regime legitimacy has declined or under specific circumstances will decline in the sample of five countries and also that the differences in terms of both levels and changes over time are considerable. These variations have to be explained in terms of specific institutional and structural properties of the countries. In the process of describing the findings I have speculated about some of these factors. What is lacking, however, is a general theoretical argument that could explain the *common* reason of the observed phenomena. I would therefore like to conclude with an attempt to outline such a general explanation. It is obvious that such an informal theoretical approach goes far beyond what can be represented in a formalized model. It is, however, my firm conviction that informal theories are required to interpret the construction and the results of formal models. In this attempt to outline a general explanation of the observed phenomenon, I focus on the classic question of political sociology, namely, the relationship between social structure and political order, or, in other words, the kind and scope of interest articulation and organization and how these interests are aggregated into political decisions.

Following an initial phase of expansion, beginning at the end of the last century, the capitalistic economic order has activated social differentiation processes that have been further accelerated by technological impulses in the wake of two world wars. An indication of this development might be the number of new occupational designations. A variety of new professions has most certainly offset the gradual extinction of the blacksmith (who may yet survive), and moreover, occupational designations like farmer or agronomist tend to obscure the degree of division of labor within those professional categories. The increasing number of occupations and the descriptions of their respective activities are evidence of a vast social differentiation process. This process means that people increasingly have a growing diversity of interests, and all of them have an at least implicit—if not yet very articulate— belief in their right to consideration in the allocation of resources (resources in the broadest sense). An unequal distribution of wealth, property, and income can no longer be justified with reference to traditional social norms and values. Indeed the latter have been weakened considerably in the process of modernization, which emphasizes individualistic rather than collective values.

Processes of social differentiation are not restricted to the realms of labor and production. In fact, it is precisely in their secondary roles that people are increasingly subject to a differentiation of interests (e.g., as automobile drivers and as spare-time gardeners) because of the increase of available leisure time. If one interprets the term *division of labor* not merely as a differentiation of professional qualification but, more generally, as a phenomenon involving increasing fragmentation of previously integral units of activity with common normative regulations, then one detects a social mechanism that can turn division of labor into a political issue. The increasing divergence of interests leads not only to a quantitative expansion of differing and to a degree contradictory interests with respect to allocation but also to centrifugal tendencies in the association of individuals with social groups. Interests can no longer be articulated by traditional groups and organizations, and thus conflicts arise. The most successful strategy for coping with crises and conflicts is further social or institutional differentiation. In other words, newly evolved "groups" are forming internal regulations and corresponding modes of action.

This strategy for settling conflicts and crises, one that has led to an immense expansion of productive power in nations of the Western Hemisphere (cf. Max Weber's analysis of the institutional separation of state, city, and church during the Renaissance), does have its disadvantages. These are primarily owing to the fact that actions based on internal decision making of institutions and organizations have consequences for other units of the larger system. One may characterize these consequences as external costs charged to others, and very often externalities have the character of collective "bads" (e.g., pollution of the environment). One could argue that politics in modern societies has the function of protecting property rights and individual self-interest, of maximizing economic activity against internal and external attacks. Increasingly, however, politics is preoccupied with attempts to cope with external problems in order to maintain the support of the general public (including the media).

It is possible, however, that the existing institutions are ill suited to perform such a function. For some time now, one has been able to observe functional changes in the environment of parliamentary, executive, and judiciary bodies of all Western industrial nations without any adequate institutional differentiations actually taking place. In the Federal Republic of Germany, especially, there is little inclination to make structural changes in central institutions of the parliamentary democracy because of certain historical experiences. The organizational setup of governments does little to accommodate this state of affairs. Basically, politics is still organized around the classic departments of the nineteenth century. In spite of—or rather because of—the inflation of bureaucracy around the offices of the presidents or chancellors, these political figures are often overburdened. They must direct their own bureaucracies, guarantee governmental decision-making ability in the case of a coalition government, and come to grips with their own parties, which have also responded to the increased differentiation of interests by increased fragmentation. In order to react to the complexity of social differentiation and the resulting externality problem with a reasonably "congenial" structure on the side of the political system, a whole series of coordinating, steering, and integrating committees has been created. A common characteristic is their minimal parliamentary control (Lehner and Schubert 1984).

Another problem is that in a society in which interests are increasingly organized, distributional conflicts cannot be fought out in a competitive, market-type way. That way would mean extremely severe, essentially destructive controversies among the groups involved (think of the anarchistic organizational battles in the early days of industrialization). Neither the state itself nor the groups involved find this method desirable. That is why organized interest group networks try to maintain a certain autonomy or monopoly, so as to be able to deal more effectively with such questions as membership and regulation.

For many of the same reasons, the state bureaucracy prefers to settle problems by negotiating with only a *few* groups. This method of operation has the advantage, among others, of making the issues manageable so that a negotiated compromise has a better chance of actually being put into effect. However, this method induces a segmentation of the relations between the state and the interest groups. Certain interaction systems screen themselves off from one another to avoid direct competition and high decision costs. As a consequence of this strategy, overall political consistency of decision is lost, and further externalities are created. In other words, the problem of political decisions, within the logic of organized group activities, lies in the fact that organized groups and government agencies negotiate and pursue their interests in partially autonomous subsystems. The results of this form of bargaining have an unanticipated impact on the entire system or on other groups. Complex systems become victims of their own strategy of encouraging differentiated, autonomous or semi-autonomous subunits in order to reduce the pressure of conflicts on the overall system. This result is the core of the so-called government overload problem and one explanation for the political inefficiency that damages the legitimacy of regimes.

The complex industrial nations of the Western Hemisphere seem to have outgrown the phase of steerability and to have entered a drifting stage. Steerability, in this connection, means the possible integration of differing interests and needs into political programs with a high degree of consistency and efficiency. Drifting is taken to mean a state in which the rationale for and motivation of political decisions are determined to a large degree by the need to compensate for unanticipated or latent effects that proceed from one or several other political decisions. This "logic" of political decision making has increased in all Western countries, but it can hardly be sold to the political consumer as an attractive product.

The bureaucratic segmentation of politics caused by the factors outlined (and others) has logically paralleled the differentiation of interests in society and generated a substantial degree of inefficiency in the legitimacy and authoritative allocation of values (Easton 1953). The traditional integrative institutions of Western liberal democracies—parliaments, presidents, chancellors, prime ministers—are no longer in a position to integrate the pieces. Their political bases—the parties—are themselves subject to an increasing segmentation of political decision making. The formation of so-called distributional coalitions (Olson 1982) and their suggested impact on economic development could be taken as an example for a general "segmentation of politics" hypothesis.

The voter's political decision, in the stricter sense, consists of choosing among several candidates for a political office (Lipset 1960). The candidates are usually recruited, selected, and presented by the political parties, but the citizen only has a "real" choice if the candidates are not only personally diverse but also politically distinct in their perceived intentions and qualifications for solving individual, group-oriented problems and/or problems of general interest.

However, it appears to be a structural problem of party democracy that in spite of the specific foundations of the party system, differences among the party programs are minimized on the assumption of uni-modal (normally distributed) voter preferences (Downs 1968). The growing lack of differences in programs alone would not necessarily be a problem if politicians and parties would actually demonstrate different records on the solutions to particular problems. But as I have tried to show, political inefficiency in avoiding externalities joins forces with a lack of differences in political programs. Let it be understood that this situation need not imply the disappearance of political controversies. On the contrary, conflicts are waged vehemently on three levels:

- personal defamation of political opponents (personalizing politics)
- elevation of technical details to matters of principle (stylizing politics)
- mobilization of general ideologies as the supposed basis of one's own politics (symbolizing politics)

The last method is particularly well-suited for political confrontations since, as we know, general axiomatic principles can serve as a basis for just about any set of precepts (policies). Such ploys can readily be observed during election campaigns, and this ritualized form of political conflict is sure to gain even more ground in inverse proportion to the disappearance of differences in the capacities offered by political parties for a consensual solution of problems.

One should not exclude the fact that politicians may be very popular over a certain period. Indeed, I think that exactly this personalization of politics by public relations campaigns supports the argument. Thus, from the citizen's point of view, the trouble with voting decisions is not so much dissatisfaction with the political achievements of a specific government but a growing feeling, especially among younger citizens, that political personnel are simply and utterly superfluous.[12] The political elite and the institutional and organizational bases supporting it become expensive shows while political confrontations are seen as superfluous performance numbers that present ritualistic fights between equally incompetent opponents. Election results yield no direct indications (such as a growth of radical parties) of the fact that the legitimacy of political systems is being undermined, because inherent properties of the electoral system can exclude radicals and generate comfortable majorities in a legislative body for nonmajority parties.

From the perspective of the political consumer, political regimes (and not only governments) are experiencing a governing crisis: Convincing political conceptions have given way to the strategy of muddling through. The rise of ecological parties and regional movements in some political systems can be seen as a response to the failure of conventional politics to deal with externalities.

It should be noted, however, that the problem is not solely a governmental one. In a certain way the governmental failure to generate consistent, planned, and long-term political decision making—which is very often demanded by the public—is caused by the pursuit of rigid, self-interested, and egoistic activities by the citizens and their various associations. In other words, governments with less or greater talent suffer from the increasing and basic problem in modern societies: the growing gap between the provision of private or individual goods and those of a collective nature.[13]

The argument on the causes of decline of regime legitimacy in Western democratic political systems has neglected or even ignored alternative explanations. Especially I have not dealt with theories of value change (Inglehart 1977) or political alienation (Kaase 1980, Gamson 1968, Muller 1979). I do not want to imply, however, that these approaches are invalid or less relevant. In fact, they seem likely to work in the same direction, and riptide effects of their impacts on the basic pressures of growing differentiation, externalities, and aggregation failures are possible. I have just focused attention on the degenerating ability of political systems to incorporate increasingly differentiated and organized interests into reasonable and consistent decision making. This problem seems to me to be one important and often overlooked cause of declining regime legitimacy in the polities under study. Furthermore, theories on and hypotheses about alien-ation, political protest, and political trust or support describe or even explain the phenomena very well on the *individual* level but lack a causal link to the aggregate level, i.e., system performance. I have tried to supply that link.

To conclude, I should like return to the question raised at the beginning of the chapter: How can political regimes maintain legitimacy under the conditions of a modern society characterized by increased differentiation of organized and/or articulated interests? My tentative answer is, they cannot unless major institutional and constitutional reforms are implemented that enable political institutions to accommodate a broad spectrum of differentiated interests and to form political decisions based on a high degree of consensus. Such a consensus is defined by the lowest level of overall external costs.[14] Some smaller democracies may serve as a model.

One cannot expect perfect, conflict-free, or cost-free solutions. Almost certainly decision costs will increase. But unless the Western democratic industrial political systems make progress in the reform of their political institutions the future of regime legitimacy does not look very bright. Radical and simplifying political movements may increase and eventually endanger the democratic procedures. Some nations are institutionally and socially more prone than others to such a development, but a prediction as to where or when a collapse of a political regime will occur is beyond the scope of this chapter.

NOTES

1. In a similar way this question is also raised by Richard Rose in Chapter 8.

2. The five are the United States, United Kingdom, France, Federal Republic of Germany, and Italy. I deleted Canada and Japan from the OECD set of nations in GLOBUS, primarily for data-base reasons.

3. For details of this project see Stuart A. Bremer, *The GLOBUS Model: History, Structure, and Illustrative Results*, IICSR/Global Developments, Science Center Berlin, IIVG/dp 84-104 (Berlin, 1984).

4. Conceptually the regime layer also includes a social order layer that refers to basic property rights and relationships.

5. For further information see the Eurobarometer publications issued by the European Commission in Brussels since 1973.

6. This assumption is, of course, a rather heroic one. Given the substantial variance in political culture and history in these five nations we would expect different meanings for the term *democracy*.

7. For details see the comprehensive discussion in Muller, Jukam, and Seligson 1982.

8. The argument and the material presented by Conradt are not convincing. Despite the fact that the percentage of Germans who take pride in their governmental and political institutions has risen from 7 percent in 1959 to 31 percent in 1982, it is still considerably below the percentages for the United States (85) and the United Kingdom (46). In addition, the argument that in Germany satisfaction with democracy increased from 1967 (74 percent) to 1972 (90 percent) and 1976 (90 percent) is highly questionable because of the totally different phrasing of the question in 1967 compared with 1972 and 1976 (see Conradt 1980, 233–235).

9. This trend varies with age groups. It may even not exist in the older generation; on the other hand, it is more pronounced in the younger generation.

10. I chose this strategy instead of running the model together with an endogenized macroeconomic model (see Kirkpatrick and Widmaier 1984) to reduce the complexity of structure and results. In principal the results do not differ much for unemployment as the macroeconomic model also "predicts" around 20 percent unemployment for the five countries in the year 2000. The difference is that this time path evolves in a cyclical way. Other political macroeconomic indicators (inflation, welfare, real income, etc.) would, of course, not remain at their 1983 levels. Because of trade-offs in the model in the aggregate some compensation for the increasing unemployment rate might occur. It is precisely because of these effects that I prefer the simple scenario to the integrated model results.

11. A specific electoral system may generate comfortable parliamentary majorities (the relative majority vote in one-person districts).

12. Numerous survey studies show a clear and sharp division between the older generation and the eighteen–thirty-year-old section of the population with respect to these issues (see Berger, Gibowski, and Roth 1984).

13. These processes seem to reinforce each other. A rising importance of external side effects makes the aggregation of interests more difficult, and in turn an increasing failure of the political aggregation function leads to higher externalities.

14. The question of to whom this minimal level of external costs refers is interesting in itself. One may postulate a historical trend from a small strata of politically relevant figures to an enlarged bourgeois public to the entire mass society organized in a pluralistic/corporatist configuration of interest groups.

REFERENCES

Abramson, Paul R. 1983. *Political Attitudes in America: Formation and Change*. San Francisco: W. H. Freeman and Company.

Almond, Gabriel A., and Sidney Verba. 1963. *The Civic Culture*. Princeton: Princeton University Press.

Bagehot, Walter. 1867. *The English Constitution*. Ed. with Introduction by R.H.S. Crossman. 1963. Ithaca: Cornell University Press.

Barnes, Samuel H., Max Kaase, et al. 1979. *Political Action: Mass Participation in Five Western Democracies*. Beverly Hills, Calif.: Sage.

Berger, Manfred, Wolfgang G. Gibowski, and Dieter Roth. 1984. "Wie zufrieden sind die Deutschen mit ihrem Staat?" In *Liberal*, no. 1.

Citrin, Jack. 1974. "Comment: The Political Relevance of Trust in Government." *American Political Science Review* 68:973–988.

Citrin, Jack, and Philip G. Green. 1985. "Presidential Leadership and the Resurgence of Trust in Government." Paris: IPSA-Paper.

Conradt, David P. 1980. "Changing German Political Culture." In Gabriel A. Almond and Sidney Verba, eds., *The Civic Culture Revisited*, pp. 212–272. Boston: Little, Brown and Company.

Dennis, Jack. 1981. "Public Support for Congress." *Political Behavior* 3:319–350.

Downs, Anthony. 1968. *Ökonomische Theorie der Demokratie*. Tübingen: Mohr-Siebeck.

Easton, David. 1953. *The Political System*. New York: Knopf.

————. 1975. "A Re-Assessment of the Concept of Political Support." *British Journal of Political Science* 5:435–457.

Gamson, William A. 1968. *Power and Discontent*. Homewood, Ill.: Dorsey Press.

Habermas, Jürgen. 1973. *Legitimationsprobleme im Spätkapitalismus*. Frankfurt am Main: Suhrkamp.

Hibbs, Douglas A. 1982. "The Dynamics of Political Support for American Presidents Among Occupational and Partisan Groups." *American Journal of Political Science* 26:2:312–332.

Inglehart, Ronald. 1977. *The Silent Revolution*. Princeton: Princeton University Press.

Kaase, Max. 1980. "The Crisis of Authority: Myth and Reality." In Richard Rose, ed., *Challenge to Governance*, pp. 175–193. Beverly Hills, Calif.: Sage.

Kirkpatrick, Grant H., and Ulrich Widmaier. 1984. "Linking Islands of Theory and Technique in Political Economy." In Michael D. Ward, ed., *Theories, Models, and Simulations in International Relations*, pp. 133–179. Boulder, Colo.: Westview Press.

Kramer, Gerald. 1971. "Short-Term Fluctuations in US-Voting Behavior, 1896–1964." *American Political Science Review* 65:131–143.

Lehner, Franz, and Klaus Schubert. 1984. "Party Government and the Political Control of Public Policy." *European Journal of Political Research* 12:131–146.

Lipset, Seymour Martin. 1960. *Political Man*. London: Mercury Books.

Lipset, Seymour Martin, and William Schneider. 1983. *The Confidence Gap: Business, Labor, and Government in the Public Mind*. New York: Free Press.

Miller, Arthur H. 1974. "Political Issues and Trust in Government: 1964–1974." *American Political Science Review* 68:951–972.

Muller, Edward N. 1979. *Aggressive Political Participation*. Princeton: Princeton University Press.

Muller, Edward N., Thomas O. Jukam, and Mitchell A. Seligson. 1982. "Diffuse Political Support and Antisystem Political Behavior: A Comparative Analysis." *American Journal of Political Science* 26:240–264.

Offe, Claus. 1972. *Strukturprobleme des kapitalistischen Staates*. Frankfurt am Main: Suhrkamp.

Olson, Mancur. 1982. *The Rise and Decline of Nations*. New Haven: Yale University Press.

Parkin, Frank. 1971. *Class Inequality and Political Order*. New York: Praeger Publishers.

Robinson, John P., Jerolg G. Rusk, and Kendra B. Head. 1968. *Measures of Political Attitudes*. Ann Arbor, Mich.: Institute for Social Research.

Weber, Max. 1956. *Wirtschaft und Gesellschaft*. Cologne: Kiepenheuer and Witsch.

Widmaier, Ulrich. 1982. *Political Performance, Political Support, and Political Stability: The GLOBUS Framework.* IIVG/dp 82-108. Berlin: Science Center.

————. 1984. *Konstruktion, Simulation, und Schätzung kontinuierlicher dynamischer Modelle dargestellt am Beispiel eines polit-ökonomischen Makro-Modells.* IIVG/dp 84-105. Berlin: Science Center.

Table 4.1   Measures of Regime Legitimacy*

	U.S.	Britain	France	Germany	Italy
1970	97(56)**				
1971					
1972	96(54)				
1973					
1974	92(44)				
1975					
1976	91(42)	51	42	79	14
1977		62	49	78	19
1978	90(40)	51	40	77	19
1979		52	41	80	21
1980	89(38)	51	36	72	21
1981		48	53	70	20
1982		58	45	67	19
1983		53	44	74	20

Source: Eurobarometer publications and Muller,
       Jukam, and Seligson 1982.

*For figures with more than one data point the
yearly aggregates are unweighted averages.

**Figures in parentheses are the political trust
values reported by Abramson (1983).

Figure 4.1 Dynamics of Regime Legitimacy

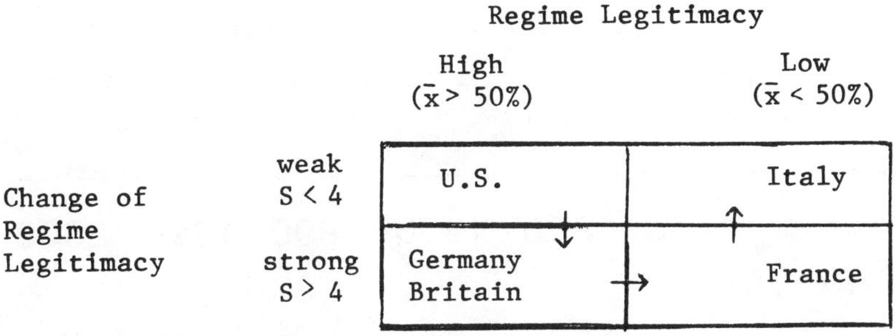

Note: The arrows across the cells indicate the hypothesized
direction of future development under the assumption that
current trends will continue.

Figure 4.2 Exogenous Indicators for the United States.

Figure 4.3 Support Levels for Italy.

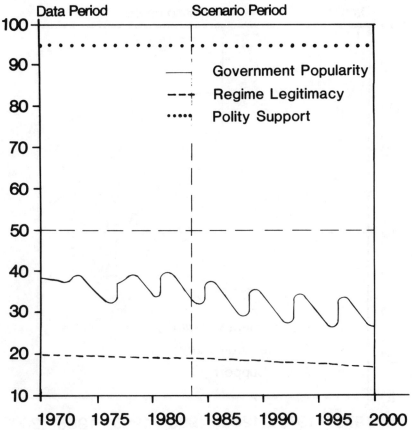

Figure 4.4 Support Levels for the United States.

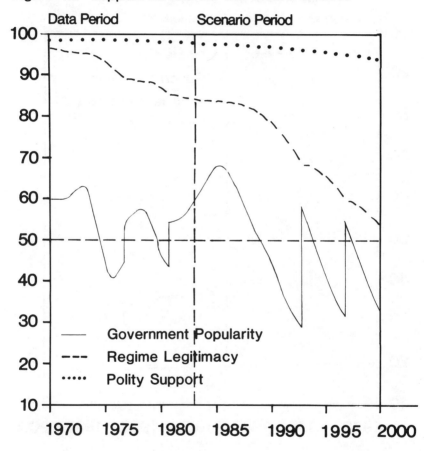

Figure 4.5 Support Levels for Germany.

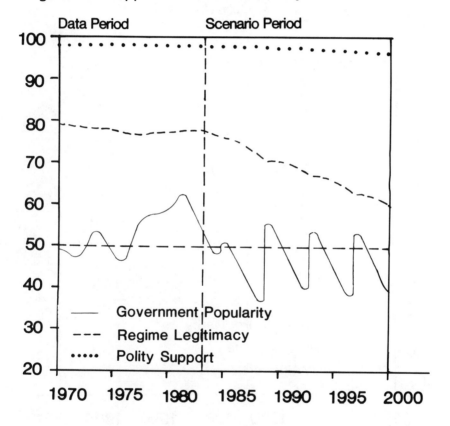

Figure 4.6 Support Levels for France.

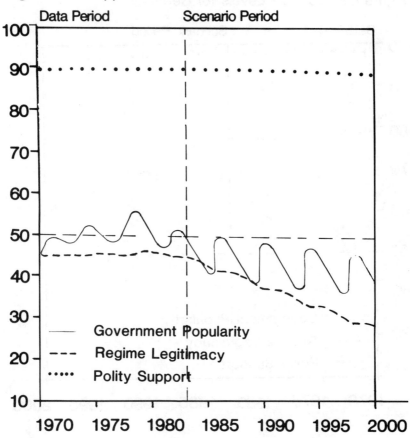

Figure 4.7 Support Levels for the United Kingdom.

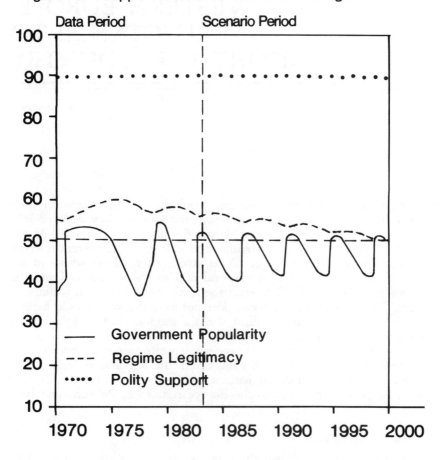

5
DEFEATISM IN WESTERN EUROPE: RELUCTANCE TO FIGHT FOR COUNTRY

Jean Stoetzel

Forty-three out of 100 West Europeans would be willing to fight for their country in case of another war. At least that is what they declared in a survey carried out in nine nations during the first month of 1981. At the same time 40 percent said they would not be willing, and 17 percent reserved their answers. When a mark of 100 is attributed to those who said no, 200 to those who gave no answer, and 300 to those who said yes, the resulting global score of 207 assesses the level of the European willingness to fight. This present-time response does not forejudge what would happen if a war actually broke out. Still, it sheds a good amount of light on the current psychological situation.

In five countries the average European score is surpassed, namely, and in decreasing order, Denmark, Britain, Spain, the Republic of Ireland, and the Netherlands. The remaining nations surveyed were France, the German Federal Republic (both close to the European average), Belgium, and Italy.

GENERAL ANALYSIS

All European answers clearly show two contrasting systems of attitudes among those who would fight versus those who would not. The attitudes of those who give no answer generally stand in between, thus legitimating, so to speak, the manner in which the scoring was carried out.

A typical example of attitude difference between the opposing groups is shown in the answers to the question, Apart from your family, in your opinion, is there anything that you would consider worth sacrificing everything for, even risking your life if necessary? Among those who said that they would fight, 42 percent answered yes and mentioned an average of 1.4 causes worthy of one's sacrifice. Among those who would not fight, only 26 percent found something worthy of their sacrifice (for 1.3 causes). It should be noticed that the difference (42 − 26 = 16) is approximately 60 percent of the smaller percentage (16 ÷ 26 = .60). This way of assessing the relative measure of a difference will be used systematically throughout this chapter.

A large difference of scores (40 percent) is found between the two groups, which is indicative of a better affect adjustment to the self, others, and the world among those who said they would fight for their country. On a very large number of attitude themes, as Table 5.1 indicates, those who said they would fight for their country responded more or less differently from those who would not fight. Compared to the latter, those who would fight actually declared a better state of health; they indicated a higher amount of control over the way their lives turn out; they were more satisfied with their lives, happier at the present time, more satisfied when comparing their situation as it had been five years previously; and they expected to be even more satisfied in another five years' time. They were more active during their leisure time, they felt lonely less frequently, and they also found life meaningless and thought of death less frequently.

In their relationship with others, the people who said they would fight belonged to more associations or organizations, and they believed more that people today are more willing to help each other than they were ten years previously, that most people can be trusted, that the young trust the old and the old the young, and that the Ten Commandments still apply today to most people. They were less reluctant to be with people whose ideas, beliefs, or values were different from their own, and they mentioned fewer types of people they would not like to have as neighbors (such as left-wing or right-wing extremists, heavy drinkers, unmarried mothers, people with a criminal record, people of a different race, immigrants). They shared more of their spouses' values concerning religion, moral standards, social attitudes, political views, and sexual attitudes. They seemed to enjoy a higher degree of leadership, and the judgment of their interviewers was that they were more sure of themselves.

In the political field, the people who would fight for their country declared a more rightist stance on the left-right political axis, allotted a higher priority to the goal of maintaining order in the nation, and had more confidence in the armed forces, the police, the parliament, and institutions in general. They were prouder of their nationality, they were more likely to consider freedom more important than equality, and they favored more free enterprise and a greater respect for authority. Conversely they found less excuse for fighting with the police or political assassination and gave less support to the notion (very much in the minority anyway) of a revolution to put an end to evils.

In the area of religion, it is possible to mention only larger sections of topics, but in nearly every section, those who would fight surpassed those who would not: For religious beliefs, the average difference was larger than 15 percent; in favorable judgments concerning the institution of religion itself, almost 10 percent. When religious needs were concerned—need to pray, finding God important for one's self—the differences were smaller (average of 5.4 percent). The same was true when the family was involved— actual sharing of religious attitudes with parents or partner, importance of same religious attitudes for a successful marriage, desirability of giving children a religious education.[1]

On topics related to the family, some differences in attitude and behavior are both material and significant. Those willing to fight are more likely to spend their leisure time with the family, they are much less likely to consider marriage an outdated institution, and they have a stricter notion of parents' duties toward their offspring—and vice versa. They are happier at home and more satisfied with their family life. However, on other topics, the differences are small, for instance, on the topic of the strictness of their own upbringing.

Interpreting such a cobweb of attitude responses with a willingness to fight on the one hand and an unwillingness on the other is a complicated task. In addition, the way the causality arrow is oriented, if there is indeed a real causality, is uncertain or at least disputable. Is it because one is satisfied with one's life that one declares oneself to be willing to fight for his or her country? Or is it rather because one is willing to fight that one is satisfied with life, at ease with the world, etc.? Moreover, is there not an interplay of intervening variables, such as sex and age, that bear upon both life satisfaction and a willingness to fight?

The causality arrow can include all the sociodemographic factors that were correlated with a willingness to fight, but the sociodemographic factor that most tightly correlates with such a willingness is actually, and quite normally, gender. The proportion of men who would fight for their country is nearly 30 percent higher than the proportion of men who would not. Another apparently weighty factor is the fact of living in a house rather than in an apartment. The difference in this case is almost 20 percent. Living in a rural area is much less influential, with an average difference of only 2.5 percent. Level of income should not be overlooked as that factor is connected everywhere (except in Italy) with a higher willingness to fight. So too, for whatever reason, the number of persons in the household.

But the most interesting factor to study for its bearing upon a willingness to fight is age. Not surprisingly, the mean age of the group of those who say they would not fight is higher than that of those who would fight. In Western Europe as a whole, the difference is three years, which is an excess of nearly 7 percent. But there is a great deal more to be learned from such an analysis because age is a quantitative and continuous variable.

The analysis is much concerned with the question, Since all variables, psychological or sociological, connected with the variation of the willingness to fight are also contingent upon age, is not the effectiveness of age hidden behind the apparent efficacy of these "factors"? To take a simple instance, life satisfaction decreases with age and so does the willingness to fight. Is not the observed fact that the willingness to fight decreases with life satisfaction simply a consequential effect of age increase?

Let us consider the connection between happiness and the willingness to fight. It was mentioned earlier that those willing to fight appeared to be happier than those who were unwilling. The score of happiness, which varies from 100 to 400, was found to be 317 for those willing and 299 for those unwilling, bringing about a difference of 6 percent in favor of the former. At the same time both the happy group and the willing group were younger. Is age responsible for the difference? The observed score of willingness to fight among the very happy is 222; the mean age of the very happy is 44 years. If this age is carried in the equation of the variations of willingness to fight by age, the expected score of willingness to fight is only 209, bringing about a positive difference of 5.8 percent, which is the measure of the "proper effect" of great happiness on the willingness to fight when the effect of age has been put aside. Similarly, the proper effect of being only "quite happy" is measured by a negative difference of 4.1 percent; for those who said they were not very happy or not at all happy, the difference is as large as minus 13.8 percent. There is no doubt that happiness has an effect of its own, independent from age, on the level of willingness to fight.

The analysis could even be carried a step further so that the variable that is associated with the willingness to fight could be expressed in steps that allow one to compute linear correlations. Under these conditions the differences between observed and expected scores of the willingness to fight increase proportionately to the successive grades of life satisfaction, political stance, and interest in politics; they decrease with increases in the feeling of loneliness and the feeling that life is meaningless.

To conclude, being willing or not willing to fight for one's country (or at least to say so to an interviewer) are not secluded attitudes (or answers). They are embedded in coherent and opposite systems of values connected with all sorts of psychological and sociodemographic attitudes and conditions. This conclusion can be ascertained, and it is even occasionally possible to derive mathematical models of these connections.

INTERNATIONAL COMPARISONS

The starting time of astonomy as a science was the day when Johannes Kepler found himself heir to Tycho Brahe's observation tables. The analyses found in the preceding pages were made possible by a store of some 200,000 data based on the responses of more than 12,000 residents of nine countries. In order to compare these nine nations on the basis of their citizens' willingness to fight, it is necessary to break down the whole of the data store into nine pieces. The number of the data to be analyzed will thus be multiplied by nine, but the statistical base for each country will be nine times less than for the European analysis, thus reducing the precision.

To take a clear instance, the high positive correlation between the score of willingness to fight and the successive steps of satisfaction with life that was found for Western Europe as a whole can be seen to prevail in each West European nation; the variation coefficient of the nine national correlation coefficients is indeed very small. One may thus say that in each West European nation, as in Western Europe as a whole, the willingness to fight increases proportionately to the satisfaction of life.

However the willingness to fight does not increase with the satisfaction of life at the same rate in every country. The rate of increase in the Federal Republic of Germany is four times what it is in Denmark. Reciprocally, the difference of the satisfaction index between those willing to fight and those unwilling to do so in West Germany exceeds by 3.65 times the differences observed in Denmark.

Where is the cause and where the effect, the available data do not show. But what may be expected to be common to the various European nations and what different are now clear enough. What they have in common is the process pattern of what is happening under the eyes of the observer. The differences lie in the parameters of the processes.

One of these parameters is the variation coefficient of the willingness to fight score according to the degrees of the variables associated with that score. In a way, the variation coefficient measures the sensitiveness of the willingness to fight score when submitted to the various degrees or steps of the associate variable. It has just been shown that the willingness to fight in West Germany is much more sensitive to life satisfaction than in Denmark—the variation coefficients are, respectively, 13.1 and 2.9.

On the other hand, the Danish willingness to fight is more sensitive to differences on the left-right political axis than is the West Germans'. In that case, the variation coefficient in Germany is 9.7; in Denmark, 12.7. It is thus possible to draft, on the basis of the national variation coefficients, a table of the sensitiveness of the willingness to fight in each country in relation to various associate variables, provided that these associate variables vary according to some objectively identifiable degrees or steps (see Table 5.2). It is then possible, by computing the European average of the national variation coefficients relative to a certain associate variable, to estimate the average potential of that associate variable upon the national dispositions to fight.

A comparison of the average potential of the different associate variables will readily detect the most influential. Of seven variables selected (because it was possible to calculate their correlations with the willingness to fight), the most influential is the political stance, the second is age, and the third is the self-estimated degree of religiousness. Satisfaction with life is fifth. But it is still more interesting, for the sake of international comparisons, to assess the sensitiveness of each of the European nations. West Germany stands out as the most sensitive, with an average variation coefficient of 9.3; next is France (7.8). The Belgians appear to be the least sensitive to the seven well-graduated associate variables (5.2).

When no graduation is available, it is still possible to measure the "effects" in the relationship between willingness to fight and the associate variable. The procedure consists of comparing the value (percentage or score) of the variable observed in the group of those willing to fight with the value among those who are unwilling. The magnitude of the effect is measured by the size of the difference, viz., the proportion by which one value exceeds the other.

Thus on a left-right scale, graduated from 100 to 1,000, the average political stance of those willing to fight is expressed by a mark of 562 while the mark of those unwilling is 487. Thus the former is 15 percent greater than the latter. Similarly, 44 percent of those who are willing to fight give priority to the goal of maintaining order in the nation among four possible goals while only 38 percent make the same choice among the unwilling. The difference now is 16 percent.

Armed with this tool, one is able to undertake both international and thematic comparisons. For instance, the average difference over eighteen political questions answered in France is 12.9 percent, a figure that is surpassed only in West Germany (14.8 percent). But a thematic analysis can also be rewarding. In the field of politics, the most discriminating topic is the confidence in the army. Among the West Europeans who declared themselves willing to fight for their country, the proportion of those who expressed a confidence in the army surpasses the proportion of the unwilling by more than one-fifth. The difference is especially large in the Federal Republic, Denmark, and France; it is especially small in Ireland. That fact does not mean that the Irish have no confidence in their army—quite the contrary. What the smallness of the Irish difference means is that their confidence in the army, be it high or low, is not influenced by the willingness to fight—and vice versa.

Three other political topics are also tightly connected with the willingness/ unwillingness to fight, namely, excusing rebellion (fighting with the police), priority given to maintaining order in the nation, and the location on the left-right political axis. In three countries—Denmark, Spain, and Belgium— those who do not want to fight excuse rebellion more than those who are willing by a high proportion, approximately one-third more.

Priority given to the maintenance of order largely contrasts those who would fight for their country against those who would not in Britain, Belgium, and West Germany. Moreover, maintaining order is the political topic for which the international variation is largest in its capacity to contrast the willing with the unwilling. Large as the variation is in the three just-mentioned countries, it is very small in Denmark and is even reversed in Ireland. Let it be remarked that this is not the only case in which the Irish show themselves at variance with people in the other nations when violence is implied. The Irish would-be fighters compared to the nonfighters excuse terrorism more by a large difference (15 percent), and although the difference is much smaller (4 percent), Ireland is the only country in which those willing to fight excuse political assassination more than the unwilling. Irish history offers the explanation.

Location on the left-right political scale has a significant international variation. This topic is nationally very discriminative in every nation except Ireland and Belgium. On the whole, the discrimination affected by political topics reaches an average value of 10 percent. This is the mean value of nine national averages, each of which is computed on the difference of attitudes between the would-be fighters and the nonfighters on eighteen political topics. The international variation of these nine national averages is measured by a variation coefficient of 43.7. In the same manner, one can compute eighteen topical averages for the attitude differences in the nine countries on each of these eighteen political topics. The arithmetic mean and the variation coefficient of those topical averages can then be computed. When all these calculations have been carried out, it appears that the variation of the topical averages is larger by one-third than the variation of the national averages.

In the area of religion, thirty-three questions have been considered in the analysis. The international variation of nine national averages is almost exactly twice the variation found in the political field, but the topical variation is of the same order of magnitude as in the field of politics. Consequently, the international variation may be said to surpass the inter-topical (or interthematic) variation by a long way in the field of religious matters.

It is in France that the religious attitudes of those who are willing to fight for their country are most disjoined from those of the nonwilling. The average difference reaches the high level of 30 percent, thirty times the average Irish difference. What sets the French apart from the Irish is not a larger difference in the importance of religion for the former than for the latter, or the reverse. It is the fact that attitudes in the matter of religion hardly influence the willingness or unwillingness to fight of the Irish but they greatly influence the French. Several meanings may be attached to the word *influence;* here it is used to state that a topic is associated with attitudes differences, large or small, between those who say they would fight for their country and those who say they would not.

It would be tedious to comment at length upon all the differences by topic and/or by country that are shown on the tables, but I would like to call the readers' attention to a few themes related to the field of personal psychology. Among the topics that are most influential, one finds on the one hand satisfaction with life, which is most influential in the Latin nations—France, Italy, and Spain. On the other hand, self-confidence, that is to say, more or less feeling "that one has complete free choice and control over the way one's life turns out," may also be considered as a rather influential topic in reference to the willingness to fight, especially in Italy. Last, it should be noted that the British are the people among whom the psychological themes entail the minimum effect.

Possibly as a matter of compensation, the British are among the most influenced in their great willingness to fight by sociodemographic factors, especially by the level of income. The level of income of the British who are willing to fight surpasses by nearly one-third the level of those who are not willing. Britain is also, together with the Netherlands and Denmark, a country in which the proportion of the homeowners among those willing to fight exceeds the proportion among those who would not fight for their country. It should also be mentioned that when the scores of a willingness to fight by occupation are computed and compared, Britain, Ireland, the Federal Republic, and Italy have among the highest variation coefficients. This is an opportunity to call the readers' attention to the levels of willingness to fight by occupation, but the sample numbers may be very small.

The most interesting sociodemographic variables are probably sex and age as they bring about large international variations. The variation coefficient of the percentage differences of the nine countries is 73 for sex, 67 for age. Table 5.3 shows the relative difference between the proportion of males and the proportion of females among those who say they would fight for their country. Table 5.4 shows the excess percent of the average age of those who would fight over the average age of those who would not.

These tables should be compared with Table 5.5, which shows the country scores of a willingness to fight. (Remember that a score of 300 was given to those saying they were willing to fight, 200 to those who reserved their answer, and 100 to those saying that they would not fight.) Is it now possible, at this stage of the analysis, to explain this table with the available data? Can one at least show some rationale for the ranking of the nine nations according to their willingness to fight? For the time being the answer is no.

It should first be observed that the correlations of the national willingness to fight with the figures in the two preceding tables are both negative and small ($r = -.21$ in both cases). People who think rationally might will surmise that when both genders are equally ready to fight for their country, the willingness to fight in that country is high. That theory is well supported by the cases of Denmark and possibly Spain, and conversely by West Germany, but the ranks of Britain, Belgium, and France contradict the notion. Moreover, the minus sign of the correlation coefficient rather points to the opposite interpretation. Turning to Table 5.4 and now taking advantage of the same minus sign, it could be thought likely that the smaller the age difference between would-be fighters and nonfighters, the higher the level of willingness to fight. The cases of Denmark, Britain, and Italy would bear out the idea, but what about France and Ireland? The smallness of the correlation coefficient is a warning that no general connection is to be found.

Looking beyond sex and age for an explanation of the international variations in the scores of willingness to fight, one might remember that in a majority of the countries and also in Western Europe taken as a whole, the affect balance scores are much higher for people who are willing to fight for their country. Is there a hope, however faint, of finding a way to a psychological explanation? The answer is no. However surprising it may be, the correlation of the national scores of a willingness to fight with the national differences in the affect balance scores between the prospective fighters and nonfighters is practically nil (0.08).

Within the limits of a reduced ambition, a comparison between the countries in which the willingness to fight exceeds the European average and those that are below the average may yield some results. Five countries belong to the first group—Denmark, Britain, Spain, Ireland, and the Netherlands. Their average willingness score is 225. The others—France, West Germany, Belgium, and Italy—have a mean score of 184. The difference is large. One rather interesting fact stands out when one compares the two groups of countries. In the countries in which the willingness to fight is higher, sensitivity as defined earlier seems to be connected mostly with socioeconomic conditions, namely, homeownership and level of income. By contrast, the citizens of the countries in which the willingness to fight is lower, appear to be mostly sensitive to nonmaterialistic values—i.e., political and religious ones. In spite of many very obvious national exceptions, the contrasts in the averages are indeed unambiguous and may well provide some food for thought.

NOTES

1. It should be noted that the relative smallness of the average European differences concerning religion (5.6 percent) is partly due to an extreme variation in the international differences. For instance, the variation coefficient of Pearson ($v = 100\sigma : \bar{x}$, where σ is the standard deviation and $\bar{x}$ the arithmetic mean) is 296 in the case of the desirability of religious education, and from nation to nation the variation of the differences on this topic between those who would fight and those who would not is very large. By contrast, the variation in the intranational average differences is much smaller: $v = 89$ is the variation coefficient of the national means of the differences on thirty-three religious questions taken together. The average difference on the observance of the Ten Commandments is still smaller (2.6 percent), and when it comes to evaluating the average difference in church attendance between those who would fight and those who would not, the result is a negative (-1.3 percent), and there is a large variation between national average differences (168).

Table 5.1   Percent of Difference of Attitude or Condition Between Those Who Would Fight and Those Who Would Not

	Europe	Belgium	Denmark	Spain	France	Great Britain	Ireland	Italy	Netherlands	West Germany
Declared state of health	7.9	3.1	9.4	9.0	4.5	6.5	5.0	6.3	5.7	8.3
Self-confidence (control over life)	8.1	3.5	6.6	4.5	6.2	1.5	2.3	11.4	4.5	4.6
Satisfied with life	8.1	5.4	1.7	10.5	7.1	1.8	4.7	10.0	4.8	6.2
Happiness	6.0	1.2	2.2	8.1	3.6	2.1	5.2	4.6	2.5	3.8
Satisfied five years ago	3.8	2.8	1.3	6.2	2.9	-0.9	3.4	1.5	4.0	2.0
Will be satisfied in five years time	7.6	5.9	2.2	9.1	5.2	1.7	5.0	8.2	6.2	3.8
Active during leisure time	4.1	9.0	6.3	8.5	6.0	5.5	9.2	10.3	8.1	5.1
Feel lonely	-12.2	2.1	10.1	18.8	8.3	6.4	11.9	2.0	11.2	17.9
Life is meaningless	-7.0	6.8	12.7	9.5	10.3	7.8	3.3	2.1	8.6	11.9
Think about death	5.1	3.0	-2.0	4.7	5.2	2.0	11.5	3.7	2.9	6.8
Belong to associations or organizations	39.4	34.2	18.5	17.9	25.0	17.4	22.9	54.5	17.2	42.9
Most can be trusted	8.8	-4.5	-4.1	2.4	3.4	6.7	4.0	7.4	0.5	7.5
The young trust the old	9.3	0.9	5.0	4.5	4.1	8.7	5.8	4.3	6.6	8.5
The old trust the young	4.9	-1.4	5.9	2.7	6.0	4.2	-1.9	0.2	2.5	2.0
The Commandments still apply to most	3.8	6.7	2.6	2.9	4.7	0.4	0.6	5.0	5.3	4.5
Dislike people with different values	8.7	13.0	3.4	7.1	5.9	5.9	10.0	7.2	5.9	8.0
Would not like some as neighbors	1.3	8.5	0.0	9.7	3.3	-2.5	7.1	-5.2	-2.5	1.1
Agree with spouse's attitudes	9.2	9.8	8.7	7.8	10.2	8.8	-14.8	3.5	13.3	12.4
Have leadership	6.3	7.7	7.1	4.8	4.6	5.2	12.8	6.9	6.2	10.5
Appeared self-assured during interview	3.8	4.6	1.7	5.2	-0.9	0.9	6.2	5.4	0.0	7.9

Table 5.1 continued:

	Europe	Belgium	Denmark	Spain	France	Great Britain	Ireland	Italy	Netherlands	West Germany
Excuse divorce	-5.8	2.9	3.8	8.5	12.7	-0.4	-10.2	3.8	-1.5	6.5
Excuse abortion	-13.0	17.3	6.2	29.6	24.9	-6.9	3.6	8.0	-0.5	10.0
Excuse prostitution	-3.1	7.2	11.1	22.9	15.9	2.0	5.2	13.0	5.1	-1.7
Excuse keeping found money	-11.5	14.6	26.2	22.0	30.1	6.8	15.3	6.0	3.5	1.1
Excuse not reporting damaging car	-5.4	27.7	4.9	15.8	27.4	-7.3	2.0	-6.3	7.7	20.9
Excuse political assassination	-7.4	3.2	15.6	27.5	30.1	5.7	-4.3	6.6	12.4	10.9
Excuse killing in self-defense	7.2	7.4	1.5	0.0	3.7	13.9	14.7	1.9	9.6	13.1
Prefer traditional virtues	1.9	3.0	0.0	10.9	13.7	-5.2	3.1	7.4	-0.3	0.7
Prefer new virtues	-1.5	-6.6	-2.7	-6.2	14.9	0.7	4.0	5.8	4.1	5.0
Prefer obedience	12.5	15.4	50.0	10.7	11.8	-11.1	3.0	19.2	13.6	-6.7
Prefer imagination	-27.3	50.0	44.4	21.7	200.0	18.2	66.7	-12.5	20.0	45.5
Prefer independence	-25.0	5.0	-3.7	21.7	90.0	18.2	11.1	36.8	24.0	9.3
Spend leisure time with family	18.6	-3.9	30.2	14.3	28.6	15.9	10.5	8.8	8.3	-2.0
Marriage is not outdated	14.3	5.3	16.4	13.6	22.0	7.5	8.8	11.4	10.7	8.1
Parents have duties to children	13.1	-1.6	6.7	17.4	11.4	7.2	-2.6	14.5	0.0	9.1
Children have duties to parents	6.3	5.6	23.3	22.2	16.9	11.3	2.7	7.8	10.5	6.4
Happy at home	6.9	2.9	4.0	7.6	2.0	3.0	3.3	4.9	3.8	7.1
Satisfied with home life	6.5	5.7	3.3	9.2	4.5	1.0	4.0	4.7	4.5	6.4
During childhood own parents were strict	1.7	0.3	2.9	-2.2	7.4	1.3	-0.7	2.7	2.0	-3.7
Male proportion of those who would fight	27.9	23.4	0.0	18.2	6.4	26.2	42.9	31.1	19.6	69.4
Live in a house	19.6	3.6	26.9	-17.1	7.8	6.0	3.4	7.7	8.2	12.5
Rurality score	2.5	4.3	8.0	-1.9	6.3	8.5	0.5	3.7	4.5	2.6
Home owners	11.3	4.5	20.8	2.8	12.8	20.0	2.9	5.2	31.0	11.9
Number of persons in the home	10.4	7.7	15.2	7.9	10.7	9.3	13.1	7.5	13.4	22.7
Income level	8.5	10.0	12.6	8.9	6.7	29.3	7.9	0.6	10.4	10.6

Table 5.1 continued:

	Europe	Belgium	Denmark	Spain	France	Great Britain	Ireland	Italy	Netherlands	West Germany
Location on political left-right scale	15.4	1.0	17.9	7.9	11.7	15.9	4.0	17.3	17.4	13.7
Priority to maintaining order	15.8	30.4	2.7	17.0	10.3	41.7	-12.8	16.3	8.1	24.4
Confidence in the armed forces	22.2	12.0	22.7	16.3	30.2	12.2	1.5	17.1	19.2	22.6
Confidence in the police	11.0	4.6	5.6	11.3	10.6	3.8	0.0	9.8	7.3	10.3
Confidence in the parliament	10.1	3.6	0.9	7.6	10.0	11.8	4.8	10.0	6.4	6.0
Confidence in the institutions overall	9.3	3.7	5.3	8.5	11.6	5.9	3.7	7.5	6.3	7.9
National pride	15.1	10.7	14.3	11.8	18.4	9.0	7.4	10.9	10.7	18.9
Prefer freedom to equality	9.2	-0.5	1.9	6.3	0.9	11.7	-2.4	1.5	6.0	8.9
Favor greater respect for authority	8.8	6.8	9.7	7.8	12.9	5.0	2.2	8.5	10.6	5.8
Favor free enterprise	5.7	-2.5	7.9	5.1	2.4	0.9	1.2	0.3	8.6	5.4
Excuse fighting with police	19.4	30.6	39.3	31.3	26.4	11.2	3.6	16.2	17.5	12.8
Excuse political assassination	7.4	3.2	14.7	27.5	30.1	5.7	-4.3	6.6	12.4	10.9
Excuse terrorism	5.3	4.2	3.9	6.5	8.1	-0.8	-14.8	0.7	-0.6	10.1
Favor revolution	3.9	3.8	-4.6	1.5	6.0	3.9	1.7	4.3	4.1	5.1
Religious beliefs	15.6	15.2	-0.9	15.0	50.7	-2.4	-0.2	18.3	32.2	2.6
Religious needs	5.4	16.9	8.4	17.0	40.4	-4.8	4.0	7.1	14.6	-1.4
Value the religious institutions	9.9	18.5	20.2	7.5	18.5	8.1	-1.7	15.1	23.4	9.4
Recommend religious education	0.0	40.0	12.5	4.5	55.5	-23.1	2.4	20.0	7.7	-37.7
The Commandments apply to them	2.6	4.1	4.8	5.3	14.7	3.0	1.8	2.1	5.1	2.4
Attend religious services	-1.3	13.8	25.7	12.4	50.4	-21.3	0.8	-2.0	16.7	4.0
Same religious values as parent/spouse	6.7	9.8	6.9	7.3	11.7	5.6	3.0	10.2	114	1.6

Table 5.2 Sensitiveness of the Willingness to Fight: Variation Coefficient
of the Willingness Score with Increasing Attitudes or Conditions

	Europe	Belgium	Denmark	Spain	France	Great Britain	Ireland	Italy	Netherlands	Germany
Political stance	8.6	3.2	12.7	5.3	13.5	12.7	3.0	9.6	13.0	9.7
Age	6.6	4.4	6.6	7.9	7.8	6.4	10.1	10.0	8.2	6.7
Religion self-judgment	8.2	6.2	4.7	9.4	11.9	4.8	12.8	4.3	4.9	8.4
Occupation	5.1	4.7	5.7	5.7	5.2	7.2	9.5	8.0	5.9	8.1
Life satisfaction	8.1	8.5	2.9	6.9	7.3	3.0	4.8	5.9	5.3	13.1
Political interest	5.2	6.2	8.1	1.5	4.9	3.5	7.6	7.8	5.7	10.8
Life is meaningless	10.0	2.9	6.0	3.8	4.3	2.7	2.3	2.7	5.0	8.4
Average	7.4	5.2	6.7	5.8	7.8	5.8	7.2	6.9	6.9	9.3

Source: European Values Study

Table 5.3 Willingness to Fight: Percentage
Difference Between Males and
Females

Federal Republic	69	Netherlands	20
Ireland	43	Spain	18
Italy	31	France	6
Great Britain	26	Denmark	0
Belgium	23		

Source: European Values Study

Table 5.4 Willingness to Fight: Percentage
Difference Between Age Groups

Ireland	17	Federal Republic	7
Netherlands	16	Great Britain	4
Italy	12	Denmark	3
Belgium	10	France	0.2
Spain	9		

Source: European Values Study

Table 5.5 Country Scores of Willingness to Fight

Denmark	237	France	196
Great Britain	235	Federal Republic	194
Spain	226	Belgium	176
Ireland	218	Italy	171
Netherlands	209	Arithmetic Mean	207

Source: European Values Study

6
BASIC VALUES: RELIGION, PATRIOTISM, AND EQUALITY

Frederick C. Turner

If values are seen as normative orientations, as underlying patterns of belief that change only slowly over time, then it becomes important for social scientists to evaluate and to understand the distinctive patterns of values that exist in the pluralist societies of our time. These patterns essentially define alternative political cultures, and the contrasts among them illustrate varied frameworks of belief in which political competition may flourish. Measuring values accurately is far more difficult than appears at first blush, and the difficulty of analysis increases substantially when the same survey questions are asked in nations with very different cultural contexts. Yet these efforts in analysis hold considerable promise. Substantively, they allow sharper distinctions to be made among the democracies of the 1980s. Methodologically, although they will not let us shape a single survey instrument that can work easily in all nations and cultures, the efforts of today can point to difficulties of past interpretations, outline specific issues for future research, and even delineate some of the best techniques through which to study those issues.

A series of crossnational studies of values carried out in the 1980s thus allows us to add an attitudinal dimension to work on comparative democratic structures that has recently been carried out on more institutional lines. In a thoughtful and extensive study of the twenty-one nations of the world that remained democratic from 1945 to 1980, for example, Arend Lijphart notes how vastly they differ one from the other in terms of population size and density, territorial extent, and societal homogeneity or heterogeneity.[1] When we analyze comparative survey research that has been conducted in these nations during the 1980s, we can add valuational contrasts to his list of differences and see that these democratic countries contain very different patterns of popular belief in God, pride in nation, and valuation of economic equality.

181

Furthermore, systematic comparisons of values among the pluralist democracies can also help us to clarify more general interpretations of political
causation, especially when they concentrate on one nation and have little
foundation in survey research. In the case of Britain, for instance, Gordon
Smith contends "that her modernity is of a very special kind—resting
precisely on the non-modernity of the total value system."[2] Assumptions
that traditional values survive in Britain are far harder to uphold in the
late 1980s than they were in the early 1970s, however, especially among
younger citizens for whom the old norms of deference and civility carry
far less weight than they did generations ago. Moreover, for the population
at large, British values are simply not "less modern" on the whole than
are the values of other citizens in the West. Before drawing out arguments
based on value premises, and especially before drawing hypotheses based
upon assumed value positions, we need to compare a broad range of values
among the pluralist democracies.

What values support democratic political systems, and how necessary is
uniformity in these values in order to provide such support? More specifically,
if democracy is seen as an institutional arrangement that protects civil
liberties and ensures the possibility for meaningful political participation
by all citizens, then what are the religious, patriotic, and egalitarian norms
that need to undergird this framework of institutions? How unified do
citizens need to be in their religious beliefs, their pride in country, and
their egalitarian sentiments? In each area, recent data point to diversity
rather than uniformity as the answer.

DIVERSITY IN VALUES: RELIGION

One of the most important efforts in crossnational survey research in the
1980s has been the Human Values Project conducted by Gallup International.
The study investigated fundamental values in Europe and the United States
in 1981 and 1982, and later many of the same questions were asked in
nations in Latin America, Asia, and Eastern Europe and even in one
community in the Soviet Union. A summary of the findings on religious
beliefs for various democracies appears in Table 6.1.

The most striking contrast comes between the United States and Japan,
with the former having the highest general level of religious belief and
Japan having the lowest, at least as measured in Western terms. Some 95
percent of citizens in the United States and in the Republic of Ireland
said that they believed in God, as opposed to only 39 percent in Japan.
Some two-thirds of the U.S. respondents said that they believed in hell,
but only 14 or 15 percent of the Japanese, the French, or the West Germans
did so.

Complex systems of belief lie behind these apparently simple, yes/no
questions, of course. A national survey in the United States conducted by
U.S. News & World Report in 1985, for example, found that although 90
percent of the respondents said that they believed in God, only 64 percent

declared belief in a personal God while some 26 percent believed—as did Thomas Jefferson and the early deists—in God as a governing force. In another area of complexity, the Gallup International data point to the French as being consistently more cynical in ethical matters than the Japanese, both in terms of behavior and attitudes, despite a higher nominal belief in God among the French. Thus only 5 percent of the French respondents agreed with the statement that "everyone is basically good" whereas 27 percent of the Japanese agreed with it. The Japanese percentage is virtually identical with the percentages in the Netherlands and West Germany and far more consistent with the general response in Western Europe than is the French.[3]

Despite the clarifications like this that need to be made in each country in order to determine more precisely what values and beliefs stand behind the data in Table 6.1, the data demonstrate conclusively that belief in God or in other elements of the Judeo-Christian religions of the West are not necessary for the maintenance of democracy. Japan has had a vibrant, pluralist system for four decades, despite having a very different religious tradition than that in the Western democracies and despite the fact that the form of Japan's democracy was largely imposed from the outside after World War II.[4] Table 6.1 also shows that the patterns of religious belief in the European democracies vary considerably, with Ireland the most and France the least like the United States. Historically, we can see that elements of traditional creeds can fall away among citizens in democracies, as, for example, in Catholic countries like Italy and Spain where today only a third of the people say that they believe in hell.

These data are not so surprising to Europeans as they must be to people who know only the environment of the United States. Europeans know from personal experience that religious belief is not a necessary cornerstone of democracy, but in the United States, the folk wisdom often points in the opposite direction. Coins in the United States still say, In God We Trust. Priests, ministers, and rabbis still give ceremonial invocations at the national conventions of the Democratic and the Republican parties every four years. In terms of the effects of religious belief on voting patterns, a Gallup survey in 1958 found that 75 percent of the people in the United States said that they would not vote for an atheist; by 1980, this percentage had fallen only to 53 percent.[5] About 42 percent of the U.S. respondents attend religious services at least once a week, as opposed to 11 percent in France and 3 percent in Denmark. The number and the electoral power of born-again Christians remain high in the United States, and fundamentalist preachers come via television into people's homes at every hour of the day and night.

Thus, in the United States, to admit publicly that one is "ungodly" is to go squarely against the accepted national norms. Here, as in other dimensions of the social sciences, we need repeatedly to ask how the nature of the data and the ways in which they are collected shape what the data tell us. In *The Spiral of Silence*, Elisabeth Noelle-Neumann writes that "the normal individual's fear of isolation sets the spiral of silence in motion."[6] That is, when we social scientists gather information on attitudes and values through survey research, our respondents are continually held back from giving completely truthful answers by their fear of social isolation—their fear in relation to the interviewer and to all of their "fellows" that a truthful answer would be too far out of line. We try, in a variety of artful ways, to take such response bias into account, but we are notably more successful with regard to some kinds of questions than to others. In the public articulation of fundamental values, especially, "acceptable" beliefs can be expected in the survey situation. This recognition does not mean that it is wrong to say that nine out of ten citizens in Ireland, or four out of ten citizens in Japan, believe in God. It does mean, however, that we need to integrate the concept of social acceptability into our interpretation of what belief in God means in the context of different nations, classes, and groups.

Even with such complexities of measurement, the differences among levels of religious commitment in the pluralist democracies are important because they correct universalistic approaches that treat these polities as though they were identical. Thus, for example, Robert L. Heilbroner writes very broadly about the "desacralization" of these capitalist societies, adding that in them, "science . . . becomes an ideology . . . fills a social requirement indistinguishable from religion."[7] The data in Table 6.1 demonstrate, however, that some capitalist societies remain traditionally religious but in others the religious values of the Judeo-Christian heritage have lost their mass appeal or never had it in the first place. Heilbroner is only half right when he writes that under capitalism, "ideas thrive but morality languishes," that there is an "absence of an organizing moral force."[8] Capitalist systems certainly permit, and in some sense thrive upon, cultural tolerance and a diversity of ideas, yet they do so in terms of religious and moral values. Crossnational comparisons reveal the variations in commitment that this tolerance allows, variations that citizens can express more openly and freely than can people in the more authoritarian states where "an organizing moral force" provides the official norms. Diversity in values is not only compatible with democratic structures, its free expression is the proof of pluralism, a self-renewing and even self-correcting manifestation of the essential tolerance of the democratic system.

A final point about religion derived from the Gallup study raises a cautionary flag in quite a different direction. Although genuine democracies tolerate a diversity of religious opinion and encourage participation by all citizens, pseudo- or limited democracies may manifest both religious belief and exclusionary political attitudes at the same time. Before and long after the Civil War in the United States, white preachers in the South regularly cited Scripture in an attempt to justify racial separation and the political exclusion of blacks. In South Africa today, as Table 6.2 demonstrates, nine out of ten Afrikaan-speaking whites say that they are religious. This proportion is far higher than for other South Africans, or even for citizens in the United States. And even though it is almost twice the proportion of French citizens who declare that they are religious, the French have achieved both a genuine democracy and a society that accepts racial differences—something that the majority of Afrikaan-speaking white South Africans stand steadfastly against. Today, as in the past, religious belief may be aligned with or against tolerance, pluralism, and democracy.

NATIONALISM AND NATIONAL PRIDE

As in the case of religious values, self-reported patriotism also varies greatly among the pluralist democracies in the 1980s. Table 6.3 reveals just how dramatic these contrasts are. It reflects the data collected by Gallup International, and the quality of the data have been confirmed by other surveys done at the same time.[9] Whereas eight out of ten U.S. respondents said that they were "very proud" to be Americans, only two out of ten West Germans made a similar statement. The values expressed in other countries range quite evenly between these two extremes. Patriotism appears to be high in Ireland and Great Britain but low in France and Japan. By implication, the data also relate to ways that citizens of one nation may think about those of another. A level of patriotism that in France or West Germany might seem to reflect a healthy skepticism toward the nation would seem, from a North American perspective, to mirror a level of pride that is "un-American."

These differences become somewhat more tangible when the issue is that of a willingness to fight for one's country. Once again, as seen in Table 6.4, the level of patriotism in the United States and Great Britain seems much stronger than in West Germany or Japan. Seven out of ten U.S. respondents said that they would fight for their country, whereas only two Japanese in ten made the same statement. Verbally at least, this question puts "pride in nation" to the test, and it turns out, crossnationally, that there is a strong correlation between taking pride in one's nation and being willing to fight for it.

In this context especially, it is important to link survey responses, where possible, with an understanding of how opinion may or may not establish limits to public policy in the democratic states. As Elisabeth Noelle-Neumann has written in her study of German nationalism, survey research offers "understanding and insight . . . for early diagnosis. For as a rule, opinions and attitudes change first and it is only then that changes in behavior occur."[10] In the 1982 Falklands/Malvinas War, for example, British opinion staunchly supported the prime minister's war policy, and a small minority of Britons was even willing to use nuclear weapons to defend the country's sovereignty over islands where only about 2,000 of her majesty's subjects lived.[11] If Argentine leaders had appropriately appraised British nationalism and Margaret Thatcher's combativeness, if they had appreciated how strongly British citizens would rally around her, then they might have used this "early diagnosis" to prevent a reckless invasion and its disastrous consequences. Analysis of underlying values at home and abroad may, then, be of very practical use to government policymakers.

Such analysis can also help us distinguish the different political cultures of the pluralist democracies and see ways in which the historical experiences of the various nations shape the values of their citizens today. To return to the most fundamental contrast on Table 6.3, that between the United States and West Germany, how except through historical experience can we explain such a vast difference in the levels of national pride? In the United States, as Everett C. Ladd emphasizes, a person's acceptance within the national community depends chiefly upon whether he or she adopts core elements of the national creed, and this acceptability, in turn, has facilitated both a powerful patriotism and an ease of ethnic incorporation, encouraging legitimacy and the durability of political institutions.[12] Until Vietnam, the United States had never lost a major war, so the military as well as the economic success of the country seemed to justify its special sense of mission. In contrast, Germany, like most of the other nations with low levels of patriotism in Table 6.3, lost World War II. It had also lost World War I, had undergone the hyperinflation and economic ruin of the 1920s, and had experienced the brutal dictatorship of the Hitler years. Intriguingly, German pride was higher at the end of World War II than it was decades later. It took time for what Noelle-Neumann calls "the syndrome of defeat" to sink in because, as she says, the media have provided the German people with an essentially negative image of their country since 1949.[13] Thus, crossnational comparisons of fundamental values such as patriotism do more than highlight existing contrasts among countries in the attitudes and values of their citizens. The comparisons also suggest how a national population interprets its collective past, a past whose images and subjective "reality," come down increasingly to the populace through the media.

In several of the pluralist democracies, the issue of historical allegiance has yet to be settled. In Catalonia, for example, citizens divide sharply in terms of their national identification. A 1979 survey found that 15 percent of them said that they were Catalan, 31 percent declared themselves as Spanish, and the largest group—some 43 percent—identified as "equally Spanish and Catalan."[14] As Table 6.5 suggests, there are significant differences between the city of Barcelona and the rest of Catalonia, but the sense of overlapping loyalties is great throughout the region, especially when compared to the Basque country where the sense of local identification is far stronger. These overlapping loyalties make divisiveness less intense in Catalonia than in the Basque country or in Northern Ireland, where the warring communities are divided in terms of religion and income as well as identification and historical animosity. National integration is certainly easiest when most citizens feel that they are members of the same nation, but when they do not, then the degrees and types of their sense of separation take on particular significance.

Even though many national communities have yet to be consolidated, it is still necessary to look to the value of internationalism as well. Some forces, such as the population explosion, that have encouraged the rise of nationalism may also give rise to more broadly internationalist sentiments.[15] Moreover, survey data suggest that the rise of nationalism may be necessary for the growth of political loyalties beyond the nation-state. As Ronald Inglehart writes: "In contemporary Europe, those who see things from a national perspective (rather than a more parochial one) have an increased potential for identifying with supra-national units. The two levels tend to function as one cosmopolitan communications network rather than as separate competing networks."[16]

Care must, of course, be taken so as not to assume prematurely that the era of nationalism is near its end. Because levels of patriotism are volatile over time in a country, it is dangerous to devise overarching interpretations that predict its demise. In the early 1970s in the United States, for example, when the Vietnam War was at its height, a sharp decline occurred among the proportion of young U.S. citizens who said that patriotism was an important value, and the decline was especially pronounced among college-educated youth.[17] In the 1980s, however, and especially by Ronald Reagan's second term, a "new" patriotism had appeared;[18] high proportions of young U.S. citizens supported the president and the Republican party, and there was a pronounced chauvinism in popular films. Just as scholars who study the nation-state have had grudgingly to admit its strengthening rather than its withering away in the late twentieth century,[19] so patriotism—the loyalty dimension of the nation-state's apparatus—remains strong as well. This fact is especially true in nations like the United States and Ireland (unlike West Germany and Japan) in which citizens have not seen destructive wars justified through nationalist appeals fought on their home territories. In the aftermath of World War II and the rise of the European Community, any lessening of old-fashioned nationalism in continental European countries should not lead us to expect a similar lessening in the United States, the Soviet Union, or the nations of the Third World. As strong reassertions of nationalism in Scotland, the Basque country, and Quebec demonstrate, loyalty patterns do not easily become uniform even decades or centuries after political communities are formed.

EQUALITY AND FREEDOM

Similar variations occur among and within nations as to the degree to which citizens value the equality of economic condition. Between two of the underlying values—freedom and equality—there is some structural conflict, so that it is revealing to compare adherence to these values among various nations. Logically, the freedom to exercise a voice politically and to enjoy civil liberties must coincide with some support for an equality of political participation, but political equity does not necessarily extend to the quality of economic condition. In order to achieve more egalitarian levels of income, governments may restrict the freedom with which the most privileged or most talented citizens acquire and keep wealth, and when the governments are electorally responsive, they must cater to the desires of the voters for greater equality or greater freedom even if there is some incompatibility between the two.

As Table 6.6 makes clear, pluralist nations in the 1980s do vary greatly in the degree to which their citizens support these two underlying values. The comparative survey by Gallup International nicely paired the two, asking the question in a balanced manner that did not require respondents entirely to negate one value while supporting the other. Respondents in Italy, West Germany, and Spain valued each to about the same degree, but in the United States the support for freedom over equality was overwhelming. The preference for equality in Britain rested nearly at the U.S. level while the degree of support for it in France and Japan was equidistant from the two extremes of Italy and the United States. From these data, gathered in the early 1980s, it is not surprising that voters chose Ronald Reagan and Margaret Thatcher and consistent to anticipate that backing for socialists or social democrats is stronger in France, West Germany, and Italy than it is in the Anglo-American countries. Of course, the reelections of Thatcher and Reagan in 1983 and 1984 depended even more on the proximate issues of the campaigns, such as the nature of the political opposition, the image that each chief executive had cultivated, and the Falklands/Malvinas War into which the British prime minister had just led her country, but the values evident in Table 6.6 form the backdrop against which the electoral contests of the 1980s have been staged.

The data on freedom are also rather striking. Agreement with freedom is vastly higher in Britain and the United States than in the other nations, the percentage of agreement being almost twice that in West Germany, Spain, and Japan. From a historical perspective, it is interesting to observe that the two nations with the highest agreement with freedom were on one side during World War II and three of the four nations with the lowest agreement fought on the other.[20]

These variations demonstrate just how disparate are the patterns of values underlying stable democratic systems, even in areas as sensitive as freedom and equality. When Robert A. Dahl notes that the Western democracies of our time contain levels of inequality that differ greatly, as he says, "in kind, in degree, and in their stability," he notes that the pluralism of interest groups may coincide with and even reinforce inequalities of income and power.[21] In such circumstances another reason why the inequalities are greater in some countries harks back to the patterns of citizens' values that stand behind them. These differences make it significant, where possible, to analyze who in a society favors equality over freedom, and vice versa, tracing the impact that these values have upon citizens and their participation in groups and in other forms of political activity.

A further benefit of analyzing these data among nations is that, even at this level, they indicate limitations to the vast generalizations that are frequently made. Verbal support for the norms of liberty and egalitarianism is so high that, understandably, many commentators assume that the two values necessarily go together. For instance, in the introduction to a volume on the challenges to constitutional democracy, E. A. Goerner writes that when radicals challenge democratic structures, they do so from an ethos "based on individual freedom and equality."[22] When we move from this level of abstraction to the more concrete issues of public attitudes, however, the data indicate considerable contradiction between dimensions of personal freedom and economic equality.

If we are going to be more precise about this contradiction, then issues of measurement become more important. In estimating the value that citizens place on economic redistribution, for example, a great deal depends on what survey questions are actually asked. As David Robertson recently observed for Britain, it depends on whether or not the questions touch "emotive symbols deeply rooted in the political culture."[23] He presents British data from 1979 showing that although only 45 percent of the voters were willing to say directly that wealth should be redistributed, some 84 percent said that it is fairly important or very important to spend more money on the National Health Service (NHS).[24] With parallel complexity, a 1984 survey conducted in England, Scotland, and Wales indicates that although 99 percent of the adult population believed that it is important for the NHS to continue to be available, 74 percent of the respondents also believed it important that private medical care should continue to be available as well.[25] Almost no one wanted to do away with the NHS, but there was also overwhelming backing for private health care—even though low-income respondents tended to feel that the rich got the best value from taxes through the NHS while high-income respondents conversely said that the poor received the greatest benefit.[26] As in other areas of survey research, therefore, it is necessary to specify concrete situations rather than to deal only with abstractions, to balance questions in terms of different points of view, and to prove for perceptions that are not obvious at all.

In pluralist political systems, it is logical that citizens should believe in the equality of economic as well as political opportunity, but there is no need for them to believe in equality of economic condition. Table 6.7 shows that this distinction exists in the Federal Republic of Germany. Eight out of ten West Germans uphold the value of equal opportunity, saying that all people should have an equal chance to make something of their lives. On this issue, there appear to be no major distinctions in response according to sex, age, or level of education. When it comes to equality of economic condition, however, only four out of ten uphold the principle, although the tendency for support here is considerably higher among those respondents with low educational backgrounds. Similarly, some 75 percent of the German sample rejects equal pay as unfair, although the people with the highest level of education are notably more likely to say that they accept the principle, which perhaps indicates a value system among some members of this group stressing verbal egalitarianism that comes from their higher levels of education.

DEGREES OF SATISFACTION

In trying to assess the results of democratic political processes, the most general issue to arise is whether democratic institutions can actually increase human satisfaction and happiness. Many people worldwide, like the civics textbooks, assume that the answer is yes—and in broad outline it probably is—but the issues are considerably more complex than they at first appear to be. The data in Table 6.8 indicate that citizens in the Western democracies and Japan are highly content with their lives, as well they might be since per capita income and personal freedom are considerably higher than for most citizens in other parts of the world. Yet even in this instance the results are culturally determined. When the "very happy" and the "quite happy" response categories are considered together, the Japanese pattern is not so different from the others, but the 15 percent of Japanese respondents who said they were "very happy" is strikingly lower than for most other nations. Japanese scholars looking at these data conclude that this response stems from the fact that younger Japanese are *not supposed* to be happy, that their culture defines satisfaction in life as coming sometime after the age of forty and after a life of hard work and struggle.[27] In the context of the survey, the mass of the younger Japanese respondents were not free in their own minds to report themselves as being "very happy," even if they were pleased with their progress in life. In other countries, such as Ireland, Britain, and the United States, it is far more acceptable to report oneself as being "very happy." Indeed, the expectation is that a great many people should be very happy, given their situations in life. Once again, the three nations that lost World War II appear distinctive and similar. Japan, West Germany, and Italy have the lowest proportions in Table 6.8 of citizens who say that they are very happy.

Thus, culturally oriented patterns of expectations both determined the ways in which people thought about their own happiness and also established the limits as to what degree of satisfaction the respondents felt comfortable in reporting in a national survey. As Sidney Verba emphasizes in his discussion of the difficulties and the possibilities of crossnational survey research, investigators must understand as far as possible the different cultural contexts in which identical questions are asked. The experience of Gallup International in Japan gives social scientists another way of dealing with the cultural problem, however—in addition to the ways Verba outlines, such as making the questions as precise as possible and allowing respondent self-definition as in the self-anchoring striving scale of Hadley Cantril.[28] Because of the very lack of "fit" in the context of Japanese culture, the Gallup questions drew forth a far better understanding of the cultural contrasts involved. Not only does this approach help us understand alternative values among specific nations at a more fundamental level, it also makes possible the selection of more finely tuned questions if the Gallup values study is replicated in the future.

From a political rather than a methodological vantage point, what do the degrees of satisfaction presented in Table 6.8 imply for the future of democratic structures? Is J. G. de Beus correct in his optimistic assumption that "the desire for real democracy is apparently in the end irresistible, as the fate of the dictatorships of Portugal, Spain and Greece . . . as well as events in Poland and Latin America has shown"?[29] Will the redemocratization of governments in southern Europe or in Central and South America during the 1970s and 1980s be able to continue given the internal pressure that those nations face? The verdict is by no means sure, but the satisfaction that citizens of the pluralist democracies manifest certainly militates in the direction of strengthening the open societies. To maintain them, the most important conditions may be success in economic policies, realistic rather than overly inflated expectations in the populace as a whole, and restraint on the part of the military establishment.

And what of happiness in the less open societies? The ideals of popular sovereignty and the responsiveness of leadership cadres win wide nominal support today, even in nations such as the German Democratic Republic in which the practice of competitive democracy remains tightly circumscribed. Those leaders who believe that a vanguard should lead the people gain popular support through the economic benefits that their systems provide as well as from a commitment to popular welfare that is usually far more than rhetorical. Democrats need to recognize that authoritarianism can win widespread approval and acceptance, not only within the top leadership but also among party members and the mass of citizens who consider themselves part of a national movement. As Milton Mayer points out in *They Thought They Were Free*, Nazi party members in small villages felt that the Nazi era had been the high point of their lives, even after the regime's defeat and the physical destruction of Germany.[30] If authoritarian systems can lead to considerable satisfaction, however, they surely curtail it for dissidents, for the naysayers, and for those citizens who are persecuted or ostracized because of religion, ethnicity, or income. Thus, it becomes necessary to look, not just at national averages, but at the locus of happiness and dissatisfaction within more limited and specific groupings of citizens. When survey researchers go from the comparatively open societies, in which dissent is tolerated and even encouraged, to the authoritarian states with their manufactured acquiescence, they can conduct surprisingly accurate research on sensitive issues,[31] but the methodological problems multiply in magnitude. In the future, our research needs include monographs on groups in which satisfaction appears lowest, more sensitivity to the sources of satisfaction that are acceptable in each culture or group, and the devising of questions that can accurately reflect true satisfaction levels in societies that are less tolerant of dissent.

CONCLUSIONS

The competitive democracies of our time differ dramatically in regard to some of the most basic values of their citizens—for example, their national patterns of religious belief, nationalist sentiment, and commitment to a wider equality of economic condition. These differences not only illustrate alternative political orientations, they also relate back to the distinctive historical experience of each nation-state and to the broader cultural norms of the citizens who live in each. The diversity of opinion and values both within and among the democracies signifies, in one sense, the healthiness of democratic systems, especially when seen in light of the generally high levels of citizen satisfaction that are also evident from the crossnational surveys of the 1980s. These patterns of attitudes suggest that Jean-François Revel is right in his criticism of de Tocqueville, in his rejection for our time of de Tocqueville's pessimistic fear that democracies could turn into "a mild dictatorship of public opinion, an age of homogeneous feelings, ideas, tastes, manners that enslave the citizenry, not to an external force, but to the omnipotence of their will toward consensus."[32]

Clearly, general consensus on political tolerance has not brought consensus in other areas, as the differences in underlying values among the democracies are far more striking than the similarities. Norms of tolerance coexist among the pluralist democracies despite very different levels of religious, nationalist, and egalitarian sentiments. The tolerance that is manifest in different democratic structures allows for considerable diversity within each country, and among countries, it demonstrates the adaptability of democratic constructs. Contemporary democracies do not require citizens to believe in a deity, to glorify the national past, or to favor an equality of economic condition. If national democracies, which guarantee all citizens civil liberties, are artifacts of the twentieth century, then their valuational adaptability and their popularity augur well for their survival—and perhaps even for their spreading—in the century to come.

NOTES

1. Arend Lijphart, *Democracies: Patterns of Majoritarian and Consensus Government in Twenty-one Countries* (New Haven: Yale University Press, 1984), p. 42. See also Arend Lijphart, *Democracy in Plural Societies: A Comparative Exploration* (New Haven: Yale University Press, 1977).

2. Gordon Smith, *Politics in Western Europe: A Comparative Analysis* (New York: Holmes and Meier, 1972), p. 40.

3. Elizabeth Hann Hastings and Philip K. Hastings, eds., *Index to International Public Opinion, 1982–1983* (Westport, Conn.: Greenwood Press, 1984), p. 530. On pp. 519–554, the Hastingses provide a detailed set of data from a Gallup International study of Japan and ten European countries. The question asked was, Some say that there is good and evil in everyone. Others say that everyone is basically good. Which point of view do you agree with?

4. There were, of course, political and cultural elements in Japan that were favorable to democracy long before 1945. As Nobutaka Ike points out, "The history of the democratic movement in the Meiji era shows conclusively that modernization was accompanied by the assertion that the masses of the people should have the right to bring the institutions of government under their control and thereby be able to run their own affairs" (Nobutaka Ike, *The Beginnings of Political Democracy in Japan* [Baltimore: Johns Hopkins Press, 1950], p. 217).

5. Harry Holloway and John George, *Public Opinion: Coalitions, Elites, and Masses,* 2d ed. (New York: St. Martin's Press, 1986), pp. 83–84.

6. Elisabeth Noelle-Neumann, *The Spiral of Silence: Public Opinion—Our Social Skin* (Chicago: University of Chicago Press, 1984), p. 40.

7. Robert L. Heilbroner, *The Nature and Logic of Capitalism* (New York: W. W. Norton, 1985), pp. 134–135.

8. Ibid., p. 140.

9. For example, in November 1981, the Roper organization asked the same question on national pride in 1,500 in-person interviews. The proportion of North Americans who said that they were "very proud" was 81 percent ("Private Initiatives and Public Values: A Survey Inquiry into the Attitudes of the American People" [Storrs, Conn.: Roper Center, 1981], p. 4).

10. Elisabeth Noelle-Neumann, "National Identity and Self-Esteem: On the Relationship Between Public and Private Virtues, Taking Germany as an Example" (Paper presented at the first panel of the Study Group on Comparative Public Opinion, World Congress of the International Political Science Association, Paris, France, July 1985), p. 5.

11. For an excellent analysis of British attitudes during the Falklands/Malvinas War, see Nancy J. Walker and Robert M. Worcester, "Nationalism in Britain" (Paper presented at the first panel of the Study Group on Comparative Public Opinion, World Congress of the International Political Science Association, Paris, France, July 1985).

12. Everett C. Ladd, "Examining the American Idea of Nation" (Paper presented at the second panel of the Study Group on Comparative Public Opinion, World Congress of the International Political Science Association, Paris, France, July 1985).

13. Noelle-Neumann, "National Identity and Self-Esteem," p. 7.

14. Juan J. Linz, "Identity and Politics in the Basque Country and Catalonia" (Unpublished paper, 1985), pp. 19–20.

15. See Frederick C. Turner, "The Implications of Demographic Change for Nationalism and Internationalism," *Journal of Politics* 27:1 (February 1965), pp. 87–108.

16. Ronald Inglehart, *The Silent Revolution: Changing Values and Poltiical Styles Among Western Publics* (Princeton: Princeton University Press, 1977), p. 337.

17. Ibid., p. 114.

18. For a detailed discussion of the rise of patriotism during the Reagan years, as measured through opinion polls, see Frederick C. Turner and Everett C. Ladd, "Nationalism and Political Leadership: The Resurgence of American Patriotism and Its Uses in the Reagan Era" (Paper presented at the Conference of the Study Group on Comparative Public Opinion, Maracaibo, Venezuela, June 1984). Together with other papers from the Maracaibo conference, a revised version of this study is scheduled to appear in the *Canadian Review of Studies in Nationalism.*

19. See John H. Herz, *The Nation State and the Crisis of World Politics: Essays on International Politics in the Twentieth Century* (New York: David McKay Company, 1976). Chapter 3 reprints Herz's much debated article on the "Rise and Demise of the Territorial State." In the Introduction and again in Chapter 8, however, Herz reflects on how and why the territorial state, rather than disappearing, has in some ways grown stronger in the late twentieth century.

20. National interests, of course, rather than public attitudes dictated the wartime coalitions, with the Soviet Union fighting alongside Britain and the United States, so that too much should not be made of the data on freedom in Table 6.6. Nevertheless, some three and a half decades after World War II, it is noteworthy

that a high percentage (19 percent) of West German citizens volunteered that they agreed with neither equality nor freedom. The next highest rejection of both values (15 percent) occurred in Japan, although the combined total of 31 percent for "neither" and "don't know" responses in the Japanese case suggests that the dichotomy between "equality" and "freedom" may not fit particularly well in the context of Japanese culture.

21. Robert A. Dahl, *Dilemmas of Pluralist Democracy: Autonomy vs. Control* (New Haven: Yale University Press, 1982), pp. 40, 75.

22. E. A. Goerner, ed., *Democracy in Crisis: New Challenges to Constitutional Democracy in the Atlantic Area* (Notre Dame, Ind.: University of Notre Dame Press, 1971), p. xiii.

23. David Robertson, "Adversary Politics, Public Opinion, and Electoral Cleavages," in Dennis Kavanagh and Gillian Peele, eds., *Comparative Government and Politics: Essays in Honour of S. E. Finer* (London: Heinemann, 1984), p. 223.

24. Ibid., pp. 222-223.

25. Peter Taylor-Gooby, "Pleasing Any of the People, Some of the Time: Perceptions of Redistribution and Attitudes to Welfare," *Government and Opposition* 20:3 (Summer 1985), p. 403. For the NHS, 93 percent of the respondents rated continuance "very important" and 6 percent rated it "fairly important"; 33 percent rated private medical care "very important" and 41 percent, "fairly important."

26. Ibid., pp. 401-402. Some 48 percent of low-income respondents said that the greatest benefits went to the rich, and 64 percent of the high-income respondents said that they went to the poor.

27. From discussions at the annual meeting of Gallup International in Baden, Austria, May 1982.

28. Sidney Verba, "The Uses of Survey Research in the Study of Comparative Politics: Issues and Strategies," in Stein Rokkan, Sidney Verba, Jean Viet, and Elina Almasy, *Comparative Survey Analysis* (The Hague: Mouton, 1969), p. 85.

29. J. G. de Beus, *Shall We Make the Year 2000? The Decisive Challenge to Western Civilization* (London: Sidgwick and Jackson, 1985), p. 156.

30. Milton Mayer, *They Thought They Were Free: The Germans, 1933-1945* (Chicago: University of Chicago Press, 1955).

31. See Brian H. Smith and Frederick C. Turner, "The Meaning of Survey Research in Authoritarian Regimes: Brazil and the Southern Cone of Latin America Since 1970," Chapter 37 in James W. Wilkie and Adam Perkal, eds., *Statistical Abstract of Latin America*, vol. 23 (Los Angeles: Latin American Center Publications, University of California, Los Angeles, 1984).

32. Jean-François Revel, *How Democracies Perish*, trans. by William Byron (New York: Harper and Row, 1983), p. 12.

Table 6.1 Religious Values (in percent)

	United States	Ireland	Spain	Italy	Great Britain	West Germany	France	Japan
Believe in God[a]	95	95	87	84	76	72	62	39
Are a religious person[b]	81	64	63	83	58	58	51	25
Believe in heaven[a]	84	83	50	41	57	31	27	20
Believe in life after death[a]	71	76	55	47	45	39	35	31
Believe in Hell[a]	67	54	34	31	27	14	15	15

[a] The question was, Which, if any, of the following do you believe in: God, life after death, heaven, hell?

[b] The question was, Independently of whether you go to church or not, would you say you are a religious person?

Source: A privately circulated report from Gallup International written by Gordon Heald in 1982 (Gordon Heald, Social Surveys, Ltd., 202 Finchley Road, London NW5 6BL, England).

Table 6.2 Self-Definition as a Religious Person (in percent)

	Afrikaan-speaking, white South Africans	United States	All South Africans	France
Citizens claiming to be religious	90	81	80	51

The question was, Independently of whether you go to church or not, would you say you are a religious person?

Source: A privately circulated report from Gallup International written by Gordon Heald in 1982.

Table 6.3 Pride in Nationality (in percent)

	United States	Ireland	Great Britain	Spain	Italy	France	Japan	West Germany
Very Proud	80	66	55	49	41	33	30	21
Quite Proud	16	25	31	34	39	43	32	38
Not Very Proud	2	5	8	8	8	8	28	18
Not At All Proud	1	1	3	4	4	9	3	11
Don't Know	2	3	3	5	5	7	7	12

The question was: How proud are you to be a citizen of [name of respondent's country]?

Source: A privately circulated report from Gallup International written by Gordon Heald in 1982.

Table 6.4 Willingness to Fight for One's Country (in percent)

	United States	Great Britain	Spain	Ireland	France	West Germany	Italy	Japan
Yes	71	62	53	49	42	35	28	22
No	20	27	27	31	46	41	57	40
Don't know	9	11	10	20	12	24	15	38

The question was: Of course, we all hope that there will not be another war, but if it were to come to that, would you be willing to fight for your country?

Source: A privately circulated report from Gallup International written by Gordon Heald in 1982.

Table 6.5 Patriotism and the Sense of Belonging in Spain,
1981 (in percent)

	All Spain	Basque Country and Navarre	Catalonia (except Barcelona)	City of Barcelona
Proud to be Spanish[a]	83	53	90	78
Belong first to:[b]				
Locality	40	70	39	26
Region	17	12	16	24
Country	34	10	38	42

[a]The question was, How proud are you to be Spanish?
The results reported here combine both the "very proud"
and the "fairly proud" response categories.

[b]The question was, To which of these geographical groups
would you say you belong first of all: the locality or
town where you live, the region where you live, the
country as a whole, Europe, the world as a whole?

Source: Charles S. Spencer, Jr., Basic Values in Spain:
The Underpinnings of Democracy (Washington, D.C.:
Office of Research, United States Information Agency,
1985), pp. 8, 24, 25. The data are from Gallup
International.

198

Table 6.6   The Values of Equality and Freedom,
1981-1982 (in percent)

	Italy	West Germany	Spain	Ireland	France	Japan	Great Britain	United States
Agree with equality	45	39	39	38	32	32	23	20
Agree with freedom	43	37	36	46	54	37	69	72
Neither (volunteered)	5	19	13	5	8	15	4	3
Don't know	7	5	12	11	7	16	4	5

The question was: Which of these statements comes
closest to your own opinion?
  (a) I find that both freedom and equality are
     important. But if I were to make up my mind
     for one or the other, I would consider personal
     freedom more important, that is, everyone can
     live in freedom and develop without hindrance.
  (b) Certainly both freedom and equality are
     important. But if I were to make up my mind
     for one of the two, I would consider equality
     more important, that is, that nobody is under-
     privileged and that social class differences
     are not so strong.

Source: Elizabeth Hann Hastings and Philip K.
Hastings, eds., Index to International Public Opinion,
1982-1983 (Westport, Conn.: Greenwood Press, 1984),
p. 604.

Table 6.7 Belief in the Equality of Opportunity and
          Condition, Federal Republic of Germany,
          1984 (percent)

Belief In	Total Sample	Low Education	Middle Education	High Education
Equality of Opportunity[a]	79	80	80	82
Equality of Condition[b]	43	50	34	34
Reject Equal Pay[c]	75	78	80	57

[a] The statement was, All people should have an equal
chance to make something of their lives. For this and
the other questions below, the percentages in the table
are for the respondents who agreed.

[b] The statement was, If all people in the Federal Republic
of Germany were at about the same level economically,
circumstances would be more just.

[c] The question was, There has to be different pay for
different work for the simple reason that not all
people are equally productive. Identical pay for all
is unfair.

Source: Elizabeth Hann Hastings and Philip K. Hastings,
eds., Index to International Public Opinion, 1983-1984
(Westport, Conn.: Greenwood Press, 1985), p. 482.

Table 6.8   Happiness in the Democracies (in percent)

	Ireland	Great Britain	United States	Spain	France	Japan	West Germany	Italy
Very happy	39	38	32	20	19	15	10	10
Quite happy	55	57	60	58	70	62	69	65
Not very happy	5	4	7	18	8	14	12	19
Not at all happy	0	0	1	2	1	1	1	4
Don't know	0	0	1	2	2	7	8	2

The question was: Taking all things together, would you say you are very happy, quite happy, not very happy, not at all happy?

Source: A privately circulated report from Gallup International written by Gordon Heald in 1982.

7
CRISIS OF
THE WELFARE STATE

Mattei Dogan

In the most advanced and richest countries, a crisis of the social security systems has developed independently, progressively, and simultaneously since the 1970s. The fact that this crisis has arisen independently in all these countries at about the same moment incites the comparatist to focus as much on the basic analogies as on the differences among the countries. It could be documented that certain decisions made in a few countries on social security matters were inspired by legislation adopted in neighboring countries, but even if "imitation" did play a role, the fact remains that in all of them we witness the same basic phenomenon. If the same phenomenon occurs so many times—even if we admit some political "contamination"—it obviously cannot be by historical accident but must arise from constant factors in each of the societies and from their combined effects.

A set of quantified indicators distinguishes these advanced countries from the rest of the 160 independent states. These indicators include high per capita incomes, a large number of physicians and hospital beds per 1,000 inhabitants, very low infant mortality rates, birthrates that are insufficient to reproduce the living generation, and considerable longevity. The concept of postindustrialization applies closely to these countries insofar as they are undergoing a process of deindustrialization in favor of tertiary economic activities, which is reflected in the slow but regular decline of the number of industrial workers in the overall work force. Quite obviously, the advanced countries must face and resolve problems of a very different nature than those of the developing countries. To people in the poorest countries the analysis of the dysfunction of social security in the most advanced nations must indeed indicate a topsy-turvy world. The richest countries are also pluralist democracies, in which a number of political forces compete at free periodic elections and conflicts are mediated through different institutions and political organizations.

These countries are further described as "welfare states." "Paternal state" would be better, but terminology does not matter. Even if the definition of this concept varies from writer to writer, one may say that fundamentally it designates the political recognition of certain social rights—"rights" being opposed to charity or relief. Among these social rights the most important are those to health care, old age pensions, and unemployment benefits. In this chapter I shall deal with the first two of these, while recognizing the importance of the third and without neglecting the significance attached, in certain countries, to child allowances or housing subsidies.

The linkage of the three notions of postindustrial society, pluralist democracy, and welfare state is not a haphazard one. There is only one country in the world that has been a pluralist democracy without interruption for more than a generation but is not a postindustrial society, and that country is India. There is only one that is postindustrial but does not possess pluralist democratic structures, the German Democratic Republic. If one considers a large number of countries, let us say about a hundred, a very significant statistical correlation appears between wealth, as measured by GNP per capita, and the proportion of the GNP set aside for social security. This relationship between the economic level of a nation and the proportion of national revenue redistributed for welfare purposes has been studied by several authors (Flora 1981, Aharoni 1981, Wilenski 1975). The fact that such countries have pursued the same direction for several decades and have adopted very similar social security systems calls for an interdisciplinary explanation that takes into account changes in family structures and roles, changes in the nature of work resulting from technological development, cultural changes, longer life spans, low birthrates, etc. This evolution has recently raised psychological and philosophical problems relating to attitudes toward incurable diseases, senility, euthanasia, and death.

I will consider fifteen Western countries—the United States and Canada and thirteen West European countries—but not Ireland, Portugal, and Greece, which, although Western, are not yet postindustrial. Japan is a rich postindustrial society and a pluralist democracy, but it is not western in the sense that it has a different historical background and it is only to a limited degree a welfare state. It is unnecessary here to trace the recent development of social security in Europe and the United States. Suffice it to say that the social security system, by a sort of dialectic, having resolved a number of the fundamental problems thrown up by industrial civilization, is, through its extraordinary expansion, generating certain major problems at about the same time in all the most advanced countries.

This analysis is centered on fundamental similarities to such an extent that I am sometimes impelled to speak of all these countries as if they were but one. Nevertheless, one must admit that significant differences do exist, such as those between Western European countries and the United States. Outlays for health, for example, were reimbursed in 1985 from public sources at the rate of 90 percent in the United Kingdom, 70 percent in France, but only 42 percent in the United States. Yet it is the Americans who are best insured against health risks, even if such insurance is largely private. Harold Wilenski notes that "the Welfare State is at once one of the great structural uniformities of modern society" and then asks "why rich countries having adopted similar health and welfare programs diverge so sharply in their levels of spending, organization and administration of services and benefits" (Wilensky 1975, 1). My question is the opposite: How did it come about that countries with such different party systems, social stratifications, ideologies, and traditions of social security institutions today face the same imperative: to cure the elephantiasis of the social security system and the perverse effects of its overdevelopment?

The social security crisis is threefold as it concerns spending for health, old age pensions, and unemployment benefits. The gravity of the crisis arises from cumulation, for the three components do not manifest themselves in succession but add up and feed into each other. Yet their maturity is not simultaneous, for health has already reached a level that many observers—to the right, at the center, and to the left of the political spectrum—consider intolerable yet spending for health continues to rise, absorbing an increasing share of national revenues. That is the first point I will discuss. Spending on old age pensions has increased steadily in all the countries considered, but for demographic reasons the situation has not yet reached its most critical point. The crisis is inevitable over the medium run—that is the second point to be discussed. The third area examined is unemployment, which has spread in all Western countries. Such massive unemployment results in part from the recent decline in the ability of countries to compete economically in international trade, a decline that in turn is linked to the social overhead costs of industrial production.

CHEATING DEATH: FOUR AGENTS
OF THE FINANCIAL CRISIS
OF SOCIAL SECURITY FOR HEALTH

Spending for health in the United States represented about 11 percent of the GNP in 1983, as much as in Sweden in the same year, and it was expected to rise to 15 percent within ten or fifteen years. In this context the dichotomy between capitalism and socialism is irrelevant. In the other Western European countries, the proportion of the GNP devoted to health expenses, both private and public, was a little lower, but it was expected to rise proportionally at a faster rate in the ensuing years. The social security budget in France is larger than the national budget. For every 100 francs that a French employee received in 1984, social security got 43–47 francs, and most of the money went for health expenses. If direct taxation is added, the French middle-class white-collar employees work from January 1 to June 15 for the state, and only for the rest of the year for themselves.

There is a widespread stereotyped belief that social security is a device to redistribute national income from the rich to the poor. In reality, so far as health care is concerned, it is much more a redistribution from healthy people to sick people across all social classes. The French minister of social

204   MATTEI DOGAN

security declared in 1983 that 70 percent of the social security budget was
spent on 10 percent of those insured, of all social classes. Some analysts
claim that for various sociological reasons, the rich spend more than the
poor. It is true that all insurance systems are based on the same principle:
The more than 90 percent of the people who insure against fire or automobile
accidents are paying for the 10 percent or so who will collect. As illness
is largely unpredictable, the philosophy of the social security system is
justified. But it should be recognized that it is mostly a transfer of resources
from the healthy to the sick rather than from the rich to the poor.

"Absolute levels of health expenditures are not in themselves as alarming
as the accelerated rate of growth in those expenditures. The annual rate
of increase between 1965 and 1981 was, in the United States, 12.8 percent.
. . . In 1980 and 1981 alone, national health expenditures rose 15.8 percent
and 15.1 percent, respectively. The nation's economy has not yet expanded
at an equivalent rate. The average annual percentage increase in the GNP
was only 7.5 percent for 1965-70, 10.2 percent for 1970-80 and only 8.9
percent for 1980" (Lohr and Marquis 1984, 13). The growth of public and
private spending for health in recent years has been too spectacular to be
attributed to one factor alone. I perceive four agents that are directly or
indirectly responsible for the financial crisis of health insurance. There is
no conspiracy among them but, rather, a convergence of interests. Before
considering each of these agents, it is essential to stress the financial
consequences of the technological advances in medicine.

Medical Technology

For generations, medicine was relatively inexpensive, or at least it appears
that it was so in retrospect—even penicillin and other antibiotics rapidly
became affordable by the poor. Expensive medication and forms of treatment
are a relatively recent phenomenon, and that fact has resulted in an ethical
problem that, curiously enough, is not sufficiently discussed in the literature
of medical sociology. When a critically ill person cannot be helped medically,
there is no ethical problem. But as soon as a technique is discovered that
could help such a person, a moral issue is raised as Judeo-Christian ethics
hold that life is precious, even for those who believe in paradise (and more
for those who don't).

Medical research has received the highest priority in scientific endowments
in the last third of a century in all Western countries except Switzerland.
Therefore, "the rate of development of new medical technology is greater
than it has been at any time in the past" declared the director of the U.S.
National Institutes of Health in 1984.

There is considerable questioning of the value of technological interventions
or of the desirability of further support for research and technological
development . . . many technological innovations are adopted in spite of high
costs and high risks to individual patients . . . because physicians have been
successful in maintaining a mystique of expertise. As a consequence, few
patients question either the cost or the efficiency of the procedures to which

they are subject . . . the nation, collectively, cannot provide the resources necessary to support all the technologies now available. [Aiken and Freeman 1980, 547–549]

When someone invents the artificial heart or the technique of coronary transplantation or the kidney dialysis machine, he or she becomes a scientific hero and receives the highest accolades and rewards. But between the scientific discovery and its widespread application is a gulf that must be filled, not by science, but by money. Society could easily supply funds for the most expensive surgical operations, but only for a limited number of persons. Who should decide who the privileged persons shall be (setting aside the very rich who can pay for themselves)? It is possible to provide artificial hearts for thousands of people, but not for millions. It may be essential for society to delay the death of a person who could make an important contribution, which is precisely what has been decided recently in Britain where kidney dialysis is no longer to be provided for people over the age of 65 except in the case of persons judged by committee to be of great national importance.

But a moral and political problem arises: inequality in the face of death, the last link in a concatenation of inequalities during life. What is more important for an individual: to enjoy life as much as possible when healthy or to prolong life by a few weeks or months when mortally ill? It could be calculated that more money has been spent on keeping hundreds of thousands of patients on life-support systems in hospitals than they contributed to the society in their entire lives. Is it right to prevent people from dying peacefully in the name of a so-called medical deontology when they themselves or their families do not wish them to linger on? Such an absurd situation results from the convergence of interest of four unintending "plotters"—doctors, hospital administrators, politicians, and patients and their relatives. The same agents are found in all the fifteen countries, though the relative importance of each varies from country to country.

Doctors

It is obvious that there are greater similarities among doctors across nations than among doctors and members of the other professions in the societies in which they live (this is not to say that there are no differences; it is well known that British doctors have a much lower income than their European or U.S. counterparts). Everywhere in the world, doctors enjoy a privileged status. A teacher or a professor has a higher status in developing countries than in advanced societies, but the same does not hold true for doctors; they constitute a privileged class even in the United States. In addition, in Europe as well as in the United States, doctors are the major agents of the growth in medical spending. One of the main reasons is that many of them want to adopt as soon as possible the most expensive apparatus, the use of which will contribute to their personal prestige and income as "high specialists." High technology has two immediate financial consequences of unequal importance: the cost of the equipment and the need for operators. The issue is clearly summarized as follows:

> The existence of diseases which lead to untimely death has always challenged the medical profession to seek daring new remedies. The value which has traditionally been placed on doing the job as well as it can be done and on persevering in the face of defeat, in part explains the lengths to which some have gone in attempting to treat catastrophic illness. . . . Optimal treatment of patients with catastrophic diseases requires specially trained teams of professionals from many disciplines, including internists, surgeons, immunologists, psychologists, nurses, social workers, and paramedical personnel. Moreover it demands sophisticated hospital and out-patient facilities, organ registries, specialized laboratories, computers, and a regional or national network of organ exchange. [Katz and Capron 1975, 29]

Liberal medicine, medicine practiced outside hospitals in many European countries, has incontestable merits, but it also encourages spending in another way. In France, for example, doctors' fees must not exceed a certain level if they are to be reimbursed from social security, and this level is periodically adjusted by negotiations between the medical council and representatives of the state. But it is not easy to control the number of medical acts that a doctor may consider necessary to treat an illness. To reduce abuses, computerized controls have been established. In Italy, faulty legislation governing medical studies has allowed for a considerable increase in the number of doctors, some of whom cannot find enough patients.

Hospital Administrators

There was a time when the number of hospital beds provided for every 1,000 inhabitants was one of the most reliable indicators in measuring social and economic development. The need to construct new hospitals and modernize old ones has been a priority in most of the European democracies and the United States, but some of these countries have now arrived at a saturation point with respect to the number of available hospital beds. This is particularly the case in the United States, where in some states there are too many hospitals in the sense that it is difficult to fill the beds with patients. The result is a tendency to keep patients in the hospital longer than necessary since a hospital cannot balance its budget with empty beds. The financing of a hospital is a question of scale. Without entering into details, it can be mentioned that in the United States many hospitals employ on the average 400 people for each 100 beds. According to some observers there is a waste of human resources, in public more than in private hospitals, in part because each specialist wants to have his or her own group of assistants.

It could be argued that it is good for a city or region to have available hospital beds in case of emergencies, but the point is that the administrators want to fill beds in normal times without real need. The hospital administrator has an interest in increasing hospital revenues and in doing so, is in conflict neither with the doctors nor with the patients since the expenses are most often paid by a third party, the state or a private insurance company. "The extensive adoption of third-party payments and particularly the government-sponsored programs allow the use of complex and expensive technologies in diagnosis and treatment with only limited concern for cost to the patient. Health care charges are determined mostly by groups and lobbies of medical care providers, not by the third parties who typically pay for health care" (Aiken and Freeman 1980, 548).

"The recent explosion in hospital costs is generally blamed for pushing up the overall health care bill. The nation spent about 46% of all personal health care expenditures on hospital care in 1980. That was 16.2% more than hospital care cost in 1979" (*Congressional Quarterly* 1982, 10). In order to reduce the incentive for all hospitals to acquire the most sophisticated technology, a new mechanism was adopted in the United States in 1983, the Diagnosis Related Group. Another hidden cost of hospitals, particularly in surgery, relates to the training of young doctors. This training is classified as health care, even if the patient who receives an artificial heart or undergoes an operation for a hernia is in his or her late seventies. In addition, scientific medical research is also concealed under the label of health care.

People who need only simple care are hospitalized to be "cured," and in all the fifteen countries, there has been a considerable increase in hospitalization of the very old. "Technological advances have made it possible for older people to undergo surgery and complicated medical procedures, . . . but mortality statistics show that increased hospitalization has not increased the life expectancy of the elderly" (Stahl 1982, 104).

A survey conducted in France in 1984 covering 2,500 doctors and relating to over 100,000 elderly persons revealed improper hospitalization in psychiatric hospitals, which had a considerable number of people over 65 years of age. More than 40 percent of those aged people had been badly advised and could have stayed at home without any medical assistance, but the ceiling for home care is very low while hospitalization costs are fully reimbursed. Thus, the families of the old people participate, with the complicity of the hospitals, in depleting social security resources. "Despite the continuing difference in organization of services, in every country the hospital is consuming an increasing share of national health care expenditures" (Somers and Somers 1977, 382).

Politicians

If there are national funds to build hospitals, politicians will do their best to have one built in their own constituencies in exchange for promises of support for a hospital construction bill. Such was the case in the United States with the Hill-Burton Act, by which the federal government subsidized the building of hospitals. In France, politicians have been told that small hospitals, including ones in their own constituencies, should be eliminated in favor of larger, more modern hospitals. Naturally they have resisted such proposals. In some cases politicians have even opposed the elimination of hospitals for reasons not connected with medical considerations; one example will suffice. In the state of New York there are twenty-two mental hospitals. According to some specialists, five or six would be enough to deal with the demand because most mental patients are not dangerous and do not need to be committed. But according to the local politicians, the elimination of the superfluous hospitals would entail the loss of jobs, so we have an absurd situation: People are needlessly committed to mental institutions to the possible advantage only of their families, resources are misused, state and insurance company moneys are misspent, and skilled manpower is misapplied.

If citizens are more sensitive to the benefits of the social security system than to its cost, this is so in part because of the lack of courage of political leaders when faced with the issue in the electoral arena. It is easier to increase taxation for social security by 1 or 2 percent every year than in any way to limit the benefits. This situation is particularly clear in France, but it holds true for almost all European countries. In Italy, the demagoguery of politicians on the issue of social welfare has reached an intolerable level. For instance, in Italy there were 5,419,500 disabled people in 1980: One out of every ten citizens (including children) was considered "unfit for work." In 1969 at least 30 percent of all former parliamentarians had been declared "unfit for work"; by 1978 the proportion had risen to 40 percent (Fausto 1983, 50). The responsibility of the politicians is obvious: "The essential problem with these welfare programs is that they occur over a vastly longer period than the relatively short time perspective of most politicians. As a result, they are extremely vulnerable to the politicians' temptation to vote short-term benefits, transferring the much longer term costs into the future—to their successors or to future taxpayers, some of them not yet even born" (Chickering and Rosa 1982, 208).

Union leaders also push for spending on social security, but not for identical reasons on either side of the Atlantic. In Western Europe, union leaders are ideologically in favor of social redistribution in general, but they also favor an increase in social security funding because they help manage the funds (with high civil servants and employers). In some countries unions obtain indirect help from the social security system; in other countries, such as France, they have succeeded in shifting the burden of financing the system mainly to the employers. In the United States, labor unions have become financial corporations as they manage enormous pension funds.

Patients and Their Relatives

In most of the fifteen countries the medical expenses are paid almost entirely by a third party. In a few countries, like France, the patient has to pay for a *ticket moderateur* on a sliding scale, which varies according to the type of medical care from 20 to 33 percent. But a large proportion of the people have a secondary insurance policy, on a voluntary basis, which means that 100 percent of all medical expenses are covered. Consequently, the patient tries to get the best possible care without worrying about the cost and will not hesitate to consult more than one specialist. Despite the diversity among countries in systems of health delivery, the patient is financially protected in almost all of them and reducing medical costs is not a preoccupation. Only in the United States is the financial coverage partial for a fraction of the population. "Most analysts agree that the near-total reliance on third-party payers interrupts the traditional relationship between supply and demand that might otherwise restrain use and thus expenditures" (Lohr and Marquis 1984, 17).

Health care expenses will continue to increase, particularly for the older part of the populations because the elderly need medical care much more than other adults or children. In the United States, "the aged are accounting for a larger and larger share of the escalating bill on health . . . (in 1978, 29.4 percent of all personal health care expenditures were for the aged— even though the aged made up only 11 percent of the population). . . . The type of diseases common to the elderly—arthritis, hypertension, diabetes, emphysema, heart disease—are generally chronic, requiring constant, long-term and more expensive care" (Congressional Quarterly 1982, 9). In Sweden, more than 50 percent of the health care resources are spent on the 16 percent of the population over 65 years of age (Stahl 1982, 94). Death is inevitable, but life can be prolonged. Is it the state's function to cheat death? Or should the matter be a prerogative of the individual? The ethical issue must be addressed, but how can it be resolved? Can an ethical issue be resolved by financial means? Perhaps not. In the final analysis it is a political issue, one that will dominate the political scene for many years to come.

SPIRALING COSTS OF OLD AGE PENSIONS

Several aspects of the problems of retirement and old age pensions merit brief examination: longer life spans, the increasing imbalance between the active work force and the number of retirees, the shift from capitalization to intergenerational redistribution, the worsening financial imbalance because of early retirements, the relatively privileged position of the majority of retired persons, and the financial deficits. In all advanced countries, the increase in the length of the average life span is slow but regular so that one must distinguish between retired people and the really old. On the one hand, more people reach the age of retirement; on the other, elderly people tend to live longer. Thus, in the United States in 1940, 583 out of every 1,000 men and 687 out of every 1,000 women reached the age of 65. In 1980, the proportions were, respectively, 711 and 839 per 1,000. In 1950, life expectancy at the age of 65 was 13 years for men and 15 years for women. In 1980, it was 15 years for men and 20 for women (Ginzberg 1982, 55 and 57). In the Federal Republic of Germany in 1980, life expenctancy at the age of 60 was 16.2 years for men and 20.6 years for women (Tamburi 1983, 322), and similar figures could be produced for nearly all the fifteen countries studied.

Two demographic currents may be observed. The decline in the birthrate experienced over the past twenty years, which curiously enough occurred in all the countries concerned at about the same time, will have a strong but gradual impact. When the relatively few children of today join the work force, they will have to subsidize the pensions of today's adults who will have retired. To this phenomenon, another, equally important generational one will be added, the effects of which will also arise over the medium run. The relatively large generation born after World War II, between 1946 and 1965, at work today, will start to retire in about twenty years, around the year 2005, with results that can already be anticipated.

Longer life spans for a greater number of people mean that retirees will collect retirement benefits for a longer period of time and also that older people are likely to incur greater health costs in the long term. Both of these costs will have to be covered by a relatively restricted working population, unless there is considerable immigration. That possibility seems unlikely in Western Europe because of current structural unemployment there, but the working populations in the United States and Canada are continuing to be rejuvenated by immigration.

The decisive factor with regard to old age pensions is the numerical relationship between the working population, which contributes the money for the pensions, and the retired population, which receives the benefits. In the United States in 1945, there were fifty working people for every retired person; in 1980, there were only three. "Germany is [also] facing an extremely unfavourable ratio between pensioners and contributors to the pension scheme. Taking all pensions in payment into account, one finds that in 1979 there were 56.5 pensioners for 100 contributors. The ratio was 34.1 in 1960, and 43.9 in 1970" (Tamburi 1983, 322).

The ratio of workers to retirees in West Germany will remain fairly constant until 1990, declining from 2.19 in 1980 to an estimated 2.11 in 1990. After that, however, the ratio will decline significantly to 1.56 by 2010 and to an incredible 1.12 by 2030. (Jüttemeier and Petersen 1982, 182). These figures mean that 112 children born in 1985 will have to underwrite the pensions of 100 people aged 20 who entered the work force in 1985 and who will retire in 2030 at the age of 65—and most of them will live on past the age of 85. In Italy, "in 1955 the ratio of insured workers to pensions was 3.62; in 1980 it had fallen to 1.41 and it is expected to decline further." From 1950 to 1980, the "much more rapid increase in the number of pensioners than in the number of workers (36.9% as against 14%) had led to a five-fold increase in the payroll tax rate" (Castellino 1982, 50 and 55). In France, on the basis of certain projections, "the future solvency of the retirement system has been put in question, and public confidence in the system's ability to meet its commitments has been turned to mistrust. Millenarianism has therefore come back into fashion and the year 2005—when the first full post-war generation will reach retirement age—has become the moment when Satan is to appear" (Kessler 1984, 71).

To finance retirement, nearly all the fifteen countries have adopted the principle of intergenerational redistribution, also known as pay as you go, abandoning capitalization because of continuous inflation, especially during and after World War II. In the United States, however, retirement benefits are still partly based on the capitalization principle. Under the pay-as-you-go principle, retirement benefits depend on contributions, which are in turn tied to the growth or shrinking of the working population in relation to the number of retired persons as well as economic boom or depression.

The imbalance between the number of contributors and the number of beneficiaries has worsened recently because of the spread of early retirement. In an effort to resolve unemployment among young people, the governments of France, the Federal Republic of Germany, and the Scandinavian countries offer generous terms to people who are willing to retire at 60 or 62. In the Federal Republic of Germany, the average age of retirement has been 63 years since 1978; in Sweden, the proportion of working men in the age bracket 55–64 declined from 88.3 in 1965 to 78.7 in 1980 and in the age bracket 65–74, from 37.7 to 14.2 over the same fifteen-year period (Stahl 1982, 112). Also, lowering the age of retirement has become a matter of priority for the trade unions.

The similarities between Sweden and the United States are striking. The percentage of men aged 55–64 in the U.S. labor force dropped from 86.9 percent in 1950 to 73 percent in 1979. Similarly, labor force participation by men 65 and older fell from 45.8 percent in 1950 to 20 percent in 1979 (Ginzberg 1982, 55). Legislation encourages early retirement: An employee who retires at the age of 62 instead of 65 loses only 20 percent of the full pension for three years. As a result, three-quarters of the workers retire before 65. There is no need to look at the statistics to confirm how important the phenomenon has become: Anyone who has traveled in the United States will have had occasion to note how many of the tourists are retired, but not really elderly, people. In Italy, the problem is aggravated by the massive award of pensions for reasons of unfitness for work to people in their forties and fifties, particularly in the rural regions of the south.

Even though people are living longer and longer, they are leaving the work force earlier and earlier. Although longer life spans should encourage legislators to set the retirement age as late as possible, they in fact shorten the length of time people work. The nearsightedness of politicians and union leaders causes them to take the short-term view. They perceive today's unemployment, but they miss the inevitable bankruptcy of pension funds the day after tomorrow.

Demographic laws will nevertheless continue to prevail. In the first phase of industrialization, when birthrates were high, children were put to work. By the same token, when people in their seventies become even more numerous, it will no doubt become necessary to make them work half time or three-quarter time.

The redistribution of money through the social security system operates between generations as much as between the rich and the poor, to such an extent that the incomes of the retired appear relatively higher than those of the active working population of the same social category. In France, many older householders are said to control "a large estate, appreciably higher than that of active households. Statistics show that the average financial resources of households over 60 are considerably higher than those of the households of younger generations" (Kessler 1984, 75). Old age pensions in France increased threefold in twenty years, in constant francs, and the increase in retirement benefits was 50 percent higher than the increase in wages (Chesnais 1984, 94).

In Sweden, the elderly absorb an "excessive proportion" of the GNP (Stahl 1982, 118). Their situation in the Federal Republic also seems relatively advantageous since it is possible to receive pension benefits from different sources, so that "net benefits for individual pensioners frequently equal more than 100% of the wage, after tax" (Jüttemeier and Petersen 1982, 183). In Italy, retirement benefits are so generous that one must wonder to what extent they are linked to political patronage. Civil servants who begin their careers at the age of 20 can claim retirement at 40, at 60 percent of their salaries. They then take their pension—and coverage for medical expenses—into the clandestine economy, which the Italians call the "submerged" sector, a point to which I shall return later. They keep all of their pensions even if they accept new work. The same advantages are offered to women at the age of 35 if they are married and have children.

One can make the rounds of Western Europe, from Helsinki to Vienna and from Madrid to Brussels and not find a single country in which the financial crisis of pension funds has not been exposed and analyzed by experts and its worsening over the medium run has not been foreseen and calculated. But the demographers, the economists, and the administrators preach in the desert most of the time: The politicians have more urgent business to settle, and "planning French style" is, in this context, a bureaucratic legend. Nevertheless, on both sides of the "Atlantic lake" the political debate on this issue is open, and in a few countries action is beginning to be taken.

Schematically, one can approach the financial crisis of pension funds in three not at all incompatible ways: by the reduction of benefits; by a rise in rates of contribution; by delaying the age of retirement (rather than advancing it). To postpone the age of retirement, inevitable though this action is over the medium run, can be but a partial solution. The dilemma, which is the same everywhere, remains: increase contributions or decrease benefits?

In the Netherlands, "because the level of taxation is already so high, there is scarcely any extra source for additional taxation: any further increase of the level of taxation, or, to put it in more general terms, any governmental effort to create a further shift from private budgets to the government's budget, seems to have significant counter-productive effects, such as fraud, black circuits and decreased working efficiency" (Schendelen 1983, 225). For the Federal Republic of Germany experts have calculated that if there are no changes in the legislation, the demographic trends might require a contribution rate on a pay-as-you-go basis of 30 percent of the payroll, just to pay out the pensions. The situation in Sweden, whose social security system served as a model for many years, merits special attention. "The overriding political question here is how much the present working generation is willing to decrease its own consumption in order to support the older non-working generation . . . [because] increasing payroll tax would drastically reduce the real disposable income of the working population and thus cause further harm to the economy" (Stahl 1982, 103 and 105).

But it is in Italy, where politics for over a third of a century were dominated, not by the Socialist party as in Sweden, but by the Christian Democrats, that criticism of the social security system is at its sharpest. The figures speak for themselves: Between 1955 and 1980 the contributions automatically deducted from payrolls rose from 9 percent to 24 percent. Despite this increase, the contributions were not enough to cover the pensions, one-third of which had to be financed by a considerable increase in the national debt. Either one increases contributions, or one increases the national debt since, in such a *partitocrazia* ("reign of parties"), it is difficult to imagine even a nominal reduction of retirement benefits. But there is another solution, cynical but efficient: galloping inflation, which reduces the real benefits. "The most distinctive features of the Italian pension system are haphazard redistributions and huge deficits." The workers themselves, who should be the principal beneficiaries, chime in with management: "Workers and firms alike resist further increases in payroll tax rates. Voters and tax evaders object to further increases in general taxation" (Castellino 1982, 68).

The same dilemma and the same song exist in France as in Belgium, in Austria as in Denmark, and even in Canada despite the fact that it is a country of immigration. Many of the people who will be paying contributions in the year 2005 were, in 1985, still children or adolescents. Will they, when they grow up, accept the situation that three of them work several months a year in order to pay a pension to some anonymous retired person by virtue of legislation adopted by the pensioner's generation? Will today's adults, when they have retired, be able to impose such a burden on today's children who will then be adults in their working prime? Since the number of the active workers will be too small in relation to the mass of the inactive ones, it will be necessary—barring a currently unforseeable technological revolution—to reduce both pensions and the number of retired people by postponing the age of retirement. A further rise in social security charges, while theoretically conceivable, would have a deleterious impact on the most advanced countries, especially on their international competitiveness.

THE WELFARE STATE AND
INTERNATIONAL ECONOMIC COMPETITIVENESS

If one adds to the 8–11 percent (according to country) of expenditure for health benefits that part of the GNP that is allocated for pensions (10–12 percent) and that part that goes to the unemployed or the "assisted poor" (8–12 percent), the total for some countries is one-third of the GNP and for the others more than one-quarter. This amount is taken away from direct creative production, which means that only two-thirds or so of the national resources remain for all the other needs of society: investment in industry, education of the young, higher incomes for the people who work, reduction of the work load, and increase of leisure time.

The choice to spend such a large portion of the GNP on the social security system is politically legitimate, since it has been adopted by governments elected according to democratic rules. Socially, it is largely necessary and corresponds to the expectations of large strata of society. It would be justified even from the economic point of view if all countries that play an important role in international economic life would spend as much for social welfare as the fifteen richest Western democracies.

The economy of each of these countries, except that of the United States, is trade dependent for more than one-third of the GNP; in some, such as the Netherlands, for more than half of the GNP. Italy, for instance, has few natural resources except sunshine: It has to have exports to pay for everything that its industry needs. The U.S. GNP is less trade dependent because of the continental size of the country: The United States has its own internal "common market."

These countries can survive at their present level of wealth as long as they are still able to trade, not only among themselves but with the rest of the world, by exchanging finished products and services for raw materials. At the right moment, a third of a century ago, they wisely decided not to build a new "Chinese wall" around the shores of the Atlantic to protect their scientific and technological advancements. They sold their technology to all comers, including the Soviet Union. Now it is too late. Foreign trade is vital; autarchy, impossible.

If the cost of labor is much higher than in Japan, the new industrial nations of the Third World (Taiwan, the Republic of Korea, Hong Kong, Singapore, Brazil, etc.), or the developing countries like India, the industrial products of countries where social expenditure is a high priority become noncompetitive. Consequently, despite their technological advances, these countries experience a kind of deindustrialization. In turn, deindustrialization engenders unemployment, which reduces the amount of contributions to the social budget. In order to rectify the imbalance, more contributions are needed. Higher contributions in turn have a direct impact on the cost of labor. The higher the cost of labor, the less competitive industrial products become on the international market. It is a vicious circle or, more precisely, a mounting spiral.

The economic difficulties the Western countries have experienced since 1974 are not temporary. In fact, these countries are facing a profound and long-term structural change. The time is gone when they imported raw materials and exported finished products: They must today import what they traditionally exported. This is the reason for the crisis in certain industries (steel, textile, energy, etc.). The simultaneous growth of unemployment in so many Western countries reflects this process of deindustrialization more than it does the process of automation of industry. Moreover, the so-called British disease—economic decline engendered by too much social redistribution—is spreading.

The growth of the tertiary sector more or less implies deindustrialization, but part of the tertiary sector is not directly productive; it is, rather, an aspect of consumption. For instance, education, which belongs to the tertiary sector, absorbs about 20 percent of the national budget in nearly all advanced societies. The insurance and the banking systems are not directly profitable, except in a few countries like Switzerland and Britain. The technological advances that these countries enjoy in some domains have not been important enough to compensate for the deindustrialization of the traditionally vital sectors of the economy, and even the technological advances are slowly or rapidly extending to the developing countries. In the near future India and China will produce their own computers. The only flourishing industrial domain for some of the major countries is the production of arms, which can still easily be exported. Even in the area of high technology, optimism should be moderate. The failure of the Concorde supersonic airplane is a good cautionary example.

As these Western societies grow older, spend more on health, and are no longer able to take surplus value (in the Marxist sense) out of their industrial potential, they can invest less, and so their capacity for future growth is undermined. They are already spending more than they produce. A society that over a long period of time consumes more than it produces cannot invest, and without investment there is no growth. Such a society lives by devouring its capital. The national debt of so many advanced countries—including the United States, France and the United Kingdom— is a measure, so to speak, of the imbalance not only between government revenue and spending but also between production and consumption, since many social expenditures are part of the national budgets. Even if tomorrow the national debts were reduced—by deliberate inflation, for instance—that would not necessarily imply a reversal of the trend.

The ongoing slow economic decline of the advanced Western countries is a complex phenomenon involving a series of factors: levels of productivity, relations between management and employees, military expenditures, the power of organized groups to impose their will, etc. But social expenditures for health, for pensions, and for unemployment also play an important role.

Society manages, to an extent, to resist the encroachment of the state. One of the most obvious symptoms of resistance to the social security system is the rise of an underground economy everywhere, its importance varying from country to country. The underground economy, moonlighting, tax evasion, fighting shy of ventures, the brain drain, the decline of the work ethic are, in part, perverse effects of excessive taxation. Too much taxation finally impoverishes the community as a whole even if it does reduce inequalities. Warnings are being heard everywhere.

The same diagnosis is made for socialist Sweden: "Public spending at present runs at about 65% of Sweden's G.D.P. and recent budget deficits amount to almost 5% of G.D.P. To support public spending, marginal tax rates have been raised to levels where they stifle industrial productivity" (Stahl 1982, 118). In the Federal Republic of Germany, there are similar anxieties: "We fear a growing movement into the tax-free and contributions free underground economy. This would limit revenues more than ever, and would probably lead to a complete collapse of the social insurance system" (Jüttemeier and Petersen 1982, 198). But it is Italy, a society that for 2,000 years has sought to resist power, that has succeeded in producing the largest underground economy. Some people estimate that a quarter, others one-third, of the share of national production escapes state control and social security. The government itself tolerates the clandestine economy since it knows that without it, Italy would be plunged into economic and financial disaster, for it is the underground economy that enables Italy to more or less balance its foreign trade. This pessimistic thesis has also been expressed by Richard Rose and Guy Peters in a book in which they show how the mutilation of take-home pay, which is unacceptable psychologically, would produce "political bankruptcy," which they define as "undermining constitutional authority by joining civic indifference to institutional ineffectiveness" (Rose and Peters 1978, 32).

So the welfare state, which was created to cushion the negative effects of the capitalist economy and the logic of the free market, produces in its turn its own dysfunctions: bureaucratic hypertrophy, overcentralization, incompetence of public servants to deal with social problems, lack of rationality in the decision-making process, and so on. The services the welfare state renders do not compensate sufficiently for the level of taxation required.

If this trend continues for many more years, what is now forseeable only by analysts will become obvious to many people, particularly to politicians, whose myopia can be excused because they have more immediate problems to resolve. The cumulative effects of an aging population, increasing health costs, and deindustrialization in the fifteen more advanced Western countries considered will inevitably engender a relative economic decline by a kind of dialectical process. This forecast may be specified as a decline in the quality of life for most people, or, in more technical terms, a decline in the GNP per capita. It remains to be seen whether such a decline in mean income will be accompanied by higher or lower inequalities, or, in technical terms, by a higher or lower standard deviation. It seems very probable that such a decline will be accompanied by a reduction of social inequality. There will be fewer very rich people, because of the redistribution of national income, and fewer very poor people, because of the inevitable extension of social programs under democratic regimes. A decline in the quality of life means, first of all, a greater uniformity of life-styles, brought about by an impoverishment of the very rich that is greater, relatively, than the improvement in the condition of the very poor. It is decline, so to speak, in absolute terms of the statistical mean, a leveling down. It is also a decline in relative terms of the West as opposed to the phalanx of Third World countries. This double decline will probably be a relatively slow process and, consequently, painless.

REFERENCES

Aharoni, Yair. 1981. *The No-Risk Society*. Chatam, N.Y.: Chatam House.

Aiken, Linda H., and E. Howard Freeman. 1980. "Medical Sociology and Science and Technology in Medicine." In Paul T. Durbin, ed., *A Guide to the Culture of Science, Technology and Medicine*, pp. 527–580. New York: Free Press.

Alber, Jens. 1979. "The Growth of Social Insurance in Western Europe: Has Democracy Made a Difference?" Paper presented at the International Political Science Association Congress, Moscow.

Altman, S. H., and R. Blendon. 1979. *Medical Technology: The Culprit Behind Health Care Costs*. Hyattsville, Md.: National Center for Health Services Research.

Beauchamp, T. L., and L. Walters, eds. 1978. *Contemporary Issues in Bioethics*. Belmont, Calif.: Wadsworth Publishing Company.

Browning, K. Edgar. 1975. *Redistribution and the Welfare State*. Washington, D.C.: American Enterprise Institute.

Castellino, Onorato. 1982. "Italy." In Jean-Jacques Rosa, ed., *The World Crisis in Social Security*, pp. 48–91. Paris: Fondation Nationale d'Economie Politique.

Chesnais, J. C. 1984. "Evolution démographique et charge de financement des retraités." *Revue Française des Affaires Sociales* (June), pp. 85–102.

Chickering, Lawrence A., and J. J. Rosa. 1982. "A Political Dilemma." In Jean-Jacques Rosa, ed., *The World Crisis in Social Security*, pp. 207–220. Paris: Fondation Nationale d'Economie Politique.

Congressional Quarterly Weekly Report. 1982. November 28.

Fausto, Domenicantonio. 1983. "The Proliferation of Disability Pensions: An Application Not Limited to the South of Italy." *Mezzogiorno d'Europa* (January-March), pp. 49–69.

Flora, Peter, and J. Arnold Heidenheimer. 1981. *The Development of Welfare States in Europe and America*. London: Transaction Books.

Flora, Peter, et al. 1983. *State, Economy, and Society in Western Europe 1815–1975. A Data Handbook*. Frankfurt am Main: Campus Verlag.

Fuchs, R. Victor. 1974. *Who Shall Live? Health, Economics, and Social Choice*. New York: Basic Books.

Ginzberg, Eli. 1982. "The Social Security System." *Scientific American* (January), pp. 51–57.

Illich, Ivan. 1975. *Nemesis medicale*. Paris: Seuil.

International Labour Office. 1984. *Into the Twenty-first Century: The Development of Social Security*. Geneva.

Janowitz, Morris. 1978. *The Social Control of the Welfare State*. New York: Elsevier.

Jüttemeier, K. H., and H. G. Petersen. 1982. "West Germany." In Jean-Jacques Rosa, ed., *The World Crisis in Social Security*, pp. 181–205. Paris: Fondation Nationale d'Economie Politique.

Katz, Jay, and Alexander Morgan Capron. 1975. *Catastrophic Diseases: Who Decides What?* New York: Russell Sage Foundation.

Kessler, Denis. 1984. "Les retraités en péril?" *Revue Française des Affaires Sociales* (June), pp. 69–83.

King, Anthony. 1973–1974. "Ideas, Institutions, and the Policies of Governments: A Comparative Analysis." *British Journal of Political Science* 3 (1973), pp. 291–313, and 4 (1974), pp. 409–423.

Lohr, N. Kathleen, and M. Susan Marquis. 1984. *Medicare and Medicaid: Past, Present, and Future.* Santa Monica, Calif.: Rand Corporation.

Morison, Robert S. 1979. "Misgivings About Life: Extending Technologies." In G. Holton and R. Morison, eds., *Limits of Scientific Inquiry,* pp. 211–226. New York: Norton and Company.

O'Connor, James. 1973. *The Fiscal Crisis of the State.* New York: Saint Martin's Press.

Organization for Economic Cooperation and Development (OECD). 1978. *Public Expenditure Trends.* Paris.

Rosa, Jean-Jacques, ed. 1982. *The World Crisis in Social Security.* Paris: Fondation Nationale d'Economie Politique.

Rosanvallon, Pierre. 1981. *La crise de l'Etat-providence.* Paris: Seuil.

Rose, Richard, and Guy Peters. 1978. *Can Government Go Bankrupt?* New York: Basic Books.

Schendelen, M.C.P.M. van. 1983. "Crisis of the Dutch Welfare State." *Contemporary Crises* 7:209–230.

Somers, R. Ann, and M. Herman Somers. 1977. *Health and Health Care.* Germantown, Md.: Aspen Systems Corporation.

Stahl, Ingemar. 1982. "Sweden." In Jean-Jacques Rosa, ed., *The World Crisis in Social Security,* pp. 93–120. Paris: Fondation Nationale d'Economie Politique.

Tamburi, G. 1983. "Escalation of State Pension Costs: The Reasons and the Issues." *International Labour Review* 122:3 (May-June).

Wilensky, L. Harold. 1975. *The Welfare State and Equality.* Berkeley: University of California Press.

World Bank. 1980. *Health Sector Policy Paper.* Washington, D.C.

8
COMPARATIVE POLICY ANALYSIS: THE PROGRAM APPROACH

Richard Rose

Par ma foi! il y a plus de quarante ans
que je dis de la prose sans que j'en susse rien.
—M. Jourdain, *Le Bourgeois Gentilhomme*

Whether we think of a world of nations or a world of people, variability is inevitable. In fact, it is so much taken for granted that for more than four times forty years social scientists have been making prose comparisons of variability within and between societies. But just as philologists are challenged because prose statements may be similar though in different languages, so comparative social scientists have a formidable task. Languages differentiate researchers by nations, and there are also many differences in language between academic disciplines. In social science, as in philology, comparison is inevitable.

Why comparison in policy analysis? (Rose 1973, 68–73). The major problems that face one government are often the same as those that face its neighbors; this is the rationale of such intergovernmental organizations as the OECD and the IMF as well as of academic researchers. Although the existence of common or similar problems need not imply that every nation should or will respond in the same way, it does mean that each may draw lessons from the relevant experience of others. Crossnational lesson-drawing is particularly important when a given program, for example, a national health service, is meant to be uniform within a nation. Just as Americans make comparisons among fifty states, so Europeans should be able to compare more than a dozen independent nations. Comparison removes ethnocentric blinkers and shows what is possible within the framework of a democratic, Western society. It also offers a far more realistic way to investigate the

219

actual consequences of adopting a particular program than a necessarily speculative and abstract *gedanken-experimenten* (cf. Rose 1973, 68ff.).

How to do comparative policy analysis is a different and more difficult question to answer. Dogan and Pelassy's (1981) review describes and evaluates many different types of comparison. Attention is concentrated upon relatively abstract questions of considerable intellectual interest to social scientists rather more than upon the concrete, specific problems facing policymakers. The book is a review of pure *Wissenschaft* rather than *angewandte Wissenschaft* in the Lazarsfeld tradition. Policymakers are not only concerned with understanding the causes of problems but also seek help in understanding alternative policies for dealing with the problems (Rose 1976).

The object of this chapter is to consider important issues in comparative policy analysis. In this branch of social science, intellectual and practical concerns cannot be kept separate. Policy analysts in government as well as academic social scientists share a common concern with the questions addressed here: What is the unit of analysis in comparing public policies? What are the most important comparisons practicable within nations? What are the most important comparisons across nations? What priorities for future investigation follow from the comparative analysis of public policies?

PROGRAMS: THE CENTRAL UNIT OF ANALYSIS

Comparison requires conceptualization; statements about the similarity or dissimilarity of a public policy in two or more countries or at two or more points in time presuppose the prior stipulation of a concept that is clear and robust enough to survive translation across linguistic as well as national boundaries. The terms *policy*, *politics*, and *polity* (and, for that matter, *police*) all have the same Greek root. The anglophone use of the word *policy*, as distinct from *politics*, is not normally matched in other languages (cf. Heidenheimer 1984).

When the use of the word *policy* is examined in U.S. writings, the source of the great bulk of publications in this field, confusion results: The term *policy* is used in at least four distinctly different ways. First of all, it is used as a synonym for a problem or issue area; for example, when one speaks of housing policy or economic policy. Second, it is a statement of intentions about what government ought to do; for example, during an election campaign candidates and parties often refer to policies they intend to promote if elected. Third, the term can refer to a program; that is, a set of laws that confer specific competence upon public organizations to deliver particular services for more or less clearly stated purposes. Fourth, the term can refer to the impact of a government program; for example, the consequences of an urban renewal program may not be the same as was intended nor vary as the program design intended. When such different meanings can all be attributed to the same word, then there is a risk that policy scientists may communicate informally in a common language— colloquial American—yet be referring to such different things that the result is an intellectual Tower of Babel. As it stands, the term *policy* is not precise enough to be the unit of analysis.

Logically, one can stipulate many different ways in which policies may vary. Each distinction can be a dimension in a multidimensional typology. The more distinctions made, the more complex the resulting typology—and the more improbable it is that social scientists will ever find data to fill all the resulting cells. For example, if each of the seven analytic categories identified by Dogan and Pelassy (1981, part 3) were employed, then one would need forty-nine different cases to have one example for each cell and at least ninety-eight in order to test possible variation between two cases within each cell. At best, one may use such a matrix of possible combinations as a device to question why some cells are crowded and others are empty. Comparison cannot succeed by the elaboration of typological concepts; it requires the selection of one concept as a central organizing idea, that is, the crucial dependent or independent variable.

The principal unit of comparative analysis will vary with the purpose at hand, and this principle is a fortiori true in an instrumentalist field such as policy analysis. Many approaches that are valid for some intellectual ends are not relevant for policy analysis. Many sophisticated efforts to explain public policy (e.g., Cameron 1978) focus far more attention upon the independent variables deemed to cause policy variation than upon the definition and measurement of that which is to be explained. For instance, analyses of stages of development presuppose that there is clarity and consensus about what political development is, or that economic development is a suitable proxy indicator for political change.

Studies of political cultures are inevitably bedeviled by the problem of determining whether cultural norms are a consequence or a cause of that which is to be explained (cf. King 1973, Almond and Verba 1980). Survey-based studies of popular preferences beg many questions about the disjunction between diffuse individual attitudes and specific government action; they reflect the "individualist fallacy" (Scheuch 1966), assuming that the actions of institutions such as governments can be inferred from attributes of masses of individuals.

Political scientists frequently concentrate upon two elements in the production of public policies, namely, government organizations and the policy process. But studies of the policy process confront a dilemma: If attention is focused upon only one stage, what stage should this be? To examine only the input of demands by voters and parties is to confuse policy demands with program outputs. To examine every stage is to anatomize a lengthy and complex process without identifying what may be specifically crucial. To select government organizations as the unit of analysis is reasonable, inasmuch as they cannot be excluded from the production of public programs outputs. But most organizations are intervening influences between demand inputs and outputs; they are not the thing itself (cf. Rose 1984c, chapter 6). Nor is there sufficient empirical support for theories of organizations to draw reliable or valid inferences about program outputs from properties of organizations (see Hood and Dunsire 1981).

The ambiguity of the word *policy* makes it more useful as a modifying adjective than as a substantive. Policy analysis requires concentrating attention upon the *outputs* of the policy process. The most commonly employed output measure—aggregate public expenditure as a proportion of the national product—is deficient in two very important respects (Rose 1983). First of all, it assumes that all relevant attributes of government programs, from the declaration of war through abortion policy, can be reduced to the common measuring rod of money. Studies that use money as a measure assume that the money input of a program equals the value of the output, whereas the relationship is contingent and often disputable.

Second, inasmuch as most studies concentrate upon public expenditure as a proportion of the national product, all government programs are reduced to a single homogenized entity. It is assumed that there are no differences between programs, and it becomes impossible to test *whether* this assumption is true. Years ago, in *A Critique of Welfare Economics*, Ian Little (1963, 81f.) succinctly noted that pure welfare economics risks becoming "an uninterrupted stream of deductions which are not about anything at all." Today, the greater risk is that politics is thought to be about only one thing—money—and that anything not expressed as public expenditure is of no political consequence.

To understand what government does we must analyze public policies in terms of *programs,* that is, resources of laws, money, and personnel mobilized by government organizations and converted into outputs meant to realize more or less clearly identified political purposes (Rose 1984c, chapter 1, Rose 1985b). To see the activities of government in program terms incorporates public expenditure data, but it does not assume that the multiplicity of government's activities can be reduced to a single money measure. The laws that authorize programs and the public employees who carry them out are also taken into account by the program approach. It differs from the functionalist definition of government, which concentrates upon system maintenance, by considering what systems do with their capabilities. Organizations are central because they mobilize the resources that become program inputs and convert them into program outputs. But organizations are not complete in themselves. The object of public policy is to produce programs, not to produce or maintain organizations.

Analyzing government in terms of programs puts the purposes of government first. Government is not just about office holding or about vote gathering; it is also about doing things for some public purpose. In contemporary mixed-economy welfare states, it is evident that what ordinary citizens receive from government consists of its program outputs. In Britain, for example, 89 percent of the families are regularly in receipt of such major program outputs as education, hospital treatment, or a pension (Rose 1984b). The programs of government constitute the benefits and create the costs of a mixed-economy welfare state. A quantitative description of government that ignores the nominal purposes of programs (cf. Ted Gurr's dictum, "The most important variables are nominal") risks becoming no more than "recreational mathematics" or statistics in the abstract (Larkey, Stolp, and Winer 1981, 203).

Analyzing the programs of government emphasizes the hundreds of different activities of a mixed-economy welfare state. The activities of government are heterogeneous, not homogeneous: It maintains an army, provides health care, subsidizes agricultural production, regulates the adoption of children, pays pensions to the elderly and debt interest to bankers, and gives prison sentences to criminals. To understand what government does, we must understand the variety as well as the scale of its activities.

Defining resources in terms of three different but related terms—laws, money, and public employees—makes it possible to understand fundamental differences in the instruments of government. Pensions, for example, are relatively money intensive; they require a computer and a bank account, rather than a large number of bureaucrats, and the most important pension laws are not easily altered. Education is relatively labor intensive—to educate children it is necessary to employ teachers—and the money spent on education does not provide cash incentives to pupils to learn but to pay the salaries of teachers. Marriage and divorce and matters of public morals such as drugs are law intensive; acts set out conditions under which certain social activities may be undertaken.

The major programs of government are those that make a substantial claim upon one or more of its resources. Education, health, income maintenance, debt interest, economic infrastructure, defense, and law and order together account for about five-sixths of public expenditure and public employment, and for a substantial proportion of the laws as well.

The program approach turns the incommensurability of government's resources from a liability into an advantage: The mix of money, public employees, and laws used by one program can be compared with the mix used by another. The elements in the mix must be analyzed separately. Money and public employees cannot be added together, because they use the incommensurable scales of money and people. The fact that laws are not readily quantified is positively challenging, emphasizing the extent to which nominal influences may be just as important as continuous variables (cf. Rose 1984a, Van Mechelen 1984).

The program approach greatly extends the repertoire of comparisons that can be made. First of all, programs can be compared within a nation, a crucial step in testing whether or not the current convention of treating all programs as if they were alike is justifiable. Second, comparisons can be made across national boundaries to test for similarities in the same program in different countries. This type of comparison is crucial in order to determine whether the appropriate unit of analysis is better conceived of as the United States, Great Britain, or West Germany or, alternatively, attention should be directed to health, defense, or energy programs.

The program approach readily lends itself to empirical and quantitative analysis, for it defines the activities of government in terms of concrete concerns of operating agencies and the Ministry of Finance rather than abstractions about never-never land. By definition, programs are located in public sector organizations. Since public agencies are good recordkeepers, there is a host of information available, even if not always in readily usable form, about public employment (Rose 1985a) as well as program expenditure. Laws too are indexed, if not codified, under a variety of program-relevant heads (cf. G. B., Statutory Publications Office 1982). Programs of major resource significance are usually the responsibility of a particular ministry and receive careful attention in public budgets and other official statistics.

COMPARING PROGRAMS WITHIN NATIONS

The practice of comparison often assumes within-nation homogeneity and then proceeds to test for crossnational similarities or differences. This procedure is inevitable when the subject is an attribute of the nation as a whole, such as public expenditure as a proportion of the aggregate national product. But there are many ways in which a nation can be differentiated internally. The original French title of Dogan and Pelassy's book, *Sociologie politique comparative*, makes no prior assumption about geographical focus. The U.S. edition's title—*How to Compare Nations*—demonstrates how easy it is to assume that comparative analysis is confined to the study of "other" or "alien" societies. But comparison can be practiced within a country as well.

Furthermore, the homogeneity within a country of different programs can only be established by empirical testing. A variety of theories can be adduced to indicate why programs might be very similar within a given country. Theories of bureaucratic empire building ought to apply to all bureaucrats, whatever their particular program responsibilities. Theories of party competition may postulate that all parties will produce what the median voter wants or, insofar as parties matter, that a change in party control of government should be equally important for all programs. To the extent that economic conditions tend to determine program outputs, then the rate of growth in the national product can influence all programs equally, and so too can inflation, rising unemployment, or fiscal stress.

In fact, there are major differences within every nation among programs, whether the indicator used is that of money, employment, or laws (cf. Rose 1985b). This fact is even more true if the stated purposes of the programs are the units of comparison. There are three principal axes for comparison within a given nation.

1. *Comparison Across Time.* The simplest and most familiar type of comparison is across time *within* a program. In the compass of a single program it is straightforward to monitor change in one or more indicators for a few years or decades. Trend analysis need not reflect growth; nil change, cyclical fluctuations, or contraction are also logically possible. Within government the routine performance of unchanging activities is not news. Politics—in the sense of controversy about what government does or ought to do—occurs at the margin, where change occurs or is desired.

Budgeting conventionally involves the comparison of current year spending commitments with spending proposed for the next year. For practicing politicians, there are many incentives to confine attention to the life of the present parliament or government coalition, not to look beyond the next election. But year-by-year commitments of government have cumulative consequences. The inertia of public programs is not static, it advances steadily like a juggernaut. Political problems dealt with in the short term by incremental increases in public programs can result in bigger medium-term problems, compounding with the force of inertia (cf. Rose and Karran 1984). A challenge for policymakers today is to create political incentives that will make governors compare the positive consequences of today's choice with its negative consequences the day after tomorrow.

In a dynamic environment, few programs can be judged in isolation. For example, the money cost of a program must be related to inflation in price and wage levels. Social priorities can be measured by the proportion of the national product devoted to a given program. In a period of growing affluence, a program can claim more and more resources in absolute terms while keeping constant its share of a growing national product. Changes in demand are also important; for example, providing a constant volume of university places in the face of an increase in demand alters the proportion of those people receiving a particular social benefit.

Within a cabinet, comparison between programs is one way in which a government collectively establishes priorities. When each cabinet minister wants more resources, and if political consensus is the overriding concern, each minister can be given the same proportionate increase. But this line is difficult to hold when there are external pressures for increasing some programs. Moreover, activist governments wish to change the relative balance among programs. For example, President Reagan signaled a shift in political priorities by increasing defense expenditure and debt interest rather than increasing social security expenditure and/or taxes.

2. *The Mix of Resources.* The resources of public programs are neither singular nor commensurable. When designing a given program, policymakers can consider which resource to use, for example, whether to seek a program goal by a money-moving strategy of cash payments or by employing skilled professionals (cf. Hood 1983).

Laws come first among the resources of government. Government is not the only employer or spending organization in society, but it has a monopoly upon the enactment of binding rules and upon law enforcement. Moreover, statutes are used differently than public employment expenditure.

Laws remain on the statute books by their own inertia. If a parliament enacted no new laws in the course of a year, government could continue as before. When major laws about pensions, education, or health create open-ended entitlements, then public expenditure and public employment are likely to alter in response to demographic pressures and changes in relative prices. When the number of elderly people increases, income-maintenance and health programs grow. After laws are enacted, then, as

Heclo (1974) shows, programs can expand by a gradual process of organizational learning, which can lead to new or amended legislation that expands a program. Wildavsky (1979) sees a similar process of expansion, but evaluates it as a response to shortcomings in programs that cannot be routinized, which leads to "policy as its own cause."

Changes in the resource mix have meta-program implications, for government budgets incorporate the sum total of changes in all programs. An increase in income-maintenance or health claims will increase aggregate public expenditure or, if the government of the day is opposed to an increase, compel a reduction in allocations to other programs. In the 1980s the chief question facing many national ministries of finance is not how to increase program expenditure or how to cut it but rather whether both can be done simultaneously.

3. *Comparison Across Client Groups.* In contemporary welfare states, nearly every family will benefit substantially from programs for education, health, and pensions and often from insurance against contingent risks such as unemployment. But the widespread provision of benefits does not mean that they are necessarily proportional to group size or need. The exact distribution of benefits—as well as the extent, if any, of redistribution—is a major policy concern.

Within any Western nation, the provision of programs can be compared spatially; there is a substantial potential for locational differences in the distribution of most public programs. Even collective goods such as military defense have substantial spatial skewness in the location of military bases, reflecting political as well as strategic concerns, and in the distribution of military contracts. If cities, countries, or *Länder* are made the units of analysis, then each unit of government is an authoritative source of data for program outputs as well as a decision-making agency.

Necessarily, any analysis of the redistributional element of public programs must be comparative among groups within a program. Comparison of the provision of contemporary welfare state services is likely to emphasize commonality, for the spatial distribution of benefits to individuals and households ought to be in accord with population—which is in fact the case for education, health, housing, and income-maintenance benefits. If the national level of provision is set at 100, then the differences around that norm are usually limited in degree, e.g., within a range of 90 to 110 rather than a range of 0 to 200. Moreover, even where differences exist they are often diminishing, because of trends toward convergence (see, e.g., McAllister, Parry, and Rose 1979). For lumpy goods such as capital-intensive automobile manufacturing or national forests, then a mixture of geographical and economic constraints work against territorial proportionality (cf. Parry 1981); each member of Parliament cannot have a steel mill and a national park in his or her constituency—or even a choice of one of the two.

Analyses of equality and inequality typically involve comparisons between individuals or families; the clients for some major public programs, such as health care or education, are individuals, whereas the recipients of other benefits, such as housing or children's allowance, are families. The choice of the unit of analysis is contingent. It is logically possible to compare incomes of individuals or family incomes. A comparison of individual incomes will typically identify differences between husband and wife (waged versus unwaged, or full-time wage versus part-time or lower wage) and between parents and offspring. It is practicable to generate statistical information that shows the extent to which people of different classes, races, or sex differ in their receipt of the benefits of a given public program.

Comparing the distribution of program benefits invites controversy, insofar as comparisons are invidious. The first point of potential controversy arises in choosing whether to use equality of procedural treatment (all applicants are to be treated equally); equality of resources (all persons are to be given the same resources); equality of need (each person is to be given what is appropriate to his or her particular condition); or equality of outcome (everyone is to end up in the same condition). The first two criteria imply uniformity, e.g., in the case of applications for higher education, all applicants are to be treated the same and if accepted, receive the same resources. The latter two imply positive differentiation or discrimination: People who have most difficulty in education may receive more resources until equality of outcome is achieved.

COMPARISON ACROSS NATIONS

National governments are introverted, and with good reason. Elected officeholders place their fates in the hands of a national electorate, and civil servants identify their careers with the success of a national system, or of the ministries responsible for particular programs within it. Furthermore, most public officials are likely to be parochial because they do not work in the national capital but are employed in (and often by) regions or localities (Rose 1985a, tables 1.9–11).

Most public officials are concerned with a specific functional program rather than interested in fungible knowledge. They may have program-specific skills, as, e.g., nurses or teachers, or they may be employed to work for a specific ministry, for example, a clerk in the Ministry of Labor. Trade union and professional memberships reinforce organizational lines of authority. The proportion of public employees with responsibilities cutting across programs is low, only a few higher civil servants and persons clustering around a prime minister and a finance ministry.

Insofar as a ministry or program effectively commands the loyalty of a public employee, the potential for learning from between-program comparisons within a nation is limited. Highway engineers will have little to exchange with health visitors, and teachers little to learn from post office clerks. Comparison within a program is confined to distributional concerns that take the national standard as given.

The basic hypothesis of between-nation comparison is simple: Similarities are greater within a given program across national boundaries than among different programs within a country. Instead of programs being determined by nation-specific characteristics or the choices of national political leaders, they can reflect program-specific characteristics. The broader the canvas, as in Third World versus First World comparisons, the greater the likelihood of finding that program differences may be explained as reflecting differences in national economic development (cf. Tait and Heller 1982, Taylor 1981). Conversely, analysis that is confined to the Organization for Economic Cooperation and Development or, in default of OECD data, to such major Western nations as Britain, France, West Germany, Italy, Sweden, and the United States is likely to find substantial crossnational similarities in a given program.

Within any one OECD nation there are differences among programs in their relative claims upon particular resources and major differences in the mixture of resources claimed by money-intensive as against employee-intensive or law-intensive programs (see Table 8.1). Everywhere in the OECD world income-maintenance programs now claim a larger share of the national product than does defense, and defense claims a far larger share of the national product than agriculture, which in turn claims far more than such relatively inexpensive programs as parks and recreation or diplomatic representation abroad.

Similarly, public employment in health and in education outstrips employment in the provision of income-maintenance grants, and employment in the labor-intensive post office is greater than in the publicly owned but capital-intensive field of electricity generation (cf. Rose 1985a, chapter 1). There is no relation between the amount of money that a ministry spends and the amount of legislation it promotes. About three-quarters of the acts of Parliament in Britain concern programs of departments such as the Home Office, the law officers, the Foreign Office, and the Treasury, which spend about one-quarter of public revenue. About three-quarters of all revenue is spent for programs such as health and social security, education, and those of other ministries, which account for about one-quarter of the legislation (Rose 1984a, table 1).

Comparing similarities in programs across national boundaries need not imply that education in, say, Britain and Italy, is identical, but one must reject the assumption that just because education is authorized by statutes written in English in one country and in Italian in another that education will be as different in substance as in language. Although teaching reading and writing in Italian sounds different from teaching reading and writing in English, the methods and objects are broadly similar: to promote basic literacy. In such public enterprises as the post office and state-owned airlines, the need for standardization is even greater, because of crossnational interdependencies. The different sound made by the ringing of English, American, and German telephones does not mean that they operate on different scientific principles. The process of pluralization—the multiplication of such standard service-delivery units as primary schools and hospitals— follows from program standardization within a country (Kochen and Deutsch

1980, 35ff.). As the Coca Cola Company has shown, standardization makes possible pluralization across national boundaries as well.

For any given program, nearly all OECD countries can readily be grouped into several more or less similar models of program provision. For example, all Western nations have much the same goals and methods for primary education. There are however, differences in the selective element for secondary and tertiary education, and in some countries, the role of the church in education is still salient. In health care, the aims—preventive medicine plus recuperative treatment—are very similar; the differences arise in the method of organizing and paying for medical and hospital services. In regard to pensions, organizational forms differ, but the provision of a cash payment for elderly persons is general. The existence of different program means should be treated not as proof of differences in ends but as an example of flexibility in a universe that spans continents and cultures.

When the resource claims of a variety of programs within a country are compared, the differences are measured in magnitude. Spending on income maintenance tends to be double that on education and health, and about three times that on defense, and public employment in education and health tends to be eight to ten times that for income-maintenance programs. At the extreme, employment in major welfare programs is hundreds of times greater than that required to write the checks that pay debt interest.

Statistically, the most straightforward way to test for similarity or dissimilarity is to calculate the standard deviation around the mean and derive the coefficient of variation (the mean divided by the standard deviation). When public employment within each major Western nation is divided under more than a dozen headings for social welfare, economic activities, and defining conditions of the state, the extent of variability revealed is very high: The coefficient of variation is more than 1.00 for five of the six countries and averages 1.21 (Table 8.2). Governments employ very large numbers of people in education, health, defense, the post office, and public transport; they employ small numbers for such programs as agriculture, tax collection, and judicial administration.

When national budgets are examined, a similar pattern is found: There is a high degree of variability in expenditure under different program headings. Variability in spending under the eighteen major program headings of the British budget is high, with a coefficient of variation of 0.90. The coefficient of variation for the eighteen major program headings of the U.S. budget is higher still, 1.47 (G.B., Treasury 1983, 1:11; U.S., Office of Management and Budget, 1984, summary table 3).

If national boundaries make less difference to a given program than the boundaries between programs within a nation, then the coefficients of crossnational variation for a specific program should be low. Public expenditure data to test this proposition are available for up to twenty OECD countries, much the same number of cases as for public employment. Moreover, the data are available for six major programs that together account for more than two-thirds of total public expenditure.

Within a given major program category, there is consistently little crossnational difference in the claims that a program makes upon public revenue. The coefficients of variation range from as low as 0.18 (education) to 0.51 (defense and debt interest). By contrast, the coefficients of variability for public employment are several times higher (cf. Tables 8.2 and 8.3). Across the six programs, the average coefficient of variation is 0.34. The similarity in program expenditure has been consistent across the decades: In the 1950s and early 1960s, the coefficients ranged from 0.28 for health to 0.60 for defense, averaging 0.43. Programs making the greatest claim on resources of money and employment, such as health and education, consistently show very low variability. The reduction in the coefficient of variation across time for five of the six programs is an indication of convergence.

When the dynamics of programs are examined, the first point to note is the direction of change. There are extreme contrasts in public employment in major Western nations: It goes up by several magnitudes for a few programs, such as education and health; it goes up a limited percent for many programs; and for some programs, such as defense and public transport, it actually falls as these became less important (Rose 1985a, table 1.8). An increase in public employment in the aggregate is the result, not of many programs changing in the same direction, but the net effect of programs changing in opposite directions.

However, crossnational comparisons within a program show consistency in the direction of change. This fact is best demonstrated by examining public expenditure data, since they are available for a substantial number of countries for a period of up to twenty-one years.

In every OECD country, spending on health and on pensions has risen as a share of the national product, and in sixteen of seventeen countries, spending on education has risen as well (Table 8.4). It is easy to explain these trends as an indication that people want more "good" goods and services, and politicians court immediate popularity by making them available. But there are also patterns of increased spending on a less visible and popular program, economic investment, and on a "bad" program, debt interest. The relative downgrading of expenditure on defense is reasonably consistent among nations; had Austria, Germany, and Italy not had defense expenditure in the mid-1950s abnormally depressed by wartime defeat, the fall in defense spending during most of the 1970s would have been just as consistent as the upward trend in welfare programs. Only in the 1980s did conservative governments in Britain, the United States, and West Germany try to reverse these trends.

The money spent to provide program outputs initially enters the fisc as tax revenues. It is thus possible to test the degree of crossnational variability in the proportion of the national product raised by particular taxes and compare this result with the within-nation variability among tax components (see Table 8.5). Systematic analysis of the proportion of the gross domestic product claimed by ten different taxes within twenty OECD countries confirms that the variation within each tax category (median coefficient of variation, 0.59) is much less than the variation among categories within a nation (coefficient of variation, 1.21). Moreover, the greater the share of the national product raised by a tax, the lower its variability tends to be crossnationally. The coefficient of variation for income tax, the most important, is 0.39; that for the least important category, miscellaneous taxes, is 1.81.

To emphasize crossnational program similarities is not to assert that there are no differences. To think in terms of a principal axis of comparison need not exclude secondary sources of differentiation. The foregoing analysis allows for differences in the resource claims of every major program, but these crossnational differences are relatively minor when compared to the differences between programs within a country.

IMPLICATIONS FOR POLICY ANALYSIS

Because comparison is a methodological tool rather than a theory, its uses in policy analysis are multiple. Here it is sufficient to point out several different ways in which comparisons may improve the awareness of policy-makers. The first illustration is the comparison of the two sides of the budget, taxing and spending; the second, comparison of public sector and private sector resources mobilized for the same end; and the third, conscious lesson-drawing through crossnational comparison.

Because the budget has two sides, taxing and spending, budgeting is intrinsically comparative. Although that suggestion sounds obvious, it is nonetheless necessary to emphasize this point in view of the distortions introduced into the budget process by an excessive emphasis solely on one side (cf. Pliatzky 1982). In the interwar period, it was typically the revenue side that constrained expenditure; since then, it has been the spending side that has dominated (see, e.g., Buchanan and Wagner 1977).

In the postwar era, politicians have tended to practice "one-eyed Keynes-ianism" (cf. Rose and Peters 1978, 135ff.), spending more money when revenues increase and spending still more as a countercyclical measure when revenues fall. In Britain, the cash revenue constraint was buried beneath "real" or "constant value" figures that were meant to represent a constant volume of goods and services purchased, though it is impossible to fully index tax revenue, which must be collected in current money values (see, e.g., Tanzi 1980). Academic analyses have followed the prevailing Keynesian trend: In political science a dozen articles have appeared about the spending side of the budget for every one about raising revenue to finance that expenditure. The word *budget* today is biased toward expenditure.

Organizationally, governments tend to have a one-eyed perspective. The political interests of spending ministers are different than the interests of either tax administrators, who raise revenue, or finance officials, who allocate revenue. In academic terms, materials currently segregated in journals such as the *National Tax Journal* and the *Journal of Social Policy* logically need to be considered together. Spending on social policy and taxing to finance it are two complementary sides of the policy process, albeit currently two unrelated academic disciplines.

The simple way to give equal concern to revenue *and* expenditure is to think in terms of a fiscal system. The fisc refers to a state's treasury, without any particular connotation of taxing or spending; the system emphasizes the interdependence between the two sides of the budget—and the deficit or surplus that constitutes its bottom line. The Italian term for budget, *bilancio*, emphasizes the significance of balance in the system.

A second within-country comparison is of public sector and private sector resources devoted to public concerns. In the contemporary mixed-economy welfare state, the state is *not* the only source of welfare services. Logically, total welfare in society (TWS) is the sum of outputs from three different sources: the state (S), the market (M), and the household (H) (cf. Rose 1985c).

$$TWS = S + M + H$$

The state's contribution to the welfare mix is substantial, but it is not exclusive. In anything other than a totalitarian society, the state's contribution is less than the total welfare produced by the market, the household, and the state combined.

When comparisons are made solely on the basis of state and market provisions of major welfare programs, the contribution in Britain to the welfare mix varies from 90 percent for education to less than one-third for housing (cf. Rose 1985c). For the most basic of all necessities, food, the state's direct contribution is virtually nil. Nearly all the food that people consume is bought in the market or else homegrown, and most meals are prepared in the home rather than by the market. The food stamp program in the United States is exceptional and was partly designed to benefit the farm bloc.

When the welfare produced by the nonmonetized household economy is added to that produced by the two monetized sectors, the state's contribution to welfare is lessened. Although there are problems in estimating household inputs to welfare, they are nonetheless real. For example, health maintenance can be better secured by an individual's taking regular exercise and following a balanced diet than by frequent attendance at a public clinic or hospital to repair ill health. Education requires nonmonetized inputs from pupils to learn lessons as well as inputs from teachers presenting lessons. The personal social services provided by relatives and neighbors are often of greater value than those provided by employees of local authorities.

Once it is recognized that welfare in society is produced by a multiplicity of sources, then comparison of welfare provision by the state, the market, and the household follows. Comparisons of alternative sources of supply may concern equity in distribution or efficiency, the potential for substitutability between one source and another, and the contribution that each makes to the society's total welfare.

A third implication of the program approach is that comparisons across nations can aid in drawing lessons about how to alter a program in the light of experience elsewhere. Lesson-drawing, like the use of prose, is already part of our everyday life. Every time a local authority official— whether a policeman, a librarian, or a teacher—talks to someone from another authority, there is the potential for learning. Studies of the diffusion of innovation show that people do learn from outside their immediate organization as well as from within it. Particularly for people on top of an organization, looking outward offers the only prospect of learning about alternatives, since by looking within they see only what they already know.

Crossnational lesson-drawing assumes that professional tribalism is as strong as national ethnocentrism. People who work in a given field—whether policemen, postmen, or pedagogues—have many professional concerns in common. This fact is made evident by a variety of transnational professional organizations that mirror almost every activity of government. It is also evident in the organization of many OECD working parties and in the structure of the European Commission, which is organized along functional rather than geographical lines.

The art of lesson-drawing (and it is at least as much art as science) lies in understanding which national differences are important rather than in denying their existence. The European Community has found that there are no functional imperatives that lead member nations to adopt uniform policies, or if they exist they are too weak to override national differences. National differences are palpable in institutions that make and deliver policies, in the inertia of preexisting commitments in a given program area, and in the partisan direction of government and cultural values. Notwithstanding all these considerations, it is nonetheless possible for policymakers to learn from the experience of other nations; for example, when considering the introduction of a Value Added Tax (VAT), already in use in many continental European countries (cf. Johnston 1975, Aaron 1981).

Social scientists have taken comparative policy research two-thirds of the distance toward systematic lesson-drawing. The comparative analysis of the dependent variable—a specific program—is sufficiently advanced to permit identification of similarities and differences among national programs directed toward a common concern. In addition, a substantial effort has been invested in explaining the causes of differences. In order to make crossnational lesson-drawing relevant, a further step is necessary: to distinguish among those identified influences that are subject to manipulation by government (e.g., money inputs), those identified influences that are not readily subject to manipulation by government (e.g., cultural values), and those that cannot be manipulated because they are not identified.

The next major task in comparative policy analysis is to understand under what circumstances desirable features of a program in country A might be introduced in country B and have a reasonable probability of success. The starting point of such efforts is simple: Every program has some common elements that are fungible crossnationally—tax revenues,

234   RICHARD ROSE

education, and defense each demonstrate this fact. But each program also has some specific national features that are not subject to alteration.

The task of innovation within government is more difficult than within the social sciences because the former is a team 'effort; it is not simply the product of an individual scholar's ideas put on paper. The student of comparative public policy usually lacks both the constraints and the opportunities of a public official. If applied creatively, the perspective gained by detachment can be of positive value.

Because nothing is certain in efforts to transfer programs crossnationally, imagination is needed, and risks are present. These factors are accepted routinely by many multinational companies. Many private sector goods and services are common crossnationally, such as those produced by Coca Cola, Xerox, and Sony. Although lesson-drawing about public programs is not a science, it is amenable to systematic application. In the open market of ideas, policy analysts should be as positive in their response to opportunities as clothing manufacturers such as Levi, Strauss & Co. have been. Blue jeans are not the only common international phenomenon; so too is government's concern for pensions, health, and education.

NOTES

The research reported in this chapter is part of a five-year program on the growth of government sponsored by the British Economic & Social Research Council HR 7849/1.

REFERENCES

Aaron, Henry, ed. 1981. *The Value Added Tax: Lessons from Europe.* Washington, D.C.: Brookings Institution.
Almond, Gabriel A., and Sidney Verba, eds. 1980. *The Civic Culture Revisited.* Boston: Little, Brown and Company.
Buchanan, J. M., and R. E. Wagner. 1977. *Democracy in Deficit.* New York: Academic Press.
Cameron, David. 1978. "The Expansion of the Public Economy: A Comparative Analysis." *American Political Science Review* 72:4, pp. 1243–1261.
Dogan, Mattei, and Dominique Pelassy. 1981. *Sociologie politique comparative.* Paris: Economica. 1982. *How to Compare Nations.* Chatham, N.J.: Chatham House.
Great Britain, Statutory Publications Office. 1982. *Index to the Statutes.* London: Her Majesty's Stationery Office.
Great Britain, Treasury. 1983. *The Government's Expenditure Plans, 1983–84 to 1985–86.* Cmnd. 8789-I, II. London: Her Majesty's Stationery Office.
Heclo, Hugh. 1974. *Modern Social Politics in Britain and Sweden.* New Haven: Yale University Press.
Heidenheimer, Arnold. 1984. "Politics, Policy, and Police as Concepts in Western Language." St. Louis: Washington University. Duplicated.
Hood, C. C. 1983. *The Tools of Government.* London: Macmillan.
Hood, C. C., and A. Dunsire. 1981. *Bureaumetrics.* Farnborough, Eng.: Gower.

Johnston, D. 1975. *A Tax Shall Be Charged.* London: Her Majesty's Stationery Office.

King, A. S. 1973. "Ideas, Institutions, and the Policies of Government." *British Journal of Political Science* 3:3-4, pp. 291-313 and 409-423.

Kochen, Manfred, and K. W. Deutsch. 1980. *Decentralization.* Cambridge, Mass.: Oelgeschlager, Gunn and Hain.

Kohl, Jurgen. 1979. *Staatsausgaben in Westeuropa: Ansaetze zur empirischen Analyse der langfristigen Entwicklung der oeffentlichen Ausgaben.* Ph.D. thesis. Mannheim.

Larkey, Patrick D., Chandler Stolp, and Mark Winer. 1981. "Theorizing About the Growth of Government." *Journal of Public Policy* 1:2, pp. 157-220.

Little, I.M.D. 1963. *A Critique of Welfare Economics.* 2d ed. Oxford: Clarendon Press.

McAllister, I., R. Parry, and R. Rose. 1979. *United Kingdom Rankings.* Studies in Public Policy no. 44. Glasgow: University of Strathclyde.

Organization for Economic Cooperation and Development (OECD). 1978. *Public Expenditure Trends.* Studies in Resource Allocation no. 5. Paris.

――――. 1984. *Social Expenditure: 1960-1990.* Paris.

Parry, Richard. 1981. "Territory and Public Employment: A General Model and a British Example." *Journal of Public Policy* 1:4.

Pliatzky, Leo. 1982. *Getting and Spending.* Oxford: Basil Blackwell.

Rose, Richard. 1973. "Comparing Public Policy: An Overview." *European Journal of Political Research* 1:1, pp. 67-94.

――――. 1976. "Disciplined Research and Undisciplined Problems." *International Social Science Journal* 28:1, pp. 99-121.

――――. 1983. "Disaggregating the Concept of Government." In Charles L. Taylor, ed., *Why Governments Grow,* pp. 157-176. Beverly Hills, Calif., and London: Sage Publications.

――――. 1984a. *Are Laws a Cause, a Constraint, or Irrelevant to the Growth of Government.* Studies in Public Policy no. 124. Glasgow: University of Strathclyde.

――――. 1984b. "Families at Work." *Daily Telegraph,* London, April 2-3.

――――. 1984c. *Understanding Big Government.* Beverly Hills, Calif., and London: Sage Publications.

――――. 1985a. "The Growth of Public Employment in Western Nations." In Richard Rose et al., *Public Employment in Western Nations.* Cambridge: Cambridge University Press.

――――. 1985b. "The Programme Approach to the Growth of Government." *British Journal of Political Science* 15:1, pp. 1-28.

――――. 1985c. *The State's Contribution to the Welfare Mix.* Studies in Public Policy SPP 140. Glasgow: University of Strathclyde.

Rose, Richard, and Terence Karran. 1984. *Inertia or Incrementalism? A Long-Term View of the Growth of Government.* Studies in Public Policy no. 126. Glasgow: University of Strathclyde.

Rose, Richard, and Guy Peters. 1978. *Can Government Go Bankrupt?* New York: Basic Books.

Scheuch, E. K. 1966. "Cross-National Comparisons Using Aggregate Data: Some Substantive and Methodological Problems." In R. L. Merritt and S. Rokkan, eds., *Comparing Nations,* pp. 131-168. New Haven: Yale University Press.

Tait, Alan A., and Peter Heller. 1982. *International Comparisons of Government Expenditure.* Occasional Paper no. 10. Washington, D.C.: International Monetary Fund.

Tanzi, Vito. 1980. *Inflation and the Personal Income Tax.* Cambridge: Cambridge University Press.

Taylor, Charles L. 1981. "Limits to National Growth." In R. Merritt and B. Russett, eds., *From National Development to Global Community,* pp. 97–114. London: Allen and Unwin.

United States, Office of Management and Budget. 1984. *Budget of the United States Government: Fiscal Year 1985.* Washington, D.C.: U.S. Government Printing Office.

Van Mechelen, Denis. 1984. *Has There Been a Growth of Legislation in Britain Since 1945?* Studies in Public Policy no. 123. Glasgow: University of Strathclyde.

Wildavsky, Aaron. 1979. *Speaking Truth to Power: The Art and Craft of Policy Analysis.* Boston: Little, Brown and Company.

Table 8.1   The Scale of Major Public Programs Compared

Resource Claims	Public Expenditure[a] (Mean % GNP)	Public Employment[b] (Mean% Employed)
High in money and employment		
Education	6.0	5.5
Health	5.4	4.8
Economic infrastructure	4.3	n.a.
Public enterprise	n.a.	6.7
High in money only		
Income maintenance	15.2	(very low)
Debt interest	3.5	(trivial)
Medium high in money and employment		
Defense	3.2	2.4
High in laws only		
Law and order	1.1[c]	1.5[c]
Total all programs	44.4	27.7

a. Data for Denmark, France, West Germany, Italy, Japan,
   Netherlands, United Kingdom, and the United States,
   latest available year, as reported in "Big Government:
   How Big Is It?" OECD Observer, no. 121 (March 1983),
   p. 8.
b. Calculated by the author from data for latest
   available year from Britain, France, West Germany,
   Italy, Sweden, and the United States, reported in
   Richard Rose et al., Public Employment in Western
   Nations (Cambridge: Cambridge University Press, 1985).
c. Public expenditure figures are for European Community
   countries as of 1970 as reported in Kohl 1979, vol. 2,
   table 3.5. Employment estimates are based on totals
   for police and fire services, plus an allowance for
   court and prison staffs.

Table 8.2 High Variability Between Programs Within Major
Western Nations

	N Programs	Mean (000 employees)	Stand. Dev'n.	Coeff. Nar'n.
United States	18	976	1,540	1.58
Sweden	22	63	88	1.39
Italy	20	212	261	1.23
France	18	305	360	1.18
Britain	21	365	410	1.12
Germany	18	370	289	0.78

Source: Calculated from tables giving functions of
public employees by nation in Richard Rose et al.,
Public Employment in Western Nations (Cambridge:
Cambridge University Press, 1985).

Table 8.3   Low Variability Within Programs
            Across OECD Nations

	Mean	Stand. Dev'n. (%GDP)	Coeff. Var'n.
Pensions			
1960	4.5	2.3	0.51
1961	8.7	3.2	0.37
Health			
1960	2.5	0.7	0.28
1961	5.7	1.3	0.23
Education			
1960	3.5	1.2	0.34
1961	5.9	1.1	0.18
Economic Investment			
Mid-1950s	3.5	1.3	0.37
Mid-1970s	4.3	1.1	0.25
Defense			
Mid-1950s	3.6	2.2	0.60
Mid-1970s	2.8	1.4	0.51
Debt Interest			
Mid-1950s	1.7	0.9	0.50
Mid-1970s	2.8	1.4	0.51

(All coefficients of variation calculated
before rounding off.)

Source: OECD, Public Expenditures Trends
(Paris: OECD, 1978); 14f, 25, and
Social Expenditure 1960-1990 (Paris: OECD).
For debt interest, 20 countries; for
pensions, education and health, 19
countries; for defense, 12 and then 19
countries, and for economic investment,
12 and 16 countries.

Table 8.4 The Direction of Change in
           Major Programs in OECD Nations

	Change in share of GDP 1950s/60s to 1981	
	Up	Down
Health	18	0
Pensions	17	0
Education	16	1
Economic Investment	15	1
Debt Interest	15	5
Defense	5	12

Source: Same as for Table 8.3.

For economic investment, defense and
debt interest, the initial observations
are three-year averages for 1955-57;
for the welfare programs, three-year
averages for the early 1960s. The
latter observation for economic
investment, debt interest and defense
is normally an average, 1974-1976.

Table 8.5   Variability Within National Tax
Systems is Greater than Within
A Single Category of Taxation

Variation in Tax Revenue as % GDP	Coefficient of Variation
Within each of 20 OECD nations across 10 categories of taxes (mean)	1.21
Within each tax category across 20 OECD nations (mean % GDP)	
Income tax (12.7%)	0.39
Excise & use (4.6%)	0.51
VAT and sales (5.7%)	0.53
Wealth & estate (0.9%)	0.53
Corporation (2.8%)	0.56
Social security (9.9%)	0.63
Customs (0.7%)	0.80
Property (1.0%)	1.18
Miscellaneous (0.2%)	1.81
Payroll (0.4%)	1.84

Source: Calculated from 1981 OECD revenue statistics in Richard Rose, "Maximizing Revenue and Minimizing Political Costs: A Comparative Dynamic Analysis" (Salzburg, Annual ECPR Joint Workshops, 1984), Tables 3, 4.

9

WHAT KIND OF PLURALIST DEMOCRACY TOMORROW: CIVIC OR STATE CONTROLLED?

Mattei Dogan

What kind of society will people born today in the pluralist democracies be living in when they are thirty years old? We might consider two hypotheses, deliberately polarized as ideal types for clarity: first, that the proportion of the GNP controlled by the state[1] will increase by half in the next generation, that is to say, it will expand from approximately 50 percent to approximately 75 percent; second, on the contrary, that it will decrease by half, being reduced to approximately 25 percent. According to the first hypothesis, the pluralist democracies will more or less approach a model that we may call the "state-controlled society," characterized by the socialization of a large part of incomes and in many cases also by a centralized capitalism limiting the market economy. According to the second hypothesis, they will move toward a model of "civic society," with moderate penetration of the society by the state and a limited public expenditure. The two types of societies could be equally complex, but the first would be dominated by the state while the other would be organized without the state's being omnipresent. It is the financial intervention of the state that I aim to observe, not the degree of complexity of the so-called postindustrial society or the amount of regulations decreed by the central authority. For instance, the system of pension insurance could be entirely managed by the government or it could be almost entirely private—even if mandatory and regulated in detail by law. The proportion of GNP dedicated to pensions can be the same in both cases, but the consequences for the relations between state and society are obviously contrasting.

A good example of regulation without etatization is the system of codetermination in West Germany (*Mitbestimmung*), which offers employees more influence over company decisions than state ownership in France or

242

Britain does. The best example is the Swedish "functional socialism," which socializes some functions of management while avoiding state ownership.

All pluralistic democracies face these alternatives. It is best not to take a position in this debate by recommending an ideal dosage of etatization for injection into tomorrow's society. I will only indicate some of the means for reaching one or the other type of society. I will also abstain from adopting theories based on economic models, along the lines of scholars such as Milton Friedman or Charles Lindblom; civic society, as considered here, does not correspond to the individualistic perspective of the neoclassical theory of market society. I also will not discuss here the various theories about the growth of government formulated by economists. However, I do find convincing the theorem that "an important component of the explanation for the growth of government lies in government's redistributional activities" (Mueller 1987, 128). I shall look directly at these activities.

I prefer to start from existing realities, as revealed by comparative analysis, with the guiding idea that if an experience has succeeded in one of the thirty advanced pluralist democracies, there is no a priori reason to exclude the possibility of its reproduction in the other countries, which are, after all, similar in many respects. It is irrelevant if the repetition of such experiences results from a similar and parallel maturation or from a kind of contagion by some socialist or liberal virus.

One would suspect the existence of an unavoidable determinism, responding to the electoral logic of pluralist democracies and its leveling effects. Yet, by analyzing the intervention of the state sector by sector—in health, family allocation, pensions, unemployment assistance, nationalized enterprises, educational subsidies, housing subsidies, public transportation, and so on—one sees significant differences from one country to the next. My starting point is the enormous disparity in levels and rates of growth in state expenditure by sectors in spite of some similarity in the total amount of public expenditure. Comparing the role played by the state in Britain, France, West Germany, Canada, and the United States, Anthony King has shown the wide divergencies among these countries in state ownership (particularly in the areas of airlines, banking, oil, iron and steel, electricity, coal, gas, etc.) and in social services (such as old age pensions, unemployment insurance, sick pay, housing, higher education, and so on). The existence of such differences shows that the future is not written in advance, that there is no mechanical determinism.

In 1982, at the moment when the socialist government in France was rapidly nationalizing, the Conservative government on the other side of the English Channel was proceeding with the denationalization of many enterprises. A few years before, the Labour Party had adopted at its 1977 party conference a long list of proposed nationalizations, including banks and insurance companies, but then-Prime Minister James Callaghan declared that his government was not prepared to implement the party's "suicidal" recommendation. What appeared suicidal to Callaghan was at the same moment presented by the candidate François Mitterrand as a "hope for

France." A mountain of data analyzed by the most sophisticated methods could not explain such a divergence of opinion between the two socialist leaders, except perhaps the need to obtain the electoral support of the Communist voters in French presidential elections.

At the famous Bad Godesberg Congress in 1959, the German social democrats gave up the doctrine of nationalization of enterprises. In France, however, the socialists will still proposing nationalization fifteen years later, in the 1974 presidential campaign. Again, in 1981, Mitterrand and the French Socialist party, along with the Communist party, presented the electorate with a program wherein priority was given to the nationalization of most of the largest enterprises and banks. What was considered on one side of the Rhine in 1959 as risking "to become a sect without influence in the political struggles of our time" (Erich Ollenhauer's introductory speech to the congress) appeared on the other side of the Rhine in 1981 as an acceptable proposition for half the French electorate before being, after three years' experience, rejected by a large majority in public opinion polls. Such a reversal suggests that the future is not predetermined, except in the minds of ideologues.

With few exceptions, socialist governments in Sweden, Denmark, and West Germany did not nationalize the large corporations, as did the British and French socialists. "Contemporary economic democracy plans, in Denmark as well as in Sweden, all have one thing in common: they break with the orthodox prescription for nationalization and state ownership of the means of production" (Esping-Anderson 1985, 291).

Is the difference between a society's having 50 percent of its GNP controlled by the state and a society's having 75 percent a difference of degree or of kind? At what point does a quantitative change become a qualitative leap? Rather than getting involved in theoretical considerations, it might be more suggestive to respond by asking another question: Is there a difference of degree or of kind today between Poland, where approximately three-quarters of the GNP is socialized (taking into account both the private agricultural sector and the underground urban economy), and Sweden, where 54 percent of the GNP is controlled by the government? If the degree of etatization of Swedish society were to increase to 75 percent of GNP tomorrow, would this competitive democracy be transformed, *volens nolens*, into a political regime with a heavy hegemonic party? If, in Poland, the control of the economy by the state were to weaken to the point where one out of every two companies relied on the free market, would this country exhibit a tendency toward becoming a pluralist system?[2] Such a question is implicit throughout Charles Lindblom's *Politics and Markets*.

In the exposition of these hypotheses, a number of parameters could be examined,[3] but in this debate we may, for the sake of brevity, limit the imaginary protagonist of each hypothesis to only six arguments. The reader, who may belong to one camp or the other, can certainly add other arguments, except an unpredictable one, military expenditures, which correspond to a traditional and an essential function of the state. These arguments are different in nature. Extrapolating a historical trend is not the same as discussing the possibility of reactions against trends.

THE STATE-CONTROLLED SOCIETY: THE STATE COLLECTS AND REDISTRIBUTES 75 PERCENT OF GNP

The protagonist of the statist thesis chooses the following six arguments: the continuation of a long trend, the ubiquity of a strong Social Democratic party in almost all pluralist democracies (except the United States and Ireland), the role of the new political mandarinate, the aging of the population, the decline in birthrates, and the eventuality of a high level of unemployment.

Extrapolation of a Historical Trend

Government expenditure was accelerated shortly after both World War I and World War II. A nation cannot transform millions of its citizens into soldiers without rewarding the veterans. In the trenches, the distance between social classes was enormously reduced. Several advanced countries adopted universal suffrage just after World War I, which favored the expansion of the welfare state. Because of these abrupt increases in public spending, longitudinal analysis of the causes of government growth has limited explanatory power. It is sufficient to indicate here that the size of public expenditure in the GNP in Germany grew from about 8 percent in 1900 to 10.5 percent in 1913-1914, 29.2 percent in 1924-1925, and 45.3 percent in 1982 (the last figure refers to West Germany), and one can observe similar progressions in Britain (10, 11.3, 24.8, 43.7 percent), France (15, 14, 20, 46.9 percent), and the United States (7.7, 7.7, 11, and 32 percent) (Mueller 1987, 117). These trends are impressive; it is nevertheless more meaningful for our purposes to consider here only the later years.

As Table 9.1 shows, some countries had relatively high general government expenditures by 1960, such as Austria, France, Germany, the Netherlands, Norway, and Sweden. But almost a quarter of a century later, we find only a few of these among the countries with the highest expenditures, and some others have surpassed them—particularly Belgium, Denmark, Ireland, and the United Kingdom. Why did some countries increase so much more rapidly than others, without any relation to their starting levels in 1960? Some scholars have analyzed the causes of this growth in a sophisticated way without always arriving at impressive results. Why did the share of government expenditures in Denmark and Ireland increase almost 100 percent while that in the United States increased by only 22 percent during the same period? Only by carefully examining the political history of these three countries could this question be answered, taking into consideration a series of factors such as the political culture and the size of each country. Was the United States less democratic than the other two? Maybe the Irish government became an ambitious entrepreneur. Anyway, it is worthwhile to note that my starting hypothesis of an increase of 50 percent of the proportion of GNP controlled by the state over thirty-five years has been surpassed by an increase of almost 100 percent in only twenty-five years in the cases of Denmark and Ireland. In Sweden, government revenue as a percentage of GNP also doubled between 1950 and 1972, from 25.9 percent to 50.1 percent (Peacock 1979, 81).

In the Western European democracies the proportion of the GNP collected by the state has, since 1950, increased by a yearly average of 0.8 percent. It is a reasonable hypothesis that such a trend could continue by injecting society with small unpainful doses of the statist drug. An increase of taxation by 0.8 percent per year is tolerable, even over a long period. No one revolts against a percentage! Nevertheless, this rate maintained over thirty years means, by cumulative effect, a nearly 30 percent increase. Then one has, without being really conscious of it, a state-controlled society. One could observe that this extrapolation is a rigid one that does not take into consideration the hazards of history. It is useful to recall here a history lesson.

Almost a century ago, the German economist Adolf Wagner wrote that the progress of human civilization is reflected in the increase of the proportion of the GNP managed by the state (Wagner, vol. 3). An analysis of 116 nations in 1973, comparing per capita GNP and the portion of GNP controlled by the government, seems to confirm Wagner's law, if one excludes the oil-producing countries (Taylor 1981). Nothing proves that there is an absolute threshold over which taxation could become unsupportable. In 1926, John Maynard Keynes wrote the French minister of finance an open letter in which he estimated that it would be politically impossible to have public expenditures surpass one-quarter of the GNP, and there is a long list of economists from Leon Say through Colin Clark to Joseph Schumpeter who have estimated that a new increase of social expenditures was unsupportable. When President Giscard d'Estaing estimated in 1974 that the tax threshold of 40 percent of GNP should not be surpassed, it had already reached 50 percent in the Netherlands and Sweden and almost that in Norway and Denmark. Ironically, at the end of Giscard's term in 1981, the state collected 42 percent of GNP, and by 1984, three years after the beginning of the socialist experiment, the percentage had climbed still higher, to 47 percent. A real decline of taxation has not been realized, not even in the United States as the decrease during the first Reagan administration was insignificant. In a few countries, the reduction in direct taxation has been compensated for by an increase in indirect taxation. From this point of view, the 1987 British budget was similar to the French budget of the same year: There was a slight decrease of expenses but not of taxation, since it was urgently necessary to reduce the national debt.

The progression of the interventionist state will probably continue with economic growth. Thirty years from now we might see observers asking if state control of 60 or 65 percent of the GNP represents an unbreakable barrier, after which the qualitative change will be such that it will no longer be possible to talk of democratic pluralism, since too much power would be concentrated in the higher state bureaucracy. Such debates will undoubtedly take place if the economies of the postindustrial societies become even more heavily controlled by those who hold the reins of the state.

The Ubiquity of Social-Democracy in Western Europe

It is necessary to distinguish between the budget for the functioning of the modern state and the social budget of the nation. The first varies little over time, except for military expenses. Historically, before World War I it was tied to the growth of GNP, escaping the left-right cleavage, and seemingly incompressible. In many countries, its amount changes by less than 2 or 3 percent when the electoral pendulum passes from right to left or back again. Just as their predecessors had not significantly changed this budget, the governments of Thatcher, Reagan, and Chirac have not reduced it. Their successors will probably maintain it, except in some details. In this domain of the indispensable, irreplaceable, and incompressible state, yearly parliamentary debates are only rituals and formalities—except, of course, for military expenses.

It is the social budget of the nation that changes, and it changes in two ways: in the short term and in the long term. This distinction is not clear enough, because any increase of the social budget in the short term tends to be irreversible, each short-term increase becoming long-term by accretion. A lot of time could pass between the moment when a decision is made in principle and the moment when the budgetary consequences of the decision fully appear.

It is the short-term change that interests us here, taking into consideration an important political fact: There is a strong Social Democratic party in all pluralist democracies except the United States and Ireland (in Canada, socialism is a regional phenomenon). A question has been clearly formulated by several scholars: Is there any relation between the participation of the Social Democratic party in power and the increase in the portion of the GNP controlled by the state? To answer this question, some political scientists and economists have utilized sophisticated quantified methods, some of which have lacked not a grain of naïveté. It is true that the reply is not as easy as it might seem at first, and we will not advance very much by considering examples of conservative leaders who accomplished great social reforms, from Bismarck and Disraeli to contemporary leaders such as de Gaulle and de Gasperi.

There are two main difficulties in trying to ascertain the importance of the Social Democratic party in the growth of government. The first stems from the fact that a strong Social Democratic party in opposition (or even a Communist party, as in Italy, Finland, and, until recently, France) may have an impact on the policy of their conservative adversaries in power. This phenomenon is known, in French politics, as *sinistrisme*, the tendency of the centrist parties to imitate and adopt, because of the electoral competition, part of the program of their leftist rivals.

The second difficulty arises because in many of these countries economic growth has usually been associated with conservative government, as in France and Italy. It was easier to expand the state's role in society and to promote social reforms whenever there was a budget surplus in the treasury. Yet, even those authors who stress the relationship between the growth of government and the growth of the economy also recognize the impact of the socialist presence in government:

> The rapid economic growth of the recovery period after World War II enabled Western democracies to increase public spending in almost all fields because of greater fiscal resources. Now, as the prospects for sustained economic growth diminish, political pressure is exerted on governments and parliaments to maintain and even expand the present level of public expenditures. Both former obligations and increased needs during economic crisis suggest that relative expenditure growth (public spending as a percentage of GNP) is disproportionately expanded when economic development slackens. Thus, public expenditure development is less a function of economic growth and is instead primarily determined by political and ideological factors. [Kohl 1986, 307–308]

Tom W. Rice has done a longitudinal analysis of twelve European countries for the period 1950–1980, measuring the increase of public expenses and the strength of socialist parties in parliament. His regression models are inconclusive: Too many factors are involved. On the other hand, David Cameron compared eighteen Western democracies and found a significant relationship between the increase of civil expenses and the presence in the government of a leftist party—a Social Democratic party in the European countries. When the left governs, he concluded, the extent of government control of GNP increases.[4]

There is also no ambiguity in John D. Stephens's analysis of seventeen Western democracies in which he measured socialist participation in government between 1945 and 1970 and the proportion of GNP allocated to civil public expenses in each country. His conclusion is that increases in social expenditures vary positively with the length of time socialists are present in government (Stephens 1979, chap. 4).

Jens Alber distinguished several historical phases for twelve European countries, examining the relationship between socialist electoral success and the extent of social redistribution during the five years following such success. He showed that social expenditures depend on the strength of the socialists in parliament and government: "The extension of social programs was usually pushed forward more strongly when socialist parties formed part of the governing coalitions" (Alber 1979, 10). Edward R. Tufte arrived at similar results:

> Parties of the Left traditionally favored a more powerful central government than parties of the Right. Governing political parties have translated these preferences into policy. [There is a] very strong relationship between government receipts, as a percent of GNP, and the extent of Socialist-Labor control of

the executive in 13 countries. From 1945 to 1969, each additional decade of the left-wing control meant an additional 10 percentage point increase in government receipts. [Tufte 1978, 97]

Because of the strong ties between the socialist parties and the unions, the presence of socialists in government, alone or in coalition, facilitates cooperation between government and unions. It is for this reason that neocorporatism flourishes in countries where the socialists have held executive power for a long time. In Austria, for instance, "the vertical interconnections of the left camp form a cornerstone of the neo-corporatist network. Since within the OGB [the trade union federation] the Socialist *Fraktion* has a solid majority this means that both are intensely interconnected through overlapping membership" (Lehmbruch 1984, 9).

In Ireland, where there is no significant socialist party, public expenditure has nevertheless risen as much as in countries having a strong socialist party. This fact could be explained by the role assumed by the Irish state in the growth and modernization of the economy (Desmond King 1986, 86).

Undoubtedly, the socialists are changing their orientation and program, and the French socialists of tomorrow will be very different from what they were before 1983. Having experienced power in 1981–1986, they have become less ideological and more pragmatic, as has happened to socialists in many other countries before them. Other socialists, for ideological reasons, have moved away from stressing the state toward popular ownership and control under the guise of such phrases as "industrial democracy." Nevertheless, the left-right cleavage will remain essential for the degree of etatization of the society. It is enough to compare the recent electoral programs of the socialist parties with those of their adversaries to be convinced that the social budget of every European nation will have the tendency—all other conditions being equal—to inflate or deflate according to the color of the parliamentary majority—red, pink, or blue.

The New Statist Mandarins

Statism is not advocated just by social democrats; they have objective allies at the highest levels of the state apparatus. The higher civil servants in charge of the economic and social functions of the state are managers, industrialists, investors, organizers, subsidizers, regulators, treasury inspectors, planners, experts in national agencies, directors of nationalized corporations, bankers, chairmen of powerful boards, and heads of the French Planning Commission, the Italian Institute for Industrial Reconstruction, the British Economic Development Council, the Belgian Bureau of Economic Planning, the Dutch Central Plan Bureau, and so on.

The manna of the state does not profit everyone equally; the priests who celebrate its cult profit the most. The importance of this statist priesthood varies from country to country. In a Weberian ideal-type analysis, we should include in the comparison the Eastern Empire. The "New Class" was first described by Milovan Djilas: "The new class obtains its power, privileges, ideology, and its customs from one specific form of ownership—collective ownership—which the class administers and distributes in the name of the nation and society" (Djilas 1957, 45). According to Michael Voslenskii, the principal characteristic of this new class, and what sets it apart in the elitist gallery, comes from the fact that it "starts with the takeover of state power and finishes with the takeover of power in the economic field. . . . It is not the class of proprietors. It is the class of administrators" (Voslenskii 1984, 100–101). The class is registered in the "nomenklatura," the list of top positions subject to the control of the party leadership as well as the list of persons appointed to such positions or kept in reserve. In imperial China, the mandarins were nonhereditary civil servants recruited on the basis of merit demonstrated in competitive written examinations. The contemporary Soviet mandarins are selected primarily on political criteria. The Western mandarins are a hybrid variety: half political, half technical (Dogan 1975, 4).

We do not find an imitation of the Soviet nomenklatura in its full splendor anywhere else, not even in China where there are no more mandarins in silk robes. France provides the closest analogue. For some time, no category of the French ruling class has been analyzed more carefully than this state mandarinate. Some well-placed and perspicacious observers have testified to its role; a few have even exaggerated its dominance, as in a carnival-house mirror. Alexandre Wickham and Sophie Coignard have collected a rich documentation of these *privilegiatures* of French society, and Michel Schifres called it "l'Enaklatura," using the initials of the Ecole Nationale d'Administration and thus considerably reducing its size. We also have this self-portrait painted in the shades of Rembrandt:

> I am, for my part, a full product of the state technistructure and my appointment to the head of this nationalized enterprise is a typical example of a process of selection of para-public managers from the pool of the political-administrative class. My career is nothing extraordinary. Graduated from a great school in a good position, I naturally entered the civil service. . . . There I made my apprenticeship in the state *grand corps,* and then, by the hazard of relationships and friendships and mainly by the vigilance of my *corps* and its will to see itself represented in the greatest possible number of ministerial staff, I was propelled into the service of several cabinet ministers . . . from time to time, I returned to my original administration in order to climb the scale . . . my age and my career encouraged me to nourish new ambitions. In 1981, I started to look elsewhere. [Pierre Dupont Gabriel 1985, 19–20]

This painting is worth more than a mountain of statistics. Nothing is missing. Make 4,000 or 5,000 copies of various sizes, reserving a place of honor for the 800 higher civil servants and administrators appointed directly by the Council of Ministers. Retouch each one according to its prestige, power, income, and privileges, and you will have the totality of the new mandarin class, nourished by statism, with the mixed economy being its preferred meal.

The "pink elite" was in the front stage during socialist rule (1981–1986), a sample of which is presented by Monique Dagnaud and Dominique Mehl. But, according to Philippe Alexandre and Jacques Delors, "the Gaullists and the Right have also, in the exercise of power, constantly reinforced the role of the state and multiplied its interventions" (1986, 88). Bernard Gournay is as explicit: "It is true that the higher civil servants are relatively favorable to a political and social system which is semi-public, semi-private, and to highly centralized interventions of the state. It is true that in defending this system, they are reinforcing their own positions. Who would want to destroy this system? Certainly not the men who have succeeded in the governments of the Fifth Republic for twenty years" (Gournay 1981, 231). For Jean-Francois Revel, a new nomenklatura becomes theoretically possible

> when the autonomy of the economy has been so reduced or suppressed that it becomes marginal. . . . Suppose, in fact, the existence of a nomenklatura, a society where the scale of incomes and of all material, cultural and moral advantages coincide, point by point, with the hierarchy of political and bureaucratic positions. Such a fusion implies full socialism, economics being absorbed forever by politics, an ultimate stage which France obviously is not ready to reach. [Revel 1981, 136]

There are exceptions. It is possible to mention great mandarins who resisted such politicization, such as Francois Bloch-Laine, who "loved the administration indefatigably" (Bloch-Laine 1976, 75). There is also Pierre Moussa, who had the courage to criticize the system:

> The appointment of the managers of the public sector is always a prerogative of the executive power . . . the main risk is that the career of a manager of a corporation becomes the coronation of a nice career as civil servant. But, experience shows that the first-class high civil servant does not necessarily become a first-class manager, sometimes yes, sometimes no . . . the public sector of the French economy works in this way when it selects its managers from among the higher civil servants. [Moussa 1986]

Obviously, the political class in general, and its mandarinate branch in particular, have become the accomplices of the hypertrophy of the state. If these mandarins are the people who profit the most from the growth of government, is it not also in their own interest to push for an extension of the state? One could question their sincerity when they pretend to represent the general interest of the nation.

Starting with the ideal type of the French mandarin, a comparative analysis could be developed without too much difficulty. It is possible to find an impure variety of mandarins in what the Italians call *sottogoverno,* and the Scandinavian variety is recruited on a neocorporatist basis. It is in Belgium that we observe the most politicized selection of top civil servants (Moulin 1975) while on the scale of politicization the Austrian mandarins have a privileged place. In the Netherlands, the recruitment of higher civil servants is accomplished according to consociational criteria.

In Britain, the three tracks—political, administrative, managerial—are almost impermeable. In fact, whereas the higher civil servants are traditionally neutral, the managers of national enterprises are recruited from business people. The British higher administration does not, therefore, get any direct advantage from the etatization of the economy. In the United States, the interpenetration is limited to the "revolving door" in the military-industrial complex. Scholars like C. Wright Mills and others have not given enough attention to this country's federal public administration, but it is clear that the spoils system at the top of the pyramid does not offer the privileges and guarantees that benefit the top civil servants in France and many other European countries. There is not, in the United States, the equivalent of a new statist class of mandarins. It is necessary to look further, to Japan, in order to discover the cousin of the French mandarin; but the relationship is not a close one because the transfer from the public sector to the private sector is an irreversible move in Japan.

The Aging of the Population

The advanced societies are aging in the sense that the proportion of people over 65 is progressively increasing. In the United States, the expectation of life at age 60 in 1982 was 20.4 years; at 65, 16.8 years; at 75, 10.8 years; at 80, 8.3 years (United States 1986, 69). A person who retires at age 65 has a statistical chance to continue to live about 16.5 more years. Germany has more inhabitants aged 62 years and over than it has youngsters under 16.

> The ratio of contributors to retirees [in the social security system] is projected to decrease by almost half within the next fifty years, declining to 1.12 in 2030, if the present birth rate continues. If the current benefit formula were maintained, the social security tax rate would have to increase from 18 percent in 1982 to 32 percent in 2030. If the current tax rate were maintained, the ratio of social security pensions to current after tax wages would have to be almost halved. [Juttemeier and Petersen 1982, 183, 193]

Most of the European countries are approaching a demographic profile similar to that of Germany, and the percentage of septuagenarians and octogenarians is nearly as high in Japan as in Western Europe.

In the Western European countries, the state takes more care of the older population than anywhere else in the world with the exception of Israel, and the financial burdens of this lengthening of life in the advanced societies are becoming heavier and heavier. The basic values of Western culture do not allow the slightest abandonment of this population by the state, which is committed to take care of the elderly because of the contributions they have already made toward social security. The acceptance of euthanasia will not come soon because of religious resistance and because of the objective complicity of the medical profession—whose concerns are easily understood and can even be approved.

Statistical data about the financial consequences of this rapid aging of the population, using projections for the next thirty or forty years, have been presented in Chapter 7 of this book. Considering the development of medical technology in general and of gerontology in particular, some experts are very pessimistic about the financial prospect. Only later will a state be able to reduce its intervention if it now takes the necessary steps to replace the current pay-as-you-go system with a private insurance system—while nevertheless continuing to regulate insurance companies and to guarantee minimal assistance to the poorest. In Europe, a system of capitalization for pensions and for medical care, such as exists in the United States, will bear full fruit only after the thirty-five year period that I consider here. Until such a change occurs, the aging of the population will be a factor favoring the growth of the state. Meanwhile, the retardation of the retirement age will become unavoidable—contrary to what most union leaders advocate today in France, Italy, Germany, Belgium, and Scandinavia.

The Decline of Birthrates

It is well known that in most advanced Western countries the birthrate is no longer sufficient to maintain zero population growth. Consequently, the populations of these countries will decline. The reasons for this decline are many, and we need not discuss them here, as only the fact of decline is relevant to this discussion.

The issue can be clearly stated. In order for a generation to be fully replaced by another, 100 women have to give birth to 100 girls. Since at birth girls are less numerous than boys (105 boys to 100 girls), 100 women have to give birth to 205 babies. Considering also other minor factors, demographers estimate that a birthrate of 2.2 children per woman is the minimum for maintaining a population at the same level. In most European countries, the birthrate is now lower than that minimum. In France, the birthrate has remained at only 1.8 since 1976, in spite of generous family allocations; in West Germany, it has been only 1.3 for many years, and most other European countries fall somewhere in between those two figures. Such a demographic trend is typical of declining civilizations.

Theoretically, four "solutions" could be imagined, the first being currently unrealistic, and I mention it here only because we cannot be certain that it will never become acceptable. After all, most observers of China a few decades ago would have thought unrealistic a policy imposing a limit of one child per family—even if the unique child is a girl, in a culture where the family survives only through sons. This policy has nevertheless been implemented, affecting hundreds of millions of people. It is true that this would not have been possible if China had been a pluralist democratic country. Among the solutions, I do not consider possible a reverse of current policies on birth control and abortion, at least not under a democratic regime.

The first solution is to impose a mandatory birthrate for women similar to compulsory military service for men, with parallel medical exemptions.

Today, women who have no children are not "punished," but it is conceivable that one day a government might democratically decide to impose financial sanctions on childless women. Such a measure would clearly require the consent of a large proportion of the female electorate.

The second possibility is simply to ignore the problem, which could result over several generations in a kind of national suicide. Perhaps West Germany comes closest to having chosen this path. The third solution is immigration. The United States and Israel are the leaders here, both building on traditions of using immigration to populate their lands. Other countries have hesitated to use this solution since the necessary immigrants cannot possibly be forthcoming from the other Western countries, which are themselves declining, so immigrants can come only from non-Western, less-advanced, and—it must be noted—nonwhite countries. Thus, immigration entails a wider range of cultural and racial diversity than most of these countries have been willing to consider, and it may lead to increased racial tension among a population, as in the last decade in Britain, France, Switzerland, and Germany. Even in the United States, the assimilation of an even larger number of Hispanics may present many problems.

The fourth solution is to encourage an increased birthrate by providing family allocations and financial incentives for having a second or third child. Many Europeans countries have chosen this solution, to varying extents, and the fiscal implications of such large-scale subsidization give this option a place among the reasons why a more state-controlled society can be expected. If the birthrate continues to decline, the role of the state can only increase as it desperately attempts to reverse the trend. This solution is very costly. Contrary to the pessimism of some demographers, "governments can buy babies," but they would have to pay the right price.

In France, for instance, parents with several children receive important subsidies. Of course, the wealthy feel no need for these subsidies, so the policy is relatively ineffective in encouraging the upper classes to reproduce. The members of the lower classes, those most in need of the extra income, are the ones most likely to avail themselves of the money provided; as an ultimate irony, it appears that immigrants are the most likely of all to seek such subsidies.

Sometimes such programs overlap and intermix with other welfare state provisions. In Vienna, for instance, a mother may be eligible for as many as nine distinct subsidies upon childbirth, some designed to encourage having children, some designed to offset medical expenses, some designed as welfare for the poor. In such cases, the declining birthrate interacts with other factors that encourage growth of the welfare state and increases the role of the state even more.

A High Level of Unemployment

All the advanced pluralist democracies have some kind of unemployment insurance system, although the details of these systems vary widely. Some are private, some are semipublic, others are fully public; some provide almost full pay for up to a year, others half pay for a matter of weeks; some rely on the contributions of workers, others rely on contributions from employers, and most rely on both.

All these insurance systems work well in times of predictable and relatively low unemployment, since the funds from which compensation is drawn are prepared for an unemployment rate of 2 or 3 percent. Thus, all functioned smoothly throughout the postwar boom, and during the period of the Keynesian consensus, they even contributed to stability because of their countercyclical nature.

Since the two oil shocks of the 1970s, however, unemployment has been at postwar record levels in most, if not all, advanced pluralist countries. Crises of unemployment, reaching over 10 percent of the working population, have put extraordinary demands on the systems of unemployment compensation in many countries. If 10 percent of the workers of a country are unemployed for a year, that means that the 90 percent still working must support the 10 percent unemployed. If the reserves from the normal unemployment insurance system are exhausted, there is no institution capable of intervening except the state. No unemployment insurance system can deal with these unforeseen major crises, whose effects on insurance companies are like those of an earthquake. Only the state has the resources with which to confront these society-wide dislocations. These resources, like all state resources, come ultimately from taxation and will provide regular impetuses for movements in the direction of a state-controlled society. If the nine employed out of every ten must support the one who is not, simple mathematics tells us that the nine must accept an increase in their taxation of 11 percent. The state must fill the vacuum left by insurance institutions by taxing and redistributing, taking and giving.

Increasing competition from newly industrializing countries could also contribute to unemployment in the advanced democracies. As Korea, Taiwan, Singapore, Brazil, and others develop more and more dynamic export sectors in textiles, shipbuilding, steel, automobiles, and even armaments, Europe, North America, and even Japan will be under pressure to develop increasingly sophisticated postindustrial technologies. It is by no means certain that all, or even most, of the European nations will succeed in the attempt. Those that fail will need to confront endemically high unemployment, but even those that succeed will doubtless be subject to recurrent shocks such as those of the 1970s. In a world of rapidly fluctuating exchange rates, even a dynamic country such as Japan suffers when the value of its currency skyrockets. Small countries are even more sensitive to international market conditions. As Peter Katzenstein has suggested, these countries may use "domestic compensation" as part of a strategy of economic adjustment, but as market conditions reach crisis levels, the size of this compensation must increase.

Unemployment compensation is not, of course, the only possible policy with which to combat unemployment. Governments could utilize a number of measures such as employment subsidies, job training, expanded research and development, active manpower policies, investment subsidies, and severe limitations on "guest workers" either to prevent unemployment or to ameliorate it once it occurs. However, all of these measures have their costs, and all would move a country toward a state-controlled society. In addition, placing restrictions on immigration rules out one of the solutions to the declining birthrate, which highlights the interrelationships among these different possibilities.

In the case of a rise in unemployment, the people most victimized are the young who are trying to enter the labor market but for whom there is no place. Unions protect those who already have a job against those who want a job. Even by the late 1970s in several Western European countries, one in every four people under twenty-five were condemned to a parasitic existence, with all the psychological consequences such a life implies. In Britain in 1982, 23.7 percent of all those under twenty-five were unemployed compared to only 8.6 percent of those over twenty-five. In the United States in the same year, the figures were 17.8 percent and 9.7 percent, respectively (Ashton 1986, 105).

One of the lessons that must be learned from the experience of the Weimar Republic is that the young generation should not be delivered to the extremists. These young people may receive unemployment compensation, but the political consequences could be more important than the economic ones. Some policies seek to mitigate these adverse consequences (Ashton 1986, 173–181), but programs such as the U.S. Job Corps, the British Youth Opportunities Programmes, or the French Program for Apprenticeship are also expensive, bringing us further in the direction of the state-controlled society.

CIVIC SOCIETY: THE STATE CONTROLS 25 PERCENT OF GNP

Having heard the arguments of the statist protagonist, we should now turn to those of his opponent. Could the megalomanic state retreat until it collects only 25 percent of the GNP, while still assuring the essential functions of the modern state and without compromising the legitimacy of the democratic system? This second hypothetic prospective again involves consideration of six arguments, based on the experiences of several countries: popular capitalism, the capitalization of pensions, employee shareholding, the disappearance of the state as a housing authority, privatization of higher education, and the conversion of tax evasion into social welfare.

Popular Capitalism as an Alternative to State Capitalism

A new phenomenon could be observed by the comparativist today: The more popular shareholding expands, the more the entrepreneurial role of the state shrinks. The great originality of recent denationalization in several countries is the transfer of capital, not to the "capitalist-with-the-cigar-between-his-teeth," but to the millions of small shareholders. Sociologically, such popular shareholding fills the same ideological function as the nationalization of corporations. The current programs of denationalization, started in Britain under Thatcher and in France in 1986, would reduce the portion of the GNP that the state controls by about 9 or 10 percent if accomplished in their entirety: from 47 percent of French GNP in December 1985 to 37 percent if all sixty-five nationalized corporations listed in the program of the liberal coalition for the March 1986 elections are effectively denationalized.

Adolf Berle and Gardiner Means in *The Modern Enterprise and Private Property*, published in 1932, showed that on the one hand, the direction of enterprises is largely escaping from the holders of capital while on the other hand, the possession of capital is becoming more and more diffuse. All studies done since then, by James Burnham among others, confirm the Berle and Means analysis: The holders of capital surrender their power of command to managers and experts, and the shareholders are more and more numerous, that is to say, the capitalist class is growing considerably.

The increase of the number of shareholders during the last two decades—in addition to the ballooning of the middle classes and the numerical decline of the manual workers—makes the dichotomous vision of Karl Marx's epigones archaic, and the Marxist theoreticians in Europe do not grant the phenomenon of popular capital diffusion the importance that it merits. Reality is changing more rapidly than either theory or ideology.

In the United States, the diffusion of popular shareholding is not a recent phenomenon, as it is in many West European countries, Japan, and a few other advanced countries. Nonetheless, its extension in the United States has accelerated during the last thirty years. In 1983, there were 42,360,000 shareholders, as opposed to 32,260,000 in 1981 and 30,850,000 in 1970 (United States 1986, 509). In 1959, there were only 12,490,000 shareholders. In 1983, one out of every four U.S. adults possessed stocks or bonds, as opposed to one out of every six in 1965 and one out of every sixteen in 1952. As is the case with all other forms of property, this popular shareholding is not equally distributed among the various social strata. Among the shareholders in 1983, 3 percent had an income of less than $10,000; 25 percent, an income between $10,000 and $25,000; 40 percent, between $25,000 and $50,000; and 19 percent, more than $50,000. More than 14 percent were minors whose parents had invested in the name of their children (United States 1986, 509), usually to supply capital for their college education. Obviously, this sociological shareholding profile does not reflect the social structure of the population. Blue-collar workers, whose incomes are not necessarily lower than those of many white-collar workers, participate unequally in this popular capitalism, as can be seen from the 1986 distribution of shareholders according to their level of education: 27,900,000 had a college education; 11,000,000 had ended their schooling earlier. Popular shareholding tends to follow the contours of the middle classes.

How many myths and stereotypes collapse when one learns that the shares of General Motors were distributed among nearly 1 million shareholders in 1985; that the shares of American Telephone and Telegraph (New York) were held by 2,927,067 shareholders; that the telephone network, instead of belonging to a small and powerful group of capitalists or to the state as a monopoly, belonged to more than 5 million shareholders of Bell South Corporation, Bell Atlantic, Southern Bell, etc.; that IBM has 798,152 shareholders; Exxon Corporation, 776,172; Ford Motor, 274,634; General Electric, 506,000, and so on. The list of the fifty largest U.S. companies and the list of corporations that have the greatest number of shareholders greatly overlap (see Table 9.2 for thirty of them based on Moody's Industrial Manual, 1986).

Statistics about individual shareholders in the United States are not reliable because it is difficult to estimate the number of subscribers to mutual funds. According to one source, about 10 percent of the value of shares quoted in the market are owned by individual shareholders, leaving financial corporations with less than 35 percent and foreign investors with about 5 percent. Because of this popular shareholding, the United States escapes state capitalism and reduces concentrated capitalism, so well described by the Marxists of yesteryear.[5] Popular shareholding does not avoid concentration of control in relatively few hands, but even if power is retained by the large shareholders, millions of small shareholders nonetheless profit as well. Studies about the professionalization of management show, nevertheless, that at this level reality has buried stereotypes.

Popular shareholding is as well diffused in Japan as in the United States. The number of Japanese shareholders increased from 8,607,000 in 1956 to 18,072,000 in 1966 and 19,181,000 in 1976. In 1981, 19,590,000 individuals held fewer than 50,000 shares each, and they represented 99 percent of the total of 19,785,000 shareholders, as well as 25 percent of the total capital of the 1,734 companies traded on the Tokyo stock market. It is true that the capital held by "small capitalists" diminished between 1951 and 1981, going from 49.2 to 37.2 percent (Tokyo Stock Exchange Fact Book 1982). Simultaneously, banks, insurance companies, and other financial institutions increased their portion. Nonetheless, one-quarter of the capital traded in the market in 1981 was still distributed among almost 20 million individuals. One in every five Japanese, or one in every three families, owned some capital in the form of stocks and bonds. It is easy to nationalize a company belonging to a small number of persons; it is much more difficult to expropriate shares belonging to one of every three families. Popular shareholding does not lead to participation in the cult of the state.

In Germany, there were about 21,400,000 shareholders in 1985, and 13,500,000 low-income shareholders were eligible to receive state financial assistance in order to acquire shares. The best occasion for popular shareholding is the denationalization of public enterprises, but as Germany has nationalized relatively little, there is not very much to denationalize. The nationalized sector in 1985 represented only 5 percent of the total value of German industry, which contrasts heavily with the situation in Britain before 1980 and in France after 1981. In Britain and in France, popular shareholding is a recent phenomenon, deliberately encouraged by the denationalization of state-owned companies. Privatization was perceived as "an attempt to push through change on such a widespread scale that it would be impossible for any future Labour government readily to reverse it" (Young 1986, 236).

In Britain, the public sector in 1979 included about fifty companies, which were responsible for nearly 12 percent of the GNP. By 1985, about twenty of these companies had been sold for a total of £7.5 billion (Santini 1986, 47–67). The sectors touched by privatization were energy, telecommunications, aeronautics, and automobiles. To favor popular shareholding, an important advertising campaign was launched at the offering of each company. Small buyers were given priority; for instance, all orders for fewer than 400 shares of British Telecom were satisfied while orders for more than 1,200 shares were automatically reduced to 800 shares. It is estimated that more than 2 million people have purchased shares of British Telecom, half of whom had never previously acquired a share in their life. Individual investors obtained 34.2 percent of the total equity; institutional investors, 47 percent; foreign investors, 13.8 percent; and employees of British Telecom, 4.6 percent (Santini 1986, 54). For all denationalizations, the official estimates as of April 1985 were 6 million individual shareholders. After new denationalizations in 1986, popular shareholding in Britain was estimated at 9 million adults. There are in Britain today as many small shareholders as members of unions. New privatizations that will expand the popular shareholding even more are being considered by the Thatcher government, making the process of privatization irreversible. The government intends to sell parts of British Airways, the British Airports Authority, British Steel, Rolls Royce, British Leyland, British Shipbuilding, the National Bus Company, and other firms.

Selling parts of the nationalized industries is not the only way of reducing the role of the state. Discussing the meaning of the concept of privatization in Britain, Stephen Young distinguishes among eight forms, the first three being the most important: selling off public sector assets, relaxing state monopolies, contracting services out, private provision of services, investment projects, extending private sector practices into the public sector, reducing subsidies, and increasing charges. These various forms of privatization resulted in part from a "learning process," from a pragmatic strategy that became a source of inspiration for the French conservative government formed in March 1986.

In France, after two years of the socialist "experiment," there was an impressive ideological reversal in the opinion polls in 1983, at both the elite and mass levels: disenchantment with nationalization. At that moment, only 8 percent of the financing of twenty-two nationalized corporations was supplied by the enterprises' income, whereas 55 percent was financed by bonds and other debts and 37 percent by the government. About 7 percent of the national budget was allocated to cover the losses of the nationalized enterprises. The deficit of the railway network, SNCF, for instance, amounted to 30 billion francs, or about 2,000 francs for each taxpayer. The process of denationalization began in 1986, soon after legislative elections brought a conservative majority to the National Assembly. For instance, when the state-owned Compagnie Generale d'Electricite was privatized in 1987, 85 percent of the shares were reserved for small shareholders. The law severely restricted the number of shares each individual could obtain.

The first privatizations generated a massive class of small shareholders of Saint-Gobain (1.5 million shareholders), of Bank Paribas (3.8 million), and of Compagnie Generale d'Electricite (2.2 million). Between September 1986 and August 1987, eleven corporations were privatized, including Elf-Acquitaine and banks such as Société Générale and Suez. It is difficult to estimate the total number of new small shareholders in France, since some of them acquired shares in two or more denationalized companies. According to nonofficial estimates, the number of "small capitalists" was over 8 million by July 1987. The Chirac government intended to denationalize a total of sixty-five corporations. If this program is achieved, several ideological dichotomies would have to be seriously revised. In 1987, there were more "small capitalists" in France than there were union members, and their number is expected to double by the privatization of other large corporations.

In Austria, where the state controls about two-thirds of the economy, where the total taxation in 1986 reached 42.4 percent of GNP, and where all nationalized enterprises except one (the oil company OEMV) were in deficit in 1986, a new coalition between socialists and liberals formed after the November 1986 elections seems determined to reduce the economic role of the state. Subsidies for public enterprises have mounted to about 40 billion schillings each year and in 1986, to half of the national budget deficit. The coalition government has already decided on the privatization of at least one public corporation that controls 200 enterprises.

The state as entrepreneur is stepping back in most West European countries. In Italy, a new slogan is making the rounds, less state, less deficit, and the state-owned industrial empire of IRI is being dismantled. The Dutch government is selling part of its airline, KLM. In Sweden, the state does not need to step back because it has never played an entrepreneurial role: 90 percent of Swedish industry belongs to private citizens and corporations. This increase in popular stockholding may become, if it continues, one of the most challenging historical phenomena in the advanced postindustrial societies.

Capitalization of Pensions: Socialization Without Etatization

To this popular shareholding must be added the pension funds. The United States is considered the capitalist country par excellence, perhaps because it is the first economic power of the world. But, paradoxically, it is in this country that wage and salary earners constitute the greatest holders of capital. The volume of pension funds is as great as that of the capitalists' capital. The pension fund is undoubtedly a spectacular financial fact in the capitalist world today, but it is almost ignored in the European literature of Marxist inspiration and even by most liberal economists. In the United States in 1976, after thirty-five years of contributions, the pension funds accounted for about one-quarter of the capital invested in stocks and bonds in the U.S. market. To this quarter, belonging in its greatest part to "the working class"—to use a Marxist expression—it is necessary to add the pension funds of civil servants, teachers, and the liberal professions.

In most pension funds, the employees of U.S. enterprises make contributions to a network of insurance companies controlled by their representatives. Of course, the question of who controls the pension funds is an important issue—many funds are managed by employers, which is not the most appropriate form of control. The dispersion of pension funds among thousands of organizations is a source of financial pluralism, and this system has been protected since 1974 by an important law, which Congress discussed at length over two years, the Pension Reform Act.

An important part of the capital of the 1,000 most important U.S. enterprises belongs to the employees of all sectors of the economy.

If "socialism" is defined as "ownership of the means of production by the workers"—and this is the orthodox definition—then the United States is the most "socialist" country in the world. Through their pension funds, employees of American business own today at least 25 per cent of the equity capital of American business. The pension funds of the self-employed, of public employees, and of school and college teachers own at least another 10 per cent more, giving the workers of America ownership of more than one third of the equity capital of American business. Within another 10 years the pension funds inevitably will increase their holdings . . . all of this, of course, excludes personal ownership of stock by individual American workers—a small, but not negligible, percentage of the total. . . . The United States, without consciously trying, has "socialized" the economy without "nationalizing" it. The United States still sees itself, and is seen elsewhere, as "capitalist." But if terms like "socialism" or "capitalism" have any meaning at all (which is doubtful), what the United States economic system actually has become is a version of "decentralized market socialism." [Drucker 1976, 4-5]

The implementation of such a system in the European democracies would no doubt raise enormous political problems, but it is conceivable. The period of transition from a statist system of pensions to a private one would be relatively long, but possible. Such a change would have major consequences: It would relieve the states of a heavy burden; it would imply a transfer of capital to wage earners in the form of publicly traded stocks and bonds managed by banks and insurance companies for the benefit of the wage earners. The privatization of the pension systems in Western countries would reduce, by ten points today and by fifteen points tomorrow, the percentage of the GNP collected and redistributed by the states.

The Participation of Employees
in the Capital of Their Enterprise

A distinct but related form of "socialization" is the purchase of shares in each firm by that firm's own employees. The diffusion of shareholding among wage earners could be achieved in three ways: (1) Employees could be offered opportunities to buy shares, accompanied by a prohibition against selling to people outside the enterprise; (2) the enterprise could lend capital to be reimbursed by payroll deductions (this practice is even compulsory in some U.S. companies, where the holding of shares is a condition of promotion within the company); (3) shares could be distributed for free to employees of the company.

In theory, an employee's holding of shares could result in an increase of income, either in the form of dividends or by increases in the value of the stock. But such holding does not imply control over management, or even a way to participate in management. With small amounts of savings, an employee can buy only a limited number of shares, and the free distribution of shares is also limited. What is true for the individual is also true collectively: For an employee to acquire stock in his or her own enterprise is a way to increase assets, not to manage the enterprise. Shareholding by employees favors their integration into the enterprise, and a diffusion of ownership reduces social tensions.

A diffusion of shareholding among wage earners is accomplished more easily if unions are favorable to the idea. In France, Italy, and many other countries, however, unions are opposed to such shareholding in principle. It is for this reason that only 4.8 percent of manual workers held shares in France in 1965. Neither the unions nor the employers manifested a great interest in the diffusion of shareholding among employees. But, when the giant company Saint-Gobain was denationalized in 1986, its employees were offered attractive conditions for buying shares. They reacted very favorably, which embarrassed the unions. Perhaps that reaction was the beginning of a new phase in the social history of France, as well as in Britain and Japan.

In Britain, the government has encouraged the employees of denationalized enterprises to buy part of the capital. Employees who wish to purchase shares have been offered attractive conditions and given priority reservations. Thus, when British Telecom was denationalized, employees were able to obtain as many shares as they wanted, while ordinary buyers were limited to 800 shares. Some enterprises have distributed free shares to their employees, and a high proportion of employees have bought shares: 96 percent of the employees of British Telecom, 99 percent of those of Cable and Wireless, 90 percent of the employees of Associated British Post, 43 percent of those of British Petroleum, and 74 percent of British Aerospace employees (United Kingdom 1986). In 1982, the National Freight Consortium was sold entirely to the employees and pensioners of the enterprise; one-third of the shares of British Gas were bought by its employees.

In Japan, most of the largest enterprises (1,387 out of 1,734 of those having shares traded on the Tokyo stock exchange) periodically offer their employees the opportunity to buy shares in the enterprise by means of voluntary monthly payments. In 1981, about 40 percent of the employees of these enterprises, or more than 1.6 million employees, took advantage of such offers (*Tokyo Stock Exchange Fact Book* 1982, 45). In Germany, the phenomenal development of popular shareholding in general and the neocorporatist management of enterprises (*Mitbestimmung*) make the expansion of shareholding among employees as a form of control less necessary.

Sweden is also a land for social and political experimentation. In spite of the country's small size, it occupies a great place in the literature on democratic socialism, and the Swedish wage-earner fund system merits our attention. After the 1974-1975 wage explosion, the trade unions accepted wage moderation on the condition that wage earners get a share of the profits. A plan prepared by the leading economist of the trade unions, Rudolf Meidner, was endorsed by the trade union federation in 1976. The plan called for a wage-earner fund financed by a transfer of 20 percent of the companies' profits per annum; the capital would be invested in stocks and administered by directly elected worker representatives within each enterprise (Esping-Anderson 1985, 298). The fund was expected to grow progressively, and within twenty-five to fifty years to hold the majority of the shares of big corporations. It was assumed that the representatives of the employees, that is to say, the union leaders, had the expertise and the skills for the financial management of the stocks.

The plan was, naturally, criticized by the employers and the "bourgeois" parties: Economic democracy would destroy political democracy by concentrating too much economic power in the trade unions (Esping-Anderson 1985, 299). The Employers' Federation proposed a different scheme, individual shares would be in a collectively administered fund and an employee would have the right to cash in shares after a given number of years.

A new plan was prepared by the Social Democratic party and adopted at its congress in 1981. The transfer of 20 percent applies only to the portion of profits "above average," i.e., to the "excess" profits. In addition, the levy on profits is complemented by a 1 percent deduction from wages. These savings are transferred to an extraordinary pension fund, which lends money to wage-earner investment funds. The stocks are to be purchased in the open market.

The Swedish plan does not create a popular type of shareholding, which would favor individual ownership, or a democracy of small proprietors. It creates instead an "economic democracy," collective ownership, managed not by the state apparatus, as in the Soviet Union, but by the employees—in practice, by the unions. The wage-earner funds have a regional base, and they are not linked to an individual firm, the idea being that all employees will collectively own all big corporations. Such a scheme reduces the role of the state but increases the power of another oligarchic structure. Between Scylla and Charybdis!

A similar plan of wage-earner funds has been considered in Denmark where collective ownership permits individual employees to receive a dividend at retirement. The plan proposed a transfer of 10 percent of the profits of private firms into a collectively administered wage-earner fund. Initially, the fund had to be under the trade unions' control, but this idea was criticized and finally abandoned. The parliament rejected the plan in 1981.

The participation of employees in the benefits of an enterprise will cut the ideological roots of nationalization only if a large part of the benefits are effectively distributed to employees, not in cash, but as shares. There is here a potential strategy for politicians, employers, and for some unions: A progressive increase of wage-earners' shareholding will give birth to a new sociological type of wage earners, a hybrid between proprietor and employee, thereby reducing the pressure for the intervention of the state in the economy and the society.

The Disappearance of the State as a Housing Authority

The welfare state in Europe is polychromatic. Here the state prefers to nationalize enterprises, as in Austria, and there to socialize incomes, as in Sweden. In some countries, the state has a major vocation as landlord. The German state is a great owner of housing, about 30 percent of the housing units. The state constructed housing itself instead of offering the citizens loans, tax deductions, or other advantages to help them build themselves. In Britain, one-tenth of the social budget was at one time reserved for the construction of housing, and by 1971, the British state was the owner of 46 percent of the existing dwellings (Heidenheimier, Heclo, and Teich Adams 1976, 72). In other countries, the state is indirectly the principal housing constructor, having adopted cooperative or associate arrangements, as in Sweden—where semipublic agencies manage more than half of the total number of dwellings—or in the Netherlands. This policy, known as "municipal socialism," is not the monopoly of the Social Democratic parties. In postwar Germany, public authorities had to finance the construction of dwellings because a large part of most great cities had been destroyed and it was necessary to house 11 million refugees from Poland, Czechoslovakia, and East Germany—in 1955, these refugees represented 17 percent of the population. But the West German state continues even today to play this role of landlord, through municipalities, a debatable function under conditions of economic prosperity.

If it is admitted tomorrow that the vocation of the state is to help the citizen become the owner of his or her own house—not a tenant or sometimes client—and if the state decides to give up its millions of dwellings, it will rid itself of a function that other institutions could probably fulfill better. In this way, the proportion of GNP controlled by the state would diminish, without detriment to either the economy or social justice, since the selling of the dwellings could be reserved for the tenants alone. In so doing, it would reinforce the legitimacy of the democratic regime. We know since Tocqueville that the citizen-small-owner is better integrated in society and the political system than the citizen-small-tenant.

In Britain, for instance, a law adopted in 1980 obliged municipalities to sell part of their dwellings to the tenants. After six years, nearly 1 million dwellings had been sold to the people who occupied them, and the proportion of people who owned their own domiciles had increased from 54 percent to 61 percent, reaching the same proportion as in the United States. This operation brought the British treasury more than £8 billion (Santini 1986, 49).

Privatization of University Expenditures

A public expenditure can be justified if almost the entire population benefits from it, such as elementary or high school education. It becomes unfair if it advantages only a minority, which is the case with a college education. The proportion of people with some higher education in no case exceeds 40 percent, and this share is much lower in most countries. The number of people who have attained a university degree is, of course, still lower, since many of the people who begin university study do not finish. In the United States, 19 percent of family heads had a college degree in 1983, and 20 percent had had some college education (United States 1984, 682).

In most European countries, higher education is heavily or almost entirely subsidized by the state. This fact means, in effect, that the entire country finances the education of its future elite; the lower classes pay for the education of the people who will later dominate them. It is not only a question of limiting public expenditure but also a question of social justice.

It is possible for an advanced society to choose to disentangle the state from the business of paying for higher education, letting the people who benefit from such training pay for the investment themselves. Although increased earnings may not be the sole reason why students attend college, one must admit that this is the dominant basis for their decision.

The privatization of higher education need not work to the detriment of those students whose families cannot afford to send their children to college. It should be possible for the less well-off to take out loans in order to finance their educational investment. A doctor from a working-class background can expect to be just as wealthy as a third-generation doctor, and the former can use his or her earned wealth in order to pay off the loans needed to obtain a medical degree.

It is true that as higher education becomes expensive, fewer students enroll, even if they are able to finance their education by means of loans. Upper- and middle-class students are much less responsive to changes in cost than lower-class students, however (O'Neill and Simms 1982, 348–349). One could increase the costs these first two groups must pay, and they will still find the investment profitable. The lower-income students, who are very sensitive to increased costs, could have government loans more efficiently directed at them for reasons of social equity. One example of the many unfair features of educational subsidies is that the Pell Grant program in the United States is estimated to make the critical difference in the decision to attend college for 41 percent of low-income students, but it is of similar importance for only 17 percent of middle-income and 6 percent of high-income recipients (O'Neill and Simms 1982, 354).

The United States provides an example of such a system because it has traditionally required its university students to pay a much larger share of the costs of their own education than other advanced countries have. In the United States, student loans are the most important means of financing a university education: In 1981, 3.5 million students, or 33 percent of the total, received Guaranteed Student Loans, and the cost of this one program to the federal government was $7.7 billion (O'Neill and Simms 1982, 356). By obtaining loans, students finance their investment in their capacity for increased earnings by means of borrowing against their expected income. Through various regulations, in fact, it should be possible to make later loan payments reflect later earnings: Those who have benefited the most from their education in retrospect would therefore pay more for it, with the increased payments taken out of these gains as they are obtained.

Student loans are made by lenders against "human capital," not physical collateral, which presents problems of collection. Various methods have been tried or suggested to deal with this problem. In the United States, the federal and some state governments guarantee a large proportion of all student loans, making these loans attractive to banks despite the collection problem. Although such a guarantee does increase the willingness of banks to make such loans in the first place, this method obviously does little more than shift the burden of the collection problem from the banks to government, but this problem can be solved as well. Persons in default on their student loans have income tax refunds withheld; it has been proposed that default on such loans also affect one's eligibility for other state loans, such as small business loans; laws for income garnishment in such cases could also be proposed. In any case, and even if one accepts the high default figure of one in ten loans, loans are undeniably less expensive than having had the state pay for all of a student's higher education. Even if the state is heavily involved in certain aspects of such loans, the size of government support for education is substantially reduced, moving the country in the direction of a civil society.

Student loans cannot be discussed without considering the total debt burden students carry upon graduation. In 1986 in the United States, the average indebtedness at the end of four years was $6,685 for students of public institutions and $8,950 for those attending private ones; the undergraduate loan ceiling in the Guaranteed Student Loan program was $17,250, and there were undoubtedly a number of students who were at this maximum, which does not include other loan progrms (Hansen 1987, 6–10). One must admit that the fact that a student carries a large debt burden will influence his or her choice of career so that such a system may produce more MBAs than any society wants or needs while failing to produce, for instance, competent elementary school teachers. Yet, here too, careful regulations can compensate for this difficulty. If loans are in whole or in part forgiven in exchange for certain career choices—forgiveness taking place after the person has spent some years in the type of employment desired—sufficient numbers of intelligent graduates can be directed wherever a need exists. Such programs are already in existence in some countries such as France.

The investments in some students will doubtless be poor ones: Although education does increase the average income of graduates, not all graduates become wealthy. It is possible to insure students against the risks of dramatic changes in society's employment needs. In Sweden, student debt repayment is deferred if the borrower's income falls below a certain point, and if deferment persists to age sixty-five, the remaining debt is forgiven. Germany has recently introduced a similar program (Hansen 1987, 34–35).

In order to get an idea of the impact of such changes, one can examine the size of possible changes in the financing of education in the United States, even though that country already has the most privatized higher educational system in the developed world. In 1979, all levels of government combined paid 50 percent of the costs of institutions of higher education while student tuition and fees provided only 21 percent. Federal student aid programs alone, to say nothing of institutional subsidies or state and local expenditures, totaled $10 billion in 1981 (O'Neill and Simms 1982, 347–348, 351).

The question of who pays for university training is a controversial issue, and decreasing the role of the state will be politically difficult. Even in the United States, where this role is smaller than elsewhere, federal subsidies have a very large middle-class clientele. Doubtless well over half of all families include at least one potential college student, and many of those children who will not attend college nevertheless have parents who hope that they will. With such a majority, a reduction of public support is difficult, even if it is true that these same families are also taxpayers. Nevertheless, a privatized system of higher education is possible, as the case of the United States attests, and it could be adopted in the other advanced pluralist democracies. One must include it as an argument in favor of a civil society.

Such a policy would be a progressive, not a regressive, one. Today, in all advanced societies—but more in Europe and Japan than in North America—subvention of the university system results in discrimination in favor of the upper half of society. By a generalized and generous form of lending, the proportion of young people from the lower half of society who obtain a college education might be increased. Furthermore, subsidies to the upper half would be replaced by loans.

It is astounding to see that working-class unions and the most radical socialist leaders in Europe have not already proposed such a change. Class conflicts tend to be increasingly concerned with educational issues rather than with income, as in Britain. This trend is in part an intragenerational injustice since more than half of each age cohort, working in factories and fields, pay taxes in order to support the education of those who are in auditoriums.

Such a policy would apply only to higher education but not necessarily to scientific research, which will probably remain a major task of any dynamic state or, tomorrow, a consortium of states. It is likely that scientific research will increasingly be done by international teams and by multinational institutions, at least in the natural sciences.

Converting Tax Evasion into Social Welfare

One of the major problems of the hypertrophied state is collecting the revenues with which to nourish its growth. No one enjoys being taxed, and only the state mandarinate enjoys taxation. Wily taxpayers find ways of protecting their wealth and income from the specter of taxation. Some of these means are legal, such as emigration to low-tax countries like Switzerland. Emigration there occurs not only from Italy, France, and Scandinavia, but also from the United States. According to unofficial statistics, some 15,000 U.S. movie stars, singers, and businessmen are residents of Switzerland, even if most of their income is generated in the United States. Some other means of tax evasion are of marginal legality, and others are without doubt illegal. Those who have the most to gain from the evasion of taxation will be the most successful in discovering means by which to accomplish this end.

This money can go underground or it can fly overseas. If it is underground, only the state is the worse for it. But if it flies away, the entire nation suffers from a shortage of capital. This problem was clearly one important factor in the decline of Britain after World War II, where marginal tax rates reached 98 percent before the Thatcher government came to power.

The state could induce the wealthy to be generous to society by means of sizable tax deductions for charitable contributions. Prior to the tax reform law in the United States in 1986, one-half of all charitable contributions were deducted from taxable income, which meant in the highest tax brackets that one-half of all contributions were financed by the individual and one-half by the state (it is now about one-third by the state and two-thirds by the individual because of the changed tax rates). The politicians were themselves sufficiently wily to make the incentives for contributions to political action committees even more attractive by providing for a reduction of the tax bill—not taxable income—by one-half, subject to certain limits.

Because of these laws, private donations in the United States provide a range of public services and cultural institutions that many Europeans would find difficult to believe: hospitals, churches, mental institutions, universities, parks, museums, libraries, symphonies, operas, schools for the handicapped, scientific laboratories, shelters for the homeless, soup kitchens, scholarships, and overseas development assistance. Perhaps the world's wealthiest man, J. Paul Getty, was able to find the financial incentives in the United States to establish in a remarkably brief period of time one of the most important art collections in the world. The most prestigious U.S. universities are, with few exceptions, private. Private foundations supply huge sums of money for higher education, such as scholarships, research grants, and endowed chairs. A private organization, the Nature Conservancy, purchases and preserves large tracts of land in the form of parks—including the largest island in Channel Islands National Park. Churches and universities, themselves charitable institutions, own many hospitals (others are owned by municipalities or private corporations).

The functions of private philanthropy are many. Private charities innovate in the sphere of social welfare and can experiment in the field of public policy, support minority and local interests, provide services the government cannot constitutionally provide, oversee government and the marketplace, and stimulate the coordination of activities among government, business, and voluntary groups. Such organizations also stimulate active citizenship (Commission on Private Philanthropy and Public Needs 1975, 41-46) and thus contribute to the civic culture.

The incentive in the United States is such that even private corporations are induced to make sizable donations—the leader in 1983, IBM, donated $120 million. Total corporate giving in 1980 was $2.7 billion, which neglects a large amount of nondeductible donations of services and the like that could double the total (Bertsch 1982, 3). The largest and most profitable corporations give the most: Only one out of three corporations make any charitable contributions at all, but one one-thousandth of all U.S. corporations account for one-half of all corporate donations (Lord 1982, 7-8). Such donations go disproportionately to health and welfare and to higher education, areas that are more easily justified in the eyes of shareholders as investments in society as a whole. Individual corporations tend to donate to fields from which they receive indirect benefits: "Pharmaceutical companies show a greater interest in medical research, banks in economic development, oil in engineering education, food processing in nutrition, and insurance in health maintenance" (Lord 1982, 10).

In most advanced countries taxes are heaviest for the dead. With regard to inheritance taxes, the state sometimes appears to act like a hyena, scavenging among the wealthy dead, grave robbers among the documents and financial instruments of a lifetime. In Britain, the high taxes on inheritance were "connected" to nationalization as a way to prevent the collapse of unsuccessful companies. In a statement at a Labour party conference in 1957, Harold Wilson proposed paying for the purchase of shares of such companies by increasing inheritance taxes. One of the invisible effects of such a "death duty" was the flight of British brains and capital to the United States and elsewhere. The wealthy anticipate such taxes and plan accordingly. In the United States, the wealthy create foundations as they get old; only if they die by accident at an early age does the U.S. state have an opportunity to scavenge among the financial remains.

To list the names of major foundations in the United States is to list the names of the captains of U.S. industry. These foundations use their endowments to generate income, which they donate to a variety of causes. Without these foundations, the Carnegie, Ford, Mellon, and Rockefeller families would have an image as greedy capitalists; the family foundations soften the image considerably. Does it matter that the motives are not purely altruistic? Such foundations also improve the image of capitalism and contribute to the legitimacy of the economic system.

The system of tax deductions to encourage private charity has wide support in the United States. In a survey of "distinguished citizens" in both the private and public sectors, the Commission on Foundations and Private Philanthropy found that only 9.8 percent of the sample believed that tax incentives should be reduced in favor of a more active government role (1970, 203).

When one considers the huge amounts that European governments spend each year on educational and cultural institutions, one understands the remarkable effects such a system could have on the size of government expenditures in these countries. In many ways, Austria is the extreme case, combining a strong welfare state with the largest cultural patrimony per capita in the Western world. For instance, Austrian subsidies to the Vienna opera alone are immense; if private persons and corporations could be encouraged through tax regulations to make donations to the opera, the state budget would be significantly reduced.[6] The French government does not allow citizens to deduct more than 1 percent of their income for charitable contributions, but it occasionally spends the taxpayers' money to purchase paintings for museums.

Throughout Europe, as the size of the state increases, so does tax evasion. A democratic country cannot become an enormous gulag. Tax laws that encourage charitable contributions simultaneously discourage tax evasion, since one need not hide income that can be deducted on account of charitable donations. Any policy that discourages tax evasion by the rich in favor of social welfare and cultural institutions has arguments of social justice on its side as well as arguments of efficiency. Such a policy could be a part of the civic society of tomorrow.

*   *   *

DILEMMA OF THE ADVANCED PLURALIST DEMOCRACIES

Decades ago, Marxist thinkers viewed the state as "the committee of the capitalist bourgeoisie." At that time, the state was in the hands of the right, and it was the left that criticized it. With the ascent of socialist parties to power, particularly after World War II, state power was transferred to the leftist parties or to center-left coalitions. For generations, the privileged utilized the state for their own profit. Today, thanks to universal suffrage and to the electoral logic of democracy, the less-favored part of the population has taken control of the state, by the intermediary of the leftist parties, in order to obtain redistributions via taxation.

Suppose that the Austrian government came to control nearly three-quarters of the GNP tomorrow, almost as much as the neighboring Hungarian government. Would the two appear basically similar, even though one might fly the red flag of state socialism and the other the blue flag of state capitalism? Even admitting that the two societies would differ in many other fields, especially in their political systems, in financial terms both would nevertheless be equally controlled by the state. They would converge on this essential point, but of course, what they would control is also important.

Neocorporatism leads slowly to state capitalism. The growth of public expenditures—and consequently, of various kinds of taxation—has been continuous and more or less cyclical. In a democratic regime, this growth cannot be exponential, but it is cumulative. Several European countries already seem to be traveling this path, particularly Austria, the Netherlands, Sweden, Norway, and to a lesser extent, West Germany, but obviously they cannot do so indefinitely.

The opposite model, the civic society, implies a serious risk of partial delegitimation of the political regime in the poorest sectors of the population. Some people will see such an attempt to reduce state intervention as a social regression, a return to an earlier and a less-developed state, a "reactionary" move. But what if it is simply a reaction against the hypertrophy of the bureaucratic state? As some of the civic society hypotheses suggest, it is also a question of social justice.

A deflationary policy is not a way to reduce the national budget. In the past, particularly during the interwar period, deflationary policies generated serious political discontent and caused the collapse of several pluralist democracies—most notably the Weimar Republic. Transferring public expenditure to the private sector is not an easy task. Opinion polls show that in most Western European democracies, a majority is in favor of the maintenance of social security benefits, but the results of these surveys are too often misleading because alternative solutions are not suggested in the questions asked. The dilemma of "more contributions or less benefits" could be resolved in a more legitimizing way by referendum than by competition among party platforms.

The civic society hypothesis does not imply a reduction of the complexity of society, only a transfer of responsibilities from the state bureaucracy to private organizations, a transfer of ownership and functions from the state to the people, by privatizing some of the present economic and social functions of the state. Popular shareholding, the capitalization of pensions, a compulsory private social security system, the participation of wage earners in the capital of their enterprises, a policy favoring the private ownership of housing, a university system partially based on private loans to students, and the conversion of tax evasion into social welfare are some of the means, among others, to emancipate society from the tentacular state. The protagonist of the civic society preaches, "Render unto Caesar the things that are Caesar's and unto the people the things that are the people's."

The advanced pluralist democracy today is already neither purely capitalist nor purely socialist but a hybrid. It has a mixed economy, and its welfare system is partly private, partly public. It might metamorphize, as Tocqueville speculated, into a new type of society based on a large popular diffusion of property with positive consequences for the integration of citizens into society and for the legitimacy of the regime. There is no real term to capture what is happening today. Perhaps it is popular capitalism. It might also become a more meritocratic society.

MIDWAY BETWEEN STATIST SOCIETY
AND CIVIC SOCIETY

It is quite possible that the factors favoring the statist hypothesis and the factors playing in favor of the civic society might compensate for one another. For instance, it is realistic to expect an increase in state expenditure for pensions as well as a reduction of state subventions to deficit-ridden state enterprises. In France, for instance, public opinion polls show that the majority of the population is in favor of the maintenance of pension plans but also against maintaining high subsidies to the railway system (in spite of the fact that it is one of the most efficient in the world). It is difficult to justify the fact that almost half the entire direct income tax serves to cover the deficit of the SNCF (the state railway enterprise). Similar examples of apparently absurd situations could be found in almost all European countries, with the most beautiful cases in Italy and Austria. No country would escape such an inventory, and an amusing book could be written just on absurdities committed by states as entrepreneurs. It would be relatively easy to denationalize enterprises and to reduce the role of the state as industrialist, banker, insurer, and landlord, but it would be extremely difficult to reduce significantly the social subsidies. In all European countries, and even in the United States, the issue of the social security crisis is chronically present in the mass media and political debates; however, at the same time, more than half of the populations remain favorable to the social security system. Everyone admits that there is a limit to its growth, but once in power, politicians do exactly the opposite of what they advocated earlier. The most recent example is the French conservative government, which increased contributions to the social security system in 1986, a few months after having promised the contrary. This behavior is understandable when the government has to face new elections, when it is preoccupied with attracting the vote of the median citizen, without whom there is no majority in a presidential system.

The median voter behaves as an accountant, knowing intuitively if he or she will gain or lose by an increase in taxation and redistribution, in the sense that it will cost more than he or she will get back. "With nearly universal suffrage, the median voter has less income than the average earner. The voter with an income below the median can gain if incomes above the average are taxed, and the benefits are distributed to himself and others. Large governments thus result from the difference between the distribution of votes and the distribution of income" (Meltzer and Richard 1978, 6). This interpretation assumes that all redistribution is from rich to poor, but as Dennis Mueller remarks, "much redistribution is difficult to categorize in terms of rich or poor . . . the most salient feature of this process of redistribution is probably its lack of a single-directional flow" (Mueller 1987, 127–128).

Obviously, voters do not think only of taxation and redistribution issues. Everywhere cultural factors play a role as well, but these cultural factors change slowly over time, and for this reason, the accounting strategy of the democratic game can be considered here with all other motivations remaining the same. The accounting voter is certainly more frequent around the median of the electoral system or near the cultural cleavages; he or she switches most easily. Those in the center of the political spectrum largely control the electoral pendulum, and they judge whether the state is too large or too small. They choose, much more than others, between the state-controlled society and the civic society.

The state-controlled society tends to reduce inequality but also to reduce the freedom of the upper half of the society. The dichotomy of equality versus freedom underlines the dichotomy between a state-controlled society and a civic society. The floating voter decides when too much freedom is detrimental to equality, or vice versa.

NOTES

1. By the proportion of the GNP controlled by the state, or total public expenditures, we understand not only the national budget but also taxation at the regional and municipal levels as well as social security and the nationalized enterprises. Of course, in addition to taxation, one should take into consideration all forms of regulation.

2. If, instead of the portion of GNP controlled by the government, we take into consideration the proportion of the working population in government service, the analogy between Sweden and Poland remains. Sweden has one of the highest collective public services in the world—27 percent of the working population—and the chief economist of the Swedish Trade Union Federation, Rudolf Meidner, has predicted that the public sector will employ more than 50 percent of the working population by the year 2000. ·

3. The question could also be formulated as a rather complex model. But, in so doing, we might lose in clarity what we gain in formalization.

4. Some scholars consider the Democratic party in the United States the functional equivalent of the European Social Democratic parties: one white pear among pink or red apples.

5. Obviously, popular shareholding and the distribution of wealth should not be confused.

6. The phenomenon of huge cultural subsidies is widespread, from the Berlin opera to the British Columbia Provincial Museum in Victoria, Canada. As one example among many, the total budget of the four national theaters in Vienna was 1,363,800,000 schillings in 1979, only 287,000 of which came from those who directly benefited—ticket purchasers (Esslin 1982, 180). I do not suggest that this is unwise policy—on the contrary—but I do hypothesize that if ticket purchases and voluntary contributions were tax deductible, the price of tickets could be increased and state subventions reduced.

REFERENCES

Alber, Jens. 1979. "The Growth of Social Insurance in Western Europe: Has Social Democracy Made a Difference?" Paper presented at the World Congress of Political Science, Moscow. August.

Alexandre, Philippe, and Delors, Jacques. 1986. *En sortir ou pas.* Paris: Grasset.

Ashton, David N. 1986. *Unemployment Under Capitalism: The Sociology of British and American Labour Markets.* Westport, Conn.: Greenwood Press.

Barbé, A., and Messier, J. M. 1986. "Les privatisations en R.F.A." In Ch. de Croisset et al., *Denationalisations.* Paris: Economica, pp. 47–68.

Bertsch, Kenneth A. 1982. *Corporate Philanthropy.* Washington, D.C.: Investor Responsibility Research Center Inc.

Blaug, Mark. 1983. "Declining Subsidies to Higher Education: An Economic Analysis." In Herbert Giersch, ed., pp. 125–143.

Bloch-Laine, Francois. 1976. *Profession fonctionnaire.* Paris: Seuil.

Butler, Walter. 1986. "Les denationalisations au Japon." In Ch. de Croisset et al., *Denationalisations.* Paris: Economica, pp. 19–45.

Cameron, David. 1978. "The Expansion of the Public Economy: A Comparative Analysis." *American Political Science Review* 72, pp. 1243–1261.

Castles, Frank, and McKinlay, Robert D. 1979. "Does Politics Matter: An Analysis of the Public Welfare Commitment in Advanced Democratic States." *European Journal of Political Research* 7, pp. 169–186.

Cazzola, Franco. 1979. *Anatomia del Potere D.C.* Bari: De Donato.

Commission on Foundations and Private Philanthropy. 1970. *Foundations, Private Giving, and Public Policy: Report and Recommendatioins of the Commission on Foundations and Private Philanthropy.* Chicago and London: University of Chicago Press.

Commission on Private Philanthropy and Public Needs. 1975. *Giving in America: Toward a Stronger Voluntary Sector.* Washington, D.C.: Commission on Private Philanthropy and Public Needs.

Dagnaud, Monique, and Mehl, Dominique. 1982. *L'Elite Rose: Qui Gouverne?* Paris: Ramsay.

Djilas, Milovan. 1957. *The New Class.* New York: Praeger Publishers.

Dogan, Mattei, ed. 1975. *The Mandarins of Western Europe.* New York: Halsted Press-Sage.

Drucker, Peter F. 1976. "Pension Fund Socialism." *Public Interest* 42 (Winter), pp. 3–46.

Esping-Anderson, Gosta. 1985. *Politics Against Markets: The Social-Democratic Road to Power.* Princeton: Princeton University Press.

Esslin, Martin. 1982. "The Performing Arts." In Kurt Steiner, ed., *Tradition and Innovation in Contemporary Austria,* pp. 177–185. Palo Alto, Calif.: Society for the Promotion of Science and Scholarship, Inc.

Federal Reserve Bulletin. 1984. *Survey of Consumer Finances, 1983.* September.

Giersch, Herbert, ed. 1983. *Reassessing the Role of Government in the Mixed Economy.* Tübingen: Mohr.

Gournay, Bernard. 1981. "L'influence de la haute administration sur l'action gouvernementale." In F. de Baeque and J. L. Quermonne, eds., *Administration et politique sous la Cinquieme Republique.* Paris: Fondation Nationale des Sciences Politiques.

Hancock, Donald, and Logue, John. 1984. "Sweden: The Quest for Economic Democracy." *Polity* 17:2 (Winter).

Hansen, Janet S. 1987. *Student Loans: Are They Overburdening a Generation?* Washington, D.C.: Washington Office of the College Board.

Heidenheimer, A.; Heclo, H.; and Teich Adams, C. 1976. *Comparative Public Policy.* New York: St. Martin's Press.

International Monetary Fund. 1985. *Government Finance Statistics Yearbook.* Vol. 9. Washington, D.C.

Juttemeier, Karl Heinz, and Petersen, Hans-Georg. 1982. "West Germany." In Jean Jacques Rosa, ed., *The World Crisis in Social Security,* pp. 181–205. Paris.

Katzenstein, Peter J. 1984. *Corporatism and Change: Austria, Switzerland, and the Politics of Industry.* Ithaca: Cornell University Press.

_____. 1985. *Small States in World Markets: Industrial Policy in Europe.* Ithaca: Cornell University Press.

King, Anthony. 1978. "Why Do Different Governments Make Different Decisions and Pursue Different Policies?" In P. G. Lewis, D. C. Potter, and F. G. Castels, eds., *Comparative Politics,* pp. 101–118. London: Longman.

King, Desmond S. 1986. "The Changing Role and Scope of the State in Ireland Since 1950." *West European Politics* 9 (January), pp. 81–96.

Kohl, Jurgen. 1986. "Trends and Problems in Post-War Public Expenditure Development in Western Europe and North America." In P. Flora and A. Heidenheimer, eds., *The Development of the Welfare States in Europe and America,* pp. 307–344. London: Transaction Books.

Lehmbruch, Gerhard. 1984. "An Interorganizational Perspective on Neocorporatism." Paper delivered at the European Consortium for Political Research, Salzburg. April.

Lord, Benjamin. 1982. *Corporate Philanthropy in America: New Perspectives for the Eighties.* Washington, D.C.: Taft Corporation.

Meltzer, Allan H., and Richard, Scott F. 1978. "Why Government Grows (and Grows) in a Democracy." *Public Interest* 52 (Summer).

Moody's Bank and Finance Manual. 1986. 3 vols. New York: Moody's Investor Service, Inc.

Moody's Industrial Manual. 1986. 2 vols. New York: Moody's Investor Service, Inc.

Moulin, Leo. 1975. "The Politicization of the Administration in Belgium." In M. Dogan, ed., *The Mandarins of Western Europe,* pp. 163–186. New York: Halsted Press-Sage.

Moussa, Pierre. 1986. "Comment privatiser les societes nationalisees en evitant l'outrance et la demesure." *Le Monde,* February 4.

Mueller, Dennis C. 1987. "The Growth of Government: A Public Choice Perspective." *International Monetary Fund Staff Papers* 34:1 (March), pp. 115–149.

Olsen, Edgar. 1983. "The Role of Government in the Housing Sector." In Herbert Giersch, ed., pp. 199–224.

O'Neill, June A., and Simms, Margaret C. 1982. "Education." In John L. Palmer and Isabel V. Sawhill, *The Reagan Experiment.* Washington, D.C.: Urban Institute Press.

Peacock, Alan. 1979. "Public Expenditure Growth in Post-Industrial Society." In B. Gustafson, ed., *Post-industrial Society,* pp. 80–95. London: Croom Helm.

_____. 1983. "Reducing Government Expenditure Growth: A British View." In Herbert Giersch, ed., pp. 1–24.

Pierre Dupont Gabriel (pseudonym suggesting a President-Director-General). 1985. *L'etat-patron, c'est moi*. Paris: Flammarion.

Revel, Jean-Francois. 1981. *La grace de l'Etat*. Paris: Grasset.

Rice, Tom W. 1986. "The Determinants of Western European Government Growth, 1950-1980." *Comparative Political Studies* 19 (July), pp. 217-232.

Santini, Jean Jacques. 1986. "Les denationalisations britanniques: objectifs et realisations." *Economie et Prevision*, no. 76, pp. 47-67.

Saunders, Peter, and Klau, Friedrich. 1985. *The Role of the Public Sector: Causes and Consequences of the Growth of Government*. Economic Studies no. 4. Paris: OECD.

Schifres, Michel. 1987. *L'Enaklatura*. Paris: Lattes.

Stephens, John D. 1979. *The Transition from Capitalism to Socialism*. New York: Macmillan.

Tamburano, Giuseppe. 1975. *L'iceberg democristiano: Il potere in Italia*. Milan: Sugar Company.

Tarschys, Daniel. 1975. "The Growth of Public Expenditures: Nine Modes of Explanation." *Scandinavian Political Studies* 10, pp. 9-31.

Taylor, Charles Lewis. 1981. "Limits to Government Growth." In R. L. Merritt and B. M. Russett, eds., *From National Development to Global Community*, pp. 96-114. London: Allen and Unwin.

Taylor, Charles Lewis, and Hudson, Michel C. 1972. *World Handbook of Political and Social Indicators*. 2d ed. New Haven: Yale University Press.

Tokyo Stock Exchange Fact Book. 1982.

Tufte, Edward R. 1978. *Political Control of the Economy*. Princeton: Princeton University Press.

United Kingdom, Exchequer. 1986. *Privatisation in the United Kingdom: Background Briefing*. London.

United States. 1984. *Survey of Consumer Finances, 1983*. Federal Reserve Bulletin. Washington, D.C., September.

————. 1986. *Statistical Abstracts*.

Vaubel, Roland. 1983. "Reforming Social Security for Old Age." In Herbert Giersch, ed., pp. 173-190.

Voslenskii, Michael S. 1984. *Nomenklatura: The Soviet Ruling Class*. Preface by Milovan Djilas. Garden City, N.Y.: Doubleday.

Wagner, Adolf. 1912. *Les fondements de l'economie politique*. French translation of *Finanzwirtschaften* (Leipzig), vol. 1 (1883), vol. 3 (1901). Paris: Giard.

Wickham, Alexandre, and Coignard, Sophie. 1986. *La Nomenklatura francaise: Pouvoirs et privileges des elites*. Paris: Belfond.

Young, Stephen. 1986. "The Nature of Privatisation in Britain 1979-85." *West European Politics* 9 (April), pp. 235-252.

Table 9.1   General Government Expenditure
            as Percent of Gross Domestic
            Product

	1960[a]	1973[b]	1983[b]
Australia	25.4	28.5	35.8
Austria	31.0	40.8	46.8
Belgium	27.5	45.7*	47.6
Canada	26.0	--	45.4*
Denmark	27.3	47.6	54.1
Finland	30.0	37.2	40.3
France	34.9	37.5	46.5
Germany (Fed.)	35.1	42.5	45.9
Greece	21.1	26.5	30.4*
Ireland	24.8	34.9	47.0
Israel	--	40.8	43.7*
Italy	28.8	29.4	41.5*
Japan	20.7	--	30.2*
Luxembourg	32.5	35.5	34.8
Netherlands	33.9	51.4*	55.1
Norway	33.1	54.0	52.7
Portugal	17.6	--	33.2*
Spain	18.8	21.1	30.7
Sweden	32.2	47.4	62.8
Switzerland	23.3	30.6	37.3
United Kingdom	30.3	37.2	45.9
United States	27.3	32.3	33.8
Industrial Countries	--	35.6	39.7

Sources: a. Saunders and Klau (O.E.C.D.),
            1985, p. 29
         b. International Monetary Fund,
            1985, p. 78
*1982, or the nearest available year.

Table 9.2   The Thirty U.S. Industrial Corporations Having the
Largest Number of Stockholders

	Number of Stockholders	Sales in $ Millions	Rank by Sales	Assets in $ Millions	Rank by Assets
1. American Tel. & Tel. (New York)	2972.067	34909	8	40462	5
2. General Motors (Detroit)	927000	96372	1	63832	2
3. Inter. Business Machines	978152	52774	4	31603	8
4. Exxon (New York)	776172	86673	2	69160	1
5. General Electric (Fairfield, Connecticut)	506000	28283	10	26432	10
6. Occidental Petroleum (Los Angeles)	346000	14534	19	11585	26
7. Ford Motor (Dearborn, Michigan)	274004	52774	4	31603	8
8. Texaco (White Plains) (New York)	272392	46297	6	37703	7
9. Mobil (New York)	268589	55960	3	41752	4
10. DuPont de Nemours (Delaware)	240842	29483	9	25140	12
11. Chevron (San Francisco)	220000	41741	7	38899	6
12. Atlantic Richfield (Los Angeles)	215793	22357	12	20279	14
13. Eastman Kodak (Rochester, New York)	188972	10631	33	12142	24
14. U.S. Steel (Pittsburgh)	182169	18429	15	18446	15
15. Amaco (Chicago)	171697	27215	11	25198	11
16. Reynolds Industry (Winston-Salem, North Carolina)	155138	13533	23	16930	18
17. ITT (New York)	146657	12714	25	14272	19
18. Westinghouse Electric (Pittsburgh)	134096	10738	32	9681	23
19. Chrysler (Michigan)	131999	21255	13	12605	23
20. DOW Chemical (Michigan)	122600	11537	28	11830	25
21. Minnesota Mining Manufacturing (St. Paul)	112100	7846	47	6593	42
22. Allied Signal (Morris Township, New York)	110254	9115	37	13271	21
23. Rockwell International (Pittsburgh)	104866	11337	30	7332	37
24. LTV (Dallas)	98400	8198	43	6306	45
25. Xerox (Stanford, Connecticut)	92179	8947	40	9816	31
26. Sun (Radnor, Pennsylvania)	89345	13769	20	12923	22
27. Union Carbide (Danbury, Connecticut)	85385	9003	39	10581	28
28. Phillips Petroleum (Oklahoma)	84830	15676	17	14045	20
29. Coca Cola (Atlanta)	74963	8138	44	6897	40
30. Digital Equipment (Massachusetts)	74833	6886	55	6368	43

Boeing, McDonnell Douglas, Lockheed, Goodyear Tire & Rubber, Pepsico,
General Dynamics are among the 50 corporations with the largest
number of shareholders, but not among the first 30.

ABOUT THE CONTRIBUTORS

Jean Stoetzel died on February 21, 1987, at the age of seventy-six. He was Fellow of the Academie des Sciences Morales et Politiques, professor at the Sorbonne, founder and longtime president of the Institut Français d'Opinion Publique, director of the Centre d'Etudes Sociologiques, president of the World Association of Public Opinion Research and of Faits et Opinions, a new survey research center in Paris, and founder and editor of the *Revue francaise de sociologie*. He was the author of many books in French, particularly *Les valeurs du temps present: Une enquete europeenne, Jeunesse sans chyrsantheme ni sabre, Theorie des opinions, Francais et immigres*, and *La psychologie sociale*.

Mattei Dogan is senior research director at the National Center of Scientific Research, Paris; professor of political science at the University of California, Los Angeles; chairman of the Research Committee on Political Elites (International Political Science Association) and of the Committee on Comparative Sociology (International Sociological Association); and a former member of the French National Committee for Scientific Research. He has published fourteen books and contributed chapters to forty others.

Max Kaase is professor at the University of Mannheim and former director of the Zentrum für Umfragen, Methoden, und Analysen. He is a coauthor of *Political Action: Mass Participation in Five Western Democracies, Wahlen und politisches System*, and *Empirische Sozialforschung* and author of many articles on comparative politics.

Juan J. Linz is professor of sociology and political science at Yale University, former chairman of the Committee on Political Sociology (International Political Science Association and International Sociological Association), and former president of World Association of Public Opinion Research. He is the author of essays in many books, coeditor of *The Breakdown of Democratic Regimes*, and coauthor of six books published in Spanish.

Peter H. Merkl is professor of political science, University of California, Santa Barbara; a former member of the Steering Committee of the Council for European Studies; currently president of the Conference Group on German Politics; and secretary of the Research Committee on Comparative Sociology. His recent publications are *Political Violence Under the Swastika*, *The Making of a Stormtrooper*, *Political Violence and Terror: Motifs and Motivations*, and *Parties Fail: Emerging Political Organizations*.

Richard Rose is professor at the University of Strathclyde and director of the Center for the Study of Public Policy, Glasgow. A native of the United States, he has reversed the historical trend by emigrating to Britain. He is also former secretary of the Research Committee on Political Sociology (International Political Science Association and International Sociological Association) and author, coauthor, editor, or coeditor of thirty-six books including *Understanding Big Government* and *Do Parties Make a Difference?*

Frederick C. Turner is professor of political science at the University of Connecticut. The author of several books on nationalism, religion, and demographic change, he chairs the Study Group on Comparative Public Opinion of the International Political Science Association.

Ulrich Widmaier is a research fellow at the Science Center, Berlin, and has taught at the Universities of Mannheim and Berlin. He has published articles on political violence, global modeling, and empirical political economy and is the author of *Politische Gewaltanwendung als Problem der Organisation von Interessen*.

INDEX